Idols of Modernity

Movie Stars of the

1920s

EDITED BY

PATRICE PETRO

RUTGERS UNIVERSITY PRESS

NEW BRUNSWICK, NEW JERSEY, AND LONDON

LIBRARY OF CONGRESS CATALOGING-IN-PUBLICATION DATA

Idols of modernity : movie stars of the 1920s / edited by Patrice Petro.
    p. cm.
  Includes bibliographical references and index.
  ISBN 978–0–8135–4731–2 (hardcover : alk. paper)
  ISBN 978–0–8135–4732–9 (pbk. : alk. paper)
  1. Motion picture actors and actresses—United States—Biography.   I. Petro, Patrice,
1957–   .
  PN1998.2.I36 2010
  791.4302'80922—dc22
  [B]

                                            2009021735

A British Cataloging-in-Publication record for this book is available from the British
Library.

This collection copyright © 2010 by Rutgers, The State University

Individual chapters copyright © 2010 in the names of their authors

Visit our Web site: http://rutgerspress.rutgers.edu

Manufactured in the United States of America

For Andy

CONTENTS

☆☆☆☆☆☆☆☆☆★

ACKNOWLEDGMENTS

☆☆☆☆☆☆★★★★

I would like to thank Leslie Mitchner, editor in chief at Rutgers University Press, as well as the Star Decades series editors, Murray Pomerance and Adrienne McLean, for their assistance with this volume. In the early stages of preparation, Chuck Wolfe and Nataša Ďurovičová provided invaluable insights and ideas that helped me think through the shape and scope of this project. As always, I owe them both an enormous debt of gratitude for their friendship and boundless generosity over so many years. I would like to acknowledge the superb work of all of the contributors, whose essays are included here. I invited each of them to be part of this project, because I so admire their scholarship and commitment to the highest standards of our field. David Gerstner deserves special thanks for his contributions to this volume; although not included in this collection, his essay on Ramon Novarro helped to shape both my introduction and my thinking about stars in the 1920s and beyond. I would like to express my gratitude to the Center for International Education's Research Coordinator, Thomas Maguire, for assisting me with the detailed logistics of putting this collection together. Sara Tully, my longtime colleague in the center, also merits special acknowledgment, not only for her help with all matters, large and small, but especially for listening to me talk about this project for more than two years, and for reading several drafts of my own essays, which are stronger as a result. Finally, I would like to extend my deepest thanks to Andy Martin, the love of my life, for his help with this project and his unwavering support of all that I do. For that, and for so much more, I dedicate this volume to him.

Idols of Modernity

Introduction
Stardom in the 1920s

PATRICE PETRO

No one ever leaves a star. That's what makes one a star.
—Norma Desmond

Billy Wilder's *Sunset Blvd.* (1950) provides an auspicious way to introduce this volume. Released twenty years after the end of the silent era, Wilder's darkly ironic film about cinema and stardom promotes a particular view of 1920s Hollywood by juxtaposing it with what was then the current studio system. One of the first conversations between financially struggling writer Joe Gillis (William Holden) and aging silent film star Norma Desmond (Gloria Swanson) captures the film's attitude toward Hollywood, both old and new, silent era and sound: Gillis: "I know your face. You're Norma Desmond. You used to be in silent pictures. You used to be big." Norma: "I am big. It's the pictures that got small." Gillis: "Aha. I knew there was something wrong with them."

Later in the film, Norma and Gillis watch Norma's performance in a silent film in the private screening room of her cavernous and dilapidated Hollywood mansion. Over the sound of the flickering projector, illuminated by the light cast by the moving images, Norma caustically remarks: "We didn't need dialogue; we had faces." These faces from the silent era return to the big screen through the brilliant casting and performances of *Sunset Blvd.* Former director, now butler Max von Mayerling is played by Erich von Stroheim, among the most eccentric, controversial, and respected directors of the 1920s, whose credits include *Foolish Wives* (1922), *Greed* (1923), and *Queen Kelly* (1929), glimpsed briefly in Wilder's film. Appearing as themselves are journalist Hedda Hopper and director Cecil B. DeMille, who featured Swanson in such lavish films as *Don't Change Your Husband* (1919), *Male and Female* (1919), and *The Affairs of Anatole* (1921). There are also the infamous "wax works," Norma's card-playing friends from the silent days whom Gillis derisively writes off as has-beens of a forgotten era:

Gloria Swanson, as Norma Desmond, impersonating Charlie Chaplin in *Sunset Blvd.* Frame enlargement.

the incomparable silent clown Buster Keaton; the actor H. B. Warner, best known for his performance as Jesus in DeMille's *The King of Kings* (1927); and the Swedish-born actress Anna Q. Nilsson, who starred in the William S. Hart vehicle *The Toll Gate* (1920). Although not one of the wax works, Charlie Chaplin nonetheless makes an appearance in the film via Norma's impersonation of the international superstar. Norma Desmond's name itself was derived from combining the names of silent comedienne Mabel Normand and director William Desmond Taylor, whose murder, along with other scandals in Hollywood at the time, hastened the establishment of industry self-censorship and regulation.

Sunset Blvd. exemplifies significant and enduring transnational and cross-cultural influences (especially German) on the development of classical Hollywood style. Its director, Billy Wilder, began his career in cinema as a writer hawking scripts in Weimar Germany before coming to the United States in the 1930s, only to finally find success in 1934 when paired with Charles Brackett as a screenwriting team. In his recent book, Gerd Gemünden shows how Wilder writes his own history into *Sunset Blvd.* by exploring the complex relationship between writer and star "as a mixture of rivalry and mutual dependency in controlling the narrative of one's life and films" (89). Indeed, if Gloria Swanson/Norma Desmond stands in for those who failed to survive the industry in its transition to sound ("the Fairbankses, the Gilberts, the Valentinos!" as Norma exclaims), Wilder himself, not to mention the character of screenwriter Joe Gillis, personifies those drawn to Hollywood (especially its exiles and émigrés) who never entirely assimilated or embraced its industrial policies or practices.[1]

And yet while Wilder's film offers us a way into remembering Hollywood in the twenties, it also strategically misrepresents the era, catering to a popular mythology about stardom in the period that the essays in this volume set out to complicate, counter, and explore. For instance, Holden's persona of cool detachment is meant to offer a striking contrast to Swanson's broader, more mannered, and histrionic performance, thus implying a fundamental difference between silent and sound film acting styles. But the roots of Holden's modern style can be traced in part to that of silent film stars like Keaton, the Talmadge sisters, and Greta Garbo, as several of the contributors to this volume show. More than this, the notion that dialogue alone brought sophistication to the movies, a view that Wilder's film promotes, is certainly open to question, at the very least when it comes from a screenwriter-turned-director, who had his own reasons for touting the superiority of a dialogue-driven cinema over that of the silent screen.

In any case, close study of the careers of key stars of the twenties reveals a range of complex social, institutional, and aesthetic issues at work in American cinema that take us well beyond *Sunset Blvd*. This film nevertheless provides a useful way to get started in thinking about patterns and contexts of stardom in the twenties, and to frame the major themes of this collection: the relationships between stardom, industry, and technology; performance styles in silent and sound films; stars as models for behavior and screens for desire; stardom as an ensemble of texts, contexts, and social phenomena stretching beyond the cinema; the movies themselves as traces of the recycling, myth-making, and translation of national, transnational, and cross-cultural trends. Much contemporary scholarship has focused extensively on early cinema, with "early" understood to be cinema prior to 1915. While there have been important studies of stardom and cinema in the twenties in recent years,[2] this decade has received less attention than it merits, suspended as it is between what has come to be known as an early "cinema of attractions" and a later, more classical, thoroughly codified commercial narrative style. This collection aims to rethink such oppositions by showing how stardom in the twenties reveals strong connections and dissonances in matters of storytelling, style, and performance that can be traced both backward and forward, across Europe, Asia, and the United States, from the teens into the thirties, and from the silent era into that of sound.

★★★★★ Stars, Scandals, and Celebrity Culture

Whether one finds connections or experiences dissonances when looking back at this history is all a matter of perspective. In *Sunset Blvd.*, for instance, the twenties appear to us as remote, otherworldly, and strange—literally, a world forgotten, lost in decadence and decay. But today, as we live through the worst economic downturn since the Great Depression, the 1920s seem more familiar and proximate than ever. Indeed, there remains something distinctly modern about twenties Hollywood, especially when we consider stardom and celebrity as social phenomena shaped by the period.

Historians often describe the twenties as a decade of great affluence and great hardship, beginning with the end of World War I and ending in worldwide economic depression. The decade sustained a dizzying array of changes and conflicts in American life: the end of war, a new internationalism, and a discernable shift from rural to urban life, including the Great Migration of African Americans from the South to the North; the passage of groundbreaking amendments to the Constitution, one granting women the right to vote, the other prohibiting the consumption of alcohol (which didn't stop drinking on- or offscreen); the ascendance of consumer culture, department stores, and commercial amusements, accompanied by an array of new freedoms in dress, behavior, and sexual attitudes that clashed with traditional morality and values. This was an era fascinated with exoticism, colonialism, and the innovations of the Harlem Renaissance, ranging from poetry to literature to music, especially jazz. Heady and expansive, the twenties were also racked by racism, poverty, and labor unrest. By 1924 the backlash against eastern and southern European immigration was put into U.S. laws that established strict quotas favoring northern Europeans. Amid virulent antisemitism and racism against African Americans, the twenties witnessed race riots, lynchings, and the revival of the Ku Klux Klan.

Needless to say, Hollywood stars were both symptomatic of and contributory to these changes. In his essay for this collection, for instance, Krin Gabbard captures the contradictions of race, ethnic assimilation, and performance style that made Al Jolson a star. Jolson, he explains, was a white entertainer who often performed as a black man, wearing burnt cork as both costume and mask. "He was an immigrant Jew who spoke in a dialect that was pure American street argot. And he was extremely successful at invoking a plantation idyll that he could never have experienced." Gabbard nevertheless suggests that Jolson is much more than a blackface minstrel, since his style of speaking represented "an authentic, working-class patois" (Jewish, Irish, and Lower East Side), not just a white imitation of Negro dialect. For those African American performers who tried to make their way into film, Paula Massood suggests that their options were rather more limited. Indeed, at a time when most black performers were not even credited for the small roles they played in studio films, African American actors could either take small and often demeaning roles or appear in independently produced all-black "race" films, exhibited in mostly segregated venues. While performers like Ernest Morrison, Lincoln Perry, and Paul Robeson enjoyed recognition, even notoriety, for their work in Hollywood, many talented and experienced African American performers such as Noble Johnson and Evelyn Preer got their start in the race film industry, where to have recognizable stars at all was a coup for the underfunded and often technically inferior productions.

While minstrelsy and blackface produced a star like Jolson and limited the options of African American performers, encouraging some, like Josephine Baker, to leave the country for careers in Europe,[3] even bona fide Hollywood legends could not escape xenophobic hostilities and anxieties. Rudolph Valentino's career, for instance, paralleled the decade's notorious trial of Italian-born laborers and anarchists Sacco and Vanzetti, who were executed in 1927. As Amy Lawrence points out in her contribution to this volume, studio executives attempted to transform Valentino's Italian origins into a non-specific pan-ethnicity in order to construct him as the ideal immigrant (ready to be anything while claiming no special gifts), even as the press criticized him as woman-dominated, childlike, and effeminate. In the context of bitter debates over immigration and press-stoked fears of Italians as bomb-throwing anarchists, Lawrence writes, anything was preferable to being associated with radical members of the immigrant working class: "There were worse things than being seen as a fashionably dressed actor with a bossy wife and artistic pretentions."

Indeed, like Valentino, stars of the period embodied the contradictions and promises of the decade, particularly in relation to emergent views of sexuality and gender. As scholars have recently shown, the twenties witnessed the emergence of an open and unapologetically queer culture, as commercialized venues—from speakeasies in New York City's Greenwich Village, nightclubs in Harlem, cabarets in Times Square, and jazz clubs on Chicago's South Side—gave visibility and acceptability to homosexuality as a vital part of urban nightlife.[4] While the sexual proclivities of major film stars often went undetected onscreen, they were well known by studio bosses and gossip columnists, who worked with publicity departments to keep such matters from public view. Some closeted married couples upheld the pretense of heterosexuality while maintaining separate bedrooms (Cedric Gibbons and Dolores Del Rio, Edmund Loew and Lilyan Tashman, Charles Bryant and Alla Nazimova); others were the subject of persistent rumors (Rudolph Valentino and Natasha Rambova), while openly gay stars like leading man William Haines lived with his partner Jimmie Shields and was, as one commentator put it, "gay in everything except magazine interviews" (Musto). Touted as "the next Valentino," Mexican-born actor Ramon Novarro's homosexuality was a relatively open secret in Hollywood of the twenties; nonetheless, he zealously guarded his sexuality from the film-going public, maintaining his superior status as male romantic lead while simultaneously navigating his own conflicted relationship to Roman Catholicism and homosexuality.[5]

The careers and personas of Clara Bow, Colleen Moore, and Swanson, moreover, reveal what Mary Desjardins describes as ever evolving versions of the American "new woman" in the teens and twenties that, while differing in ways specific to class status, all suggest a woman seeking her own pleasures outside the traditional patriarchal family. Versions of the new woman expanded over the course of the decade to include foreign-born or foreign-looking stars, such as Swedish Greta Garbo or Chinese American Anna May Wong. As Lucy Fischer explains, Garbo combined aspects of the new woman's sexual and social autonomy with a new sophistication, tied to the novel and cutting-edge design aesthetic of Art Deco (known in the twenties as "modernism" or the *style moderne*). Like Garbo, Wong also drew on Art Deco aesthetics in performances that exploited her sexual and "oriental" appeal. Unlike Garbo, however, Wong's status as a heritage actress (U.S. born but equated with her "Chinese" characters) resulted in what Yiman Wang contends was a complicated racial masquerade that exposed the permeability and intransigence of both racial and gender divides. In sum, each of these stars had a profound cultural impact, which proved at the time to be cause for celebration and alarm. As one historian explains:

> Commentators throughout the 1920s were gripped by the certainty—exhilarating to some, troubling to others—that their society had moved headlong into a sexualized modernity marked by sophistication and complexity. The 1920s saw an increasingly intense public debate over what seemed radically nontraditional sexual behavior: a newly aggressive and public middle-class female sexuality, exemplified by women who streamlined their bodies into sleek instruments of pleasure, embracing styles of dress and expression previously associated only with prostitutes; and new forms of specifically sexual identity—male homosexuality and lesbianism—that blatantly detached sex from procreation, and from traditional notions of masculinity and femininity, and made it into a style of life.   (Hamilton 118)

Public debate and even outrage over styles of sexual behavior were not new to the 1920s.[6] A series of sensational scandals early in the decade nonetheless had far-reaching effects on the development of modern notions of stardom and celebrity. The most infamous of these involved the case of comedian Roscoe "Fatty" Arbuckle, who was arrested in 1921 for the alleged rape and murder of actress Virginia Rappe at a wild San Francisco party; tried three times, he was ultimately exonerated and acquitted. A month into Arbuckle's second trial, director William Desmond Taylor was murdered in his apartment and actress Mabel Normand was implicated in the crime. Like Arbuckle, she was also tried and acquitted, but her reputation suffered irreparable damage as a result of sensationalist press coverage. As scholars have shown, these scandals and others, such as the morphine addiction and early death of actor Wallace Reid in 1922, only seemed to prove what many in the country had suspected all along; namely, that the movie colony was immoral, its films inherently dangerous and corrupt.

The industry responded by creating a new trade association, the Motion Picture Producers and Distributors of America (MPPDA), headed up by Will Hays. Hays had been chairman of the Republican Party, a Presbyterian deacon, campaign manager for President Warren Harding, and Harding's postmaster general. Under his leadership, the Hays Office was established to stave off threats of national government censorship and to repair the industry's broken reputation. But this and other efforts failed ultimately to stem the larger and more significant cultural transformation already under way.

Indeed, as Mark Lynn Anderson suggests in his contribution to Lucy Fischer's Screen Decades volume devoted to the 1920s (which serves as a companion to this collection), the sensational scandals of the early twenties were actually a "continuation of a series of developing contradictions in the creation and dissemination of modern personalities by the press and by the movies" (53). Corporate consolidation and vertical integration of film production, distribution, and exhibition succeeded in establishing control over independent filmmakers and exhibitors. And yet complete standardization and control of stars, stories, and audiences were by no means assured in a vastly expanded media environment. "While the luxurious lifestyles of the stars had furnished the industry with a concrete demonstration of Hollywood's transformative potential to elevate both taste and standards of living," Anderson explains, "the scandals point to the corruptive possibilities of this new form of class mobility and leisured consumption" (54). Corruptive possibilities, moreover, meant new marketing opportunities, such as provided by the nation's 2,335 daily newspapers (with a circulation of over thirty million). As Anderson argues:

> The stories the movies now told bore the traces of a significant cultural transition: from a Progressive Era concern with finding happiness through solving life's problems to a new and sustained fascination with the experiences and fate of the unusual person. For some, this development marks the transition from a socially conscious cinema to one of mere entertainment, but it also announces the arrival of the contemporary media personality, one of the principal categories through which we now experience the world.   (46)

Modern celebrity culture emerged in the twenties across the overlapping media of film, newspapers, magazines, musical recording, and radio. It destroyed the careers of Arbuckle and Normand and catapulted the careers of others—including Douglas Fairbanks, Mary Pickford, Charlie Chaplin, Valentino, and Swanson herself—onto the world stage. As Scott Curtis points out in his essay on Fairbanks, after the formation of United Artists and his marriage to Pickford, Fairbanks became the unrivaled "King of Hollywood." With Pickford at his side, the two "were arguably the first celebrity couple, treated like royalty by the press, by their adoring fans, and even by actual aristocrats." Their residence in Hollywood, known as "Pickfair," was touted as a sanctuary against the glare of publicity, even as it was located in (and was promoted by the press as) the capital of modern celebrity. Traveling the world for months at a time, Fairbanks and Pickford were greeted by crowds of fans the world had never before seen. In the process, Fairbanks's earlier "democratic" image and kinship with the common man, forged in the teens, became in the twenties more difficult to sustain. As Curtis explains, his marriage to Pickford propelled his status as Hollywood royalty—a status that found its way into his film roles and star persona and the way he conducted business both on- and offscreen.

But as Fairbanks's career trajectory suggests, even the most successful film stars were not immune to the fate of modern celebrity, or to the meteoric rise and fall of fame, as entertainment and reportage became interconnected and often indistinguishable. Over the course of the twenties, Fairbanks's clever manipulation of his image and of the press would not be enough to ward off his decline; "with the coming of sound and the weakening of his bond with Pickford," Curtis writes, "it became increasingly clear that Fairbanks's position as King of Hollywood was securely tied to the silent era." Other stars, too, understood well how an actor could both exploit and be exploited by celebrity culture. After his unsuccessful lawsuit against Paramount/Famous Players–Lasky, for example, Valentino was effectively "on strike" from the industry between August 1922 and August 1924. During this time, he and his advisors came up with creative ways to promote his interests offscreen, using a range of media and entertainment venues. As Lawrence points out, in addition to a widely celebrated dance/personal appearance tour (which allowed Valentino to address fans in person in eighty-eight separate venues across the country), Valentino extended his reach into publishing and kept his image in circulation with a steady stream of still photographs that became fundamental to his appeal.

In sum, while the film industry promoted itself as uniquely positioned to both create and shape (through self-censorship) the appeal of its stars, the ascendancy of the modern "personality" was part of a much broader media landscape with its own extensive myth-making powers. As Max tells Gillis, who vaguely recognizes Norma's face but can't entirely place her: "She was the greatest of them all. You wouldn't know, you're too young. In one week she received 17,000 fan letters. Men bribed her hairdresser to get a lock of her hair. There was a maharajah who came all the way from India to beg one of her silk stockings. Later he strangled himself with it!"

★★★★★ Hollywood and the World

It is ironic that European-born director Max von Mayerling feels compelled to educate American writer Joe Gillis about the global reach of twenties stardom. After all, von Stroheim (and Wilder) experienced the phenomenon at first hand. Of course *Sunset Blvd.* engages in its own myth-making, of which the revelation about the maharajah from India is only a part. It is nonetheless indisputable that the early scandals, which created new media personalities and led to industry regulation, were fundamentally bound up with international considerations, as Ruth Vasey has shown in her detailed history of the period, *The World According to Hollywood, 1918–1939.* Prior to World War I, Hollywood catered largely to its domestic market. Beginning in 1917, as the major film companies derived an average of 35 percent of their gross revenue from abroad, the international market became an essential part of Hollywood's highly capitalized economic structure and business practice. Studios had to satisfy audiences of vastly different national, cultural, religious, and political values with "a recipe for movies that could play in the North and the South, on the West Coast and in the East, and from Capetown to Capri" (4). Hollywood was big business and its films were emissaries of U.S. commercial and political interests. As Vasey explains, "Just as the American industry had to persuade its domestic audiences that its products were harmless and morally sound, its domination of the markets of the world depended at least in part on its ability to convince its foreign customers that its output was inoffensive and ideologically neutral" (8).

But in the context of a burgeoning celebrity culture, the industry's efforts often proved easier to put into policy than into practice. Indeed, Vasey points out that Hollywood films were never "foreign" to their fans, whether they lived in the United States or elsewhere, and as active interpreters in an expanded media environment, audiences made sense of the movies in their own cultural terms:

The movie-going habit was a familiar, domestic ritual around the world, and American movies and their stars were a significant part of millions of non-American people's daily experience. . . . Foreign audiences constituted a market not only for the movies themselves but also for fan magazines which encouraged personal identification with American stars. Douglas Fairbanks and Mary Pickford visited Norway in 1924 and Moscow in 1926, and on both occasions they were given rapturous receptions by spectacular crowds. Harold Lloyd was familiarly known in the USSR as "Harry," as Charlie Chaplin was known as "Charlot" in France. Even in Japan, where a thriving national industry produced more than half the films exhibited, American stars had become household names, and they were thoroughly assimilated into the popular imagination.   (69)

It is noteworthy that contemporary film scholars interpret the impact of Hollywood's global reach on the kinds of films it made in significantly different ways. Lee Grieveson, for example, maintains that industry policy in the twenties resulted in films that promoted "a self-contained universe, melodramatic but fundamentally benign" (34). He enlists Vasey's book to support his argument, claiming that her research "has shown how the industry's attempts to create noncontroversial films pushed companies in the direction of the construction of Hollywood as a 'mythical kingdom,' to the production of films that submerged political issues into the universal, and into an agreed 'industry policy' that sought explicitly to avoid controversial and politically sensitive images and stories" (208). Vasey, however, seems to suggest something very different when she writes: "But for a world that eschewed any explicit representation of sex, it was strongly erotic; for a social world designed to be consumable everywhere on earth, it was strangely ethnocentric; and for an industry that was often denigrated for providing entertainment for the masses, its mode of representation was often extraordinarily sophisticated, ironic, and self-conscious" (12).

Vasey's assessment resonates with the one proposed by Lea Jacobs in her new book, *The Decline of Sentiment: American Film in the 1920s*. Here, Jacobs likewise discerns a remarkably sophisticated aesthetic sensibility in the era's Hollywood cinema, one that rejected the sentimentality and highly moralized view of life that characterized American filmmaking in the prewar period. Jacobs, who contributes an essay on the Talmadge sisters to this volume, makes the important point in her book that "the problem censorship posed for the industry was not simply one of enforcing a particular moral agenda but also, and more importantly, of negotiating very different sets of assumptions about the subject matter deemed fit for inclusion in a film and the manner in which it could be presented: it was an issue of decorum as much as of morality" (22). The subject matter of Hollywood films and its treatment, in other words, were points of negotiation (not enforcement) in the quest for the widest possible audience—an audience that was defined regionally, nationally, and internationally. Contrary to scholars like Grieveson, who look back to the early, prefeature, and preclassical cinema to imagine cinema's "relationship to the rebellions and cultural perturbations that presaged modernism" (17), Jacobs insists that it was in fact in the 1920s that some Hollywood films "came to be identified as 'sophisticated,' on the edge of what censors or more conservative viewers would tolerate," distinctive from "films that were dismissed as sentimental or simply old-fashioned" (2).

Jacobs's book is not about stars or stardom. Instead, it describes a shift in taste that was manifested in the trade press, in filmmaking techniques, and across four popular narrative types: the sophisticated comedy, the male adventure story, the seduction plot, and the romantic drama. Her larger argument about the transformation of Hollywood cinema nevertheless provides insights into the construction and reception of stars in this period. Indeed, for Jacobs, what was new was not the decade's much vaunted sexual permissiveness or subject matter of conspicuous consumption. It was rather its rejection of sentimentality and a morally cohesive worldview in favor of a modernist sensibility rooted in the vernacular, free from the restrictions of genteel good taste. This sensibility was as much European as American, involving the talents of directors such as Ernst Lubitsch, F. W. Murnau, and von Stroheim, as well as those of Buster Keaton, whose distinctly American, and indisputably modernist, approach to filmmaking is explored by Charles Wolfe in this collection. It was also a sensibility that infused acting and performance styles, spanning silent and sound film, which helps us to rethink the longstanding critical notion that "sound changed everything," especially for actors who failed to make the transition—a point of view espoused by Norma Desmond and by theorists of the cinema as well.

★★★★★ Silent/Film/Sound

"There once was a time in this business when I had the eyes of the whole world! But that wasn't good enough for them, oh no! They had to have the ears of the whole world too. So they opened their big mouths and out came talk, talk, talk!"
                                                                    —Norma Desmond

It has become commonplace to assume that the coming of sound changed everything about filmmaking in Hollywood, from dramaturgy to direction, film stardom to film style. German film theorist and perceptual psychologist Rudolf Arnheim eloquently expresses this view in his essay "The Artistry of the Silent Film":

> Naturally, the silent film had often shown the actor in close-ups. But more importantly, it had created a union of silent man and silent things as well as the (audible) person close-by and the (inaudible) one at a far distance. In the universal silence of the image, the fragments of a broken vase could "talk" exactly the way a character talked to his neighbor, and a person approaching on a road and visible on the horizon a mere dot "talked" as someone acting in close-up. This homogeneity, which is completely foreign to the theater but familiar to painting, is destroyed by the talking film: it endows the actor with speech, and since only he can have it, all other things are pushed into the background.   (56–57)

Commentators ever since have suggested that the introduction of synchronized dialogue in *The Jazz Singer* (1927) destroyed the highly sophisticated visual aesthetic of the silent era, effectively ending the careers of some of its most accomplished artists (Keaton, von Stroheim, Swanson, John Gilbert, Louise Brooks, and many others). But as we now know, *The Jazz Singer* was not the first talking film. Warner Bros.' *Don Juan* (1926) is often considered a more important milestone, but it had a synchronized orchestral score and was not a talking film. Vocal performance shorts, including those on the *Don Juan* program of 1926, however, did open up a key path in the development toward talking features. Orchestral scores for features such as *A Better 'Ole* (1927) and *The First Auto* (1927) also began to include vocal effects, in advance of *The Jazz Singer*, while the Vitaphone shorts unit developed two-reel, all-talking "playlets," although none were released until after *The Jazz Singer* went into distribution. Which of these events was most decisive in the development of the sound film is still a matter of scholarly debate.[7]

What is not debatable is that the widespread adoption of sound technology made the movies far less malleable, restricting their cultural adaptability. Vasey points out that, unlike silent films, which could be modified in distribution and exhibition in line with the sensitivities and predilections of their intended audiences, "sound films made it far more important to be 'correct' at the point of production" (10). Still, the transition to permanent commercial sound film production took much longer than previously assumed. The production challenges, disasters, and success stories that the American industry faced between 1926 and 1930 are the subject of new scholarly studies and historical revision, just as they were once the focus of classical films like *Sunset Blvd.* and *Singin' in the Rain* (1952). (The conceit of the latter film, of course, is that sound technology exposed the silent film diva's lack of talent and shrill New York accent, and that this, more than anything else, represented the greatest hurdle to the studios' successful conversion to talking films.) It is not surprising, then, that on the basis of new research, contributors to this volume contend that while the coming of sound may have marked the end of an era, sound technology itself neither destroyed most careers nor completely buried the aesthetic innovations of the period.

As Jacobs argues in her essay on Norma and Constance Talmadge, the famous sisters were among the most important stars of the 1920s, evidenced not only by contemporary fan magazines but also undeniable given their family connections (Norma was married to independent producer and later chairman of the board of United Artists Joseph M. Schenck, and middle sister Natalie was married to Buster Keaton). Today, however, the Talmadges are nearly forgotten, in large part due to the inaccessibility of their films. Still, the lore persists that their careers were brought down by the coming of sound. Jacobs's essay goes a long way toward dispelling this myth, showing how hackneyed and overly melodramatic stories rather than a Brooklyn accent hindered the subtlety and grace of Norma's acting in sound films (as such stories had done during the silent era), and noting that Constance, still at the top of her profession by the end of the decade, did not even attempt to make the transition to sound.

Mary Desjardins similarly overturns the legend of Norma Desmond's demise by showing that Swanson herself made the transition to the talkies with relative ease. Swanson's indecision over whether to make a sound film nevertheless set the stage for later career problems. In 1929, in her new capacity as independent producer for United Artists, Swanson hired von Stroheim to direct *Queen Kelly* and ultimately decided not to make it with sound. Von Stroheim, notes Desjardins, "already notorious by 1928 for an unwillingness to stay within budget, insisted on lavishly detailed sets, the inclusion of perverse sexual details (such as the character of the prince sniffing the panties of Swanson's character, who at that point in the narrative is a young convent-educated orphan girl), and shooting more film than could easily be edited into a conventional running time for theatrical release." *Queen Kelly* was shelved before it was completed, and Swanson, motivated to salvage what was left of her finances, supported films produced by others rather than build upon her own established acting career.

The examples go on. Novarro, for instance, was not hampered in the transition to sound by his Mexican accent as has often been assumed. Indeed, his speaking voice, and especially his singing, carried over well with the new technology. His performance in *The Pagan* (1929), a film with syn-chronized numbers much like *The Jazz Singer*, was a critical and popular success; the film's theme song, "The Pagan Love Song," was thought at the time to secure his future in the industry. However, intimations of Novarro's closeted homosexuality began to make their way into public discourses, and this, more than his voice or ethnicity, accounts for the slow decline of his career in the 1930s.

So why do the myths persist about sound technology's challenge to the abilities of 1920s stars? Paula Massood suggests at least one possibility when she references the cabaret vogue, already associated with Harlem's cafes, clubs, and theaters, which created an almost overnight demand for African American singers and dancers at the beginning of the sound era. To be sure, early jazz shorts featuring African American performers Noble Sissle and Eubie Blake appeared as early as 1923 in films by Lee de Forest, well before Warners and Fox began experimenting with sound films. But by 1929, Holly-wood sought to capitalize on the theatrical success of a number of Broad-way musicals (including *Shuffle Along*, 1921) and released two popular feature-length musicals with all-black casts: *Hallelujah!* and *Hearts in Dixie*. Almost as soon as it started, however, the rage for black entertainers ended. By the mid-thirties, Massood says, "the studios had moved on to other fads." It was not for the lack of talent, ambition, or ability, but rather the long history of institutionalized racism that accounts for the brief vogue for African American stars.

Buster Keaton's case raises further questions. As Charles Wolfe argues in his contribution to this volume, Keaton's career spans nearly seven decades, but he produced his most enduring work during the twenties. This was a period in which comedian-centered physical and visual comedy was widely regarded as a distinctly modern American art form (represented by Chaplin and Keaton, but also Harry Langdon and Harold Lloyd), much like the sights and sounds of African American jazz traditions. Among a hand-ful of silent comedians schooled in vaudeville who came to exercise control over the production of their films, Keaton made a successful transition from short comedies to features, achieving international stardom as well as crit-ical acclaim. At the end of the twenties, he signed on as a contract star at MGM. No longer in control of his productions, he found himself increas-ingly constrained by studio practices and policies. In one of his early sound films, *Free and Easy* (1930), a multilingual production, he and his fellow actors shot each scene in English, in Spanish, and in either French or Ger-man. Keaton complained about having to shoot and perform in cumber-some sound-laden movies, not just once, but three times.

So does the burden of dialogue account for the demise of Keaton's singular aesthetic? In her essay on Marie Dressler, whose career spans the teens through the 1930s, Joanna Rapf suggests not. Dressler first found stardom as Tillie, the overweight "plain Jane" of the vaudeville stage. In 1910, she had a hit with "Tillie's Nightmare," which Mack Sennett adapted to film in 1914 as *Tillie's Punctured Romance*. Dressler took top billing over a young Chaplin in this first six-reel comedy, which also featured Mabel Normand. But her career soon stalled and by the end of the teens, she was out of work. Blacklisted for her role in the chorus girls' strike of 1917 and out of place in a Hollywood focused on youth culture, Dressler considered becoming a housekeeper in the mid-twenties. In 1927, her friend, MGM screenwriter Frances Marion, got her small parts and then a co-starring lead with Polly Moran in *The Callahans and the Murphys* (1927). Her popularity continued to grow until she became a break-out sensation in the role of Marthy, the waterfront rat in *Anna Christie* (1930), the film Marion had adapted for Garbo's first talkie. Dressler's success in that film shocked her as well as everyone else. Nearly sixty years old and weighing two hundred pounds, she was no conventional female star, although her popularity would explode over the course of the early 1930s. As Rapf notes, Dressler became the number one star in Hollywood in 1932, more popular than Garbo or Chaplin; her earning power alone topped that of Garbo, Jean Harlow, Joan Crawford, Clark Gable, and Mickey Mouse.

Although schooled in silent comedy, Dressler's age and persona, not to mention her active body, blank expression, and intensity around the eyes, made her uniquely positioned to appeal to a Depression-era audience. Her ability to combine verbal wit with visual gags also earned her the moniker "The Thief of the Talkies" (for scene-stealing through small but visually effective "bits of business"). Rapf provides a telling comparison of Dressler and Mae West, another older, untraditional female star who made the transition from the theater to the movies at around the same time. Both stars were "survivors," Rapf contends, but while West was cynical, Dressler was not. Both challenged conventional notions of femininity and both were comfortable with their formidable bodies. And yet, as Rapf puts it, "West puts hers on display for the male gaze that she then returns with a sharp one-liner, whereas Dressler is deliciously indifferent to her looks. West's technique is essentially that of farce—hostile, aggressive. Dressler's comedy, on the other hand, like Buster Keaton's, is not mean, bitter, or hostile."

While Keaton himself suffered during the transitional years to talkies, the physical and visual comedy he and others like Dressler perfected was not entirely lost to the screen. Although later films like *Sunset Blvd.* imagine slapstick comedians as quaint and antiquated relics ("the wax works"), this reflects a critical sensibility of the late 1930s and 1940s—and not the view promoted in the trade press or among intellectuals in the twenties.[8] Wolfe shows how Keaton refined a screen persona informed by "an engineer's imagination freed of civil or industrial obligations." This allowed him to play with notions of functional planning in non-utilitarian ways, and to produce an aesthetic at once sophisticated and vernacular, based on principles of technological design. During the twenties, this approach was thought to connect art with public life in a more dynamic and democratic way than did genteel forms of literature or fine art. For European observers especially, Keaton's films revealed a distinctly modernist sensibility akin to Dada, surrealism, constructivism, and other modern art movements. Keaton's career declined, then, not because his aesthetic was old-fashioned or that he himself was incapable of adjusting to sound, but because of an array of other factors, including his health and because he was aging and his comic persona would have had to change accordingly.[9]

Interestingly, Wolfe points out that Keaton's modernity as a comic performer was bound up with his emotional reserve and refusal to amplify psychological states for dramatic effect. Drawing on Luis Buñuel's remarks regarding distinctions between European and American acting,[10] Wolfe further comments that "precisely at the historical moment when Hollywood turned to European actors, directors, and cinematographers to enhance the cultural value of their product—in fact, ironically, at a time when [Emil] Jannings, brought to Hollywood by Paramount, was presented with the first Academy Award granted a movie actor—European critics praised Keaton's cooler, introspective style and practical route to dream-like states." While Wolfe's assessment of Keaton resonates with Jacobs's larger view of the rejection of sentimentality in 1920s Hollywood, it also opens up a wider consideration of modernism in the popular cinema, which was never confined to Hollywood alone.

Indeed, in his essay on Jannings for this volume, Gerd Gemünden reminds us that Weimar cinema and culture were truly international and had an enormous impact on the development of the Hollywood film. But influences and exchanges went both ways, as German studios imitated Hollywood genres, promotional strategies, and stars, and American producers imported German directors, screenwriters, and film personnel, sufficiently complicating any question of "origins."[11] These developments, moreover, were closely watched by industry executives, cultural critics, and the public at large. "While some Germans claimed that American mass culture foreshadowed a homogenization of the world," Gemünden explains, "others

The Blue Angel (1930).
Marlene Dietrich (Lola Lola)
and Emil Jannings (Emmanuel
Rath). Frame enlargement.

considered it to be a force that could subvert the pretentiousness of traditional elite culture." If neither modernist sensibilities nor technological
know-how belonged to any one national film industry, Hollywood did have
an edge over Germany in its ability to lure the finest talent to its studios
(directors like Lubitsch, Murnau, and E. A. Dupont, screenwriters like
Hanns Kräly, and actors like Jannings, Conrad Veidt, and Pola Negri all
came to Hollywood in the 1920s). Jannings offers a case in point. He arrived
in Los Angeles in 1926, yet another in a long line of German and European
film professionals to sign a contract with a Hollywood studio. Gemünden
suggests that Jannings's career is nonetheless unique, not only because his
American star persona and screen roles were grafted onto an already established image, but mostly because "the studio gave the star extraordinary
control over scripts, roles, and choice of directors, allowing him power in
the artistic creation of his films which few domestic stars and no other foreign stars enjoyed at the time."

Jannings enjoyed enormous popularity in Hollywood and with the
American filmgoing public. His nearly three-year sojourn in the United
States nevertheless came to an abrupt end when the major studios converted to sound and he returned to Germany to begin planning his own,
critically important, German film sound debut. Wolfe underscores the irony
that Jannings's performances were recognized in America with the first
Academy Award at the very same time that Keaton's films were being celebrated by European intellectuals. But perhaps the even greater irony was
that just one year after the success of *The Last Command* (1928) and his
Oscar for best actor, Jannings brought Josef von Sternberg to Germany to
direct *Der blaue Engel* (*The Blue Angel*, 1930), Jannings's first talking film. For
the project, von Sternberg enlisted the talents of a relatively unknown and

untested Berlin actress, Marlene Dietrich. As critics noted at the time and have emphasized ever since, Dietrich surprisingly overshadowed Jannings in her performance and was signed by Paramount in 1930.[12] Thus, the film that was supposed to solidify Jannings's reputation as international cinema's premiere star performer instead became known as the film that launched Dietrich's spectacular Hollywood career.

This brings us, finally, to issues of film acting and film style. Trained in an expressionistic, theatrical tradition, Jannings, it seemed, could not com-

Buster Keaton, in an MGM studio portrait made in 1928 for *The Cameraman*.

pete with Dietrich's cooler, surface-oriented, cinematic style. Dietrich's style, moreover, might be usefully compared with Keaton's understated approach, since both reflect larger international and modernist trends that marked both Weimar and Hollywood filmmaking during the silent era which were ultimately reclaimed, in the 1930s, for a U.S. national cinema alone. This cinematic aesthetic encompassed more than styles of acting, however, and at its finest, its economy of narration and performance captured the highly accessible yet irrepressibly modern and sophisticated sensibility analyzed by the contributors to this volume.

In this regard, it is useful to recall the strange and wonderful contradictions Vasey describes as central to Hollywood cinema in the interwar period. Hollywood, she says, created a world that "eschewed any explicit representation of sex" yet remained strongly erotic, designed films "to be consumable everywhere on earth" yet was strangely ethnocentric, and was denigrated for producing "entertainment for the masses" yet retained a mode of representation at once sophisticated, ironic, and self-conscious. Erotic, ethnic (as much as ethnocentric), ironic, and self-conscious—these words describe the stars of the twenties whose careers and personas are explored in this volume. They had names, and they had faces: Douglas Fairbanks, Buster Keaton, Norma and Constance Talmadge, Rudolph Valentino, Gloria Swanson, Clara Bow, Colleen Moore, Greta Garbo, Anna May Wong, Emil Jannings, Al Jolson, Ernest Morrison, Noble Johnson, Evelyn Preer, Lincoln Perry, and Marie Dressler. Billy Wilder couldn't have imagined that scholarly studies of stardom would one day give credence to Norma Desmond's seemingly deluded claim, which opens this introduction: "No one ever leaves a star. That's what makes one a star."

NOTES

1. "Of the many incidents Billy Wilder was fond of recalling for the benefit of his biographers and interview partners," Gemünden explains, "there may have been none he relished retelling more than the one about using the f-word to insult studio boss Louis B. Mayer after the very first Hollywood screening of *Sunset Blvd.* Mayer had been incensed not only about the film's attack on the industry but particularly by the fact that it was written and directed by someone whom that very industry had made rich and famous; for having bitten the hand that fed him, Mayer shouted, Wilder 'should be tarred and feathered and run out of town.' The fact that Mayer addressed his scorn only to Wilder and not toward coauthor and producer Charles Brackett suggests that it was largely fueled by the fact that a foreigner had dared to shine an unflattering light at 'Hollywood from the inside' (as the movie poster caption had it), and one critic claims that Mayer explicitly called Wilder a 'goddam foreigner son of a bitch.' Obviously, Mayer attacked Wilder for what he perceived as a lack of gratitude to his host country and a sign of halfhearted assimilation, a stance to which he himself provided the perfect counterexample" (95).

2. See, for instance, Hansen; Higashi; Staiger; and Studlar *This Mad*.

3. On Josephine Baker in Europe, see Nenno.

4. See, for example, Faderman and Timmons, Mann.

5. On Novarro's conflicted relationship to Roman Catholicism and homosexuality, see David Gerstner's unpublished essay, "Ramon Novarro: The Performance of Deception." I am indebted to Gerstner's work on Novarro, which helped shape this introduction.

6. In this regard, see Mahar and Grieveson.

7. I owe this insight, and many others, to Charles Wolfe. For recent research on the coming of sound, see Altman; Crafton; Eyman; Gomery; and Wolfe *On the Track*.

8. As Wolfe notes in his essay for this volume, screenings at the Museum of Modern Art played a key role in keeping the reputation of Keaton's silent films (barely) alive. In his forthcoming book, he also explains that, despite strains of nostalgia, James Agee, in his 1949 essay on silent comedy, cut through the fog of condescension toward slapstick comedy in popular culture by evoking the social aggression and imaginative energy that fueled the work of top slapstick comedy performers and, in the case of Keaton, emphasized the strange beauty and deep emotional reserve of the work. See Wolfe, *Buster Keaton and American Modernism*.

9. For a full account of Keaton's career, see Wolfe, *Buster Keaton and American Modernism*.

10. The full text, referenced in Wolfe's essay in this collection, reads as follows: "School of Jannings: European school: sentimentalism, prejudices of art, literature, tradition, etc. John Barrymore, Veidt, Mosjoukine, etc. School of Buster Keaton: American school: vitality, photogeny, no culture and new tradition: Monte Blue, Laura la Plante, Bebe Daniels, Tom Moore, Menjoy [sic], Harry Langdon, etc."

11. As Jacobs's research suggests, the impact of Chaplin's *A Woman of Paris* (1923) on Lubitsch and others complicates questions of "origins" regarding German/American influences on the development of sophisticated comedy in 1920s Hollywood.

12. For a history of the critical reception of *The Blue Angel*, see Petro's essay in *Dietrich Icon*.

Douglas Fairbanks
King of Hollywood

SCOTT CURTIS

By 1920, Douglas Fairbanks was one of the most popular stars in Hollywood and, indeed, the world, along with Mary Pickford and Charlie Chaplin. If the formation of United Artists the year before consolidated his position as a major star and producer, it also prepared the public for an even more powerful merger: the marriage of Fairbanks and Pickford. No one—least of all Fairbanks and Pickford themselves—anticipated the enormous boost this union would give their already lofty stature. They were arguably the first celebrity couple, treated like royalty by the press, by their adoring

Douglas Fairbanks as *The Thief of Bagdad* (1924). Courtesy of the Academy of Motion Picture Arts and Sciences.

fans, and even by actual aristocrats. If we look closely at the publicity covering the marriage, we can see certain themes begin to take shape. These themes are especially familiar, since they also appeared in the films of each star and in their individual star discourse as well. But these motifs—namely, rescue, royalty, and the unity of opposites—seem to be borrowed from Fairbanks's films and publicity in particular. The Fairbanks persona, in other words, shaped the discussion of the marriage in general. While Pickford's persona was clearly a factor in the way journalists wrote about the couple, many of their motifs make use of ideas already established in the publicity and films of Douglas Fairbanks.

Though it was motivated by love, we cannot discount the strategic advantage Fairbanks enjoyed from this union; it gave him the confidence and security to change his star persona and his product from westerns and modern-era comedies to costumed adventure films. This risky transformation eventually paid huge dividends: his swashbuckling persona delighted audiences, his films were lauded as the pinnacle of silent film art, and his imitators were legion. But this period also represents a significant shift in the Fairbanks persona. If his films from the 1910s emphasized his democratic instinct, the films of the 1920s present fantasies of nobility. Furthermore, the star discourse on Fairbanks in the 1920s emphasizes his role as producer over any other aspect that was underlined in the 1910s, such as author, popular philosopher, patriot, or even film star. Instead, the Fairbanks persona transforms into manager, industry spokesman, artist, and Hollywood aristocrat. As his stock continued to rise in Hollywood, he was hailed as not only a major producer, but also as a civic leader and industry captain. Indeed, it could be argued that his position of leadership in Beverly Hills and as the first president of the Academy of Motion Picture Arts and Sciences was due primarily to the enormous success of the Fairbanks star persona. In the late 1920s, with the coming of sound and the weakening of his bond with Pickford, it became increasingly clear that Fairbanks's position as King of Hollywood was securely tied to the silent era.

★★★★★ Rescue and Royalty

Upon their arrival in London in late June 1920, the first stop on their six-week honeymoon tour of Europe, Douglas Fairbanks and Mary Pickford were mobbed. Whether the crowd was the result of carefully crafted publicity (everyone knew exactly where and when they would arrive) or due to a long, pent-up desire to see them both in the flesh, the display of fan enthusiasm was unprecedented and even frightening. One

Mary and Doug on the Pickford-Fairbanks studio back lot, circa 1925. Courtesy of the Academy of Motion Picture Arts and Sciences.

correspondent, Algonquin Round Table member Alexander Woollcott, reported that fans "hung from factory windows and mounted running boards and fell under the wheels. To the authorities was left only the task of protecting the visitors from being trampled to death or having their clothes lovingly torn from them. In this they were not entirely successful, but then only thirty policemen were detailed as bodyguards" (*Everybody's Magazine*, November 1920, 36–37). At one point, in a moment that would become exemplary of not only their honeymoon but their marriage, "when Mary was in danger of being enthusiastically but fatally trampled under-foot, her husband rushed to the rescue of his lovely and prosperous bride, lifted her in his justly celebrated arms and started to plow his way to safety" (37). A fan, undeterred by this melodramatic rescue, asked for his auto-graph. While some Londoners were puzzled or disgusted at this display, no one could question its authenticity, or that the crowds treated Doug and Mary with a uniquely modern mixture of reverence and familiarity. They were indeed monarchs of the screen, but everyone felt they knew them personally. Woollcott reports that the King of England did not call on the couple, but that "he had his car drawn up on the distant outskirts of the crowd, and for twenty minutes watched the seething multitude that had turned out with an interest they would be unlikely to show for anyone else in the world, save his own son and heir" (37). George V might not have been caught up in the awesome funnel cloud of modern celebrity, but he could certainly see it from where he stood.

Keen observers would have recognized its contours on the horizon years earlier, of course, with the rise of fan culture in the 1910s, as studios capitalized on the increasing interest in film actors by organizing their pro-ductions and publicity around stars (on the early star system, see deCor-dova). In April 1918, Pickford, Fairbanks, and Chaplin embarked on a nationwide tour for the Liberty Loan bond drive, which was the govern-ment's attempt to stir up money and national fervor for the war (for more on the tours, see Kennedy *Over Here* 98–106; on Fairbanks and the war effort, see Curtis). The tour's patriotic publicity combined with the mount-ing passion for film stars (especially these three) to create a perfect storm of celebrity: the crowds for this tour were enormous (e.g., *Chicago Daily Tri-bune*, 5 April 1918, 12). During this tour, fans also got their first extended look at Doug and Mary together, a public pairing that did not sit well with Fairbanks's wife, Beth Sully. Coincident with the tour, Sully announced to the press that she and her husband had separated, citing an unnamed "actress" as the cause (*Chicago Daily Tribune*, 12 April 1918, 10). Everybody knew who this "actress" was, of course, even if Fairbanks disingenuously denied the story as "German propaganda." Owen Moore, Pickford's hus-band, knew, too, and released his own thoughts on the topic, accusing Fair-banks of being the "aggressor" and declaring that "the other woman" had been "much victimized" (*Los Angeles Times*, 14 April 1918, 2:1). This was the beginning of an irreparable breach, even if Pickford and Fairbanks, who had met in New York in November 1915, had been seeing each other regularly since 1916 (Pickford 195–223). Now that the affair was public, there was no turning back. Sully was granted a divorce in December 1918, which became final in March 1919 (*Los Angeles Times*, 1 December 1918, 1:5; 6 March 1919, 2:10). That divorce was relatively uncomplicated compared to the Moore-Pickford separation. Out of the blue in March 1920, Pickford was granted a quickie divorce from Moore in Minden, Nevada. Pickford and her mother had been in Minden since February and claimed to have plans to move there permanently. Meanwhile, Moore just happened to be in nearby Virginia City, where he was served with papers (*New York Times*, 4 March 1920, 9). Immediately after the divorce, reporters were already asking if she would wed Fairbanks, which she vehemently denied, but by the end of the month she had already moved back to Los Angeles and married him (*Los Angeles Times*, 31 March 1920, 2:1). All of this raised the suspicions of the Nevada attorney general, who claimed that Pickford had acted in bad faith in order to get around the Nevada residency requirement for divorce (*Chicago Tribune*, 4 April 1920, 3). He vowed to sue to void the divorce; the case moved through the Nevada legal system until Pickford prevailed in June of 1922 (*Los Angeles Times*, 1 May 1922, 2:1).

Pickford's divorce could have been disastrous for her and Fairbanks, especially given the celebrity scandals of the early 1920s. They were, in fact, very worried about how their fans would take the news; Pickford was especially anxious that divorce and remarriage, which would lead to her excommunication from the Catholic Church (to which she had converted upon marrying Moore), would cost her her Catholic fans (Pickford 204–05; *Photoplay*, June 1920, 74). But they had three things working in their favor. First, their individual popularity was such that fans were already eagerly anticipating their marriage. The top two box-office stars seemed perfect for each other. A May 1919 feature on Pickford, for example, tells of fan mail asking when she would marry Fairbanks (*Boston Daily Globe*, 11 May 1919, E3). Second, their established personas—Mary's innocence and purity, Doug's honor and gallantry—were already squeaky clean, so it would have taken much worse to tarnish them. Third, they worked quickly to develop sweet-smelling publicity that would overpower any whiff of scandal. Indeed, this publicity borrows its characters and narrative arc from the Pickford and Fairbanks personas. An important example is a June 1920 *Photoplay* feature on the couple, which appeared in early May, just after the Nevada divorce brouhaha erupted in April. Notably, this article was distributed to a variety of newspapers nationwide, where it was reprinted word for word in whole or in part (for example, *Washington Post*, 9 May 1920, 49); the piece thereby shaped much of the subsequent coverage of the couple in the national press. The *Photoplay* article calls their romance "one of the great love stories of all time" and creates a sympathetic (if not pathetic) portrait of Pickford as a long-suffering woman who deserves a little happiness in her life (*Photoplay*, June 1920, 70, 73–74, 113). According to the article, hers is "a love that has come after great sorrow" (73)—even if it is vague on the details of the source of that sorrow—and while cynics and gossips may snigger, no one who knows her story would deny her this crumb of joy. It paints the Fairbanks-Pickford marriage as the quintessential happy ending, making her personal story an echo of her films. Particularly interesting is that, even while it tells the story in terms of a Hollywood happy ending, the article equates the cynicism of the press with the "relentless eye of the camera" (70). That is, the camera works as a metaphor for the critical, unforgiving intrusiveness of modern publicity, even while that same machinery creates the criteria by which the success of their romance is measured. By framing their delicate, ephemeral, and "moonlit" romance against "the glare of the mid-day sun of publicity," the article admonishes the cynical Hollywood gossip (or fan) who does not believe in "romance," thereby validating not only the marriage, but their films. This piece on Pickford and Fairbanks, like others that followed, demonstrates how much their films and characters set the terms by which writers and journalists approached the couple.

Three themes serve as examples of the way in which the Fairbanks persona, in particular, framed the story of their marriage: rescue, royalty, and the "unity of opposites."[1] First, as Christina Lane has pointed out, "rescue" was a prominent theme in coverage of the marriage from the beginning (Lane 78). The *Photoplay* article, for instance, illustrates their shared destiny with this story: "One day there was an accident on the Lasky lot. Miss Pickford was suspended high in the air at a rope's end. It began to spin and twist. There was grave danger that she would be injured. Fairbanks, acting on instinct, climbed to her rescue. He carried her to safety and her arms went about his neck" (Bates 74). Whether this was true or not (likely not) is immaterial. The narrative created around the two is scattered with such stories. Even Pickford remembers the beginning of their romance in terms of a rescue. Recalling their first meeting, she describes a cold November evening when she and Elsie Janis are playfully chasing after Fairbanks and Moore to escape a boring party. Suddenly she finds herself stepping on a log in the middle of a stream: "I knew I couldn't possibly negotiate it without falling into the icy water. What followed was typical of Douglas. At the precise moment of my sudden panic he decided to turn back. What a relief it was to see his friendly face smiling at me. 'Do you mind?' he said. And I frankly replied, 'No,' when I saw how he planned to rescue me. 'Please do'"

(Pickford 197). And he did indeed. It has not been noted, however, that the rescue theme is pervasive in the Fairbanks publicity from the 1910s onward. According to promotional and publicity materials, he always seems to be at the right place at the right time: "Douglas Fairbanks Finds Dying Man on the Desert," "Fairbanks Rescues Child; Proves Hero of the Day," "Fairbanks Gives Blood to Save Employee's Life" (all from Douglas Fairbanks Scrapbook #5, circa 1917–18, AMPAS), "Fairbanks Routs Wolves, Saves Dog" (*Los Angeles Times*, 10 January 1920, 2:7), "Fairbanks and His Merry Men Subdue Blaze" (*Los Angeles Times*, 9 March 1924, B13), and "Doug Fairbanks Rescues 3 Under Overturned Auto" (unsourced, 25 June 1931, Douglas Fairbanks bio clipping file, AMPAS)[2] are just some of the headlines strewn through the discourse on Doug, who apparently saved more lives than the Red Cross. Fairbanks rescued damsels in his films, too, and in this he was not unique; but the insistence of this motif in his publicity from the beginning to the end of his career is rather unusual. When he married Pickford, the publicity about them appropriated this theme in order to validate and make sense of the union for their film audience.

A second frequent theme is "the unity of opposites." Commentators never failed to note the difference between Pickford and Fairbanks—one demure, the other brash; one calm, the other boyishly energetic. One interview describes their entrances into the hotel room in a typical, if picturesque, way: "Something happens. At first one doesn't know just what. Then realization comes. It is Doug." If Fairbanks is lightning, Pickford is rain: "Suddenly there is a deep quiet, as tho a flower, a cool, white pond-lily, perhaps with a heart of clear gold, falling into a pond, had sent out broad circles of peace. It is Mary" (*Motion Picture Magazine*, November 1920, 32). This piece lays it on especially thick, but thinking about the Pickford-Fairbanks marriage as an idyllic unity of complementary forces was common. We should also think of this motif in terms of Fairbanks's films. Sometimes publicity about the couple would be tied to publicity about his films in a painfully obvious way, as when a feature story on the two declares that "Mary and Doug will become a Legend" or "They bring the Age of Chivalry, when men were brave and women fair, into an Age of Commerce," just after *Robin Hood* had opened (*Motion Picture Classic*, February 1923, 47).

But publicity that focuses on the "unity of opposites" theme also recalls similar motifs in the Fairbanks oeuvre starting from his earliest films. This theme, however, has little to do with the romantic subplots of his films; even the most memorable heroines in the Fairbanks films function as little more than pretty faces. Yet these heroines are usually a calm presence in contrast to Doug's flamboyant stunts and personality. Ruth Renick's character in *The Mollycoddle* (1920) is a little more active than usual: she plays a secret agent on the trail of a smuggler. Even so, her activity is limited predominantly to the first half of the film, in which Fairbanks plays a foppish ex-pat American who has grown "soft" from too much time in Europe. In the second half of the film, the Fairbanks character ends up in Arizona and, from this encounter with the land, finds his "true" American blood within; during this transformation, we see little of Renick and when we do, she is a damsel in need of rescue. Accordingly, Fairbanks blossoms into a western hero, saving the girl from the clutches of the evil smuggler. There are two levels, then, in which the "unity of opposites" theme usually works in a Fairbanks film. On the first level, the female lead often functions as blank, calm canvas against which the energetic Fairbanks character can fully display his colors. Interviews with Doug and Mary often rehearse this configuration by contrasting his boyish exuberance against her tranquil, even maternal demeanor. The comparison between Madonna and child or Wendy and Peter Pan, for example, is presented as particularly apt (*Photoplay*, February 1927, 35).

On the second level, the Fairbanks character itself usually displays an inner duality. In such films as *The Lamb* (1915), *Double Trouble* (1915), *Manhattan Madness* (1916), *The Mollycoddle*, or especially *The Mark of Zorro* (1920), the Fairbanks character is divided in two along the East/West axis. *The Lamb* anticipates *The Mollycoddle*: Fairbanks plays an eastern mama's boy who finds his spine out west and rescues the girl. In *Double Trouble*, he plays a bookish twerp from the East who, after a blow to the head, wakes up as a rowdy mayor of a western boomtown. In *Manhattan Madness*, he plays a son of eastern schools and exclusive clubs who returns to New York after life on the range and consequently finds the city life incredibly boring. This theme of western rejuvenation, of the West as an antidote to degeneration, has a long history in American literature (see Slotkin and White), but the most proximate influence on Fairbanks was his hero, Theodore Roosevelt, who adopted this theme as his own and transformed his political career (on Fairbanks and Roosevelt, see Studlar, *Mad Masquerade*). When he entered the film industry, Fairbanks, too, took on this motif as a way of differentiating himself from his Broadway past and aligning himself with his new Hollywood home. Even when his films from the 1910s were not explicitly western-themed, they incorporated some aspect of this duality, usually in the form of a transformation from dissolute or distracted to focused and determined characters (see Curtis). *The Mollycoddle* is a summary—by way of caricature—of these Fairbanks motifs, but *The Mark of Zorro* (1920) is their culmination and conclusion. In *Zorro*, Fairbanks plays Don Diego Vega, the son of a titled landowner in Spanish California, which is ruled by a corrupt governor. Vega returns to California after many years in Spain. By day, he presents himself as a feminized, fey, easily fatigued fop who is concerned with little beyond his slight sleight-of-hand parlor tricks (which nevertheless hint that all is not as it appears). By night, however, he is the dashing masked avenger known as Zorro, who protects the exploited poor from the whip of tyranny. The original inspiration for leagues of superheroes, *Zorro* combined thrilling swordplay, secret identities, and intrigues with a historical setting. Fairbanks had been interested in costume dramas for some time; *A Modern Musketeer* (1917) featured a winking historical prologue in which he plays a swashbuckler. But he was wary of putting his successful generic formula of westerns and modern comedies at risk. The rise of United Artists, his marriage to Pickford, and the enormous boost in celebrity that came with both gave him the confidence to try his hand at the costumed adventure film. It paid off: *Zorro* was his most profitable production yet (Vance 99) and a pivotal film. After *The Nut* (1921), a minor modern comedy mostly ignored by the contemporary press and historians, Fairbanks never returned to his earlier formula. *Zorro* also concludes the East/West, weak/strong duality of the former persona and looks forward to his preoccupation with costume films and nobility.

Fairbanks's longstanding interest in aristocracy is inseparable from publicity about the couple as "Hollywood royalty," the third theme about the marriage that is framed in terms of the Fairbanks persona. This motif first shows up at the time of their honeymoon in June 1920. Upon their arrival in New York, they were hailed as "Filmland Monarchs" and "given a royal welcome by fans" (*Los Angeles Times*, 2 June 1920, 1:8). But the metaphor becomes even more common after their return from their European trip; the adoration of crowds overseas seemed to cement their claim to international fame and entitlement.[3] One set of interviewers was especially smitten when meeting Doug and Mary after their European tour, writing that they "begin to realize how it feels to be presented to royalty. Life can never again hold any thrills" (*Motion Picture Magazine*, November 1920, 31). Subsequent European trips (in 1921, 1922, 1924, and 1926) were instrumental in securing this association between the couple and aristocracy. The trips were not simply vacations; Pickford and Fairbanks also spent time forging business ties with foreign exhibitors, a necessary part of the job, given that United Artists was a distribution company (*Los Angeles Times*, 6 August 1924, A1). But this workaday aspect of the trips was overshadowed by press that focused on their meetings with royalty and heads of state. During their

1924 trip, one paper reported that "the movie sovereigns will be the guests of Lord Louis Mountbatten, cousin of King George," and that "they are also 'commanded' to appear before the king and queen of the Belgians" before calling on "the court of Sweden" later in the season (*Chicago Daily Tribune*, 20 April 1924, 5). They were, however, rebuffed by the king of Denmark on this same trip (*New York Times*, 8 May 1924, 21) and the Spanish king apparently did not appreciate that they attracted bigger crowds than he did, so he asked them to leave (*Los Angeles Times*, 15 August 1924, 2). But in 1926 they had a long, friendly chat with Benito Mussolini, so it all evened out in the end (*New York Times*, 11 May 1926, 29).

As a result of these trips, Mr. and Mrs. Fairbanks assumed the appearance of unofficial American ambassadors (see "Our Unofficial Ambassadors," *Motion Picture Magazine*, June 1927; "'Doug' Fairbanks Called 'Greatest Ambassador,'" *Pittsburg (Kansas) Sun*, 14 December 1926). They often hosted dignitaries at their residence in Hollywood, known as Pickfair. They presented their home as a sanctuary against the glare of publicity, even as it was located in the capital of modern celebrity. In one month, for example, they hosted the British foreign secretary and an Italian duke (*Los Angeles Times*, 30 September 1928, 14). They even offered Pickfair as a summer vacation home for President Calvin Coolidge (*Los Angeles Times*, 26 January 1927, A1). Lord Mountbatten testified, "It was run very much on English country house lines and in fact they really kept court there. It was like Buckingham Palace in London" (Vance 65). And it was well known in Hollywood that Fairbanks and Pickford rarely went out, but receiving an invitation to Pickfair was a special thing indeed. So by 1927, the royalty theme had become an inescapable element of the publicity surrounding the couple, to the point of cliché: "Doug and Mary are, of course, the King and Queen of Hollywood, providing the necessary air of dignity, sobriety, and aristocracy. Gravely they attend movie openings, cornerstone layings, gravely sit at the head of the table at the long dinners in honor of the cinema great, Douglas making graceful speeches, Mary conducting herself with the self-abnegation of Queen Mary of Britain" (Talmey 33).

Perhaps this equation with royalty was inevitable, given their place at the top of the Hollywood hierarchy. But it can't be entirely coincidental that its use corresponds with significant changes in the Fairbanks persona in the 1920s. Certainly, he flirted with the royal fantasy even in his films of the 1910s. *Reaching for the Moon* (1917), for example, features Fairbanks as a regular fellow obsessed with hints of his quasi-royal heritage; much of the film is a dream sequence in which he finds himself defending that heritage in a crumbling European monarchy. Likewise, *His Majesty the American*

(1919) finds Doug playing a restless roustabout who discovers that he is heir to a Balkan throne; he rushes over to set the degenerating monarchy straight using old-fashioned American know-how. But these fantasies were exceptions to his distinctly down-to-earth, democratic persona of the teens. Even in *His Majesty*, the Fairbanks character works hard to maintain ties to the common man by entertaining the chambermaids or sharing a smoke with the hansom cab driver, for example. With *Zorro*, however, a different pattern emerges: the heroes (for example, Zorro, Robin Hood, Don Q, the Black Pirate) start out as aristocrats and use their positions and/or skills to aid the people. In other words, between the 1910s and 1920s there is a shift in the Fairbanks persona that corresponds to, shapes, and amplifies his status as "Hollywood royalty" in the publicity of the day. From a "regular fellow" in his films of the 1910s, Fairbanks is vaulted into nobility by the celebrity machinery of Hollywood. From this high pedestal, it was hard even for him to jump down—and with a sanctuary like Pickfair, he really didn't need to. So his marriage to Pickford generates a royalty trope that taps into his personal interests and finds its way into his films, which in turn continue to feed the metaphor, which eventually guides the way he conducts business.

★★★★★ Fairbanks the Producer

From 1921 to 1926, corresponding to the production of *The Three Musketeers* and the release of *The Black Pirate*, the publicity about Fairbanks focused much more on his role as producer than any other feature of his persona, save his status as Hollywood "royalty." In some ways, this emphasis follows a pattern familiar to his devotees. In the previous six years, he had been portrayed variously as cowboy, popular philosopher, athlete, super-patriot, author, and of course film star—producer/businessman was just one more facet of his persona. In fact, the discussion of Fairbanks as businessman first begins during his Broadway days as a recurring feature of a (mostly fanciful) biography that tells of a brief stint on Wall Street. That story was apparently a necessary, masculine element. As Richard Schickel states, "It was man's work—business—in the age when business was said to be the business of America" (Schickel, *Picture* 75). The motif comes up again when Fairbanks creates his own production company in 1917, and then again with the formation of United Artists in 1919. But even at these moments, his role as producer never overshadowed other aspects of his image; it functioned more as a side light bringing other roles into relief. As his productions became more expansive and his status at the top of the

Douglas Fairbanks as *The Black Pirate* (1926). Courtesy of the Academy of Motion Picture Arts and Sciences.

Hollywood food chain more secure, his role as producer outshone all other features of his star persona. One Hollywood wit even admitted, "Doug, the star, would have been out long ago had it not been for his friend, Doug, the producer" (*Los Angeles Times*, 29 April 1925, C7). During these years, Fairbanks's "producer function" had three sides: manager, industry spokesman, and artist.

If Fairbanks dipped his toe in the uncertain waters of the costume film with *Zorro*, pulling back quickly with *The Nut*, he flung himself head first into the genre with *The Three Musketeers* (1921). His initial caution stemmed from his unwillingness to fiddle with his successful formula. But costume films had been making headway in the industry without him; Germany's Ernst Lubitsch, for example, had scored box office hits with imports *Madame DuBarry* (aka *Passion*, 1919) and *Anna Boleyn* (aka *Deception*, 1920).[4] So the waters were not completely untested by the time he decided to film the Dumas novel. Adding to his enthusiasm was his long-standing fascination with the character of D'Artagnan, to whom he would return with his last silent film, *The Iron Mask* (1929). For some, such as critic Robert Sherwood, no other actor could have played D'Artagnan with as much panache: "When Alexandre Dumas sat down at his desk, smoothed his hair back, chewed the end of his quill pen, and said to himself, 'Well, I guess I might as well write a book called *The Three Musketeers*,' he doubtless had but one object in view: to provide a suitable story for Douglas Fairbanks to act in the movies" (*Life*, 22 September 1921, 78). The rest of the critics and country agreed—with a fast-paced story and some of the most amazing swordplay ever seen on the screen, it was a big box-office success. But it was also a big production, costing just under $750,000 (Vance 122). Much of the publicity for the film focused on the scale of its production: "The Louvre, with its vaulted ceilings and impressive arches, was reproduced in a set nearly 200 feet long. . . . With the King and Queen looking on from the throne, 200 gorgeously costumed couples occupy the floor . . . 'All told,' said Robert Fairbanks, production manager and brother of the famous Doug, 'we built 37 interiors and 40 exteriors, every one of them costing at least three times as much as any other set ever constructed on the Fairbanks lot'" (*Boston Daily Globe*, 11 September 1921, 60). Part of this emphasis has a nationalistic (if not testosterone-filled) ring to it: *Musketeers* "is the superior of any of the German pictures that have been brought to this country" (*Life*, 22 September 1921, 78), and it "has proved beyond a doubt that the foreign producers can still learn a lot from America" (*Boston Daily Globe*, 12 September 1921, 9). But this stress on the size of the production also points to the direction Fairbanks was taking the industry. Big spectacles would soon be the order of the day and "it appears to have greatly pleased [Fairbanks] to set hundreds of craftsmen to work on projects that would, ultimately, employ similar numbers of players" (Schickel, *Picture* 75).

This pattern holds for his next few films, but especially for the following picture, *Douglas Fairbanks in Robin Hood* (1922). *Robin Hood* was huge:

"Thirty thousand calls issued through casting department to players. Eighteen hundred players used in biggest scene. Three hundred horses used in a single scene. Total scenes shot, eleven hundred and eight" (*Moving Picture World*, 9 September 1922, 114). And so forth. It broke records at both ends, in the size of the production and in the size of the box office gross (*Los Angeles Times*, 10 February 1923, 2:16). It started a new trend toward big-budget spectacles in Hollywood, which included *The Ten Commandments* (1923), *The Covered Wagon* (1923), and others. But it was an especially significant film given the state of the industry at the time. Buffeted by the celebrity scandals of 1921–22 (involving Roscoe "Fatty" Arbuckle, William Desmond Taylor, Mabel Normand, and Wallace Reid) and increasing pressure from reform groups for outside censorship, the industry was on the defensive and in an economic slump (see Koszarski, *Evening's Entertainment* 198–210). For many inside and out of Hollywood, Fairbanks represented an unimpeachable brand of entertainment. "But the new picture is not all expensive setting. It has a clean-cut, human story" that, for Fairbanks, has none of the "sordid realism" he deplores in the pictures of the day (*Los Angeles Times*, 19 March 1922, 3:33). *Robin Hood* came to the rescue in another way. With thousands out of work during the slump in Hollywood, the scale of the production also provided a much-needed economic stimulus in the classic tradition of paying workers so that they can consume the products they help make: "The surprising total of 25,000 persons received pay for serving as supernumeraries" in the film. "This large number of people were given employment in the capacity of 'extras.' . . . Most of them have spent a portion of their money on several visits to Grauman's Hollywood Egyptian Theater, where *Robin Hood* is starting its fifteenth week" (*Los Angeles Times*, 21 January 1923, 3:32). And in every story, Fairbanks is portrayed as a figure who manages all aspects of the production, from the initial research to the set design and the final cut.

    Robin Hood, then, was undoubtedly good for Hollywood, just what it needed at just the right time. It was a "statement" film that testified to the industry's potential at a moment when that potential was in doubt. Starting with this film, Fairbanks begins to make more direct remarks to the press and public about the state of the industry. He had always had bylines, ever since his days on Broadway. In interviews and articles (ghost) written by him, he had offered an opinion on all sorts of topics, but usually within a domain that supported his established star persona. In the late 1910s, for example, he wrote about the importance of fitness and clean living for good health and wartime preparedness (*Los Angeles Times*, 1 October 1918, 14). He also wrote two inspirational books, *Laugh and Live*

(1917) and *Making Life Worthwhile* (1918), which outlined his formula for optimism and success. His interviews, too, would often lay out his keys to success in the film industry, or his immediate plans for the next film. He became more involved in the public presentation of business after the formation of United Artists, when he acted as the de facto spokesman for the company. Always good for a quote—and apparently less shy than his partners—Fairbanks was often the point man for any company announcement, such as the formation of Allied Corporation, a subsidiary distributor (*Los Angeles Times*, 21 April 1922, 2:11). But with *Robin Hood*, he offers bolder and broader proclamations about the state of the industry. He speaks against legislating censorship (*Moving Picture World*, 25 March 1922, 355); against industry overproduction (*Ladies' Home Journal*, September 1922, 117); even against Will Hays's plans for the studios (*Los Angeles Times*, 26 January 1923, 2:1). But he also has a vision for the industry, which he articulates in a series of articles for *Ladies Home Journal* in 1922 and 1924. With such titles as "As Douglas Fairbanks Sees the Film Play of Tomorrow" (October 1922); "Why Big Pictures" (March 1924); "Films for the Fifty Million" (April 1924); and "A Huge Responsibility" (May 1924), he justifies his production plans and suggests his ideas about the artistic potential of the medium. Nothing he says is groundbreaking, but they were not questions that would have been asked of him even five years earlier. If he had already become social royalty with his marriage to Pickford, with *Robin Hood* he emerges as one of the town's leading producers, the King of Hollywood, with all the responsibilities it entails. When he says, "I made up my mind that the best way to further the cause of pictures was by making good pictures," he explicitly places himself as the gallant protector—even rescuer—of an embattled industry (*Los Angeles Times*, 16 March 1922, 2:9).

His ambitions were not only industrial but also artistic. Not satisfied with making the biggest movies, he also wanted to make the best and most beautiful movies. This aspiration is most evident in *The Thief of Bagdad* (1924) and *The Black Pirate* (1926). Yet in his public proclamations, Fairbanks is ambivalent about the status of his films as art:

> Those of us who have tried and learned what is known today as film-making do not believe that we are turning out great and permanent works of art. . . . What everyone who is seriously interested in the business is trying to do is to get at the possibilities of the screen. There is something bigger and better going to come out of the films than anyone has yet found. We are all digging away for that, and meantime we are affording entertainment to millions of persons the world over.
>
> ("Why Big Pictures," *Ladies' Home Journal*, March 1924)

Nevertheless, there is no denying the self-consciously artistic aims of these two films, especially *Thief*. Even if Fairbanks himself humbly demurred, the publicity and critical reception of the films trumpeted their aesthetic qualities. Reviews for both were ecstatic, but the spectacle of *Thief* forced many critics to reach for their thesaurus, as in this advance publicity piece:

> Naught that adds iridescence and kindling beauty to scene and costume but will be embodied in the exotic pageant. Naught that has yet gone to make you gasp with astonishment, or laugh with delight at some bizarre eccentricity of pictorial motion, some photographic trick, but will be used to heighten the extravagant fascination of this new Scheherazade tale.
>
> (*Picture-Play*, September 1923, 44)

Reviews for *Pirate* were similarly positive, especially about its use of still-experimental two-strip Technicolor. No less a commentator than poet and early film theorist Vachel Lindsay compared the colors and compositions of *Pirate* to the paintings of Frank Brangwyn, Howard Pyle, and Winslow Homer (*Ladies' Home Journal*, August 1926, 12, 114). Indeed, if *Pirate* was an homage to painting, *Thief* borrowed liberally from modern dance, as Gaylyn Studlar has argued. With its "treatment of scenic décor as a 'dance space' and by the Léon Bakst–influenced style of its production design . . . the film appears as a self-consciously artful meditation of trends found in the Ballets Russes's scenic and costume design, setting, and figure movement" (Studlar, "Douglas Fairbanks" 109).

This combination of scale and artistic ambition naturally drew comparisons to D. W. Griffith, as when one reporter notes that the sets for *Robin Hood* represent the largest since *Intolerance* (1916) (*Los Angeles Times*, 16 March 1922, 2:9). Lindsay took that comparison one step further: "I say that in *The Thief of Bagdad* and *The Black Pirate*, Douglas is fighting like a gentleman and scholar for Griffith's place. The history of the movies is now David Wark Griffith, Douglas Fairbanks, and whoever rises hereafter to dispute their title" (*Ladies' Home Journal*, August 1926, 12). Today that claim might seem specious to all but the most devoted fans, but at the time Lindsay was merely confirming Fairbanks's established place in the cinema hierarchy. After a string of industry-changing successes, his stature was on a par with Griffith's after *The Birth of a Nation* (1915) and *Intolerance*. And Lindsay based his praise not on claims for Fairbanks's artistic genius, but for his *leadership*. Chaplin and Valentino have their particular genius, Lindsay argues, "but when you reflect upon the massive statesmanship required to conceive and to put across two such films of the sea and land, of mobs and of cities, as *The Thief of Bagdad* and *The Black Pirate*, Douglas Fairbanks is the statesman and great man" (114). In the late 1920s, this position of leadership would be at once confirmed through his presidency of the newly formed Academy of Motion Picture Arts and Sciences, and lost with the coming of sound.

★★★★★ An Aging King

In mid-1927, the Academy of Motion Picture Arts and Sciences (AMPAS) chose Fairbanks as their first president. Given his stature in the industry, it appeared to be a natural choice. After all, he was also very involved in the formation and development of Beverly Hills and in the effort to bring the 1932 Olympics to Los Angeles.[5] He was an active civic and industry leader. But the idea of the Academy was born in the living room of Louis B. Mayer, the MGM studio mogul, and some contended that it was merely a "producers' union" from the very start, so the choice of president was a delicate matter that might have easily gone another way.[6]

The founders of the Academy of Motion Picture Arts and Sciences, circa 1927. Standing, left to right: Cedric Gibbons, J. A. Ball, Carey Wilson, George Cohen, Edwin Loeb, Fred Beetson, Frank Lloyd, Roy Pomeroy, John Stahl, Harry Rapf. Seated, left to right: Louis B. Mayer, Conrad Nagel, Mary Pickford, Douglas Fairbanks, Frank Woods, M. C. Levee, Joseph M. Schenck, Fred Niblo. Courtesy of the Academy of Motion Picture Arts and Sciences.

Years later, in fact, director Fred Niblo, one of the original founders, remembered that it did go another way at first: "At our first big 'get-together' it was suggested Irving Thalberg [MGM producer and Mayer protégé] be made president. But Irving believed . . . that an actor should head the organization and Douglas Fairbanks was elected the first president" (Fred Niblo to Hedda Hopper, 14 November 1941, Hedda Hopper Collection, AMPAS). Thalberg was right, as he was about so many things: trouble with the actors' union was brewing on the horizon, as anyone could see, and it would be best, if the Academy were to maintain legitimacy in the eyes of the guilds, to choose not a representative from management, but from the actors. As a producer himself, Fairbanks would also be friendly to those concerns. Furthermore, he was a prominent and well-liked personality, giving the new organization a strong public face.

Looking closely at his tenure as president, however, it is clear that his role in the Academy was minimal. Others, such as Frank Woods, William C. De Mille, Fred Beetson, Mayer, and even Mary Pickford were more instrumental in shaping the direction of the organization. For example, an Academy bulletin announces De Mille's presidency in 1929: "In accepting the office of President, *the active duties of which he has been performing for the past year as Vice President*, Mr. De Mille briefly outlined the very considerable achievements of the Academy" (Academy Bulletin No. 26, 30 October 1929, AMPAS; my emphasis). We must conclude that it was precisely Fairbanks's public *face*, his persona, that the fledgling Academy required: someone perceived as honest and honorable, inherently democratic yet graced with *noblesse oblige*, as well as someone with managerial skill and a deep investment in the future of the industry. Fairbanks may have personally held all these qualities, but they were definitely elements of his established star image, which was more important to the Academy at its formation.

We can also speculate that the widening schism between Fairbanks and Pickford might have played a role in his waning interest in the Academy and in his work in general. Her mother's illness and death between 1926 and 1928, along with the death of his brother John in 1926, affected them both profoundly and put a heavy strain on their relationship (Vance 227). As a result, Pickford began to drink heavily, further alienating teetotaling Fairbanks (Vance 281). In 1927, they found consolation in the arms of others—Pickford with her co-star Buddy Rogers on the set of *My Best Girl* (1927) and Fairbanks with Lupe Velez during the filming of *Douglas Fairbanks as The Gaucho* (1927) (Vance 239). They stayed together through this, but the cracks in the relationship were beginning to show. His attention to his work decreased and his interest in travel grew, as they took trips around the world in 1928 and 1929.

Gaucho opened in November 1927, one month after *The Jazz Singer*, to mixed reviews. Though it did well at the box office, the critical response to the film was distracted by the potential of sound cinema. In public, Fairbanks was cautiously open-minded about the new technology: "While fully appreciative of the novelty and the advances made by talking pictures during the past few months, Fairbanks feels it still has serious limitations, particularly in his type of production" (*Washington Post*, 29 July 1928, A2). His son put it more bluntly: "My father's enthusiasm for his work had, by then, begun to diminish. He was interested in the advent of 'talking pictures,' and clearly admired *other* people's sound films, but he felt very strongly that *his* medium, like Chaplin's, was the silent film—story-telling through the medium of pictures. . . . Sound, for his purposes, was too literal, too realistic and restricting" (Douglas Fairbanks Bio Pamphlet #1, AMPAS). Nevertheless, he incorporated sound accompaniment into his last silent film, a sequel to *The Three Musketeers* called *The Iron Mask* (1929), which opened to good reviews and good box office; but it was only marginally profitable and became the swan song of the costumed adventure film (for the time being) as well. As Jeffrey Vance writes, "Having virtually defined the swashbuckler as a cinematic genre, Fairbanks was also the one to usher out its initial cycle" (266).

The final sign of his impending irrelevance was Fairbanks's collaboration with Pickford in *Taming of the Shrew* (1929), a talkie adaptation of the Shakespeare play. It seemed like a good idea: fans had been clamoring for them to appear together in a film for years, Fairbanks was comfortable with the Bard, and it was a chance to repair their relationship by renewing their interest in their work. Sadly, it didn't turn out that way. His normal exuberance soured to petulance under the restrictions of early sound film production. Pickford, meanwhile, tried to maintain her work ethic. Art director Laurence Irving witnessed the inevitable collision: "At times, it seemed as though a mischievous sprite incited Douglas to ruin scenes for the hell of it, in mockery of the medium in which he realized Mary had a professional edge on him" (Vance 276). The tensions on the set further unraveled their marriage. Even though the film opened to good reviews, it was not treated well by history; it was, for example, notorious for the credit, "By William Shakespeare. Additional Dialogue by Sam Taylor," which they hastily fixed (Vance 277). Pickford's confidence suffered from the experience and Fairbanks took to traveling, first alone and then with Lady Sylvia Ashley. Pickford and Fairbanks divorced in 1936, but *Taming* did them in long before.

Fairbanks made a couple of minor films in the 1930s, but his heart was not in it—it finally gave out completely in 1939. Perhaps it was clear to him, as it was to almost everyone else, that his reign as King of Hollywood lasted only as long as the last decade of the silent film and his happy collaboration with Mary Pickford.

ACKNOWLEDGMENTS

My thanks to The Alumnae of Northwestern for a research grant; to Alla Gadassik for her thorough and timely research assistance; to Jeffrey Vance and Mary Francis for a pre-publication copy of Vance's important biography of Fairbanks; and to Val Almendarez, Barbara Hall, Doug Johnson, Matt Severson, and the rest of the staff of the Margaret Herrick Library, Academy of Motion Picture Arts and Sciences, Beverly Hills.

NOTES

1. I do not want to give the impression that the Fairbanks persona was the only or even dominant factor in framing this publicity—Pickford's persona certainly played a role as well. But since this is an essay on Fairbanks, the focus is on him.

2. The Scrapbooks are located in the Douglas Fairbanks Collection, Margaret Herrick Library, Academy of Motion Picture Arts and Sciences, Beverly Hills. The clipping file is in the Biographical clipping files in the same institution.

3. We mustn't forget the importance of Doug's publicist, Bennie Zeidman, in orchestrating the receptions that the couple received. He accompanied them on their European honeymoon and made sure that crowds knew where to find them and that the press was there to witness it.

4. In fact, in 1922 Fairbanks and Pickford hired Lubitsch to be their director, testifying to Fairbanks's admiration of these films and his plans for the genre. Lubitsch ended up making only *Rosita* (1923) with Pickford. See "Lubitsch to Direct Doug," *Los Angeles Times*, 29 November 1922, 2:1.

5. On Fairbanks as "First Citizen" of Beverly Hills, see Scrapbook #1, Douglas Fairbanks Collection, AMPAS, or "Will Rogers Chosen Mayor," *New York Times*, 13 December 1926, 29. For his work for the Olympic Committee, see the same scrapbook or "'Doug' Boosts Olympics," *Los Angeles Times*, 1 April 1928, A7.

6. On the early history of the Academy, see Sands. On that history from the point of view of the guilds, see "The Academy Writer-Producer Agreement," *Screen Guilds' Magazine* (October 1935), 1–3; and Frank Woods, "History of Producer-Talent Relations in the Academy," *Screen Guilds' Magazine* (November 1935), 4, 26–27.

2 ☆☆☆☆☆☆☆☆☆☆☆

Buster Keaton
Comic Invention and the Art of Moving Pictures

CHARLES WOLFE

Buster Keaton's career covered nearly seven decades, but he produced his most striking and enduring work in the 1920s, a period in which comedian-centered, physical comedy was widely regarded as a vibrant American film genre and Keaton himself was in his physical prime. In 1920 Keaton assumed the starring role at the Comique Film Corporation, an independent production company established by Joseph M. Schenck for comedian Roscoe "Fatty" Arbuckle three years earlier. The company was renamed Buster Keaton Productions in 1922, and Keaton would continue

Buster Keaton, in character for the modern story in *Three Ages*, poses at the Keaton Studio in 1923. Publicity still.

to make comedies under this banner until 1928. He was among a handful of silent comedians schooled in vaudeville knockabout who in the 1920s came to exercise substantial control over the production of their films, made a successful transition from short comedies to features, and achieved international stardom on a scale that would not have been possible on the stage. He was regularly profiled in fan magazines, newspapers, and the trade press on topics of both professional and personal interest. Like his two principal rivals, Charlie Chaplin and Harold Lloyd, he attracted the attention of trade journalists and critics who were tracking changes in the form, style, and tone of motion picture comedy in the 1920s, and he became a focal point for discussions about the contribution of physical slapstick to the "mechanical" art of the screen.

Keaton's fortunes would change dramatically at the end of the silent era. Signing on as a contract star at MGM during the transitional years to talkies, he found himself increasingly constrained by studio policies and practices. Personal setbacks—a painful divorce from Natalie Talmadge, whom he had married in 1921 when his stardom was in ascent, and a debilitating drinking habit—also took a toll. By the mid-1930s he had settled into a steady stream of less celebrated roles in low-budget comedy shorts, cameo roles in features, and work behind the camera, chiefly as a gag writer and comedy advisor. In the 1950s and 1960s, he added television, commercials, and industrial films to the mix and, drawing on skills honed as a child star in vaudeville many decades before, occasionally appeared in stock company theatrical road shows and in circuses in France and Belgium. To a modest degree, then, Keaton remained in the public eye. But the reputation of his silent comedies depended fragilely on rare screenings of a few surviving films at the Museum of Modern Art and other art film venues in the United States and abroad.

This situation would change in the 1960s and 1970s, thanks in large measure to the efforts of entrepreneurial film collector Raymond Rohauer. Entering into a financial agreement with Keaton, Rohauer acquired and assembled prints of nearly all of the nineteen short and ten feature-length comedies Keaton made between 1920 and 1928, some of which Keaton himself believed to be lost. With this collection in hand, Rohauer organized a series of highly successful Keaton retrospectives, first in Europe, then in the United States (McGregor 32–33). These screenings generated a wave of new critical writing and popular commentary on Keaton's early movie comedies, the first European stirrings of which surfaced in the years just prior to his death in 1966. By the time of the first U.S. retrospectives in New York and Los Angeles in the early 1970s, his silent screen persona had gained new currency and definition as the "Great Stone Face," emphasizing the figure's silent sto-icism and reserve, and in short order Keaton's standing rose as a neglected American artist of the first rank. Yet even as these comedies came under renewed scrutiny, the history of their initial production and reception—of films made, publicized, viewed, and reviewed in the 1920s—remained a remote and vaguely formulated backdrop to most critical accounts.

This essay examines the history of Keaton's star image as it emerged and developed during the course of the 1920s. I begin, however, with a broader frame, placing details of Keaton's biography within the context of early-twentieth-century debates about American art and technology, the terms of which illuminate aspects of Keaton's professional training and experiences, and have a bearing on the critical vocabulary and concepts through which his comedies were assessed, both in the short and long term. In an essay on the history of the mischief gag in American silent comedy, Tom Gunning has proposed that the romance of Keaton's characters with "devices of a heroic but already fading age of machines and energy (the locomotive, the steam-boat)" are exemplary of silent comedy's inheritance of a nineteenth-century "operational aesthetic," in which pleasure is derived from the demonstration of mechanical processes (Gunning 100). In a complementary formulation, Noël Carroll has suggested that Keaton's comedy served a compensatory function for viewers in the 1920s, allowing renewed pleasure in acts of everyday, practical intelligence in an era when the economic value of such skills had eroded (Carroll 63–71). Testing propositions of this sort require that we consider Keaton's reputation in relation to historical evidence of dif-ferent kinds and on different scales: biographical accounts, institutional dis-courses close to the production and distribution of the films, and cultural criticism that unfolded across regional and national boundaries and over time. Of particular concern here are the ways in which commentaries on Keaton's comedies became enmeshed in conversations about the power of motion pictures as a modern art form—perhaps *the* modern art form—an idea in circulation far in advance of Keaton's revival in the 1960s and 1970s, and with more intricate implications for his star image than a rudimentary picture of a "Great Stone Face" conveys.

★★★★★ Technological Aesthetics and the Mechanics of Film Comedy

In an effort to define a distinctively American approach to art, cultural critics in the United States during the interwar years identified a national tradition of artful craftsmanship that emphasized the beauty of everyday objects and the technical ingenuity of the ordinary worker. American art, viewed in this light, took its most characteristic forms within the context of various functional applications: in the clarity of plain, colloquial language; in the simplicity of Shaker furniture and music; in the geometry of rural barns and urban bridges; in the movement of clipper ships, steamboats, and railroad locomotives; and in precision hand tools that were practical, free of ornamentation, and widely accessible. Equating engineering with creativity, the ideal of a vernacular aesthetic tradition based on principles of technological design was thought to connect art with public life in a more robust and democratic way than did genteel forms of literature or painting or concert music, fine art reserved for the museum or upper-class drawing room and set apart from worldly, material concerns (see Mumford *Sticks, Brown*; Pupin; Rourke; Kouwenhoven).

At the same time, the notion of an aesthetic of technological craftsmanship had to be reconciled with changing modes of commerce and a burgeoning consumer culture ushered in by the second industrial revolution. By the end of the nineteenth century, the broadening scale of industrial design and accelerating pace of technological change called into question the role of the imaginative inventor or mechanical tinker who, either individually or in collaboration with others, crafted solutions to local problems with the materials at hand. Funded by corporate capital, industrial research and design provided a new model for technological experimentation and innovation, with individual performance measured by standards of productivity and efficiency established for the operation of the system overall. The "beauty" of the assembly line production methods introduced by Henry Ford in 1907, commentators frequently noted, resided not in any single activity, human or mechanical, but in the conceptual logic of a rationalized, fully integrated economic operation. So too the public space of the city was imagined as a place in which private interests competed for control of vertically tiered spaces and required complex systems of transportation that carried mobile workers in carefully timed, coordinated patterns not wholly visible to the human eye (see Hughes, *American* 184–248; Smith, *Making* 15–158).

For many European intellectuals attuned to these changes in the early twentieth century, an older myth of an American Arcadia was now complicated by a new myth of the American Metropolis. In common parlance "Americanism" came to represent an ethos of accelerated, aggressive technological change, a primitive energy that seemed to leapfrog civilized habits and customs on its way toward a future of unprecedented velocity and power. In some quarters the future this portended was embraced. In the early 1920s artists allied with the Bauhaus in Germany drew upon American tenets of industrial efficiency in formulating new principles of design for mass-produced goods. The work of American engineers in part inspired the new International Style of architecture—clean, hard-edged, and angular—made famous by Walter Gropius (of the Bauhaus), Le Corbusier, and Ludwig Mies van der Rohe. In the USSR social planners wedded Frederick Taylor's principles of scientific management to scientific Marxism in the design of a newly centralized economic and political system. Shorn of any rational economic application, an American machine aesthetic also was celebrated by avant-garde artists in Italy, Russia, France, and Germany for the radical break it offered with bourgeois customs and norms. At the same time, critics of industrial modernity, in the United States as well as Europe, lamented the apparent liquidation of western traditions by the juggernaut of American technocratic culture, calling attention to contemporary social pathologies—alienated workers, urban poverty and disease, psychological disintegration and neurosis, class conflict and war—which seemed to belie the political logic by which economic and technological innovations frequently were justified. How reasonable, after all, were processes of corporate rationalization that fragmented human activity and ruptured community ties? If new technologies promised enhanced utility and power, critics asked, utility and power for whom? And at what cultural, psychological, or ethical cost (see Gramsci; Marcuse; Jay 173–218; Hughes, *American* 249–352; de Grazia)?

Patterns of economic and social development in the United States, however, were far more variegated than the equation of "Fordism" with "Americanism" suggests. The accelerated growth of modern industry in the 1910s and 1920s was limited largely to the northeast corridor and upper Midwest, with small pockets of rapid urban development in cities in the West and South. Vast stretches of farm and ranch land across the Great Plains and Deep South were cut off from electricity until the introduction of federal rural electrification programs in the mid-1930s. As Susan Hegeman has argued, regional differences of this kind help to explain conspicuous anomalies in linear historical accounts of America's cultural modernization in the putative "Jazz Age," including the flight of American expatriate writers to Europe, the anti-technological fervor of the Southern Agrarians, William Faulkner's imaginative commitments to rural Mississippi and Willa Cather's to the prairie lands and desert, Georgia O'Keeffe's abandonment of Manhattan for Taos, New Mexico, and the fascination of ethnographers and artists with craft traditions of Appalachia and the indigenous culture of the America Southwest. While the association of industrial modernity with America may be part of the mythology of modernism that we have inherited, Hegeman proposes, these provincial interests point to a more historically embedded, geographically variegated modernism in which urban centers operate in tension with outlining sectors, across regional and national boundaries, and contemporary social articulations are informed by provincial and transnational circumstances and inflected by the deep pull of the past (21–24). Although early cinema, including early cinema comedy, has in recent years often been linked to the rise of industrial modernity, understanding the emergence of Buster Keaton as a film star requires attention to these more variable, regional concerns.

Keaton arrived on the scene of these wide-ranging changes neither a social thinker nor a self-conscious artist but rather a comic performer and filmmaker whose activities are illuminated by contemporaneous cultural debates. His temperament and training were in accord with the nineteenth-century tradition of technological ingenuity, of practical invention and creative problem solving in local or regional settings. At the same time, his career trajectory through vaudeville and motion pictures brought him into contact with the full force of industrial modernity in an accelerated phase. As a young child Keaton briefly traveled a rough-and-tumble medicine show circuit with his parents, a life of itinerant comic performance and provisional social relations pursued through territory that only a few years before had defined for an expansionist nation notions of an American "frontier." But medicine show vagabondism by the Keaton family gave way to a modern form of regulated, urban entertainment, with schedules organized by powerful vaudeville booking offices and made possible by a network of railroad lines connecting dispersed cities and towns. Vaudeville promised unprecedented publicity for the once backwater Keaton family, and elevated Buster as a child performer to stardom at a very young age, but it also imposed new constraints that his father, known for a roughneck manner, openly resisted, at times in violent ways (Keaton 87–88).

Performance in moving pictures complicated this dynamic. Upon first joining the Comique Film Corporation in March 1917, Keaton later recalled, he was excited and fascinated by the studio environment, as well as by the mechanics of the camera in which Roscoe Arbuckle quickly schooled him (Keaton 91–93). In a 1958 interview, Keaton claimed that "the first thing I did in the studio was to want to tear that camera to pieces. I had to know how that film got into the cutting-room, what you did to it in there, how you projected it, how you finally got the picture together, and how you made things match" (Franklin and Franklin 67–68). Moviemaking at Comique offered the possibility of creative work with fellow actors, writers, and technicians in an intensely collaborative environment. Here a performance, no longer an ephemeral theatrical event, could be recorded, edited, and organized on film as a fixed work of fiction. Motion pictures also greatly expanded the audience for Keaton's comic skills. In 1908, the Keaton family performed briefly in England, the single exposure of foreign audiences to the child star during his early years on stage (Keaton 51–63). Two decades later the replicable image of "Buster" was recognizable to moviegoers around the world.

Throughout his long career, however, Keaton was averse to the trappings of stardom, deriving pleasure principally from private hobbies and retreats, apart from the world of show business and celebrity. From childhood on he was fascinated by mechanical devices and gadgets, designed and operable by hand. During his teenage years in vaudeville, he delighted in summers spent at Bluffton, a performer's colony near Lake Michigan, where practical jokes—a trick-wire fishing pole, a fly-away outhouse—could be rigged in wide open spaces (Blesh 64–76; Keaton 39–42). A Browniekar roadster, bought off the floor of Macy's department store in 1909, inaugurated Keaton's life-long ownership of eccentric mechanized vehicles, ranging in size from miniature trains to a thirty-foot motorized "land yacht" that in the early 1930s briefly doubled as his home (Blesh 69–70, 329–30). At the height of his fame, Keaton preferred an unpretentious California bungalow to the ornate "Italian Villa" favored by Natalie, the middle sister of Norma and Constance Talmadge, both stars in their own right, and both also under contract to Schenck, and at the time Norma's husband. In his last years, with his third wife, Eleanor, he settled comfortably into a modest San Fernando Valley home, nestled between a cornfield and a horse ranch, with its scattered barnyard animals, hen house, bunkhouse, vegetable garden, orchard, and saloon-style bar, a semi-rustic retreat he referred to as a "thinking man's farm."[1] Here he continued to tinker with gadgets, contraptions, and toy trains, the late comic designs of a tirelessly inventive mind.

As a working comic actor and filmmaker in the 1920s, Keaton found a haven of a kind in his own production company under the corporate supervision of Schenck. Upon advancing Keaton to the lead position at Comique, Schenck negotiated a distribution deal with Metro, a firm recently strengthened through its purchase by the entertainment powerhouse, Loews, and managed by Schenck's brother, Nicholas. Keaton was cast in a lead role in an upcoming Metro feature, *The Saphead* (1921), which served to get his name into wider circulation. Shot in the spring of 1920, the film's release the following February helped to establish his credentials as a legitimate

movie star (Krämer *Saphead*). For the production of his own short comedies, Keaton moved into Charlie Chaplin's old Lone Star studio, a small
facility in Hollywood that Metro had taken over after Chaplin departed, and
located on a city block adjacent to Metro's more expansive, factory-like
complex. By 1922 the sign above the main office at 1025 Lillian Way read
"'Buster Keaton' Comedies." Here he was able to exercise principal control
over the writing, directing, and editing of his films, even as Schenck took
advantage of the industrial clout of Metro—and for eleven of the short
films, First National—in the marketing and distribution of these comedies.
Deeply engaged by the craft of filmmaking, Keaton entrusted financial concerns to Schenck, an arrangement that served Keaton well until he joined
MGM as a contract star in 1928.

Had he not been born into a theatrical family, Keaton later speculated, he
might have found his calling as a civil engineer (Keaton 24). His penchant for
comic performance, we can infer, drew on an engineer's imagination, but
one freed of wholly practical demands, allowing Keaton the luxury of playing with the very notion of functional planning and design in non-utilitarian ways. Screenwriter Anita Loos, close friend of the Talmadge sisters in
the 1920s, recalls visiting the Italian Villa at the time of Keaton's mounting
estrangement from his socially ambitious in-laws and discovering him working outdoors alone. He "was digging a tiny ditch in which water trickled
aimlessly," she reports. "Buster was as intent as if he were constructing the
Panama Canal. When I asked what he was doing, he replied, 'Just having
fun! I can make my little ditch go anywhere I choose . . . to the right . . . or
left or straight ahead.' He paused to sigh in satisfaction. '*I sure have authority
over my little creek'*" (Loos 116). Loos's recollection condenses several familiar strands of biographical commentary: Keaton's tendency to retreat from
the social orbit of the smart set; his delight with pseudo-practical projects,
at once directed and aimless; and behind the self-deprecating humor his
edginess about matters of authority or control.

Within the framework of a fictional scenario, the authority to shape the
course of comic events could be equally absorbing. Friends and colleagues
frequently noted that Keaton brought to all his creative projects in the
1920s formidable powers of concentration and a fierce attention to detail.
We get a sense of this from Keaton's own retrospective lament for the disintegration of the family's vaudeville act in the winter of 1916–1917,
undermined by his father's intemperate drinking and a taxing schedule of
three performances a day at second-tier theaters on the West Coast. Keaton
recalled for Rudi Blesh: "What a beautiful thing it had been. That beautiful
timing we had—beautiful to see, beautiful to do. The sound of the laughs,

solid, right where you knew they would be. . . . But look at what happened—standing up and bopping each other like a cheap film" (81). Playmaking for Keaton, in short, required discipline. In contrast, a crude bop on the head, straight up—that is to say, not properly *set up*—was degrading, devoid of craft. On similar grounds he expressed dismay at the cavalier approach to moviemaking of sound-era comedy teams such as Abbott and Costello and the Marx Brothers, whom he advised in later years (Markle 161). The control or mastery to which Keaton was committed, however, was something other than the rationalizing force of corporate systems. Rather, it involved a careful, at times mathematical, approach to comic choreography, capable of incorporating surprising trajectories and playful detours.

Filmmaking under Schenck's loose supervision allowed Keaton and his collaborators—studio manager Lou Anger; co-writer-director (on the shorts) Eddie Cline; cinematographer Elgin Lessley; technical director Fred Gabourie; and writers Clyde Bruckman, Jean Havez, Joe Mitchell, and others on many of the features—time to discover and elaborate comedy business before the camera, to eliminate mistakes or revise dull action, and to assemble pieces of celluloid in a precise way. Repeated for the camera, extended or compressed, edited to different rhythms and in relation to different sequences, comic performances provided the raw material from which new plastic and kinetic forms could be constructed. Comic films, from this angle, might be thought of as complex arrangements of movable parts: the gag as gadget, the plot as a system of finely tuned levers, pulleys, springs, trip wires, and traps. To study film technique, in this broader sense, was to explore the central mechanisms of movie comedy—its familiar gags and large-scale structures; its recurring characters, settings, and themes—in search of new contexts for the engagement of a comic performer with the physical world.

☆☆★★★ The Invention of Buster Keaton

Publicity materials produced by Comique and Metro to launch Keaton's career as a solo film comedian in the fall of 1920 highlighted not only his physical agility and resiliency—key attractions of his athletic style dating back to his years as a vaudeville performer—but his experience, judgment, and authority as a craftsman of comedy. The cover story of Metro's press book accompanying the release of his first short, *One Week*, in October 1920 sketched a narrative of Keaton's personal and professional maturation. On the brink of motion picture stardom, he had "graduated" twice over, first from training onstage by his parents, then from mentorship in movies by Arbuckle. Tapped to succeed Arbuckle at Comique, the young star was now embarked "on his larger career for the screen."[2] A second press book item, designed for publication in local newspapers, reminded readers that audiences for the Keaton family vaudeville act had "marveled that Buster didn't have every bone in his precious young body broken in the pursuit of his theatrical career." Having earned his stripes as young vaudevillian, he then entered the field of movie comedy where his work with Arbuckle "astonished and pleased motion picture fans throughout the world." All of which led to the present moment, in which Keaton's responsibilities had expanded and his commitments deepened. "Buster Keaton's heart and soul are in his new productions," the article explained. "To show how much in earnest he is about being funny, he himself wrote and directed 'One Week,' in association with Eddie Cline."[3]

In its report on the release of *One Week*, the exhibitor's trade journal *Moving Picture World* immediately picked up the themes outlined by Metro, stressing Keaton's fame as a knockabout performer in vaudeville, his selection as Arbuckle's successor in two-reel comedies, and his partnership with Cline in the writing and directing of the films in which he now appeared (2 October 1920, 671). The last point was reinforced two months later when, reporting on the success of Keaton's debut short, *Moving Picture World* again stressed that "Keaton collaborates with Eddie Cline in the authorship and direction of his comedies" (4 December 1920, 633). In an ad in the 1920–1921 edition of *Wid's Year Book* (370), Comique went so far as to poke fun at its promotion of Keaton and Cline's collaboration, while also acknowledging a lack of parity to the partnership. Under the title "Buster Keaton and his Director," a photo showed the two sitting side by side. Adopting the demeanor of his screen persona, Keaton covers Cline's face with a rumpled version of Buster's familiar porkpie hat. An oval within an oval, its light-colored fabric matching that of the director's coat, the hat is perfectly angled to double as Keaton's face in abstracted form. In a dialogue balloon a cartoon stick figure reveals what the hat hides—the identity of Cline. Drawn with bright eyes and a broad grin, the stick figure also stands in stark contrast to the photograph of Buster who, unsmiling, looks blankly if somewhat dreamily in the direction of the camera, assuming a mock-formal pose. Keaton is depicted here in comic character, but the ad also humorously points up his emerging role as a director as well as a movie star.

As a child star onstage, it is important to note, Keaton had not been regarded exclusively as a sober-faced comedian. In 1901 the *New York Dramatic Mirror* described the youngest member of the Keaton family act "a

Buster Keaton ^{AND} _{HIS} Director

Now making two-reel releases for Joseph M. Schenck
Released through Metro.

Forthcoming Releases

"ONE WEEK" "CONVICT 13" "The SCARECROW"

Keaton as star and co-director: an ad in *Wid's Year Book, 1920–21.*

healthy, roguish child with a lively dash in him that is irresistible" (6 April 1901, 18). According to reviewers, he also on occasion punctuated his otherwise solemn acrobatic performances with a smile. The Metro advance story for *One Week* emphasized this, observing that in the act with his father Buster "landed on every part of his anatomy, but always came up smiling, so that it looked as if he were made of rubber instead of flesh and bones." As Peter Krämer suggests, these smiles, as well as press comments about the smiles, may have been designed to allay fears that the boy had suffered injury, buffering objections to the roughhouse act ("Battered Child" 258). In addition to his athleticism, moreover, Keaton was known onstage for his skills as a vocal performer; reviewers lauded his ability to deliver comic banter, recitations, monologues, and songs. An Akron, Ohio, newspaper reported in 1907 that Buster's rendition of "No, No, Never, Nox" on the local stage "brought down the house."[4] In 1909 the *Dramatic Mirror* declared Buster's singing of "Father Brings Home Something Every Day" the "big hit of the act," and predicted that by "working along this line he should develop into an excellent comedian, singer and possibly a monologist" (30 October 1909, 19). Furthermore, Keaton did not wholly abandon an exuberant performance style when joining Arbuckle in 1917. In the early two-reel comedies at Comique he occasionally laughs, smiles, recoils, grimaces, and weeps, to broad comic effect.

Beginning with his solo efforts in 1920, however, Keaton's style of acting acquired new discipline, and his sober expression became a fixed trait. In an era when a virile, vibrant masculine personality was associated with the smiling countenance of the equally athletic Douglas Fairbanks, and when the fan magazine *Photodrama* published a series of articles, credited to movie star Wallace Reid, modeling and extolling the virtues of the "smiling habit" (Barbas 52), Keaton's elimination of a smile from his actor's toolkit was considered worthy of note. Reviewers of his short films labored to find fresh ways to describe this distinctive aspect of Keaton's screen demeanor. A reviewer of *One Week* found him to be "as sober as a judge" (*Exhibitors Herald*, 2 October 1920, 85); of *Cops*, "a somber blue note in a bedlam of jazz" (*Moving Picture World*, 11 March 1922, 198); of *The Boat* (1921), possessing "the gravity of a church beadle or an undertaker's apprentice" (*Exhibitors Herald*, 22 April 1922, 31). Keaton's resolutely sober expression was especially a topic of interest to journalists assigned to interview him. Some reported him ready with a smile, others as unwaveringly solemn, but the question of the relation of his screen image to his authentic personality remained central to most profiles of the comedy star.[5] The fact that Keaton did not broadly announce or underscore a gag through facial expressions, moreover, contributed to a general impression among trade press and newspaper reviewers that his physical comedy was innovative and clever, admirably lacking in "hokum"—overused or overdone gags or bits of comedy associated with older and cruder forms of slapstick. "Keaton is as a rule original," commented *Exhibitors Herald* concerning *The Paleface* (1922), "and his solemn mien gets laughs where no amount of comedy hokum would" (25 February 1922, 61).

From early on Comique and Metro saw benefits in linking the seriousness of Keaton's comic persona with his labors behind the scene. Waxing enthusiastic about Keaton's prospects, Metro president Richard A. Rowland told *Moving Picture World* in 1920 that "this young comedian has the priceless gift of gravity so pronounced, for instance, in the work of Chaplin and other great funmakers. Without ever smiling himself, he is able to convulse audiences in a manner that would be another impossibility to the comedian who wears a grin" (11 December 1920, 751). The studio's efforts to read the sobriety of "Buster" in terms of Keaton's conscientiousness proved to be shrewd. Exploiting popular interest in the biographical figure behind the mask, it directed attention toward the professional arena in which he now competed for attention with other gifted comedians. "Buster Keaton Can Smile After Business Hours," announced the headline to an interview by Dorothy Day published in the *New York Telegraph* in October 1923, the text of which made clear that Keaton's "business hours" encompassed his work behind the camera as well as before it. Given the friendliness with which he had greeted her, Day reported asking, why did Keaton not smile on screen? To which he replied, he "didn't consider his work a joke."[6] Reiterated in press accounts throughout the 1920s, this theme at times took slightly mannered form, as when the *Los Angeles Times* reported that "the serious business of making pictures is engrossing the attention of Buster Keaton. He is daily becoming more frozen-faced, working out the details of the plot of his next feature comedy, now in the continuity stage" (10 May 1925, 18). Conceits of this kind allowed the studio, in alliance with a cooperative press, to keep Keaton's double role as comedian and writer-director in the public view.

In assessing Keaton's short comedies, reviewers often explicitly translated questions of control and craftsmanship into a vocabulary of "mechanics." The metaphor no doubt seemed pertinent given the displays of engineering in the early films, including a build-it-yourself house in *One Week*, trick gallows in *Convict 13* (1920), a cottage filled with convertible appliances in *The Scarecrow* (1920), complex backyard rigging in *Neighbors* (1920), and an arcade shooting gallery and a Victorian home with trick walls and floorboards in *The "High Sign"* (1921). On the occasion of the release of *The Electric House* in October 1922, trade reviewers found ample opportunity to compare the electronic appliances on display in the film with Keaton's comic strategies (*Moving Picture World*, 28 October 1922, 804; *Exhibitors Herald*, 4 November 1922, 60). Describing the film as "charged with dynamic sparks which generate large amount of humor," Laurence Reid of *Motion Picture News* went on to secure the analogy by conflating Keaton's comic persona with the creator of the comedy. "Keaton is a fellow ever in search of novelty," Reid wrote. "You never find him repetitious. This time he is not only a funmaker but an ingenious inventor. . . . Keaton's inventions would make Edison look worried whether someone had stolen his stuff" (4 November 1922, 2316). Not simply a function of the presence of gadgets in the films, Keaton's "mechanical" ingenuity was understood to reflect a comic attitude, a disposition toward objects, actions, and events pervading the film overall.

Notions of "mechanical comedy" also carried negative connotations when associated with gags or situations that seemed formulaic, externally imposed, or otherwise contrived—in a word, *mechanized*. Here again, the inclusion of visible gadgetry in Keaton's comedies offered an entry point for comment. Reviewer P. W. Gallico for the *New York Daily News* found the opening to *The Electric House* the "funniest part of the picture," but judged that the remainder was "more a comedy of mechanical surprises" (quoted in *Exhibitors Herald*, 28 April 1923, 30). Noting that Keaton's balloon trip in *The Balloonatic* (1923) featured "some clever situations," C. S. Sewell reported in *Moving Picture World* that "the mechanics of some of the scenes, however, are quite evident and tend to destroy the illusion" (17 February 1923, 706). Even when employed more descriptively than prescriptively, a distinction between mechanical and more "natural" forms of comedy was on occasion drawn. *Moving Picture World* differentiated between the "ingeniously contrived comedy situations and stunts" provided by the script to *The Playhouse* (1921), in which Keaton played multiple roles, and "a wealth of fun that springs from more natural sources" (14 January 1922, 206). In an interview with Keaton in *Picture-Play Magazine*, titled "Low Comedy as High Art," Malcolm H. Oettinger praised the originality of Keaton's gags and his mastery of comic form, observing that Keaton's "art is to work up a situation deliberately, to build it logically and systematically as a carpenter builds a house," citing *One Week* and *The Boat* as examples. "But can Keaton 'transcend' artful mechanical comedy?" Oettinger asked. He went on to express concern that "though one of the most adroit technicians of comedy, Buster fails to reach the heart." His conversation with the star, moreover, had failed to convince him that Keaton considered himself "anything more than a trouper" able to dress up "hokum" by "draping it different styles" (1 March 1923, 59–60).

⭐⭐⭐⭐⭐ **The New Features of Buster Keaton**

While the terms of Oettinger's argument concerning "higher" forms of film comedy were familiar ones in the 1920s, his account of Keaton's view of his own profession was atypical. When speaking with the press about questions of craft, Keaton often displayed keen interest in the future of film comedy and an understanding of changing industry standards and differences in audience taste. For the *Los Angeles Times* in May 1922, he described how, in contrast to slapstick methods in vogue when he first entered motion pictures, producers of comedy shorts now worked under new constraints: "comedy must be clean and wholesome," "the comedian must be neat," and "gags . . . must be original" (26 May 1922, 3:5). In an interview with Gertrude Chase, on the eve of the production of his first feature film in the fall of the same year, he spoke about the challenge of devising comic action that "will be appreciated outside of New York and Chicago," while at the same time appeal to more sophisticated viewers (*New York Telegraph*, 8 October 1922, 2). His experience in feature filmmaking appears to have quickened this concern. Prior to beginning production on *Seven Chances* (1925), perhaps with the assistance of Harry Brand, Keaton offered a detailed account of his efforts to craft a new kind of slapstick film. Film comedy based simply on "stunts" was nearly exhausted, he explained. He now sought to apply "principles of conventional picture comedy to a story that is good enough to stand on its merits." This entailed awareness of the expectations of different viewers, since comedy films should "be broad enough to please the large body of the public" but also "have enough subtle satire to satisfy the most critical, discriminating person in the audience." Reconciling the demands of "highbrows," who would be "antagonized by nothing but hokum," and "the overwhelming majority who insist on being made to laugh no matter what methods" was a problem he was "bothered with day and night."[7]

If exhibitors' trade press reports are a reliable guide, the reactions of exhibitors to Keaton's first feature, *Three Ages* (1923), may have raised concerns at the studio on this score. Predicting that *Three Ages* would attract a wide audience, Mary Kelly in *Moving Picture World* took pains to ground this optimistic assessment in an appreciation of the varied tastes and expectations of viewers, and the unusual structure of the comedy, which intercut three parallel stories across different time periods. "The choice of original subject-matter and a clever treatment of it should insure the picture's appeal with the discriminating patron," noted Kelly. "At the same time, those who are partial to slapstick will not be cheated" (8 September 1923, 155). However, comments by local theater managers indicate that this ambitious goal had not been met. In their reports to the trade press, some managers explicitly contrasted their own favorable reactions to *Three Ages*, or that of "high brow" patrons, with the responses of most patrons. "Personally I consider this one of the best feature comedies ever produced," wrote the owner of a small-town theater in Wellington, Ohio, "but I found after showing it that I was somewhat in the minority" (*Exhibitors Herald*, 6 September 1924, 24). An exhibitor in Tombstone, Arizona, reported, "While some of our people wonder what it was all about, the highbrows thought it was the best thing, satirically, we have ever shown. . . . Just a question of mixed audiences getting its points" (*Exhibitors Herald*, 13 September 1924, 63).

Laments for Keaton's abandonment of a two-reel slapstick format recur in exhibitors' reports throughout the 1920s, but they wane in number from mid-decade on, as new criteria for evaluating the box office appeal of his longer-format films come to the fore. Keaton's second feature, *Our Hospitality* (1923), a comedy-drama set in the Old South, represents a turning point in this regard. Exhibitors frequently identified the film's two major set pieces—a train trip aboard the Old Stephenson "Rocket" and a climactic river rescue—as prime attractions, the former for its novelty, the latter for its suspense. "Old train [is] the real 'puller' and bound to cause some comment," observed a North Loop, Nebraska, manager (*Exhibitors Herald*, 20 September 1924, 63). "Some of the comedy kidding the south is a bit subtle," wrote another, from Grand Haven, Michigan, but "a thrilling finish made up for this" (*Exhibitors Herald,* 2 August 1924, 241). According to the operator of a large, "mixed classes" theater in Harlan, Kentucky, *Our Hospitality* was a "picture made to order for my town. Good action with other merits make this one good entertainment for any patronage. Everybody satisfied" (*Moving Picture World*, 26 July 1924, 273). An exhibitor in Rochester, Indiana, reported, more telegraphically: "Unlike any other Keaton picture. Was humorous and serious. Everybody pleased" (*Moving Picture World*, 21 June 1924, 723). Viewers less engaged by the movie's more subdued passages, these reports suggest, had incentives to stay with the story as it unfolded.

Commentary on *Our Hospitality* by regular reviewers addressed more directly a point only implicit in these comments by local theater managers.

At issue was not simply the running time of shorter or longer comedies, but Keaton's ability in *Our Hospitality* to meld different kinds of attractions—physical comedy, romantic comedy, and dramatic suspense—into a feature-length fiction with broad appeal. While a few critics thought the very effort to mix elements of slapstick with historical drama misguided, most considered *Our Hospitality* a successful if not landmark effort. "It has about everything in it an audience seeking an enjoyable hour's diversion wants," wrote C. S. Sewell in *Moving Picture World*. "There is straight drama, melodrama, farce, and comedy, all in high order" (8 December 1923, 53). "The usual low comedy and slapstick allotted to Buster have been modified and woven into a consistent story that is as funny as it is entertaining," asserted the reviewer for *Variety*. "It marks a step forward in the production of picture comedies and may be the beginning of the end of the comedy picture without a plot or story that degenerates into a series of gags" (13 December 1923, 22). Less than a year after its release, a plot synopsis and analysis of *Our Hospitality* also was included by Scott O'Dell in his screenplay handbook, *Representative Photoplays Examined,* set forth as a model for the effective integration of comedy and pathos in a feature-length movie. "If the subject is treated as burlesque," O'Dell concluded, "the plot structure is just as striking and close-knit as in straight drama" (301). To follow these remarks is to observe the emergence of a new critical template for discussing physical comedy within the conventions of classical cinema.

In certain respects this shift in critical discourse parallels commentary during the same period on "sophisticated comedy," definitions of which, as Lea Jacobs has demonstrated, was also premised on a distinction between "naïve" and "sophisticated" viewers (Jacobs 79–126). Key elements of the genre identified by Jacobs—understated dramaturgy, economy of narration, efficient direction, a limited use of intertitles, and comic structures based on a misapprehension of events—are also found in *Our Hospitality*, as well as other Keaton features to follow. Slapstick comedy in the Keystone style, critic Gilbert Seldes proposed in 1924, was "one of the few places where the genteel tradition does not operate, where fantasy is liberated, where imagination is still riotous and healthy." In language that echoed discussions about an American technological aesthetic in other quarters, Seldes added: "In its economy and precision are two qualities of artistic presentation; it uses still everything commonest and simplest and nearest to hand; in terror of gentility, it has refrained from using the broad farces of literature—Aristophanes and Rabelais and Moliere—as material; it could become happily sophisticated, without being cultured" (32–33). But, then, how to make it so? Keaton's feature films constituted a possible answer, offering

Blending acrobatics and dramatic acting:
Keaton in the rescue sequence in
Our Hospitality (1923). Frame enlargements.

what James Agee would later describe as "dry comedy" (144), a combination of understated humor, physical action, and craftsmanship not bound by conventional distinctions between "genteel" and "slapstick" comic forms.

With the shift to features, new appraisals of Keaton's comic persona surfaced as well. Although most closely identified throughout the 1920s with the porkpie hat, clip-on tie, vest, wide pants, and slap shoes that he donned in most of his short comedies, he abandoned this outfit in many of the features as he assumed a much wider range of fictional roles. The embedding of the familiar figure of "Buster" in different narrative contexts fostered increased appreciation among critics for his skills as an actor and greater sensitivity to the "authentic" or "human" qualities that he brought to different roles. Keaton's familiar trick of acting serious hence was rethought in relation to his abilities as a serious actor. The 1924 Metro press book for *Sherlock Jr.* promoted criticism of this kind by recalibrating the studio's maturation narrative in terms of Keaton's acting style:

> The reason Keaton has been able to graduate from the field of oldtime slapstick into the more ennobling realm of suggestion is because he knows how to put his "gags" over. He gets the most out of any part he plays. He never registers "hate," "love," "arrogance" or "fear" but rather suggests them by the way he deports himself in the scene. He is like Chaplin in this respect. . . . The frank way in which he impersonates the parts assigned to him brings a quick response from the audience. He does not try to exaggerate any emotions or play up gags till they lose their point, but rather leaves it to the imagination to build upon the delicate slapstick he portrays.[8]

Reduced affect, from this perspective, was not a prompt for laughter but an invitation to the viewer to project emotions upon the character, granting a figure psychological depth. Closely following developments in feature comedy in the mid-1920s, Edwin Schallert of the *Los Angeles Times* praised this new direction in Keaton's work. "The laurels are again going to the comedians," he reported at the time of the release of *The Navigator* in November 1924, "and this time it appears as if Buster Keaton were the special victor. . . . There is a much more human note in the production . . . one does not feel the creak of so much machinery as is used to put over some of his productions" (11 November 1924, C33). With Keaton's shift to features in 1923, New York critic Robert Sherwood, who consistently lauded Keaton's "amazing ingenuity" throughout the decade, expressed regret that the "humbler days" of Keaton's two-reelers had been exchanged for features in which the physical comedy was dispersed and thinner (*Life*, 10 April 1924, 24). By the time of the release of *Steamboat Bill Jr.* in 1928, however, he viewed the transition in a more favorable light. "While in *One Week* and *The*

Electric House Keaton relied almost entirely on mechanical gags and ingenious contrivances," Sherwood observed, "lately he has been going in more for dramatic art and has developed into an extraordinarily good actor. The merit of *Steamboat Bill Jr.* depends not on premeditated gags, but on the individual and unaided work of Keaton himself" (*Life*, 31 May 1928, 23).

Responses to Keaton's comedies by artists and cultural critics in Europe in the 1920s provide yet another perspective on these developments, one at a remove from the institutional concerns of the studios, the trade press, fan magazines, and exhibitors. The showcasing of Keaton's films in art cinema houses helped to blur distinctions between high and lowbrow tastes and fostered new ways of thinking about his silent comedy in relation to experimental art practices. Between 1924 and 1927, three of Keaton's feature-length films—*Our Hospitality*, *The Navigator*, and *Go West* (1925)—were screened at the leading art cinema house in Paris, the Théâtre de Vieux Colombier, where they shared billing, as did comedies by Chaplin and Lloyd, with the films of the European avant-garde (Friedberg 206–08). Upon its founding in 1928, the Cineclub Español in Madrid likewise incorporated American silent comedies into its programs, most notably in a session organized by Luis Buñuel on May 4, 1929, in which excerpts from thirteen comedy films—including Keaton's *The Navigator*—were shown, with Rafael Alberti reading poetry inspired by the films of Chaplin and Lloyd as well as Keaton at the intermission (Aranda 52–53; Morris 80–111, 121–39). Homages to Keaton also can be found in literary works by poets Paul Nougé and Federico García Lorca, who composed surrealist film scenarios in which imagery from Keaton's film was prominently featured.

Concern for a possible drift in American slapstick away from more aggressive forms of knockabout is occasionally registered by these commentators, although for different reasons than those expressed in the pages of the exhibitors' trade press in the United States. Surrealist poet Robert Desnos, an early admirer of slapstick, and author of an essay for *Le Soir* titled "Mack Sennett, libérateur du cinéma" (166–68), became alarmed at the changes he discerned in the feature-length films of Keaton, Chaplin, and Lloyd, arguing that the precision and self-conscious craftsmanship of these movies had robbed them of the freer imagination on display in the slapstick shorts. From the point of view of technique, Desnos contended, *Our Hospitality* was an admirable success, but one achieved at the expense of the more radical playfulness and eroticism of a less assuming comedy such as *Convict 13* (117–18). Other critics, however, saw in the more classically structured features evidence of a new aesthetic, born of the relationship between physical comedy and the substratum of technical elements and genre patterns that supported it. They stressed the salutary, invigorating aspects of Keaton's mastery of the techniques of the medium, on occasion contrasting the frenetic quality of early Keystone to the dreamlike composure of Keaton's films and its power to freshen perception anew.

For example, Robert Aron, French critic and co-founder of the avant-garde "Théâtre Alfred Jarry," proposed that films like *The Navigator* and *Steamboat Bill Jr.*, while devoid of overt artistic or social pretension, plumb the constraints of both social and narrative forms. In the process they registered disturbances that the work of avant-garde filmmakers—consciously committed to a cinema of revolt—failed to tap. "Liberated from tradition," Buñuel wrote of *College* in 1927, "our outlook is rejuvenated in the youthful and temperate world of Buster, the great specialist against all sentimental infection." *College*, Buñuel claimed, was "as beautiful as a bathroom," an analogy that echoed Marcel Duchamp's submission of a porcelain urinal as a "ready made" art work to the 1917 Society of Independent Artists Exhibition in New York, repositioning a mass-produced American object from a "low" cultural space so as to challenge conventional conceptions of art and artists, and where one goes to find them. Keaton's performance style, Buñuel asserted, was attuned to the "rhythmic and architectonic gearing" of cinema and hence distinctly cinematic (Aranda 272–73). The same year French critic Judith Érèbe made a similar point in a wide-ranging essay for *Crapouillot*, arguing that Keaton's films could productively be thought of as ensemble pieces in which all the parts meshed. However sad or melancholic a dramatic moment, the action in Keaton's film drew the viewer's attention to a broader canvas alive with unexpected harmonies, rhythms, and striking pictorial effects.[9]

Keaton's preoccupation with mechanical objects as props strengthened the connection critics drew between the style of his comedies and the refinement of a new cinematic aesthetic: dynamic, constructive, reproducible for a mass audience, highly accessible yet irrepressibly modern. For these European observers, his films revealed a distinctly American sensibility at work, perceptible, Érèbe claimed, in the interplay between a "lunar" and a "practical" dimension to Keaton's comedy, a sense of fantasy that was also mathematical. Érèbe thought this traceable in American letters back to the fiction of Edgar Allan Poe (11). Buñuel linked Keaton's performance style to an "American school" of acting, vital and free of cultural tradition, and contrasted it with a "European school," exemplified by German actor Emil Jannings, that was mannered, sentimental, and bound by the prejudices of conventional literature and art (Aranda 273). In a review of *Camille* published around the same time, Buñuel explicitly contrasted Keaton's performance style with a growing sentimentality in Chaplin's work. "Remember the Christmas Eve sequence in *The Gold Rush*," Buñuel advised. "In this sense Buster Keaton is superior" (Aranda 268–69). For these commentators, Keaton's modernity as a comic performer was bound up with his emotional reserve, a compelling refusal to amplify or exaggerate psychological states for the purpose of a dramatic effect. Hence, precisely at the historical moment when Hollywood turned to European actors, directors, and cinematographers to enhance the cultural value of their product—in fact, ironically, at a time when Jannings, brought to Hollywood by Paramount, was presented with the first Academy Award granted a movie actor—these European critics praised Keaton's cooler, introspective style and practical route to dreamlike states.

★★★★★ **Prospects: Keaton as Comic Artist**

Keaton's star image took shape and evolved in the 1920s through this interplay of screen performances, studio publicity and promotion, journalistic reportage, and critical commentary. While there were broad areas of agreement concerning the distinctive aspects of Keaton's comic persona and his style of comedy, assessments of their significance varied. Publicity material generated by the producers and distributors established a framework for the description and evaluation of Keaton-as-star in newspapers, fan magazines, and the trade press. Published remarks by journalists that fit this framework were on occasion quoted in studio advertising, establishing a circular loop in the marketing of the man and his films. But responses to Keaton and his style of comedy exceeded the studio's range of control. At a regional level, this is evident in exhibitors' reports, which often included pithy summaries of audience reactions by theater managers who were acutely aware of variations in their patrons' tastes, and whose role in their communities depended on their connection to, and filtering of, the product distributed by Hollywood. Circulated widely, Keaton's comedies were also analyzed and appropriated in cultural contexts far removed from these root economic concerns. Different standards of evaluation colored commentary on "Buster Keaton" at every stage.

This was true of stars associated with other genres, but may have especially been the case for leading performers of slapstick comedies, which attracted spectators of different cultural backgrounds and dispositions, and with different investments in the modern experience of moviegoing. Slapstick proliferated in diverse formats in the 1920s; even as major stars such as Chaplin, Lloyd, and Keaton moved into feature filmmaking, low-budget slapstick shorts remained a staple item throughout the decade. Multivalent works, slapstick comedies were valued for multiple and sometimes conflicting reasons: falls and chases that triggered boffo laughs, stunts that generated thrills, star comedians with intriguing personalities, wildly implausible scenarios, stories told efficiently and clearly, the evoking of dream-like states, social critique. The national and international circulation of Keaton's films offers a window on the changing contours of comic stardom in the 1920s in this regard.

Still, beginning with the initial efforts of Comique and Metro to establish Keaton's credentials as a seasoned comic craftsman, through the cross-cultural speculations of European critics concerning his sensibilities as an artist, we can discern a line of thought attentive to recurring stylistic or thematic patterns in Keaton's work. Emerging across these various discourses was a set of precepts for imagining another "Buster Keaton," an "authorial" Keaton, based on an impulse to identify and personify a wider frame for the ensemble of performances on the screen, and attributing traits of personality to the distinctive manner in which his films were collaboratively composed. In 1929 French critic J. G. Auriol asserted that "we can speak of 'the films of Buster Keaton' because all the stories in which he appears are marked from beginning to end by his fascinating personality." There existed a distinct "Keaton atmosphere," evident in the response of other performers to Buster, "this man whose eternal gravity soon makes you a little grave yourself," and in possession of "the most moving face in cinema" (*La Revue du cinéma* 15 October 1929, 68–69; translation mine).

As fate would have it, Auriol's comments came in response to the release of Keaton's second and final silent feature at MGM, *Spite Marriage* (1929), just as the contract star was in the process of losing control over his own productions. Keaton's career and popular reputation proceeded to take a radically different turn, with his silent slapstick sometimes remembered, in patronizing fashion, as the quaint antics of a fading, sad-faced clown. Occasional screenings of *Sherlock Jr.*, *The Navigator*, and *The General* at the Museum of Modern Art, however, allowed for earlier impressions of Keaton's mastery of comic forms to take root, impressions that resurfaced in the writings of James Agee, Walter Kerr, and Rudi Blesh after World War II. Moreover, new critical paradigms emerged to lend greater specificity to earlier claims for Keaton's artistry as a visual stylist. Influenced by the writings of French critic André Bazin, Eric Rohmer, under the pseudonym Maurice Sherer, brought critical consideration to bear on Keaton's long shots and long takes—scenes filmed without cutting—with the activity of the director understood as an act of keen attention to the relation of actors to objects and landscapes.[10] By the time of the new wave of Keaton criticism in the 1960s, the critical concept of an authorial signature—as evident in the particular visual strategies a film director employed—had sufficiently taken root in French and Anglo-American film criticism so as to grant greater specificity to the connections made between the figure of the comic actor and a comic artist with the machinery of cinema at hand. Thus the tendency of Keaton's films to frame comic action in long shot has been likened to Buster's "frank" gaze (Robinson 61), and geometrical compositions and shifting narrational perspectives have been traced to the specific ways in which Buster moves or behaves on screen.[11] In this regard, European responses to his silent film work came to inform new critical writing on Keaton in the United States as well. Following the pathways of this criticism is instructive, for it helps to explain the logic of the route by which Keaton's films were revived in the 1960s, when retrospectives in Europe paved the way for the rise in Keaton's reputation and his recognition as an American artist *par excellence*.

NOTES

1. See Dick Williams, "Buster Keaton Looks to Life of Rural Bliss," *Los Angeles Mirror* (1 November 1960), Keaton Clipping Microfiche #3, Margaret Herrick Library, Academy of Motion Picture Arts and Sciences, Beverly Hills; and Dean Miller, "Here's Hollywood," WNBC-New York (10 August 1961), transcribed in *The Keaton Chronicle* 4:3 (Summer 1996), 1–3.

2. "Treating Your Patrons to a Live One," *One Week* Pressbook, Buster Keaton Clipping Microfiche #1, Margaret Herrick Library, Academy of Motion Picture Arts and Sciences, Beverly Hills.

3. "Arbuckle Cloak on Buster Keaton," *One Week Pressbook*, Margaret Herrick Library, Academy of Motion Picture Arts and Sciences, Beverly Hills.

4. "At the Casino," unsourced newspaper, Akron, Ohio (4 June 1907), Myra Keaton Scrapbook 30, Buster Keaton Collection, Margaret Herrick Library, Academy of Motion Picture Arts and Sciences, Beverly Hills.

5. See Gertrude Chase, "Buster Keaton Can Smile and Yawn, Too, If He Wishes," *New York Telegraph* (8 October 1922), 2, and at http://www.public.asu/~bruce/Taylor68.txt, accessed 6 July 1998; Willis Goldbeck, "Only Three Weeks," *Motion Picture* 22:9 (October 1921), 28–29, 87, and at http://www.public.asu/~bruce/Taylor68.txt, accessed 6 July 1998; Mulligan; and Werner.

6. Dorothy Day, "Buster Keaton Can Smile after Business Hours," *New York Telegraph* (31 October 1923) and at http://www.public.asu/~bruce/Taylor68.txt, accessed 6 July 1998.

7. Buster Keaton, "Originality—Comedy's Salvation," unsourced publication date 16 August 1924, MFL/x/n.c./1473, Billy Rose Theatre Collection, New York Public Library.

8. *Sherlock Jr.* Pressbook, MFL/+/n.c./187/#5, Billy Rose Theatre Collection, 3, New York Public Library.

9. Érèbe 10–13.

10. Sherer 6–7.

11. See Mardore 34–37; Martin 18–30; and Perez 113.

3 ☆☆☆☆☆☆☆☆☆☆☆

The Talmadge Sisters
A Forgotten Filmmaking Dynasty

LEA JACOBS

Norma and Constance Talmadge were among the most important stars of the 1920s. Not only do many contemporary fan magazines and industry publications, and more recent memoirs, attest to their popularity and renown but, given their family connections, it is clear that they occupied the highest social echelons in the small community of Hollywood (Talmadge; Loos; de Groat). Until her divorce in the late 1920s, Norma was married to Joseph M. Schenck, independent producer, partner and eventually chairman of the board of United Artists, and brother to

Constance and Norma Talmadge. Courtesy of the Wisconsin Center for Film and Theater Research.

Nicholas Schenck, a partner in Loew's/MGM. While not prominent as an actress, the middle Talmadge sister, Natalie, was married to Buster Keaton. The Schencks/Talmadges/Keatons amassed large personal fortunes and were frequently in the news. The *Los Angeles Times* consistently covered their movements between New York and Hollywood and their trips abroad. Joseph Schenck's decision in 1921 to close his Manhattan studio and move his operation to the West Coast was covered in great detail over a period of months, and, according to the *Los Angeles Times* (15 November 1921, 3:4), a crowd including the mayor of Los Angeles greeted the Schencks upon their arrival. There was extensive press coverage of the Talmadge/Keaton alliance, a marriage rumored between Constance and composer Irving Berlin that never materialized, and Constance's dramatic elopement with tobacco magnate John Pialoglou and her subsequent divorce. Ads for Norma Talmadge perfume and cosmetics were accompanied by reports of the New York fashions favored by the Talmadge girls. For example, the *Los Angeles Times* (28 July 1921 3:4) reported that Norma had purchased the first "fish dress" to be seen in America, designed by Mme. Francis.

The contrast between the Talmadges' visibility in the 1920s and their obscurity in the present day could not be greater. I do not know of any other major Hollywood stars who have so completely vanished from our collective memory. As Greta de Groat has argued, one reason for the neglect of the Talmadges is that Norma, who was the more prominent of the two sisters, has generally been dismissed as a bad actress by film historians (de Groat 10). A second reason for this neglect is that, until recently, the films of both sisters were largely inaccessible. This situation changed when, over a lengthy period from 1989 through 2001, the collection of Raymond Rohauer was deposited at the Library of Congress. Rohauer had acquired prints of many of the films Schenck produced as well as his papers. The library's preservation efforts have made it possible for us to begin to reassess the films of the Talmadge sisters and their place in the canon of 1920s American cinema.

★★★★★ The Talmadge Family Dynasty

Like Mary Pickford and Lillian and Dorothy Gish, Norma and Constance Talmadge grew up in a household without a father's support and became actresses at a fairly young age to provide for their families. For all of these actresses, filmmaking was at least initially a family enterprise. Margaret ("Peg") Talmadge, like Charlotte Pickford, sometimes unfairly castigated as a "stage mother," functioned as a theatrical agent and advocate

The Talmadge Family: Peg, Constance, Norma, and Natalie. Courtesy of the Wisconsin Center for Film and Theater Research.

for her daughters; in addition, Norma supported Constance's career just as Lillian supported Dorothy's. Even Natalie had a few minor roles in her sisters' films as well as a major role in Keaton's *Our Hospitality* (1923). Thus, to understand the careers of the Talmadges, it is important to consider the family dynasty that had its roots in the 1910s, of which they were a part.

While still in high school, Norma was hired at the Vitagraph Company, whose main studio was on Flatbush Avenue in Brooklyn, near the family home. It is likely that her sister also began appearing in bit parts about this time, although Constance did not have big enough roles to appear in the credits for Vitagraph films until 1914 (see Spehr, *American Film* 575). Norma first attracted notice in a small part in the three-reel *A Tale of Two Cities* (1911) as an aristocrat who is comforted on the way to the guillotine by Sidney Carton (played by Vitagraph star Maurice Costello). She was promoted to ingénue lead in the units directed by Charles Kent and then Van Dyke Brooke, and was given a significant role in the Vitagraph feature *The Battle Cry of Peace* (1915). After the family moved to California, the sisters eventually obtained work at Fine Arts, the division of Triangle Film Corporation supervised by D. W. Griffith. Norma starred in six of the seven films she made at Fine Arts and she established working relationships with people who would be important throughout the careers of both sisters. Three of Norma's films at Fine Arts were directed by Sidney Franklin and his brother Chester, including *Going Straight* (1916), about a couple of reformed crooks who get on the wrong side of the law. She also appeared in the charming comedy *The Social Secretary* (1916), directed by John Emerson and scripted by the writing team of Emerson and Anita Loos. Constance had her first major role while at Fine Arts as the Mountain Girl in Griffith's *Intolerance* (1916), and she appeared in a number of comic parts thereafter, including *The Matrimaniac*, starring Douglas Fairbanks. Some sources (Loos 25; Slide 63) attribute this script to Emerson and Loos, and if so it provides another instance of an early collaboration between the Talmadges and the Emerson/Loos team.

The last two films Norma made for Fine Arts, *The Social Secretary* and *Fifty-Fifty*, were shot not in California but in New York, where Norma met Joseph Schenck. Schenck established the Norma Talmadge Film Corporation on 4 October 1916 (*New York Times*, 5 October 1916, 20) and the couple was married on 20 October (Talmadge 143). At this point in his career, Joseph Schenck, his younger brother Nicholas, and Marcus Loew had formed a triumvirate invested in real estate, vaudeville, nickelodeons, and film theaters (*New York Times*, 23 October 1961, 1). It is sometimes asserted by unsympathetic critics that Norma Talmadge only became a star through her association with Schenck. It would be more accurate to say that Schenck's connection with the Talmadges provided his entree into film production. He may have been the mastermind behind the Talmadge dynasty, but it was only by working with them and, often, their former associates from Fine Arts, that he built up a highly successful company and launched his own career as an independent producer.

The first Talmadge/Schenck production, *Panthea* (1917), was completed by director Allan Dwan at the Willat Studio in New Jersey (Koszarski, *Fort Lee* 312–13). Schenck then set up a studio of his own in Manhattan at 318 Forty-eighth Street (the studio advertised in the *New York Times* for a stenographer to apply at this address on 1 February 1917). Apart from visits to her mother and sisters and location work, Norma remained in New York until 1921, but it appears that Constance remained on the West Coast with her mother at least for a time, since she made four films for Fine Arts in 1916–1917. In addition to Norma's films, Schenck signed Roscoe Arbuckle in early March 1917 to produce slapstick shorts under the Comique label. Buster Keaton, recruited by Arbuckle, appeared in their first film *The*

Butcher Boy, released in April 1917. After making five two-reelers in New York, Arbuckle's unit left New York for the Balboa studio in Long Beach, California, in the fall of 1917. An interview with Natalie in the *Los Angeles Times* (2 October 1917, 2:3) indicates that she was now working for Comique as an administrator.

Norma Talmadge's features were initially distributed by Lewis Selznick as Selznick Pictures, but some time later in 1917, after Adolph Zukor contributed an infusion of capital, the company became Select Pictures (Koszarski, *Fort Lee* 312–13; Spehr, *Movies Begin* 98–100). It seems likely, given Zukor's investment in Select and Paramount's perpetual shortage of features at this time, that the films made under the Select label were distributed as part of Paramount's yearly program. The Comique films were directly released through Paramount.

Sometime in the spring or summer of 1917, about the time that Griffith left Fine Arts, Constance also signed with Selznick and eventually made sixteen films distributed by Select. Although legend has it that Norma, Constance, and Keaton (at Comique) were all at work in the Forty-eighth Street Studio at the same time, this could only have happened briefly during the spring and summer of 1917. Not only did the Comique unit move to Los Angeles at this point, but Constance did as well. Her first three films for Selznick—*Scandal* (1917), *The Honeymoon* (1917), and *The Studio Girl* (early 1918)—seem to have been made in the East, but she returned to Los Angeles in December 1917 and worked at the Morosco studio at 201 North Occidental Boulevard, by this time owned by Lasky/Paramount (*Los Angeles Times*, 15 December 1917, 2:3). Thus, for much of 1918, Norma was in New York while Natalie and Constance were in Hollywood, presumably living with Peg.

Norma starred in from four to six pictures a year for Select. She worked most frequently with Sidney Franklin, with whom she made *Her Only Way* (1918), *The Forbidden City* (1918), *The Safety Curtain* (1918), *The Heart of Wetona* (1919), and *The Probation Wife* (1919). She played a wide range of roles in a variety of genres at this point in her career. In *The Heart of Wetona* (1919), she is the daughter of an Indian chief. In *The Secret of the Storm Country* (1917), which follows upon Mary Pickford's *Tess of the Storm Country* (1914), she plays the daughter of a squatter family who is abandoned by the rich landowner's son and left to bear her baby alone. In *The Forbidden City* (1918), she has a double role as San San, who is killed when her secret marriage to an American diplomat interferes with the emperor's plan to include her in his harem, and then, many years later, San San's grown daughter. Most often, however, she played women of high society in stories that revolved around marital infidelity, separation, or divorce. In *The Moth* (1917) she is a spoiled young heiress who makes an unfortunate marriage; in *By Right of Purchase* (1918) she marries for money but comes to love her husband; in *The Way of a Woman* (1919) she is a poor girl from an aristocratic Virginia family who marries to restore her fortune. These sorts of plots provided opportunities for the display of current fashions, which became an

Norma Talmadge dolls. Courtesy of the Wisconsin Center for Film and Theater Research.

important aspect of Norma's star persona onstage as off (in this period actors provided their own clothes for stories with contemporary settings). As de Groat has noted (5), the fact that Schenck's studio was in New York meant that the Talmadges had access to the best fashion designers, such as Lucile and Mme. Francis, and this gave them an edge on the actresses restricted to shopping in the more provincial Los Angeles.

During the years at Select, Selznick cast Constance Talmadge in a series of comedies, many directed by Walter Edwards, largely drawn from the contemporary Broadway stage. These films involved the complicated plots typical of romantic comedy: multiple and intersecting lines of action, often with one or more characters assuming a false identity, which place the heroine in what seem to be sexually indecorous situations while maintaining her fundamental innocence. In *A Pair of Silk Stockings* (1918), from the play by Cyril Harcourt, Molly, a divorcée, unexpectedly arrives at the country home of friends who are entertaining her ex-husband. In an attempt at reconciliation, he goes to her room late at night still wearing a burglar costume for a part he was playing in an amateur theatrical. In the dark, she thinks he is a real burglar and, along with an old boyfriend who has unexpectedly turned up, locks him in the bathroom. The house is roused, the supposed "burglar" makes his escape unseen, and Molly is left with the difficulty of explaining the presence of the former boyfriend in her room. In *Mrs. Leffingwell's Boots* (1918), based upon a play by Augustus Thomas, two marriages are threatened by complications arising from the fact that two women own identical footwear. In these and similar films, Constance perfected a light, slightly arch, style of comic performance quite distinct from the knockabout slapstick style of her work in *Intolerance*.

Schenck's operations altered radically in 1919. He broke with Select and, hence, at one remove, with Paramount, to join First National. The *Los Angeles Times* announced Norma Talmadge's move to First National on 23 December 1918. Constance shifted to First National in April 1919. At this point, Schenck set up Constance Talmadge Productions to make films starring Constance at the Forty-eighth Street Studio, where both sisters would work until 1921 (the last film produced at the Forty-eighth Street Studio was *Smilin' Through* [1922]). According to the *Los Angeles Times* (9 November 1921, 3:4), Joe Schenck then purchased the Brunton Studio in Los Angeles to make Norma Talmadge, Constance Talmadge, and Buster Keaton Productions (although, in the event, Keaton never worked at the renamed United Studios), and the Talmadges moved back to the West Coast. Although Schenck assumed a position at United Artists as early as 1924, the films he produced under the labels Norma Talmadge Productions and Constance

Talmadge Productions continued to be released by First National until 1927. At that point, Constance retired from filmmaking and Norma followed Schenck to United Artists, where she made her last three films.

The years at First National were the most fruitful for both sisters; in this period they made their most ambitious and interesting films. Production budgets seem to have been substantially higher at First National than at Select. For example, in the early 1920s, Norma made two historical costume pictures under Frank Lloyd's direction: *The Eternal Flame* (1922), set in eighteenth-century France, and *Ashes of Vengeance* (1923), set in sixteenth-century France. These demonstrate the high budgets typical of the First National/Schenck productions and were praised for their elaborate sets and costumes. *Variety* (22 September 1922, 41) wrote of *The Eternal Flame*: "Miss Talmadge, as always, exhibits a ravishing assortment of frocks—an important production feature where this star is concerned. . . . The settings are an independent feature of the picture. Astonishing effects of space are secured in the interiors, which have an atmosphere of authentic reproductions. The ballroom scene must have represented a considerable investment." The *New York Times* (7 August 1923, 20) wrote of *Ashes of Vengeance*: "One of the remarkable scenes in the production shows an interior of the Louvre thronged with dancers in beautiful costumes. It is said to be one of the largest interior sets ever built, and on the screen it is very impressive, with the swaying forms dancing in rhythm." In addition, in this period, Norma was able to work with a much wider range of top-rank directors including Herbert Brenon, Frank Borzage, and Clarence Brown. Constance, reunited with Emerson and Loos, and directed by the likes of Sidney Franklin and Victor Fleming, was given much better scripts and established a much more distinct star persona.

★★★★★ Norma

Norma was primarily associated with two kinds of films in the 1920s: costume dramas, sometimes labeled romantic dramas in the period, and more or less prestigious theatrical adaptations. Although the film industry trade press asserted that some of Norma's films had a feminine appeal, and, presumably, the displays of fashionable clothes that were an important component of her films were attractive to women, it should be stressed that, like Pickford or Gish, Norma Talmadge was a big star, and her films were usually assumed to have a wide general audience. Her films should not be considered "women's pictures" in the sense that this term came to be employed within the film industry trade press of the 1930s, or

Norma Talmadge. Courtesy of the Wisconsin Center for Film and Theater Research.

in the sense that it is used today by film critics (on the assumptions about feminine taste and women's genres in the 1920s, see Jacobs 217–23). In addition, while some of Norma's films were said to be "melodramas," this term meant not pathetic stories of domestic upheaval (its present-day usage), but rather, as usual in the 1910s and 1920s, stories of crime and intrigue with complicated plots (see Neale; Brewster and Jacobs 25–27).

Although many films of the 1910s and 1920s derived from the stage, Norma featured in adaptations of a number of especially prominent and enduringly popular plays. One of her signature roles, *Smilin' Through*, was adapted from the play first produced on Broadway by the Selwyns with Jane Cowl in 1919.[1] A dual role provided one of the attractions of the original play (although it was criticized by *New York Times* critic Alexander Woollcott in 1919 for its obvious contrivances). At the turn of the century, an Irish colleen, Moonyeen, is inadvertently killed by her fiancé's jealous rival on the day of her wedding. Her spirit lingers to watch over those she has left behind when, twenty years later, Kathleen, Moonyeen's niece, falls in love with that rival's son. The story proved so popular with audiences (and actresses) that it was remade twice, once again by Sidney Franklin with Norma Shearer in 1932 and then as a musical by Frank Borzage with Jeanette MacDonald in 1941. Another perennial favorite, Bayard Veiller's crime melodrama *Within the Law*, ran on Broadway for 541 performances in 1912, also with Jane Cowl in the leading role. It was adapted for Vitagraph with Alice Joyce in 1917 before Schenck produced a version with Norma Talmadge in 1923. It was remade in 1930 as *Paid* with Joan Crawford, and in 1939 under the original title with Ruth Hussey. David Belasco's successful musical comedy *Kiki* ran for 233 performances in 1921. Clarence Brown directed Norma in the first film version in 1926, and Sam Taylor directed a sound version with Mary Pickford in 1931. According to the review of Talmadge's *Kiki* in *Variety* (7 April 1926, 36), Schenck paid Belasco a large sum (the amount quoted, $75,000, was disputed by the participants) for the rights to the story, which "almost anybody in a city of any size will remember" about a French gamine who falls in love with a manager of a large revue. Norma's success in this comedy was followed in 1927 by *Camille*, perhaps the most venerable of theatrical war horses.

As this litany suggests, and quite contrary to her present-day reputation, Norma Talmadge was celebrated for her acting ability in the 1920s. Although one New York critic found some of the roles assigned Norma too stereotyped and shallow, he wrote approvingly of *The Eternal Flame* (1922): "It demonstrated her versatility, for it compelled her to range from unassailable virtue to sly deviltry, from blank innocence to cynical sophistication, from tyrannical dominance to abject submission, and from bored worldli-ness back to spiritual regeneration" (Sherwood 25). *Wid's Daily* (10 April 1921, 2) praised her "power of repression" in *Passion Flower* (1921). The *New York Times* (25 March 1924, 25) praised Norma's performance in *Secrets* (1924), which it characterized as "a charming romance told with dignity and restraint." Talmadge was generally thought to have a refined and grace-ful acting style. She usually abjured large bodily gestures, and even arm movements, preferring to work with her mobile facial muscles. She had very good control, not only of eyes and eyebrows, but of cheeks, mouth, and chin, and therefore had a great range of facial expressions that she manipulated smoothly and effectively. Indeed, her generally quiet demeanor sometimes worked against her. Although her performance as Mary Turner in *Within the Law* was approved by *Variety* (3 May 1923, 23) and *Moving Picture World* (12 May 1923, 157–58), Frederick James Smith complained in *Photoplay* (July 1923, 68): "Norma Talmadge's performance in this adaptation leaves us cold. Miss Talmadge, like many of our estab-lished stars, seems afraid to act." Robert Sherwood characterized this same performance as an example of Norma's "fine flair for polite melodrama" (106). While Sherwood may have intended to damn with faint praise, "polite melodrama" strikes me as just. Norma was avowedly histrionic, adept in the creation of facial expressions and gestures that forcefully expressed a story conceived as a suite of dramatic situations, but she also preferred to work on a relatively small scale, and rarely lost her composure or graceful bearing, hence the adjective "polite."

Even when Norma's films derived from less than illustrious theatrical sources, they demonstrated a marked preference for what might be termed "actorly" parts, roles in which the actress was called upon to demonstrate her versatility and control. In addition to *Forbidden City* and *Smilin' Through*, Norma appeared in four other dual roles in the late 1910s and early 1920s. One of the best, *Yes or No* (1920), featured her as two women, one rich and one working-class, both neglected by their husbands and tempted by other men. In the play by Arthur Goodrich, the parallel stories were staged side by side on a split set, but the film presents them in alternation (on the play see *Motion Picture News*, 7 August 1920, 1122). Norma as the rich wife, resplendent in fine clothes and a blonde wig, chooses the other man, a path that eventually leads to her suicide. Norma as the poor wife, simply dressed but certainly not plain in her own hair, stands by her husband and is rewarded when his invention of a washing machine makes them rich. Natalie Talmadge, in one of her rare performances, appears as the poor heroine's sister Emma, who is also the rich heroine's maid—and the only link between the two stories. Trade-press reviewers thought the film's plot trite, with its contrast between the happy and virtuous poor and the wretched and vicious rich, but argued that the acting redeemed it; as *Wid's Daily* (11 July 1920, 2) headlines it, "Fine Characterizations by star succeed in substituting for situations." Norma's performance as the poor wife, Minnie, is particularly interesting for the understated but comic way in which she reacts to the assortment of characters who share her tenement apartment. For example, in the scene in which she serves dinner, she tries to get food on the table and simultaneously keep the peace while the sharp-tongued and high-stepping Emma quarrels with her ill-mannered brother, and the family boarder pays her unwanted compliments in her husband's absence. Sometime later, after her husband comes home from work, she loyally listens to him lecture her brother about how to get ahead and shyly greets the rotund traveling salesman who, to the brother's amusement, has come to call for Emma. While not initiating any of this activity, Norma's facial expressions, emphasized in repeated reaction shots, remain the center of the scene, giving one a strong sense of the effort it takes Minnie to feed and manage her extended family.

The two Talmadge films directed by Frank Borzage, *Secrets* and *The Lady* (1925), adapted from plays by Martin Brown and May Edington, respectively, also provided opportunities for Norma to demonstrate her range, not, as in *Yes or No*, by playing two contrasting characters, but by following one character through many years and many vicissitudes.[2] In *Secrets*, aged Mary Carlton, who has been nursing her husband John for weeks, peruses her diary and, after falling asleep, relives episodes from her married life. As the *New York Times* noted, these episodes provided the actress with an extraordinary range of character states: "She is seen as a young and happy girl wearing crinolines, then as a young mother out in a Wyoming shack, as a lady of wealth in her forties, and as an aged woman who is praying for her husband's recovery at a critical period of his illness." Special mention was made of her performance as a white-haired old woman. *Variety* (26 March 1924, 26) discussed the Wyoming episode in which Mary and her husband fight side by side to hold off a group of rustlers besieging their cabin. It praised the direction, but presumably also the performance, in the scene in which her husband congratulates their rescuers while Mary "turns toward another room where her first-born lies dead. It is such a tremendous change of pace that it stands out like a Rolls-Royce in a showroom full of Cadillacs." The reviewer also mentioned the episode set in London in the 1870s when, after John has made a fortune and their children are flourishing, he takes a mistress. According to *Variety*: "The interpretation Miss Talmadge gives of the wife who never wavered, but remained firm in the belief that her husband still loved her best of all, even at the times that she knew he was unfaithful, is something that will go down in film history. It is a work of art, deftly handled with a divine touch that makes it stand out as one of the greatest screen characterizations in years."

The Lady follows the outlines of a typical mother-love story, told in flashback.[3] The elderly Polly Pearl runs a bar in Marseilles and recalls incidents from her life: her youthful performance in a London music hall; her marriage to the wealthy Leonard St. Aubyns and her eventual desertion by her husband; the birth of her child in a brothel/cabaret, which is the only place where she can find work; her father-in-law's attempt to take the child and her decision to entrust him instead to a kindly minister and his wife; years of poverty and isolation as Polly walks the streets of London selling violets and looking for her lost boy. The plot concludes with a cut back to the present where, in the course of a bar fight, a young soldier is knocked out and Polly recognizes her son. The recognition scene is handled particularly well, with Talmadge hardly moving except for her face and hands. When the boy comes to, there is only a hint of a mutual recognition (she says she once had a son "like him" and he replies in kind). *Variety* (28 January 1925, 32) and *Film Daily* (1 February 1925, 8) thought the film was among Talmadge's best, although Mordaunt Hall, in the *New York Times* (27 January 1925, 11), wrote his review from the perspective of "two grey-haired old ladies" who liked it, as if he could not admit liking it himself.[4]

Given her versatility, it is hard to identify a fixed persona for Norma, but the dignity and decorum for which she was often praised in and of themselves came to provide some sense of a typical Norma Talmadge part. This is most obvious when critics reacted to what they regarded as eccentric roles for her. For example, in *The Song of Love* (1923), made to cash in on the craze initiated by Valentino's *The Sheik* (1921), Norma played Noorma-hal, an Arab dancing girl caught between her loyalty to her people and her love for a French spy. *Film Daily* (13 January 1924, 5) noted: "Seems to have been stricken with modesty. Dancing girl garb appears to embarrass her." Although more impressed by the costume, the critic for the *New York Times* (25 February 1924, 13) also thought the part was "not Norma":

> Hitherto, Norma Talmadge . . . has confined her pantomimic art to portraying the demure, romantic heroine, the light of love to many a bold and amazingly successful hero. In "Ashes of Vengeance" she was cleverly effective, and she was charmingly sympathetic in "Smilin' Through." Now she is to be seen at the Rivoli this week in "The Song of Love," playing an utterly different type

of damsel. . . . Imagine passing into the Rivoli with a vague impression of Miss Talmadge in poke bonnet and voluminous hoop skirts that jealously guard even her slender ankles from view, and suddenly beholding a startling vision of undeniable beauty, clad expensively, but not extensively.

Although *Kiki* was judged a better film than *The Song of Love*, it provoked similar remarks about off-casting. *Film Daily* (11 April 1926, 5) noted: "Norma forgets all her dignity and throws herself in the spirit of portraying the little street gamin. . . . She proves that even slapstick can be done with refinement." *Variety* (7 April 1926, 36) described the film as a decided departure for the star: "She gives a creditable and amusing performance, which, if it isn't as subtle as it might have been, is about as effective as possible in its slapstick way. Miss Talmadge falls over couches, gets kicked out into the alley, kicks a valet around, does a little rolling over the floor and is a general roughneck." He concludes: "If any other screen actress has held up so good a record in recent years as Miss Talmadge, it might be well to recall no other actress on the stage or screen has played such varied roles with unmistakable skill and ability."

Despite the accolades accorded Norma Talmadge's acting in the 1920s, there were also fairly consistent complaints about the plots of many of her films. This component of the discourse may help to explain her later disrepute, why the first generation of serious film historians and critics such as Paul Rotha, James Card, and Iris Barry dismissed her films and found it difficult to take her seriously as an actress (de Groat 10). In the period, one finds striking disparities in the estimation of the literary or dramatic quality of Norma's films. *Variety* and the *New York Times* were the most critical of the "polite melodrama" in which she excelled, while the other trade papers—*Exhibitors Trade Review*, *Moving Picture World*, *Motion Picture News*, and *Wid's* (later *Film Daily*)—were more forgiving, and sometimes frankly enthusiastic. The uneven reception of Talmadge's films may be explained by the distinct audiences addressed by the trade press. *Variety* was oriented to the metropolitan theaters of the major producer/distributors, and particularly sought to anticipate a film's success or failure on Broadway. Similarly, the *Times*, much more of a local New York paper then than it is today, specifically addressed urban intellectual elites. In contrast, the other film industry trade papers were directed to a wide range of theater owners in the smaller cities and towns (this kind of division within the trade press, and its relationship to the distribution hierarchy, is discussed at greater length in Jacobs 19–22).

Take, for example, the reaction to *Smilin' Through*, a film that helped to define Talmadge's persona in the 1920s. *Film Daily* (5 March 1922, 2) was enthusiastic: "Here's the best picture Norma Talmadge has ever made for First National. Here is one of the best pictures she has ever made. That should be enough to get a lot of money in the box office for you." In contrast, *Variety* (10 March 1922, 41) gave it a cool if respectful review, judging the film would do well as a "program picture," that is, outside the first-run theaters on Broadway: "Miss Talmadge ably handles the leading role and gives to the production a stamp of class in the acting division that places it well up on the list of program features. . . . 'Smilin' Through' displays expert direction. The punches are landed effectively. A capable cast works up the big points. . . . The high esteem in which Norma Talmadge is held by picture patrons will not be impaired by her latest feature." The *New York Times* (17 April 1922, 25) was condescending: "The chances are that practically all those who inform themselves about 'Smilin' Through,' at the Strand this week, and then go to see it, will enjoy it. For it is entirely sentimental, and it is well done. Those who like photoplays deliberately sentimental will be attracted to it, therefore, and will find what they are looking for. Those who shy at such will not be attracted, and will stay away. So there'll be satisfaction all round."

The Sign on the Door (1921), adapted from Channing Pollock's play, provides another good example of this mixed reception. The plot builds to a situation in which Ann Regan goes to the rooms of the rake Frank Devereaux to protect her stepdaughter from an assignation with him and is trapped when her husband pays Devereaux a visit. This situation, as *Wid's* (24 July 1921, 8) noted, was "not entirely new." It occurs most famously in the plays *The School for Scandal* and *Lady Windermere's Fan*, with numerous filmic renditions, including Norma's own 1916 film *The Social Secretary*. Pollock's variant provided opportunities for a bravura performance at several junctures: when Ann challenges Devereaux, refusing to leave his room in anticipation of her stepdaughter's arrival; when, hidden in the back room, she reacts to the confrontation and escalating violence between Devereaux and her husband; when she finds herself locked in with Devereaux's body and, with mounting hysteria, takes the gun and adjusts the room to make it appear that she committed the murder in defense of her honor; and when she is cross-examined by the district attorney and the police in her husband's presence. In particular, during the cross-examination, Norma pantomimes her (false) account of the attack and murder, a set piece that presumably included dialogue onstage and was more of a virtuoso effort when done silent.

All the reviews stressed the stereotypical nature of the film's plot but most found it pleasing. *Exhibitors Trade Review* (22 July 1921, 608) noted: "It is a hard test on an intelligent person's gullibility to expect one to believe that a normal man or woman would ever allow themselves to get into the mess that the characters in this play become involved in, but in spite of this, it must be admitted that the picture is of enthralling interest and holds one almost breathless at times with its fast movement and situations that pile up to a tremendous climax." *Moving Picture World* (30 July 1921, 541) found that the play was far from "great drama," but that the main character's attempt to protect her family was extremely sympathetic and appealing: "Such a character is well within the grasp of so capable an actress as Norma Talmadge, and, in the expressive vernacular of the street, she goes after it for all she is worth." In contrast, the brief review in the *New York Times* (18 July 1921, 22) noted: "The play, though unoriginal, has theatrical, as opposed to dramatic, intensity, and so those who like 'ersatz' melodrama may like it in its present form." *Variety* (22 July 1921, 36) extended the critique of theatricality to Talmadge's performance, which for once it found problematic, attributing the fault partly to the director, Herbert Brenon: "Thanks probably to the directing, she is here at times so much the actress it is apparent to a skilled observer. The careless abandon that is life itself has given way to a trained well thought out attempt to make a graceful picture."

The reception of *Yes or No* epitomizes the ambivalent reaction to Talmadge's films. The *New York Times* (5 July 1920, 15) completely dismissed the plot, which it considered "a rut of theatrical unreality and false moralizing." The *Variety* review (9 July 1920, 26), while obviously cognizant of this kind of reaction, was still impressed by the quality of the presentation: "The same story, less classily handled, would make the cheapest kind of picture. It serves to show that a really high-class production can make of almost any tale a feature fit to be employed in these advanced days as a first run attraction in a Broadway cinema. Stripped of its aforesaid 'class' it would be commonplace, old-fashioned melodrama." For those who liked "old-fashioned melodrama," a taste presumably represented by much of the exhibitor-oriented trade press, Norma's films were embraced without reservation. But for the more sophisticated tastes represented by *Variety* and the *New York Times*, approval of the films was usually much more qualified. In many cases it was only the subtlety and grace of Norma's acting, occasionally given added force by the brilliance of a director such as Frank Borzage, that saved the films from being considered unbearably theatrical and irredeemably old hat.

Norma's career is often said to have been brought to a close by the coming of sound, although critics (de Groat; Smith "Silencing") have recently refuted claims that she had a Brooklyn accent and/or an unacceptable speaking voice. From the reviews, it appears that in her final film, the costume picture *Du Barry, Woman of Passion* (1930), badly written dialogue was a greater problem than line delivery. *Variety* (5 November 1930, 30) complained that "the dialog, being so thoroughly American seems almost sacrilegious, and the French accents are variable in every character." *Photoplay* (November 1930, 135) commented that "Norma Talmadge, as the milliner who became a king's favorite, shows a hint of her old-time vitality now and then, but gives up in the fight against long, artificial speeches." The *New York Times* review (9 November 1930, 10:5) criticized the dialogue in the scene in which Du Barry, her lover hidden in her boudoir, is confronted by a jealous Louis XV: "It is only too plain that she is repeating again and again 'I love the King' because she doesn't." Perhaps, too, Talmadge's problems when confronted with inept dialogue and the nuances of verbal performance were exacerbated by the more fundamental problem that had dogged her career throughout the 1920s: the ambivalent reaction to her story material and the difficulty of reconciling her histrionic proclivities with the dictates of modern taste. *Variety* noted of *Du Barry*: "Stuff goes melo too often to be realistic."

★★★★★ Constance

A report from New York on modern mores published in the *Los Angeles Times* (29 January 1921, 1:8) advises: "No girl really belongs now unless she looks like Constance Talmadge." In contrast with Norma, who often played ingénue leads associated with bygone days, as in *Smilin' Through* and the opening episode of *Secrets*, Constance played decidedly modern types. She thus bears comparison with actresses such as Colleen Moore, Clara Bow, and Joan Crawford who have come to epitomize the flapper in most film histories. These stars may be distinguished by the degree and nature of their engagement with comic performance traditions. Joan Crawford was primarily associated with dramatic roles, and the films that made her name in the 1920s—*Our Dancing Daughters* (1928), *Our Modern Maidens* (1929), *Our Blushing Brides* (1930)—are society dramas that self-consciously deal with the problems of modern youth.

Colleen Moore, one of the most admired comediennes of the 1920s, had a flair for gag-based humor much indebted to the best film slapstick, although in her case always employed in the context of romantic comedy. In a typical scene, from *Irene* (1926), the eponymous heroine, an Irish immigrant, delivers a package to a wealthy estate and, while waiting in the library, uses the drapes and a lampshade to posture as a well-dressed lady of fashion. She offers cigarettes to an imaginary interlocutor: "My dear, I never smoke anything but Turkish Atrocities" (for more on Moore's performance style, see Ross, *Banking* 219–27). Constance was less of a clown, and her films were much less gag-based. The films she made for First National, like many of those for Select, derived from polite Broadway farces in which comedic situations were produced through quite complicated plot mechanisms, and humor developed primarily from the interactions of the characters.

In many ways, Talmadge's roles come closest to those of Clara Bow. They both played young women who were considered "modern" in that they were sexually aggressive. For example, in the *Film Daily* review of *Don't Call Me Little Girl* (26 June 1921, 13), starring Mary Miles Minter, the reviewer notes that she "virtually steals a part away from Constance Talmadge, inasmuch as it requires a strenuous series of vampings in which the heroine steals her aunt's fiancé—a part usually associated with the bobhaired comedienne." Bow was also known for such roles, as for example in *It* (1927), in which she plays a shop girl who employs a series of stratagems, including staging a tantrum on her boss's desk, in order to win his affections. In addition to the similarities of character type, the actresses shared two directors. Both worked with Victor Fleming—Talmadge in *Mama's Affair* (1921) and *Woman's Place* (1921), Bow in *Mantrap* (1926) and *Hula* (1927) —and with Malcolm St. Clair—Talmadge in *Breakfast at Sunrise* (1927), Bow in *The Fleet's In* (1928). Their performance styles were quite distinct, however. Bow's characters were extremely direct in the pursuit of their male objects, and the actress's gestures and mannerisms often violated contemporary norms of ladylike behavior. In contrast, Talmadge's heroines were much less aggressive and her performances correspondingly more understated. Anita Loos described her style as "spontaneous, relaxing and feminine," and recalled that in her films "a sense of *fun* took the place of a sense of humor" (93).

Emerson and Loos wrote eleven of the first fifteen comedies that Constance made for First National, and they were also frequently credited as producers or supervisors on those films. Loos claimed to have invented the "baby vamp" character for the star and she recalled arguing with Peg that Constance (to whom she always referred as "Dutch," following family tradition) had to be a man chaser: "If our leading man pursues Dutch it gives all the action to *him*!" (37). Although, as noted above, many of the Emerson/Loos productions derived from the theater, they typically assign an active role to the heroine and have a remarkable consistency of tone that can probably be attributed to the adaptation. In *A Virtuous Vamp* (1919), based on the 1909 play *The Bachelor* by Clyde Fitch, the rich and aristocratic

Gwendolyn Armitage pretends to be plain Nellie Jones in order to get hired by a businessman who disapproves of job seekers trading on their social connections. After her smiles disrupt three departments, the boss takes her into his personal office, only to fall victim to her wiles himself. *In Search of a Sinner* (1920), from a 1910 comedy by Charlotte Thompson, concerns a young widow who had been bored by her angelic first husband and sets out to find a wicked man for her second (following the release of the film, Otto Harbach and W. H. Post prepared a stage version as a musical, *June Love*, which opened at the Knickerbocker on 25 April 1921). In *Mama's Affair* (1921), from the 1920 play by Rachel Barton Butler, Mrs. Orrin controls her daughter Eve by feigning hysterics whenever the girl shows the least sign of independence. While there are no explicit references to psychoanalysis, play and film were influenced by then current popularizations of the Freudian notion of repression and its role in the etiology of neuroses. Eve is about to be wed to the son of her mother's best friend—the mothers are planning to spend their lives looking after both their "children"—when Eve has a genuine fit of hysterics. The doctor who takes charge of her case removes her from her mother's care. After her "cure" Eve is not only able to call off the marriage and face down her mother, but to pursue the doctor to whom she eventually proposes.

Like the Fairbanks vehicles of the teens, also scripted by Emerson and Loos, the Talmadge films at their best are lighthearted and irreverent in tone (these qualities were apparently lost on the *New York Times* reviewer of *In Search of a Sinner* [8 March 1920, 9], who deemed the film "frivolous"). They often made use of the witty intertitles for which Loos was known. The *Variety* review (21 October 1921, 36) singled out one such title, in *Woman's Place*: "In this we have the women's club offering the prettiest flapper in Fairfax the nomination for mayor. She can't speak, but when she hurts her ankle her opponent remarks, wisely, she has twisted one of her best campaign arguments, and the battle is on." The plots often turn on palpable absurdities. In *A Virtuous Vamp*, Gwendolyn starts to date her boss when they go out to nightclubs, ostensibly to investigate the request of a shimmy dancer for insurance for her shoulders. When Georgiana goes man-hunting in Central Park in *In Search of a Sinner*, she flirts with Jack Garrison and becomes attracted to him, only to find to her horror that he is president of the Purity League. One of the few films to depart from this lightness of tone, and rather interesting as a result, is *Mama's Affair* with its rather sinister and repulsive controlling mother.

Despite their active involvement in Constance Talmadge Productions from 1919 to 1922, Loos and Emerson were only marginally involved in the last phase of Constance's career. They worked on only one of the eight films released during the years 1924–1927, *Learning to Love* (1925). Loos attributes the cessation of their relationship to her own success as a novelist with the publication of *Gentlemen Prefer Blondes* in 1925 and her decision to pursue a literary career in New York (92). However, there are decided changes in the Talmadge unit as early as 1923, well before the publication of *Gentlemen Prefer Blondes*. Constance essayed a historical drama, *The Dangerous Maid* (1923), directed by Victor Heerman with a scenario by C. Gardner Sullivan. She also played in a series of comedies directed by Sidney Franklin, the most important of which, *Her Night of Romance* (1924) and *Her Sister from Paris* (1925), were scripted by one of Ernst Lubitsch's favored scenario writers, Hanns Kräly.

The Franklin/Kräly collaborations pushed Talmadge's films in the direction of the sophisticated comedies being developed by Lubitsch, among others, in such films as *The Marriage Circle* (1924) and *Forbidden Paradise* (1924). *Variety* (14 January 1925, 30, 43) remarked of *Her Night of Romance*: "There is one thing, however, that might be desired in regard to this picture, and that would be to see the treatment that Lubitsch would have given this story in direction had he handled it." The *New York Times* (13 January 1925, 16) noted that Kräly had previously worked with Lubitsch and praised him for "giving opportunities for many novel touches, which have been aptly and adroitly handled by the director, Sidney Franklin."

The plot of *Her Night of Romance* resembles that of many previous Constance Talmadge vehicles. A concatenation of chance occurrences and mistaken identities place the heroine in indecorous and potentially risqué situations, but she is fundamentally blameless and the improprieties lead to a marriage that was never fundamentally in doubt. The film's sophistication resides in its style rather than its narrative substance. Most notably, Franklin uses detail shots ("touches" in trade press parlance) in which the humor derives from the way in which the spectator is led to make inferences about characters' motivations and events that occur in offscreen space. In one scene, the heroine's father is lulled to sleep, preparing the way for a tryst between the girl, Dorothy, and her boyfriend, Paul. Dorothy is shown at the piano, mischievously peeking at her father seated nearby. The next shot isolates the following elements: on the right her father's hand, holding a cigar; at the center, a wine decanter and two glasses on a table; on the left, Paul's hand. Paul's hand begins to refill the father's empty glass. The father's hand falls off the arm of his chair and Paul refrains from pouring. Another shot confirms that the older man has fallen asleep. Only Paul's hand is visible as he puts the stopper back in the decanter and extinguishes his own cigarette. Dorothy looks in his direction and then looks down. A detail shot of Dorothy's feet at the piano shows her depressing a pedal marked "soft."

This kind of comedy calls for an extremely reduced mode of acting. Dorothy's reactions are conveyed by slight facial expressions—a sly smile, a downcast glance—which gain meaning through the accumulation of detail shots. In the latter part of her career, Talmadge proved quite adept at this technique. Like one of Lubitsch's favorite actors, Adolphe Menjou, frequently praised in the film industry trade press for his nonchalance, her relaxed performance style was well adapted to a comedic form that depended upon understatement and economy of means of expression.

Despite Loos's malicious claim that *Her Night of Romance* was a "disaster" (91), it was in fact highly recommended by the film industry trade press. The Franklin/Kräly collaboration that followed, *Her Sister from Paris*, was equally approved, although risqué enough to provoke censorship in the Midwest (Jacobs 121). Constance did not attempt to make the transition to sound, but when she retired she was still at the top of her form: her penultimate film, Malcolm St. Clair's *Breakfast at Sunrise* (1927), was another polished example of the genre.

By the end of the 1920s, Constance Talmadge was no longer primarily associated with the self-consciously modern types played by Joan Crawford or Clara Bow. But her apparent spontaneity onscreen, and what Anita Loos referred to as her "sense of fun," contributed just as importantly to contemporary notions of the modern girl. Moreover, her last and best films might be considered quintessentially modern not only for their treatment of sexually adventurous subject matter, but, more important, for their wit and style. While not as central to the innovation of sophisticated comedy as Adolphe Menjou, its veritable icon, in 1924–1925 Talmadge, in association with Franklin and Kräly, contributed sterling performances to two key early examples of the genre. Her films deserve to be better known: both on their own merits and for the way in which they would add nuance to the discussion about the representation of gender and of femininity in the 1920s.

NOTES

1. All references to Broadway productions derive from the Internet Broadway database.

2. According to the filmography by Greta de Groat on the Norma Talmadge web site (www.stanford.edu/~gdegroat/NT/home.htm, accessed 29 August 2008), the Library of Congress has not completed preservation of its print of *Secrets*, which currently lacks parts of the middle episodes, but Hervé Dumont describes what appears to be a more or less complete print held by Gosfilmofond in Moscow (Dumont 94–95).

3. Fortunately, the Library of Congress currently holds a more complete print of *The Lady* than it does of *Secrets*, although a significant amount of footage is lacking from the episode concerning the heroine's married life.

4. *The Lady* is much admired today; Dumont (97–99) finds the film "not far short of a masterpiece" and notes that, rediscovered at the Pordenone Silent Film Festival in October 1992, it "had a house full of hardened cinéphiles in tears."

4 ☆☆☆☆☆☆☆☆☆☆☆

Rudolph Valentino
Italian American

AMY LAWRENCE

Published in 1936, *The Big Money* was the culmination of John Dos Passos's attempt to write the Great American Novel, a work that would encompass all of modernity in the first decades of the twentieth century. Part of the trilogy *U.S.A.*, *The Big Money* interweaves postwar political upheaval, popular culture, and urban life under capitalism, as it combines fiction, stream-of-consciousness meditations, "Newsreels" (found poetry plucked from the mass media of the day), and brief biographies. Among the celebrated figures of the era, only one film actor is singled out. "Newsreel LIV"

Hand-painted image of Valentino as Eastern Exotic (Shirley Blanc, 1920).

(205–06), with its fragments of stock reports, advertising copy, hit songs, murder, sensationalism, and natural catastrophe, is cut short by a newsflash: "Rudolph Valentino, noted screen star, collapsed suddenly yesterday in his apartment at the Hotel Ambassador. Several hours later he underwent—." Approximating a "cinematic" style, Dos Passos leaves the sentence unfinished and "cuts" directly to the next chapter, "Adagio Dancer."

He begins with a familiar tale: a young immigrant who "wanted to make good in the brightlights" finds himself a media sensation at twenty-six (206). But fame has a dangerous undercurrent. "Wherever he went the sirens of the motorcyclecops screeched ahead of him, flashlights flared, the streets were jumbled with hysterical faces, waving hands, crazy eyes; they stuck out their autographbooks, yanked his buttons off, cut a tail off his admirablytailored dress-suit" (207). Despite his early material success, Valentino's attempt to prove himself as an American, "to make good / in heman twofisted broncobusting pokerplaying stockjuggling America," inevitably fails. Unable to survive the flood of media sensationalism (divorces, lawsuits, rumors about his masculinity, accusations that he was a "pink powderpuff"), "he broke down in his suite in the Hotel Ambassador in New York: gastric ulcer" (207). The last words Dos Passos grants Valentino, in fact the only line the actor has in the entire piece, is this: "When he came to from the ether, the first thing he said was, 'Well, did I behave like a pink powderpuff?'" (208). Valentino the conscious subject slips away, to be replaced by his body as expressive object.

In Dos Passos, it is not Valentino but his "expensivelymassaged actor's body" that fights desperately for life while "grimyfingered newspapermen and photographers stood around bored . . . waiting for him to die in time to make the evening papers" (208). Dos Passos contrasts the actor's idolized surface with the interior's unstoppable decay. "When the doctors cut into his elegantlymolded body they found peritonitis had begun" (207). There follows a series of graphic descriptions of "the abdominal cavity," "the tissue of the stomach," and "the viscera . . . coated with a greenishgray film" (207–08). Valentino dies halfway through the chapter, details of his life supplanted by those describing his funeral.

In recounting the days following Valentino's death, Dos Passos finds his real topic—the relentless machinery of celebrity that stops short of nothing, not even the commercial exploitation of a corpse. Encouraging cult-like devotion to celebrities results in the production of passions that, once unleashed, cannot be controlled (a vision reiterated in Nathanael West's *Day of the Locust* [1939], published three years after *The Big Money*). Valentino's "managers planned to make a big thing of his highly-publicized funeral, but the people in the streets were too crazy. . . . Jammed masses stampeded under the clubs and the rearing of the hoofs of horses. The funeral chapel was gutted, men and women fought over a flower, a piece of wallpaper. . . . Showwindows were burst in. Parked cars were overturned and smashed" (208). "Even the boss," the eager owner of the funeral home, "had his fill of publicity that time" (209). "Adagio Dancer" concludes with a mordant note on the death of celebrity itself. "The funeral train arrived in Hollywood on page 23 of the *New York Times*" (209).

Admirably concise and moving, "Adagio Dancer" encapsulates the myth of Valentino as tragic figure, capturing both the brevity of his fame and the way his death and its aftermath came to substitute for, even constitute, his iconic status as a Hollywood star. It would not be the last word on the subject, nor was it the first.[1] Nevertheless, it epitomizes the way the phenomenon of Valentino's death and the events surrounding it continue to overshadow the actor's work. It is not unusual to come across those who conclude that his death was the best thing that could have happened to him. Shortly after Valentino died, H. L. Mencken wrote, "I incline to think that the inscrutable gods, in taking him off so soon . . . were very kind to him." Mencken is quite confident of this despite never having seen the actor onscreen (xi).

In *Negotiating Hollywood*, Danae Clark argues against a kind of star study that focuses on an actor's "image" and neglects "the actor as a social agent or political subject who actively participates in or resists studio discourses of stardom and the material conditions upon which they rest" (121). "Valentino's death" can serve as a paradigm for objectifying a performer by reducing him or her to "image," body, corpse, in the process creating and circulating meanings that were and are beyond the performer's knowledge or control. In an effort to restore/reconstruct Valentino as social agent and political subject, I propose to continue the work of feminist film historians Miriam Hansen and Gaylyn Studlar by exploring the way Valentino functioned as a historical subject within a specific cultural moment, paying particular attention to the actor's participation in, and reaction, negotiation, and resistance to, the formulation of his image during his life.

★★★★★ Italian American

In the 1920s, when the United States was caught up in a bitter debate over immigration and the press stoked fears of Italians as bomb-throwing anarchists, Rudolph Valentino was (and remains) the model of a silent film star. Although he made his first screen appearance in 1914, the height of Valentino's popularity stretched from March 1921 with the release of *The Four Horsemen of the Apocalypse* to the summer of 1926's *The Son of the Sheik*. This five-year period parallels some of the most intense anti-immigrant sentiment in U.S. history, much of it directed at Italians.

Anti-immigrant fires flared in November 1919 when Attorney General A. Mitchell Palmer, following a series of bombings, authorized raids against thousands of suspected "Reds" (a broad term including communists, anarchists, and otherwise unspecified "radicals"). This period came to a close around May 1920, when an Italian anarchist being "held incommunicado" by the Department of Justice fell fourteen stories to his death after having been tortured (Lyons 41–42, 45; Neville 5). As the excesses of the Palmer raids waned, debates on immigration restriction grew stronger. Mainstream publications like the *Saturday Evening Post* and *Literary Digest* launched vigorous campaigns calling for an immediate moratorium on immigration and a quota system that would ensure that the population of the United States would always maintain the ethnic balance that had pertained in 1890. (Italians began to arrive in large numbers starting in 1900.)[2] For *Literary Digest*, the only answer to the "Threatened Inundation from Europe" was "To Halt the European Invasion" (18 December 1920; 25 December 1920). The editors suggested ways to "Make the Immigrant Unwelcome" while the *New York Times* ran stories about "Italy's Criminals in the US" (30 April 1921; 21 October 1921). When wives and children trying to follow their family members to America found themselves locked out due to the new limits on immigration, the *Saturday Evening Post* dismissed such accounts as "Ellis Island Sob Stories," while the journal *Science* reminded readers of the "Proportion of Defectives from the Northwest" of Europe compared to those "from the Southeast of Europe" (28 July 1923; 14 March 1924). The passage of the Johnson Bill (called "Our New Nordic Immigration Policy" by *Literary Digest* [10 March 1924]) was met with some protest, but opponents had little chance of shifting the prevailing xenophobia. Even after the bill became law, the *Saturday Evening Post* urged Congress to "Put the Bars up Higher" and advised continued vigilance "Lest Immigration Restriction Fail" (26 September 1925; 10 October 1925).

During this period, a Dr. Antonio Stella felt compelled to refute the most common prejudices against Italians in his book *Some Aspects of Italian Immigration to the United States*. In a preface dated November 1923, he explains his sense of urgency. "Lately a disquieting outbreak of intolerance and a reign of prejudice seems to have seized the American people" (4). In his analysis, Dr. Stella ("Consulting Physician to Manhattan State Hospital for the Insane, Fellow New York Academy of Medicine, Member American Medical Association, American Statistical Association, etc. etc." [iii]) assures his readers that every "attempt has been made to pursue scientifically the objective truth by impersonal methods," and that "on the basis of the figures . . . definite deductions regarding the value of Italian immigrants" can be made (xv). These include: "Italians are the least alcoholic white race in the world"; "Italian immigrants have a lower percentage of insanity than any other race, including the native stock itself"; "the children of Italian immigrants . . . have a lower percentage of illiteracy than the native whites"; and, most important, "the average criminality of the Italian immigrant, as shown by official records, is less than that of most of the other races, in spite of public opinion to the contrary" (xv, 101–02). He also states categorically, "There are very few 'Radicals' among Italians in proportion to the population" (102).

For an actor to be perceived as "ethnic" at this time meant being relegated to playing "foreign villains, revolutionaries, and gangsters"—all three terms nearly interchangeable in regard to Italians (Winokur, "Improbable" 9). In his move from supporting player to leading man, Valentino participated in a campaign designed to open up a wider range of possibility. From the beginning, his films attempted to transform the actor's origins into a nonspecific pan-ethnicity where he was likely to be anything but Italian. He played an Argentinean in Paris in *The Four Horsemen of the Apocalypse* (1921); Spanish-French-English in *The Sheik* (1921); French in *Camille* (1921), *The Conquering Power* (1921), and *Monsieur Beaucaire* (1924); English in *Beyond the Rocks* (1922); Spanish in *Blood and Sand* (1922) and *A Sainted Devil* (1924); part-Indian in *The Young Rajah* (1922); Russian in *The Eagle* (1925); and, in *The Son of the Sheik* (1926), an Arab even less Arabian than he had been in the original. Of his fourteen leading roles, only two allowed him to play an American (the lost *Uncharted Seas* [1921] and *Moran of the Lady Letty* [1922]) and only one an Italian (*Cobra*, 1925)—the two nationalities the actor could claim. In addition, most of his films are "costume pictures," romances taking place in some distant time (*Beaucaire*, *The Eagle*) or the purposely vague, "timeless" deserts of the two *Sheik* films, the seafaring scenes in *Moran* and the bullring of *Blood and Sand*.

Such ahistorical exoticism did not disguise Valentino's status as the most famous Italian immigrant of the 1920s. In fact, it was a fundamental part of it. The public display of malleability, the willingness to appear to be anything but Italian, could be used to deflect social hostility by constructing him as the ideal immigrant—ready to remake himself as anything while claiming no special gifts (not the best actor, not the best dancer, etc.).[3]

In the classic strategy of collapsing performer with performance, contemporary interviews with Valentino re-create this all-purpose exoticism for the actor offscreen. Prior to the release of *Four Horsemen*, in one of the first articles to appear on Valentino, he is described as a man made up of contradictions and mystery. "One person could discuss Valentino and say 'What a care-free lad he is!'" C. Blythe Sherwood notes, "always joking, and romping" (18). "Those who know him best," however, suggest that "Rudie is a lonesome soul . . . [not] so much melancholic as pensive" (18). He is also "an ambitious young man" with "many friends" and at the same time "very few" (18). "Enter Julio!" (the title of the article substitutes the name of Valentino's character in *Four Horsemen* for the actor's) emphasizes not identity but contradiction and the many possible identities available to him—all in all, not a bad thing for a young actor.

An article a year later continues the theme of Valentino's fluid identity, though now a reader, having seen the films, can relate actor to character as easily as the interviewer does. In December 1921, following the success of *The Sheik*, the fan magazine *Motion Picture Classic* contributed to the construction of an Orientalized mystique in "Hitting the Hookah with Rudie." Interviewer Herbert Howe stage-manages the event, taking Valentino to a restaurant "canopied in mauve silks after the fashion of the tent occupied by Sheik Ali Hassan [*sic*], who on the screen is none other than the noble Valentino" (*Motion Picture Classic*, December 1921, 18). Senses drenched in the exotic atmosphere of "jasmine-scented cigarets" and "a frosted and absinthine cocktail," Howe details their encounter with "the trousered form of an odalisque . . . followed by cups of Stamboul café as black as Mahomet, the Turk who served them" (18–19).

Like the sheik, Valentino is described as if he exists outside of history (though Arab leaders figured large on the international stage at this time, thanks to the widely publicized exploits of T. E. Lawrence). The opposite of an immigrant, Valentino is figured as "a nomad searching out the mysteries for himself" (Howe 72). While situating the actor among many possible identities, Howe carefully qualifies those most likely to mark Valentino as an Italian. "Altho born to the rituals of Catholicism, he seems a pagan skeptical of creeds. . . . Things mystical fascinate him" (72). We are assured, too, that "there is none of the volubility that we have come to expect as an Italian characteristic thru commerce with push-cart financiers. Altho possessed of an emotional warmth that comes to the surface in moments of earnestness, [Valentino] is not florid or gesticulant" (72). On the other hand, the actor does have "the sturdy, muscled physique of the Roman gladiator"— though that is not enough to maintain his Italian identity. "Very dark-skinned, with hair that seems to be lacquered, and eyes dreamily inscrutable, he has more the facial appearance of the Bedouin than the Roman" (72)—in other words, Valentino is more Sheik Ahmed than Rodolfo Guglielmi, his real name.

At this point in his career, it is to Valentino's benefit to encourage audiences and studios to imagine him in as many roles as possible. The careful management of his characters' ethnic and racial origins, however, makes the question of the *actor's* nationality more pressing. The authors of these early pieces (both of whom refer to their subject as "Signor Valentino") assure us that this particular Italian is more tourist than immigrant. Sherwood stresses that the "youth from Italy . . . does not want to stay here forever. He longs to go to South America, China, Japan, Egypt and India" (18, 19). A year later Howe tells us that the actor, speaking "with Latin candor," "intends to become an adventurer, visiting India, Arabia and other Oriental spots" (72). In other words, this Italian is just passing through.

A recurring insistence on Valentino's class status also springs from the desire to separate the actor from the stereotype of the unlettered peasant laborer. "While thoroly Italian in his sympathies and allegiance, he has the urbanity and sophistication of the cosmopolite" (Howe 72). Five years later, *Photoplay* reminds its readers that Valentino "has the taste of a country gentleman" (Ryan 21). No less an authority than Mencken, writing of his dinner with the actor shortly before his death, opines that, to his surprise, the "simple mummer" was, in fact, "what is commonly called, for want of a better name, a gentleman" (quoted in Shulman xii, xi).

Attacks on Valentino also combine ethnicity and class. As late as 1967, Irving Shulman refuses to accept Valentino's account of his education and of his first job in the United States (92–94). Where "Enter Julio!" tags Valentino a "scientific agriculturalist," Shulman labels him a "subgardener," "aping" the ways of the upper class (Sherwood 75; Shulman 99). The connection between class hostility and anti-Italian feeling is made clear when Shulman writes that, as a new arrival, Valentino "gravitated naturally toward the cheap dance halls and cabarets where the flashier of his countrymen congregated" (101). As *Photoplay* put it, "Once a bus boy, always a bus boy" (Ryan 20).

Although contradictions are certainly present in the press's early encounters with Valentino, the familiar extremes of female adoration and male antipathy were not immediately manifested. In reviews of *Four Horsemen*, his masculinity was not questioned, nor his clothes, his wristwatch, or his hair. His acting was even singled out for praise: in "the early episode of the Argentine café . . . Julio flashed with life, passion vibrated across the screen, and the atmosphere radiated with reality" (*Motion Picture Classic*, May 1921, 81). The respectful response to the film is partly due to the nature of the project—its representation of World War I (which ended just three years before) and its status as a prestige film adapted from a best-selling novel with philosophical pretensions (what ads called "the most widely read book of all time, excepting the Bible"). Credit was spread evenly from producer/ "scenarioist" June Mathis to director Rex Ingram and Metro, the studio behind this "million dollar production." After his introduction in an elabo-rate "ethnic costume" (silk gaucho pants, jeweled cummerbund, and shin-ing patent leather boots with spurs), Valentino is presented as an ordinary (if fashionable) contemporary European in prewar Paris. A tale of redemp-tion, *Four Horsemen* is the saga of an international playboy transformed by love. Shamed by his married lover's renunciation of pleasure in favor of service to others (nursing the wounded), Valentino's character exiles himself to the front, fighting, ads proclaimed, "for France, not because it is his own country, but because it is hers." Morally recuperated by his sacrifice, Julio's death in battle puts him beyond (earthly) criticism, simultaneously certify-ing him as all man and no longer a sexual threat. Like an immigrant, he is thought "good" in direct proportion to his willingness to be gone.

Attacks on Valentino started when he began to be perceived as a threat. As the title character in *The Sheik*, his fourth film after *Four Horsemen*, he is no longer part of an ensemble but the star who carries the film from start to finish. Given credit for the film's phenomenal success (Leider 167–68), Valentino was consequently accused of undermining norms of masculinity in terms of dress, behavior, and bodily display; dislodging feminine desire from socially accepted channels involving subservience and marriage; and inverting racial values by proving the superiority (and superior appeal) of the "dark" immigrant.

As a man, Valentino's Sheik Ahmed follows the classic pattern of action-hero: an unquestioned leader of men, he forcefully pursues his own desires, risking life and limb in climactic hand-to-hand combat to rescue a damsel in distress. At the same time, he dresses in robes, wears jewels (the wristwatch is always a dead giveaway), and reclines on cushions and couches in settings crowded with Oriental rugs, Moorish tables, and a riot of pattern and fringe more evocative of Theda Bara and the exotic dancer Little Egypt than of a so-called "man's man." The attraction for women of Ahmed's "cave-man" behavior toward Diana, the Englishwoman he pur-sues, sparked debates from the beginning, with female sex-experts like *Sheik* author E. M. Hull and "It" proponent Elinor Glyn expounding on the appeal of danger and the masterful man (quoted in Leider 165–66, 194–95).

Valentino as Julio in *The Four Horsemen of the Apocalypse* (1921). Publicity still.

At the same time, a fundamental attribute of all of Valentino's characters is his tenderness and sensitivity, his finer "feminine" feelings, if you will. The balance of savagery and gentlemanliness is what *The Sheik* is about—and what allows an audience member to fine-tune a private orientalist fantasy to his or her heart's content.

If Valentino's challenging of gender identity in *The Sheik* could be dis-turbing for men, it was potentially liberating for women. Although film and novel are ostensibly about the taming of Diana, reclaiming a resistant new woman for traditional feminine submissiveness, both texts have their hands full maintaining heterosexuality as a functioning standard. In the novel, Diana is described as looking "like a boy in petticoats, a damned pretty boy"; it is as if "she was meant [to be] a boy and changed at the last moment" (Hull 2). In the film, however, the sheik's mission of straighten-ing Diana out ends up queering them both. Ahmed and Diana don a series of disguises: while the seemingly Arab sheik is actually a gentleman edu-cated in England and possessing impeccable French manners (and friends), Diana trades her "boyish" riding breeches and pith helmet for her Arab maid's "native" garb in order to sneak into a casino and watch dancing girls. Exposed as a European by the sharp-eyed Ahmed, Diana drops one of her veils to reveal a phallic gun only to be promptly disarmed by the "savage" whose dignity puts her to shame. A publicity still for the film shows Ahmed and Diana having reached parity, their companionate marriage expressed by their interchangeable wardrobes (flowing robes, harem pants, stripes, and spangles). This time she wears the wristwatch.

Valentino in *The Sheik* (1920). Publicity still.

The superiority of the suspect foreigner over the European white male turns on its head the xenophobic fear of "race suicide" (the eugenicist term for those who would make their own race extinct through miscegenation). The compounding of Valentino's foreignness with the "otherness" of Sheik Ahmed magnifies the sense of romantic and sexual transgression, paradoxically intensifying the response from female audiences rather than repelling them. In Ahmed, Diana finds the sensual excitement decidedly lacking in her pallid British fiancé and Ahmed's friend, the virtually asexual St. Hubert. Positioned between the physically enervated Europeans and the North African Arabs who are portrayed as potential rapists, Ahmed-Valentino becomes the golden mean. If the New Woman is to find her womanhood, it will take someone from south of Paris but north of North Africa to show her the way. An Italian, perhaps.

Established as a multifaceted threat, Valentino was now criticized for his acting. As a rule, he has a well-modulated naturalist style in contemporary roles (*Cobra* being an especially good example) and a broader style in costume pictures.[4] While many of these include comedy in a Fairbanksian vein (*Beaucaire*, *The Eagle*, *Son of the Sheik*), romantic melodramas like *The Sheik* and his next big hit, *Blood and Sand*, left little room for manly insouciance. Powerful, desiring, and unapologetically obsessed with a woman in *The Sheik*, Valentino in *Blood and Sand* is completely unmanned (literally gored) as his character is trapped and sapped by the competing demands of a good woman (his convent-schooled wife), a bad woman (a socialite vamp), and his mamma. Little surprise, then, that *The Sheik* and *Blood and Sand* sparked an eruption of parodies. In 1922 Ben Turpin crossed his eyes and wore a dress in *The Sheik of Araby* while Stan Laurel starred in the baseball-themed short, *Mud and Sand*, playing "Rhubarb Vaselino." A 1924 takeoff of *Blood and Sand* in *Big Moments from Little Pictures* features Will Rogers playing "Rufus," a famed matador accepting cheers from the crowd (and coins and garter belts and corsets). Revealed to be an actor exhausted after a long day's work, he is bundled into a chauffeur-driven car while prop men remove the fake horns from a "bull" restrained by ropes and covered by a sharpshooter should the tame animal frighten the delicate star.

Ridicule of Valentino's screen image bleeds directly into ridicule of the performer himself, his name being a frequent target of scorn. Throughout his career Valentino's name is remarkably unstable. Spellings change (in the sources cited here he is referred to as Rudy, Rudie, Rodolfo, Rudolfo, Rudolpho, Rodolpho, and Rodolphe, and his last name reported as Guglielmi and Guglielmo). Valentino himself, of course, changed his name more than once, which is not unusual for an actor at the beginning of his career, using seven variations of his *nom du cinéma* in as many films, including "De Valentina," "di Valentina," "di Valentini," "De Valentine," "Valentine," "Valentino," and "di Valentino" (Leider 426–27). Once he alights on "Rudolph Valentino" he does not stay there, going back to "Rodolph" for *Blood and Sand* (his eighth feature). The consistent use of variations of "Valentine" (whether spelled the English, Spanish, French, or, finally, the Italian way) signals the kind of romantic roles in which the actor hoped to be cast. When people other than Valentino stress the Italian character of his name(s), however, it is often either as a form of ridicule or, worse, a way to put him in his place. Shulman, for instance, describes an autobiographical series of essays as "formally introduc[ing] to his public Signor Rodolpho Alfonzo Raffaelo Pierre Filibert Guglielmi di Valentina d'Antonguolla" (reproducing the list of multiple names, something common in Italy, as a kind of comic excess) (220).

In 1927 a writer described the Italian immigrant's daily experience of being Italian in the United States. Upon landing in America, he writes, the Italian instantly "became a 'dago' and a 'guinea,' his name a jumble of letters and of no consequence, his language and his mannerisms fair game for the burlesquers" (Lyons 20). Whether unemployed laborer or film star, an Italian "was just another 'dago,' one of the 'goddam foreigners' who could always be told to go back where they came from" (Lyons 20–21). ("Once a bus boy. . . .") Valentino was attacked in a similar vein in an article published in *Photoplay* in May 1926. "Has the Great Lover Become Just a Celebrity?" masks itself as career advice while attempting to cut Valentino down to size by reminding him where he came from. The first line reminds readers of the actor's birth name: "And yet, Rudolph Valentino, *né* Guglielmi, is a very creditable actor" (Ryan 20). (The article is illustrated by an Orientalized caricature of the actor's face; beneath it, a small figure in Sheik's clothing tries to clamber back to fame, escaping from an open grave [Ryan 20].) After bemoaning the fickleness of fans and the actor's waning box office ("Valentino's fame is full of cracks. Can it be repaired?" [Ryan 69]), the author concludes: "And yet, Rudolph Valentino, *née* Guglielmi, is really a very good actor" (Ryan 78). The transition from "creditable" to "good" does not soften the implications of moving from the masculine to the feminine form *née*: evidently Valentino was not only born Italian but born a woman.

In an attempt to "introduce the notion of struggle into the scene of actors' labor," Danae Clark points out that "struggles over actors' subject identities [have] entered into all aspects of the cinema's production-exchange process" (120). In Valentino's case, problems negotiating his identity as an Italian added to the actor's dissatisfaction with the film industry at large. Early on, he spoke out against the racial and ethnic stereotypes that touched most closely on his career and himself as an Italian. In an interview titled "The Psychology of the Sheik" (*Movie Weekly*, 8 October 1921), Valentino is offered a chance to distinguish himself from his role as an Arab "savage" (Leider 172). Instead, he embarks on a defense of Arabs and Moors, proudly connecting them to himself and his Italian roots. "The Arabian civilization is one of the oldest in the world. I was born in Southern Italy, where Moorish influence is yet to be seen. The Moors are closely akin to the Arabs. I know them. The Arabians are dignified and keen-brained" (Leider 172). "People are not savages because they have dark skins," he adds.

It has become standard to point out the questionable status of fan magazine material purporting to quote stars or to have been written by them. But in trying "to regard the star as a social subject who struggles within the film industry's sphere of productive practices" (as well as struggling with the culture at large), we are thrown back on these potentially questionable texts (Clark xi). The extent to which Valentino expressed the opinions quoted above (whether they were paraphrased, polished, or supplied outright by an interviewer or ghostwriter) cannot be determined conclusively. Nevertheless, this speech makes it possible for fans to construct a reading of Valentino as proud of his Italian roots and willing to identify with the ethnic and racial "other."

Valentino's biographers recount other occasions where the actor responded directly to anti-Italian slurs. Although it is part of the author's vision of the actor as temperamental and given to impotent displays of rage, Shulman in 1967 describes several scenes where Valentino's anger is triggered by ethnically defamatory comments. (While these accounts may be fictionalized, the insults were real—and documented.) In April 1922, at the height of Valentino's popularity, *Photoplay* published a parody of *The Sheik*. Author Dick Dorgan rewrites the scene where Diana is told that Ahmed "is a bum Arab"—he is "really an Englishman whose mother was a *wop* or something like that" (April 1922, 92). According to Shulman, "Valentino stormed from office to office, pounded desk after desk, [and] demanded . . . that Dick Dorgan never again be allowed on the Paramount lot" (183). Jesse Lasky and Adolph Zukor backed their star one hundred percent, though the only real concession they negotiated was the editor's promise to "reprimand" the writer and to feature full-page photos of Valentino in subsequent issues as compensation. By July, though, *Photoplay* published Dorgan's "A Song of Hate" with the notorious opening "I hate Valentino! All men hate Valentino" (among the reasons listed are "his oriental optics" and

"Roman face"), causing more tension between Valentino and the studio (July 1922, 26). That August, for this among many reasons, Valentino walked out.

✰✰✰✰★ Labor Issues: An Actor Protests

There is another factor that, combined with his status as an Italian immigrant, would contribute to the hostility toward Valentino in the 1920s: from the end of August 1922 to August 1924 the actor was, in effect, on strike (an act that took two years out of his five-year career). Needless to say, his disputes with Paramount/Famous Players–Lasky were not greeted sympathetically by the industry. The 1 September 1922 *Los Angeles Times* proclaimed, "Toreador Rodolpho Wails Over New Trouble"— confusing actor and character, Italianizing his name, and infantilizing his objections to his contract in the first three words (Leider 467n). Valentino did not return until December 1923 when he agreed to make two more films for Famous Players–Lasky, over which he would have greater artistic control, before moving on to work with other production companies. Even with the contracts signed, his next film, *Monsieur Beaucaire*, would not appear in theaters for another eight months.

Valentino entered the "arena of struggle" (in which "how actors' labor is defined, and who defines it" becomes "a scene of constant negotiation" [Clark 119]) in the midst of a period of labor unrest in Hollywood. Actors Equity, which had led a successful strike on Broadway in 1919, petitioned for a standard contract for film actors in August 1922 (the month Valentino broke with Paramount), and continued to press for a basic agreement until they succeeded in 1927 (Perry and Perry 338). Producers tried to separate actors from craftspeople (who reached a standard agreement in 1926 [Ross, *Stars* 3–22; Perry and Perry 320–25]) by holding out the promise of possible stardom (and its excessive rewards), and by inviting actors to separate themselves from the less exalted "laborers" of the rank and file in return for being granted the cultural status of "artists" (Clark 6–7). When speaking publicly about his disagreement with the studio and his desire to make films that were more artistic, Valentino fell into the trap of emphasizing nebulous, immaterial qualities over "practical" business goals—something he was, predictably, ridiculed for (see James Quirk, "Presto Chango Valentino!," *Photoplay*, May 1925, 36–37).

Overall, however, his management of his labor action was quite canny and showed a sophisticated understanding of how an actor could exploit his image for his own ends (in this case, to maintain his fan base). Although his lawsuit failed and he was barred from making films during his walkout, Valentino (and his advisors) came up with many creative ways for the actor to promote his interests using a range of media. In addition to the widely celebrated dance/personal appearance tour sponsored by Mineralava (which allowed the actor to address fans in person in eighty-eight venues across the country), he extended his reach into publishing, producing articles and a book on physical fitness (a proven winner for contemporaries like Douglas Fairbanks [Studlar, *Masquerade* 41–47, 55–64]). Not abandoning his female fans, Valentino's book *How You Can Keep Fit* was serialized under the title "Valentino's Beauty Secrets" (Leider 315), and in May 1923 he published his best-selling book of romantic poetry, *Day Dreams* (Leider 242–43; Shulman 230–31). He also made a strategic peace with *Photoplay*, collaborating with Herbert Howe to produce a three-part autobiography ("My Life Story") that was serialized between January and March of 1923. Although unnamed "movie executives" were said to believe that by staying offscreen for so long Valentino "was cutting his own throat in full view of the nation" (218), the actor enjoyed considerable commercial success in his extracinematic ventures. Copies of *Photoplay* featuring his life story sold "like hotcakes" (Shulman 223).

Understanding his visual appeal, Valentino also kept his image in circulation with a steady stream of still photographs. A "stunning photograph of Valentino" accompanied the second installment of his *Photoplay* autobiography (Shulman 220). Although Clark argues against reducing actors to fetishized "objects within the representational field" (121), producing images of himself as a fetishizable object was a key part of Valentino's career. In "Enter Julio!" for example, the author directs our attention to the striking photographs that illustrate the first two pages. Describing the circumstances of their production, he stresses the actor's labor in the process: Valentino "can go one day to Shirley Blanc's to be photographed as a rigid, immobile, determined, stern mask. And the following afternoon he can drop in to have the camera catch him as illusive, lambent, unsubstantially poetique" (Sherwood 19). The photo on the top left of the article is a close-up of Valentino in a turban; the jewel on his head establishes an Orientalist atmosphere while the glinting stone visually mimics his eyes as he stares intensely into the camera, hypnotic and sensual. Below this is a full figure shot of him in a white open-necked shirt, white jodhpurs, and shiny black cavalry boots. The opposite page has another close-up and a full-figure shot of Valentino, in a tweed jacket and tie, striking a "gentlemanly" pose (a pipe in one hand and a riding crop in the other). These images establish instantly his range as an actor as well as the range of ways he might appeal to audiences—exotic and intense in close-ups, cavalier and nonchalant in full-figure display, his slicked-back hair and smooth-shaven face both modern and timeless.

In his chapter on Valentino in *The Stars* (1962), Richard Schickel suggests that (in an era before video and DVD) "still photographs" were later generations' "chief link" with Valentino (42). The theft of photographs of Valentino, frequently torn out of books and fan magazines of the 1920s, suggests that they were always fundamental to his appeal—and still are. Some of the most powerful images were initiated by the actor and his wife, costume and set designer Natacha Rambova, in collaboration with important photographers in an attempt to insert Valentino into the context of European Art, as epitomized by the Ballets Russes (Studlar, "Out-Salomeing Salome" 105, 111; Moon). More overtly sexual than the actor's film appearances, many of these photographs emphasize the fine line between nudity and adornment, the veiled and unveiled: for example, Valentino dripping with pearls and not much else in publicity stills for *The Young Rajah* (costumes by Rambova); Helen MacGregor's photographs of him as Nijinsky in *Afternoon of a Faun* (the dancer's Bakst-designed tights replaced here by paint and a hint of camouflaged G-string); or Valentino as Black Feather (taken by Russell Ball) wearing a dramatically large feathered headdress and suggestively draped loin-cloth (all reproduced in Leider).

Close-ups of Valentino, especially those featuring "the stare," form their own sub-genre extending from the turban photo in 1920 to "the so-called trance portrait by Bruno of Hollywood" in 1926. The photo reproduced here from *Beyond the Rocks* shows how photographic technique, costume, and performer combine to create an image-object that rewards fetishistic obsession. The close-up is so tight, the focal length calculated so precisely, that the image loses focus in the space between the actor's eyes and the blurred tip of his nose. The distinctions in focus highlight the texture of the fabrics the actor wears—the corduroy of his jacket, the striped velvet lapel, the crisp ruffles of his shirt, and the soft flow of the bow surrounding a starched white collar touching his skin. The pores of his skin can be counted even as it is clear that his forehead has been retouched to smooth out wrinkles. His professional investment in producing such images would continue throughout his career. They are, as a whole, one of his most notable accomplishments.

★★★★★ Women Made Him Do It

Rather than credit Valentino for his early protests regarding the actor's position in the studio system, critics and biographers have tended to look for someone to blame. Whatever mistakes he may have

Valentino in *Beyond the Rocks* (1922). Publicity still.

made regarding his career choices, they are Not His Fault. In 1925 *Photoplay* insisted that "Valentino has been badly advised. He has been swayed by absurd and silly influences" (May 1925, 117). In case there is any question to whom he is referring, the article's author points directly to "widespread reports of Mrs. Valentino's strict management of her husband" (36). The idea of Rambova as domineering wife (and/or emasculating lesbian) became a mainstay of Valentino lore; Schickel, three decades later, parrots the accepted wisdom that Valentino "was fatally attracted to women stronger than he was. The one he chose as his wife very nearly succeeded in wrecking his career" (47). It was Rambova who received the lion's share of criticism for the commercial disappointment of Valentino's "come-back film," *Monsieur Beaucaire*. The film's "powdered curls, beauty marks, and jeweled garters and the elaborately choreographed minuets set the preening, mincing tone that many American viewers found hard to stomach" (Leider 302–03). But, as these quotations suggest, the problem was not merely that Valentino could be depicted as his wife's pawn (the much commented upon "slave-bracelet" notwithstanding). The warning was starker than that: if a man was too in tune with women, he risked becoming one.

The effeminization of Valentino is part and parcel of the rampant misogyny provoked by his fame. While the actor continued to work with women as part of a strategy to attract and maintain his female fan base, critics freely expressed their scorn for those fans, referring to them *en masse* as "these thwarted women"—"postmeridian maidens, baffled wives . . . and adolescent girls, feeling the first powerful surge of Mother Eve's blood in their veins" (Ryan 78). The women involved in the production of Valentino's films are dismissed with the same casual cruelty: June Mathis reduced to a "plump and aggressive spinster" (Shipman 538), while E. M. Hull is merely the "elderly authoress of the passion-in-a-desert books" who has "concocted" *The Son of the Sheik* to "again arouse the stolid damsels of hinterland igloos" (Ryan 78). Shulman completes the picture by including gay men in his misogyny, describing recent critics as "oviparous [egg-laying] females of both sexes" (x).

The more pernicious means of keeping Valentino "blameless"— whether for his perceived hypersexual "Latin" savagery or for his woman-directed submission to effeminacy—was to argue that he was, in fact, harmless, a child. One of the first things written about him (November 1920) refers to him as "a boy-foreigner," "serious only in his mania to dance and play" (Sherwood 75, 18). In an article on "Great Lovers of the Screen," three-time co-star Nita Naldi calls Valentino "a sweet, adorable, charming boy" (*Photoplay*, May 1924, 92).

Woman-dominated, child-like, effeminized, and desexualized, Valentino by 1926 becomes sympathetic in direct proportion to his perceived harmlessness. "Valentino's house is slipping. . . . The stucco mansion so recently acquired is cracking. Something must be done," wrote *Motion Picture Classic* (May 1926, 69). Others, however, were still on the attack. Although the notorious "pink powderpuff" editorial is usually discussed as an accusation of effeminacy (and described as having led to the actor's death [Leider 372]), what incensed Valentino, according to his written response, were the ethnic slurs. He could not allow, he wrote, this "scurrilous personal attack . . . upon me, my race, and my father's name. You slur my Italian ancestry; you cast ridicule upon my Italian name" (Leider 373). Only after he has rousingly reasserted his pride in his Italian identity does he address the "doubt cast on his manhood" (Leider 373). Turning homophobia on its ear, he ends by proclaiming his hope that one day "the wrist under a slave bracelet may snap a real fist into your sagging jaw" (Leider 374).

There was one more insinuation in the editorial that Valentino did not address: "Are pink parlors and parlor pinks in any way related?" (Leider 372). There were worse things than being seen as a fashionably dressed actor with a bossy wife and artistic pretensions. To both his attackers and defenders, Valentino's infantilization was preferable to hints of radicalism. Were he to become too recalcitrant, a politically informed labor activist instead of the infinitely pliable, self-erasing immigrant, he would be at risk of being seen as a different kind of Italian: "The very bad kind," an Irish woman declares in Upton Sinclair's *Boston*—"the Eyetalian kind, the murderin' and bomb-throwin' arnychists" (50).

★★★★★ Dead Italians

As Valentino swept to stardom and John Dos Passos vacationed with American expatriates on the French Riviera (they might have met at Gerald and Sara Murphy's in the summer of 1924 [Leider 316]), two other Italian immigrants were being forcibly transformed into icons of the era. Nicola Sacco and Bartolomeo Vanzetti were tried and convicted of murder in Massachusetts in 1921. Irregularities in their trial (including "some decidedly questionable prosecution tactics" [Neville 94]) raised doubts about their arrest and conviction that linger to this day. Many at the time (including the defendants) believed that "they were being held for their radicalism" (Lyons 54), for union organizing ("goddam agitator(s)" [35]), and for their political beliefs. (The judge reportedly bragged to a friend: "Did you see what I did to those anarchist bastards?") In 1927, after six years of appeals and mounting international protest, they were sentenced to die in the electric chair.

Dos Passos became an active member of the Sacco-Vanzetti Defense Committee at the end of 1926. Besides courting arrest in multiple protests and recruiting other members of the New York intelligentsia to the cause, his major contribution was an extended essay for the *New Masses* that became a short book with the punchy title *Facing the Chair: Story of the Americanization of Two Foreignborn Workmen.*[5] "Americanization"—the point when "aliens" were considered to be "naturalized"—was widely disparaged during the immigration restriction debates as an ideal that had failed. There were certain kinds of immigrants, it was argued, that could not be transformed. Even Dr. Stella admitted (perhaps tactically) that "there is ample justification" for "a policy of exclusion as to certain types of immigrants"—though he does not specify which types that might be (5). (Trying his best as usual to prove himself a red-blooded American, Valentino applied for U.S. citizenship at the end of 1925 and succeeded only in stirring up bad feelings in Italy [Leider 351–53].)

Although what Sacco and Vanzetti experienced was on a scale vastly different from anything Valentino encountered, there are parallels between them that illuminate the period and the process by which all three came to be figures whose names continue to resonate as the controversies surrounding them continue to be debated. In addition to their status as Italian immigrants and the fact that they were exact contemporaries (Higashi, "Ethnicity" 116), there are two other major points of comparison: first, the similarity of the rhetorical moves used in their defense.

As with Valentino, those trying to arouse sympathy for the convicted Italians tended to infantilize them. In *The Life and Death of Sacco and Vanzetti* (1927), Lyons says of the latter: "There runs through all his letters a simplicity, a modesty, a gentleness. . . . His correspondence abounds in little bursts of almost boyish enthusiasm" (Lyons 119). In his novel based on the case, Upton Sinclair also infantilizes Vanzetti: "Poor old Bart! Lovable, queer, slyly humorous, fanatic, keeping his sense of whimsy" (479).[6] Sinclair even uses dialect to "humanize" Vanzetti, here discussing Dante: "Oh, da greata poet, da greata man! You reada heem, you know Italia, you lova da people!" (41). Like Valentino, the real Vanzetti (as opposed to Sinclair's pastiche) knew the role anti-Italian prejudice played in his trials and denounced it. At his sentencing he declared, "I am suffering because I am a radical and indeed I am a radical; I have suffered because I was an Italian, and indeed I am an Italian" (Lyons 141).

Second, the most obvious comparison is the way all three were, have been, and continue to be objectified by supporters and opponents alike. As dead Italians, robbed of all agency, they could be turned into legends, archetypes, and characters, endlessly refashioned by generations of historians, biographers, journalists, and fans. In "Adagio Dancer," Dos Passos creates sympathy for Valentino but only by making him a tragic victim, repeating what he and other supporters had done with Sacco and Vanzetti. It is important to remember that, despite their ultimate lack of success, when the three Italian immigrants found themselves being defined by others, they understood what was happening, spoke out, and fought back. As with Valentino, the deaths of Sacco and Vanzetti provoked an unprecedented reaction on an international scale.[7] They were executed in the early hours of 23 August 1927—one year to the day since Rudolph Valentino died.

NOTES

1. A spate of articles, books, and pamphlets appeared within months of the actor's death, including manager George Ullman's *Valentino as I Knew Him* (1926) and Natacha Rambova's *Rudy: An Intimate Portrait of Rudolph Valentino by His Wife* (1926).

2. Italian immigration hit 100,000 a year for the first time in 1900 and peaked twice at 300,000 (in 1907 and 1914). A dramatic drop-off during World War I was followed by another wave of over 200,000 in 1921. In 1922, the moratorium cut the number to 4,000 (Stella).

3. In "Enter Julio!" Valentino modestly states: "I was not a dancer, anyway. Nijinsky is a dancer" (Sherwood 75).

4. The 1925 *Cobra* directly addresses Valentino's status as an Italian star in the United States. Escaping chronic woman trouble, Count Rodrigo Torriani (Valentino) travels to New York at the behest of his new American friend, businessman Jack Dorning. Unexpectedly successful in business, the Americanized "Rod" manfully resists socialite husband-hunters, adulterous wives, and the pure love of Jack's secretary Mary out of loyalty to his friend. Finding himself an unwitting source of pain, Torriani heroically sacrifices his own happiness, arranging the marriage of the two Americans and returning to Italy, inevitably, alone.

5. Neville calls *Facing the Chair*, originally published by the "Sacco-Vanzetti Defense Committee, Boston Mass, 1927," "great propaganda, a lyrical argument explaining out-of-control law enforcement fueled by xenophobia used in the service of political persecution" (78). Dos Passos also fictionalized the case in *The Big Money*.

6. Sacco, on the other hand, "leaped from his cot and began to pound his head against a chair, in an effort to dash out his brains" in a suicide attempt (Sinclair 489).

7. Accounts of the reaction to their deaths resemble those of Valentino's funeral. "By tens of thousands men and women poured into the streets of the world to shout their resentment. It brimmed over here and there in acts of violence" (Lyons 8). As with Valentino's death, there followed an outpouring of literary production; Neville points to "countless poems, a half-dozen plays and eight novels" (152).

5

An Appetite for Living
Gloria Swanson, Colleen Moore, and Clara Bow

MARY DESJARDINS

Swanson, Moore, and Bow. Publicity stills.

The personas and careers of Gloria Swanson, Colleen Moore, and Clara Bow reveal the degree to which Hollywood of the 1920s contributed to the continual evolution of a multifaceted, controversial representation of sex and gender in modernity. As they helped shape the star personas of these actresses, the studios constructed a consumerist-inflected fantasy of female glamour and empowerment that established expectations of what female stardom—and by extension, female identity—meant for an important audience demographic (the female fan) in the twenties.

These three stars are particularly interesting in relation to one another: the characters they typically played represent permutations of the "new woman" of the teens and twenties that, while differing in ways specific to class status, all suggest a woman seeking her own pleasure and/or her own powers outside the traditional patriarchal family. These three careers also represent various possibilities and limitations of power held by the female star in the newly integrated studio system, from narratives of career autonomy exemplified by Swanson and Moore to the narrative of studio exploitation exemplified by Bow. All three made the transition to sound film, yet all are primarily remembered as actresses of the silent era. All three made huge box-office hits in the 1920s and were frequently listed in exhibitor polls of the time as top audience favorites; and two—Swanson and Moore—became, in later life, well-known chroniclers of the era, offering incisive perspectives on fame, stardom, and studio-system production and promotion practices in the 1920s (Moore; Swanson; Hastie).

The emergence of the flapper, that version of the "new woman" identified with youth culture and consumerism in the 1910s and 1920s, and associated to some extent with all three stars discussed here, can be seen as a result of the "success" of suffrage: when women finally won the vote (in 1920, after years of struggle for this goal), younger women took advantage of increased rights without the unifying goals of suffrage, and they were encouraged to embrace new freedoms entirely within a consumer context. However, feminist historians suggest that prior to suffrage there were disagreements within and between feminist groups over the relationship of sexual freedom and fashion to political and economic equality, and that suffragists themselves, rather than being "tainted" by commodity culture, used it as a tool for self-expression and advancement of political goals (Cott; Finnegan; Zeitz). Increased freedoms for women were the result of many factors of change—urbanization and expansion of the economy, increased access to birth control and lower birthrates, increased literacy and access to higher education, new forms of mass media and live public entertainment, dress reform, suffrage—so individual and group identities were neither monolithic nor permanently settled.

Different permutations of the "new woman"—flapper, companion wife, social reformer—should not be construed as merely adhering to or escaping from an outdated suffragist-inflected feminism, or as merely fulfilling personal agendas in complicity with patriarchal, consumer capitalism. For our purposes, the term "new woman" is used to indicate the myriad identities through which a variety of groups of women expressed their relation to expanded enfranchisement and increased participation in the public sphere from the late nineteenth century through the 1920s. Perhaps one expectation that all "new women" had in common was that identity—whether as wife or sexual playmate, wage worker or professional—could be forged out of the realities of one's contemporary experiences and hopes for the future, rather than predetermined by tradition. The popular success of Gloria Swanson, Colleen Moore, and Clara Bow is due, in part, to how well the representations of their private life and/or the parts they played connected with an audience who lived with those expectations and experiences.

☆☆☆☆☆ Gloria Swanson: Fashionable Companion Wife, Shop Girl, Fallen Woman

Next to Mary Pickford, Gloria Swanson was probably the most powerful female film star of the 1920s. Swanson not only produced her own films by the end of the decade but also held considerable cultural capital for female fans in relation to fashion, lifestyle, and motherhood. She sometimes inspired press wariness—for example, Adela Rogers St. Johns wrote in one of her pieces that Swanson displayed a "warmth" to her that she "barely suspected" existed in the star (*Photoplay*, February 1922, 20). However, ambition, determination, artistry, and courage were almost always qualities attributed to Swanson in fan magazine essays of the period. Usually these construct an image of Swanson as the glamorous and serious actress whose growth in ability and ambition aided her move from work as a lowly extra to star of feature-length domestic melodramas and comedies.

Indeed, Swanson, born in 1899, began her career in 1914 as an extra at Chicago's Essanay studio. Because of her short stature (she was barely five feet tall), she was even considered as partner to Charlie Chaplin, who was making films at that studio during her time there. Although she did play a bit part in Chaplin's *His New Job* (1915), he rejected her as his leading lady in subsequent films because she didn't have "a strong enough comic sense" (Swanson, *Swanson* 40). By late 1915 Swanson was in California at Mack

Gloria Swanson, c. 1920. Publicity still.

Sennett's Keystone Studios (which functioned as an autonomous unit at Triangle) where, partnered with Bobby Vernon and Teddy the Wonder Dog, she made a series of successful comic shorts. Again, she had been singled out by film producers because of her height—her co-star Vernon was short and she could be partnered with him. The challenge here for Swanson was to play her age—she and Vernon were supposed to be teens or young adults in their films—for she had become used to being cast at Essanay as an "older" woman.

When Sennett set up Mack Sennett Pictures in 1917, he sold co-star Vernon's contract to Triangle but kept Swanson in his new company to make her into "a second" Mabel Normand, an overture she rejected outright in order to return to Triangle's melodramatic formula, in which her ability to wear clothes to spectacular effect in aid of narrative economy became apparent in films such as *Shifting Sands* (1917). This and other Triangle films prepared her and her audience for more significant roles in the 1920s, when the star became associated with the "clotheshorse" femininity of Cecil B. DeMille's comedies and melodramas. Issues of class, gender, and modern marriage are relevant to Swanson's work with DeMille. The director, who was given autonomy under the Art Craft label at Famous Players–Lasky Corporation (Paramount), had long been interested in Swanson. When Triangle failed in late 1918, she was free to pursue DeMille's interest. The four sophisticated marriage comedies Swanson and DeMille made together—*Male and Female* (1919), *Don't Change Your Husband* (1919), *Why Change Your Wife* (1920), and *Affairs of Anatol* (1921)—were all immense successes at the box office and gave Swanson the kind of contract leverage that made her one of the highest paid and most powerful stars of the 1920s.

Male and Female (adapted from James M. Barrie's play *The Admirable Crichton*) caused a sensation for its bathing scene, in which Swanson's character Lady Mary disrobes and descends into a lavishly appointed sunken bathtub, as well as for its "historical" fantasy in which Lady Mary is imagined to be the "Christian slave" of Crichton's "Babylonian King" (Thomas Meighan), who throws her into a lion's den when she refuses to lose her sexual honor to him. While characters indulge in "primitive" sexual role-playing through elaborate fantasies in this film, the themes of *Don't Change Your Husband* and *Why Change Your Wife* explicitly concern companionate marriage as experienced through the daily rituals and consumer desires of man and wife. In *Don't Change Your Husband*, Swanson's Leila Porter leaves her husband, John Porter (Elliot Dexter), because he has become annoying, boring, and romantically unresponsive. In *Why Change Your Wife*, the married couple divorces because the husband Robert (Thomas Meighan) has sought companionship with Sally (Bebe Daniels), a woman more in tune with his need for sexual excitement. New spouses turn out to be not only no better than old spouses but much worse. In both films, the "left" spouses win back the spouses who spurned them by making over their bodies and attitudes. The films include scenes of these makeovers, as well as scenes revealing the duplicity of the new spouses and the moment of reawakened desire between old spouses (e.g., in *Why Change Your Wife*, the post-divorce encounter of Beth [Swanson] and Robert at a lavish tourist resort).

It is possible to read *Don't Change Your Husband* and *Why Change Your Wife* as exposures/acceptances of the reification of modern, middle-class gender relations (Higashi, *Cecil* 152–66). Certainly, one of the appeals for contemporary audiences of DeMille's films and Swanson's roles in them was the explicit referencing and visualizing of commodity goods, from phonograph records, magazines, cigars, and liqueurs, to perfumes, jewelry, and clothes that the characters use in seducing others or adorning and transforming the self. Beth, for example, gains the self-confidence to win her husband back after her transformation into a fashion plate. However, the films could also be seen as acknowledging that both men and women long for sexual compatibility with their spouses—an increasingly important tenet in the ideal of companionate marriage in a postwar American society that included young women making choices about marriage and partners with less input from families and through greater exposure to single men in an integrated public sphere.

Furthermore, while DeMille's films with Swanson employ exotic fantasies to signal the characters' hedonistic desires and their use of expensive commodities to judge the desirability of others, the married couples discover that moral character is still a necessary component for loving and holding onto a spouse. Robert, in *Why Change Your Wife*, acknowledges his former wife's glamorous transformation, but he can go back to her only when his new wife, Sally, proves herself to be of less character than Beth. Beth is willing to fight to save Robert, whose accidental fall outside their former home has rendered him unconscious. Sally, in a jealous rage, wishes to move Robert from his sickbed so that ex-wife Beth cannot be his savior. She fails after losing a literally knock-down, drag-out fight with Beth, who will risk her own physical safety to make sure that Robert remains in bed until the "crisis" has passed.

The film makes a distinction between the fashionable façade that hides the heart of a gold digger (Sally) and a transformative fashionableness that awakens the spirit of "true character" by increasing the character's confidence and consciousness of how self-presentation includes thinking of others (exemplified by Beth). This may still be a form, in Sumiko Higashi's words, of reified human relations, or, according to another critic, a form of "hokum" (Jacobs 90), but it suggests that Swanson's appeal for audiences was in part based on an onscreen persona that pleasingly mediated those old and new values about femininity relevant to the challenges of marriage and the pleasures of consumerism. These values were the source of much contemporary social anxiety and often resulted in decidedly more misogynist cultural representations than those offered by the DeMille-Swanson vehicles.

Given the contradictions in and convoluted relation between personality (complicit with commodity culture) and character (forged through virtue) in the films, it is not surprising that fan magazine articles about Swanson at the time demonstrated ambivalence about the meanings of the star's "fashionableness." According to an August 1919 *Photoplay* article, "Don't Change Your Coiffure," Swanson's influence on fashionable clothing and hairstyle is considerable—she is said to have "demoralized young America a la femme *from the skin out*" (emphasis original). Supposedly this American youth cares little about "the shut-down of theaters in Germany" or the "campaign against lynching," but "Swanson's newest head adornment means a lot to them" (Evans 73–74). While the article identifies Swanson as having this influence on the young—"Gloria is the rage . . . We'll have Gloria perfumes and powders and Gloria hats and Gloria gowns"—it also claims that "off-screen she is a well-dressed, but inconspicuously attired small person," and that it is the characters in her DeMille films who dress in the fashions that have hypnotized young America. Swanson is "laying the foundation of a career," and she "is not a modiste" but an actress who has continued to study so she can play her new roles "a little better than last" (74).

Photoplay published a follow-up article that states there has been a debate about whether it is the "head-dresses" or "Swanson herself that is responsible for that young star's success," but reaffirms that it is Swanson's acting abilities that are what make her a star ("She Changed Her Coiffure" 33). Swanson "has successfully settled the argument as to her acting" by showing her versatility in DeMille's *Something to Think About* (1920), a "problem-play of purpose rather than passion; sincerity, not sex," in which she has to wear clothes befitting a tragic woman. She is claimed to still fascinate her public, even without the "ermine tails" and "glittering trains" (33). Although fan discourse at this stage seems unable to define Swanson apart from considerations of her association with fashion, or to clearly separate onscreen and offscreen personas, Swanson-as-star emerges as a negotiation of oppositions relevant to the contemporary woman in the public sphere, including "serious professional (actress) vs. clotheshorse," "woman intent on long-term goals of self-improvement vs. one who can seize the moment," and "woman of sincerity vs. sexual playmate."

Swanson's last appearance in a DeMille film came in 1921 (in *Affairs of Anatol*, again playing a character of wifely flexibility in the face of changing expectations toward contemporary marriage), but her contract with Paramount lasted until 1926. If Paramount had proved the perfect studio environment for her at the start of the 1920s—in that it provided the structure and site for her collaboration with DeMille—it continued to be so for her in the years remaining on her contract by enthusiastically promoting her in the press (including creating a feud with Paramount star Pola Negri), bringing her together with such talents as writer Elinor Glyn and director Allan Dwan, and giving her de facto producer control over some aspects of an expensive French co-production (*Madame Sans-Gêne*, 1925). By 1923, her contract demands included choice over material and a salary of $6,500 a week.

Romance novelist and magazine writer Elinor Glyn, considered by some scholars to be more powerful as a brand name than as screenwriter or scenario writer (Morey 110; Landay 76), contributed a significant aspect of the mystique of Swanson's star persona in the early twenties. Glyn first became associated with the star in 1920 when Paramount adapted her story *The Great Moment* (1921) into a film oriented toward sensationalism (Milton Sills as Swanson's love interest sucks snake venom from her shoulder) and spectacle (Swanson wore a gown with a four-foot train of pearls and ermine). Glyn also wrote *Beyond the Rocks* (1922), in which Swanson co-starred with Rudolph Valentino, soon to become one of biggest male stars of the era. If any Swanson film of the 1920s deserves to be called "hokum," this might be it: while the film has no pretense of offering a lesson, as DeMille's films do, it also has none of the humor or believability of those films.

In *Beyond the Rocks*, the character of Theodora Fitzgerald, pressured into marriage with a wealthy older man to support her widowed father and older, spinster sisters, allows Swanson to age in film again from young girl to mature wife and romantic lover. Lord Hector Bracondale (Rudolph Valentino) rescues teenage Theodora from drowning. The shy girl gives Hector a narcissus flower; he will forever associate that scent with her. The two re-meet when Theodora is on her honeymoon with the old, wealthy, sweet—but romantically unsuitable—Josiah Brown (Robert Bolder). Hector saves Theodora again, this time in a mountain-climbing accident, and the two fall in love, spending much of their time together fantasizing scenarios of a past in which their love could flourish (for example, in pre-Revolutionary Versailles). Theodora ultimately tells Hector that she owes her husband fidelity, that they must prove themselves "stronger than [their] love." When Josiah accidentally discovers that Theodora loves Hector, he allows himself to be killed in a skirmish with Arab rebels on an expedition to the Middle East.

The scenes in which Theodora and Hector imagine themselves in the past were widely circulated in still photos to all the fan magazines and press of the time, not only allowing Swanson and Valentino to be showcased again as spectacular fashion plates (in lavish Louis XV–era garb), but associating them with a notion of timeless romance. This was one of the major contributions of Glyn to Swanson's persona—to create a discourse around Swanson that suggested that she embodied a "timeless" femininity. In 1921, Glyn declared (rather unclearly) that Swanson "has an old soul struggling to remember its former lives—not young—young—like this Great America" (*Photoplay*, October 1930, 24). This idea would be picked up by other writers: Frederick Van Vranken wrote in a 1922 issue of *Motion Picture* magazine that she "symbolizes the eternal quest of love, with all its dangers and adventures and rewards," and "represents the mystical allure of women everywhere" (*Motion Picture*, October 1922, 34–35). However much the overblown discourse suggests an ahistorical femininity for the developing star persona of Swanson, *Beyond the Rocks* does provide the actress with another role in which female desire has to struggle for expression within what are seen as unfair restraints of patriarchal institutions (i.e., Theodora's submission to marriage as an economic contract in aid of her family), and confirms Swanson as a figure most associated with modern women in relation to concerns about sexual compatibility within marriage.

Madame Sans-Gêne (1925) again connects Swanson with the romance of France's historical past. She plays a laundress who befriends Napoleon before his fame and military conquests. When she rises in class as the wife of one of Napoleon's officers, she is the only one who will stand up to the now powerful figure, including when he tries to force her husband to divorce her. Swanson had lobbied Paramount's Adolph Zukor to play the role and to film on location in France. When the studio agreed, it was Swanson who personally managed to get permission for filming at the famed Fontainebleau; in fact, she took on so many duties of a producer that Douglas Fairbanks asked her to consider coming to United Artists as producer-star when her contract at Paramount came to an end. The production used mostly French talent, including director Leonce Perret, and Swanson was given Henri, marquis de la Falaise de la Coudraye, as an on-set interpreter. Although complete prints of *Madame Sans-Gêne* no longer exist, the film has an important position in star-lore about Swanson—she took the marquis as her third husband and became the first Hollywood star to have a royal title.

As is to be expected, the romance and marriage were an asset to publicity that had already proclaimed Swanson the most glamorous woman in Hollywood, and also probably aided the film's box office, including its breaking of records at New York's Tivoli Theater when it opened there in 1925.

In Swanson's mid-decade filmography, *Madame Sans-Gêne* is bracketed by two of her greatest critical and popular successes, *Manhandled* (1924) and *Stage Struck* (1925). Both film comedies were directed by Allan Dwan, who became Swanson's favorite collaborator, one who welcomed her contribution and understood her acting versatility. Together with writer Arthur Stringer, they came up with the characters and story for *Manhandled* (a title suggested by Sidney Kent, the studio's general sales manager)—Swanson as a "shop girl" who, through a series of misadventures, hobnobs with bohemian artists and the upper classes before marrying her car mechanic boyfriend.

When Swanson had played a flapper in an earlier film, *Prodigal Daughters* (1923), critics considered her miscast and, though not a flop, the film was not as successful as Swanson's others at that time (Parrish 24–25). *Manhandled*'s Tessie Maguire is not exactly a flapper—she is not wild, consumerist, or flirty—but she sports the flapper's bobbed hair and masquerades within the flapper's milieu of parties that match young women with "sugar daddies" and artists. Tessie works in the bargain basement of Thorndyke's department store, which the film depicts as operating in a chaos of near-rioting female shoppers. After grueling workdays, she takes the subway to her boarding house residence where her boyfriend Jim (Tom Moore) also lives. Tessie rejects Jim's idea that marriage will make them happy—she sees evidence all around them that the working poor have miserable family lives.

Jim bolsters Tessie's mood by claiming that one day the car part he invented will make them rich enough to marry, but it is Tessie who first tries to find a path toward economic success. She attends a "bohemian" party with co-worker Pinkie Moran (Lilyan Tashman) and accepts an offer to pose for a famed sculptor, Robert Brandt (Ian Keith). After an embarrassingly bad (and very funny) attempt at the party to do the latest jazz dance, Tessie entertains the guests by a series of impersonations, including an impersonation of an aristocrat that briefly fools wealthy playboy and women's fashion store owner Nino Ricardi (Frank Morgan), who drops in from his penthouse next door (apparently these impersonations included one of Charlie Chaplin, but this was cut from the final print of the film).[1]

Jim takes off for Detroit to sell his invention, and Tessie keeps a calendar diary in his room that expresses how much she loves him even as she moves into the fast life. When she flees Brandt's apartment after he makes a pass, Ricardi steps in to offer her a job impersonating Russian nobility at his modiste shop. The successful Jim returns, sees her fancy dresses and late-night homecoming, and concludes that she has been "manhandled," like the goods at Thorndykes, by her new group of suitors. Tessie has been "manhandled," but not with the result that Jim's accusation implies. Part of the film's humor derives from Tessie's practical and weary responses to he-wolves and their tired come-ons. She has taken care of herself in a variety of challenging, sexually fraught situations, not becoming someone's "goods." The happy ending comes when he discovers her calendar diary and they can both share their successes.

The role of Tessie showcased Swanson's talents at convincingly playing filmic female types—the energetic, gum-chewing working girl, the fashion-able aristocrat, the loving romantic partner—and her ability to do physical comedy. The film's opening sequence includes a scene in the subway where Tessie is pushed, shoved, and almost carried away by the crowd; she loses the contents of her purse and has to retrieve them while negotiating the jostling feet, legs, and arms of other passengers. And when she finally leaves the car at her stop, she falls head-first over a chain-link barrier. When she attempts the jazz dance at the party, she ends up falling down, tripped by her own bloomers. In *Stage Struck*, Swanson pulls off similar slap-stick (such as in a scene in which she has to go into the boxing ring against a much larger woman) but also parody. Her character fantasizes playing Salome, known to audiences at that time as the role most epitomizing "seri-ous" acting, but quite beyond the talents of the film's heroine (Swanson, of course, would play another character infatuated with the role of Salome—Norma Desmond of the 1950 film *Sunset Blvd.*).

Despite her ever-increasing clout at Paramount, Swanson rejected their offer of $18,000 a week when her contract was up for renewal in 1926. She formed her own company, accepting the offer made by Fairbanks, Pickford, and Chaplin to join United Artists. Her press for some time had been sug-gesting that Swanson put her career before love (but not motherhood), and as she started her own production company, it constructed a risk-taking Swanson, emphasizing that the "possibility of failure" has never "entered the scheme" of her life (*Photoplay*, April 1926, 33) and that her new role as producer allows her to join the "Valhalla of heroes and heroines" who are masters of their own destiny (*Photoplay*, March 1927, 31). The same year that Swanson left Paramount and launched her own company, Elinor Glyn was once again issuing proclamations about the star, saying she was one of two female stars (Vilma Banky was the other) who possessed "It," a "virile quality" belonging to only the most successful, attractive people (*Photoplay*, February 1926, 31).

The first film produced by Swanson's company, *The Love of Sunya* (1927) was a remake of a Clara Kimball Young film, *Eyes of Youth* (1919). Sunya (Swanson) is the modern reincarnation of an ancient-era Egyptian maiden refused sanctuary by a priest. On the evening when Sunya has to decide whether to marry her earnest lover, marry the businessman her father is indebted to, or study opera in Paris, the priest—reincarnated as a wandering fortuneteller—arrives on her family's patio. In atonement for his refusal to help her in ancient Egypt, he lets her gaze into a crystal ball to see what lies in store for her in those possible choices. While the plot suggests Swanson had not gotten very far from the fantastic world of Elinor Glyn's stories, the depictions of Sunya's possible futures compare to some of the stark, yet lurid representations found in German silent cinema's *neue Objektivität* style. If she chooses to be an opera singer, Sunya is shown to become a drunk, decadent, and in debt. If she chooses to be the wife of her father's business partner, she will be humiliated by his womanizing, framed for adultery, and left to wander the streets after her husband divorces her. These visions make Sunya reject the pressures from exploiting patriarchs (her father and her opera teacher) and run to the arms of her lover. The film had very modest success at the box office, which managed to be a problem now that Swanson was her own producer and needed a steady supply of capital from each film's earnings to finance the next.

Swanson ended up borrowing money from Roxy Rothafel (owner of New York's Roxy Theater) to start production on her next film, *Sadie Thompson* (1928), based on W. Somerset Maugham's story of a prostitute who battles with an authoritarian minister who eventually commits suicide when he succumbs to her charms. The stage version, *Rain*, had been banned from film adaptation by the Motion Picture Producers and Distributors Association. Swanson got the MPPDA's Will Hays to agree to the production by promising to change the minister into a plain "mister" and take the film's name from Maugham's story rather than the more familiar—and infamous—play (although many aspects of the film are clearly taken from that version rather than the short story). While Swanson had played sexually knowing women before, the ease with which she played a lower-class prostitute who plied her trade among sailors and marines was a revelation to audience and critics. The film was hugely successful and earned her the first of her Academy Award nominations for Best Actress. However, Swanson's company went over budget in production and Joseph Schenck of United Artists was not forthcoming with more money—Swanson sold some of her valuable real estate and took Joseph P. Kennedy, at that time corporate head of FBO and Pathé, as a business consultant. He refinanced her company and became a co-producer of her next few films and her lover.

The decisions Swanson and Kennedy made together involving *Queen Kelly* (1929)—most famously, hiring Erich von Stroheim as director and not making it a sound film—would ultimately make it impossible for Swanson to survive as an independent producer. Von Stroheim, already notorious by 1928 for an unwillingness to stay within budget, insisted on lavishly detailed sets, the inclusion of perverse sexual details (such as the character of the prince sniffing the panties of Swanson's character, who at that point in the narrative is a young convent-educated orphan girl), and shooting more film than could easily be edited into a conventional running time for theatrical release. The film was shelved before it was finished, and Swanson lost her shares of United Artists, kept in escrow until the film's completion (Crafton 303–06). Consequently, Gloria Swanson Productions lacked the necessary economic leverage to guarantee quality films in the future.

By the end of the twenties Swanson's persona was attached to an altogether different kind of film about sex and marriage. The DeMille comedies were didactic, the Dwan comedies playful and slapsticky, but both types were romantic and optimistic in suggesting that commodified personality could coexist with virtuous character in heterosexual relations. In Swanson's last films of the decade, the economics of patriarchal sexual exchange—whether in prostitution or marriage—are seen as tragic or at least to be endured by the characters until a happy resolution years later. These filmic "new women" were comparable in some ways to the "fallen woman" of the nineteenth century who suffered the judgments of an old social order. Yet Swanson's films of the late 1920s eschewed sentimentalizing their heroines, a fact which kept them in step with modern taste, despite their lack of the comic treatment of the seduction plot that was currently the vogue (Jacobs 183). In *Sadie Thompson* and *The Trespasser* (1929, her first talking picture) she was able to parlay the fallen woman type into box office success.

Swanson worked closely with writer-director Edmund Goulding to write and produce *The Trespasser* (a melodrama about a working single mother, who accepts favors from her boss to survive after she is forced to annul her marriage to a wealthy man). The film even provided her with a hit musical tune, "Love, Your Magic Spell Is Everywhere." After this film, Swanson began to make choices motivated by a need to salvage her financial status, such as rushing into films produced by others in the early 1930s rather than refreshing or building on the strengths of her established persona. Her financial salvation ultimately came via her successful non-film-

related business ventures in the thirties and forties, and eventually a television talk show in 1949. Swanson's continual self-reinvention made her
quite unlike her most famous sound role—the crazy, deluded, has-been
silent star Norma Desmond in *Sunset Blvd.* (1950). This later film triumph
did confirm, however, that Gloria Swanson's persona exemplified a female
stardom of the silent era whose power had been felt both industrially and
culturally.

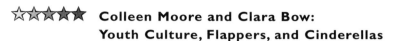 **Colleen Moore and Clara Bow:
Youth Culture, Flappers, and Cinderellas**

Colleen Moore and Clara Bow played a large variety of roles
in the twenties but both were, and continue to be, associated with the flapper (*Motion Picture*, July 1927, 28–29, 104; Basinger; Zeitz). Moore had
worked for six years to become a star before her success as the flapper Pat
she played in *Flaming Youth*; Clara Bow interspersed her flapper film roles
with others throughout her decade-long career (1922–1932), but her offscreen persona was almost always associated with this type of the "new
woman." While flappers were not exactly synonymous with adolescence,
the type was almost always young and unmarried, set in opposition to parents or other authority figures. The flapper was usually represented as
expressing her liberation from tradition in terms of consumer and entertainment fads (such as the latest jazz dance), an androgyny that included
bobbed hair and clothing that allowed for free movement and fast preparation for work and dates, and experimentation with sexual freedoms, such
as chaperone-free parties and petting with boyfriends. Some historians
have noted that this kind of new woman was also invested in and influenced by the new media, such as the movies and racy romance novels,
which represented young women as desiring subjects as well as objects
(Staiger; Ross "Hollywood Flapper"). One of the significant aspects of youth
of the twenties is that they had "greater opportunities to cultivate and to be
influenced by peer example and peer pressure" (Fass 289).

The Hollywood film industry exploited the flapper figure to secure the
continuing investment of young audiences in their productions. If the
sophisticated melodramas made by Swanson, Norma Talmadge, and Greta
Garbo in the twenties suggested an address to an adult female audience that
spanned a variety of ages, and the pleasures of the typical Mary Pickford
vehicle rested in part on their appeal to the family audience, the flapper
film was compatible with many of the popular entertainments addressed to
the youth culture of the decade. The advertising industry believed that this

particular demographic was emerging as a highly impressionable consumer majority and encouraged motion picture tie-ups and tie-ins with products, many of which were advertised in fan magazines (Felando). Colleen Moore's 1924 film, *The Perfect Flapper*, had twelve such tie-ups with clothing and cosmetic products (Ross, "Hollywood Flapper" 60).

American youth culture of the 1920s was considered to be composed of both teenagers and young adults (in their early twenties). College-age youth was of particular interest to advertisers, the film industry, and the social agents who produced discourses about this population. College life offered a generation-segregated environment where peer influence and self-regulation (through gossip, hazing, and so on) were strong and where peer-organized activities (such as parties, dances, and dates) flourished, facts that made college students the center of many discourses which speculated about the ability of this generation to take up positions of social leadership and be responsible parents in the future. Some literary stories and films about flappers were set in college life. Two of Clara Bow's flapper films, *The Plastic Age* (1925) and *The Wild Party* (1929), share this setting. Colleen Moore would later claim that she based her flapper characters on the college girlfriends of her younger brother—they were "casual about their looks and manners," but "smart and sophisticated" and didn't look "any more like the sweet young things I was playing in the movies than I did" (Moore 129).

F. Scott Fitzgerald is frequently quoted as saying, "I was the spark that lit up flaming youth, Colleen Moore was the torch."[2] Could Moore's role as a torch bearer of youth culture of the twenties have been anticipated in the teens? Like Swanson, Moore worked at developing her onscreen persona to reach stardom—before her role in *Flaming Youth* (1923) as Pat, an adolescent girl who loves wild parties and attracts fast company, Moore typically played waifish and/or plucky girls in a charming but not particularly distinguished way. Born Kathleen Morrison in 1900 (some biographical sources say 1902), Moore was a huge movie fan who wrote letters to her favorite stars and longed to be an actress since childhood. She played leading lady opposite popular male stars Bobby Harron, Charles Ray, and Tom Mix, hopping from studio to studio throughout the teens and early twenties (she made films at ArtCraft/Paramount, Selig, Universal, Ince, Fox, the Christie Brothers, Goldwyn, and First National between 1917 and 1923).

In the title role in *Little Orphant Annie* (1918) Moore entertains other orphans with stories of goblins and is abused by her guardians before being adopted by a loving couple. But Moore was right to suggest that her physicality and acting style didn't suit roles that exemplified normative femininity at the time (i.e., the "sweet young thing" type). Her role in *Sky Pilot* (1921), as the spirited girl whose miraculous recovery from paralysis climaxes the story of a young minister who struggles to establish a church in the midst of a hostile western ranching community, anticipates the type she would later develop in her popular flapper and Cinderella roles in the twenties. She is introduced in the film as a rough-rider, breaking in horses—she is a tomboy and the mismatch between her long curls and cowboy chaps startles the hero (seven years later, in *Lilac Time*, she would be introduced to the hero, played by Gary Cooper, in a similar manner—he would first mistake her for an airplane mechanic).

Moore finally settled at First National in 1923, after gaining comedy experience in Christie Brothers two-reelers such as *A Roman Scandal* (1919) and *Her Bridal Nightmare* (1920), in which slapstick was combined with mild, almost sweet, satire of bourgeois pretensions. At First National, Moore lobbied hard for the part of Pat in *Flaming Youth*, convinced that this was the part that would finally make her a star. By this time she was engaged to John McCormick, publicity agent at the studio, and she enlisted him in the lobbying effort. They would succeed when Moore took a screen test in her new bobbed hair style. As Moore became a star in the aftermath, she gained more control over material, and McCormick became her husband, production head of the West Coast First National studio, and then eventually just producer of her films (he was demoted because of his destructive alcoholism, which was also responsible for Moore's finally suing for divorce in 1929).

Only the first reel of *Flaming Youth* survives, but contemporary press accounts that summarize the plot establish a story of an upper-class girl who, following the example of older sisters and parents, participates in wild drinking and jazz dancing parties. The film adapts one of the source novel's most infamous scenes—a pool party in which some revelers swim in the nude. However, in the film the characters are shown in silhouette and Pat (Colleen Moore) is not present for the skinny-dipping. Pat eventually runs off with an older man, but when he attempts to seduce her on his yacht, she jumps ship, finally returning to her parents.

Flapper films such as *The Perfect Flapper* (1924) and *We Moderns* (1925), both now lost, followed *Flaming Youth*. Sara Ross argues that the "moral ending" and satiric treatment of the flapper in films of Moore and others (such as Olive Thomas and Clara Bow) softened potentially controversial material depicting the modern girl (Ross "Good Little"). *Flaming Youth*, with its moral ending in which Pat keeps her virtue and learns a lesson, also embraces satire, via Moore's performance. In a scene at the beginning of the film, Pat makes herself up, in imitation of her older sisters, to look like a flapper—rouging her lips, donning of a low-cut gown, affecting a seductive way of walking. Moore's interpretation of Pat's beauty ritual through exaggerated poses and excessive and enthusiastic application of makeup renders the flapper as a (comic) masquerade of femininity, mitigating the potential subversiveness of flapper sexuality.

Moore's personas, constructed both onscreen and off, convey the sexually "safe" modern girl. Diane Negra notes that contemporary publicity emphasizes her Irish American heritage (with "Irishness" seen as a European ethnicity "successfully" assimilating into American culture) and her shaping by patriarchal agents (D. W. Griffith in the late teens; husband John McCormick). Both discourses work, according to Negra, as a check on the emerging power of the new woman. Furthermore, filmic patterns associate Moore's characters with children and a girlish "sexlessness" (Negra 53). Indeed, prior to her appearance as a flapper in films, fan magazine articles with such titles as "With a Dash of Green," "The Wearing of the Green," and "The Celtic Strain" associate Moore with a sentimentalized notion of "Irishness"—she sings like a "happy little brook [in Ireland]" (*Photoplay*, March 1921, 32) and the "pixies" must have "kissed her at birth" (*Motion Picture*, June 1922, 41). Even articles touting her versatility and career achievement in later years don't fail to mention that her heart is "forever open to the little people of the Irish hills" (*Photoplay*, August 1926, 30).

To some extent, the arguments of Ross and Negra depend on an understanding of the flapper as a young woman so threatening to the social order of the twenties that Moore and/or the film industry had to create a distance from the type to make her acceptable to audiences (and/or censors). The flapper was a controversial figure, but contemporary discourse was actually divided on her moral status—many social agents, including authority figures, argued that she *was* a moral figure in her rejection of hypocritical traditions (*Literary Digest*, 24 June 1922, 17 May 1923, 24 June 1922). Perhaps what was threatening, in part, about the flapper was that she could not be reduced to a singular definition or valuation of femininity. With this context in mind, Moore's characters, even in their childlike qualities and poses, are within the definitional spectrum of the modern woman. However, the association of Moore's young female characters with children and a naïve or even absent sexuality is worth considering here in relation to some of her non-flapper roles and the roles of other female stars of the time. Despite the specificity of the age span in consumer industries' concept of "youth," as discussed earlier, age was a slippery category for some of the most important female stars of the twenties, such as Moore and Swanson, which has a bearing on how we might position their characters and personas in terms of

Colleen Moore, mid-1920s. Publicity still.

what they signified for their audiences about femininity.

Swanson's ability to act as female characters older than her own age allowed her to enact a move away from the idealized and eroticized child-woman to "the woman of sexual knowledge" who can eventually seize her own desires, even if only after patriarchal violence. Swanson's management of age transformations suggested that her acting artistry was partially displayed in performing the negotiations of a sexually knowing femininity as narratively inevitable and socially acceptable. Colleen Moore's films present the flapper or the youthful heroine as a young woman whose ambitions for recognition and romance lead her into situations in which she has to feign being more sexually knowing, of higher class, or more socially competent than she really is. If her flappers pose and masquerade, they also dream and desire, something they have in common with most of the non-flapper characters Moore played after 1925. These latter roles are of young women who don't live fast like the flapper; they are dreamy "Cinderella" types who through a series of misadventures get the prince (Negra 46–52). But they usually don't start off dreaming of the prince, or only of him—they want to be actresses (*Broken Hearts of Broadway*, 1922; *Ella Cinders*, 1926), dancers (*Twinkletoes*, 1926), successful wage-earners (*Irene*, 1927), or in wealthy and glamorous environments (*Orchids and Ermine*, 1927)—and they are all mobile, leaving home for the big city and/or stage. They don't have family (*Broken Hearts, Orchids and Ermine*), or they flee family (*Ella Cinders*), or have families who are bad role models (*Twinkletoes, Irene*). For these reasons, the Colleen Moore Cinderella narrative, like her flapper narrative, is a coming-of-age narrative, one in which the desire to be an adult who is (or appears to be) sexually knowing is less, or at least no more, important than successfully earned social recognition. Consequently, at this point in her career, romantic interests for the Moore characters are rarely fleshed out or played by important stars.

This narrative reorientation of Cinderella, where the prince is secured but not particularly sought after, perhaps makes her characters seem sexless, and the emphasis on the characters' social and career incompetence might make them seem childlike. But is the function of the undersexed, childlike woman completely subsumed by patriarchal ideology? Gaylyn Studlar argues that Mary Pickford's on- and offscreen persona of the child-woman was "a sentimentalized object of desire" that offered a controllable sexuality and idealized femininity in contrast to the modern woman. Yet this persona also offered female audiences a pleasurable fantasy of being released from the sexual demands of adult femininity in a patriarchal order (Studlar, "Oh, 'Doll'" 219). Moore's dreamy, socially incompetent, but ultimately successful young women who have adventures in the big city before the prince arrives also offer this latter possibility. But unlike Pickford's characters, the Moore characters do become conscious of their desirous feelings for the male hero, even if they prioritize other projects before marriage (Ella Cinders wants to be an actress before a wife), or are insecure about their inferior class status (shanty Irish Irene must win over her boyfriend's mother, who wants a society girl for her son). In *Orchids and Ermine*, Pinks, the small-town cement company switchboard operator who moves to a fancier setting (the switchboard at a fancy New York Hotel), has to learn which she wants most, the millionaire or the "fine feathers" he can provide. If there is some doubt about the age of these heroines, the thrust of their narrative trajectories establishes that they are moving into adulthood and will marry men of roughly comparable age in surprising, but decidedly unsentimental, fashion.

Twinkletoes, in which Moore plays Twinks, a cockney dancer committed to her talent and support of her widowed father, offers an interesting variation in this pattern. Twinks loves a married boxer who is somewhat older (he describes her as a "little bit of a girl"). When she dances on stage, she is clearly an object of desire (her dancing figure is reflected in his eyes). When their illicit love is expressed (through a kiss in a dark alley), Moore's face is lit in the soft-focus style of photography often used in close-up shots of female stars who are typically more overtly eroticized than she is. In some of her films, Moore is shot sparingly in close-up—since the films rely so much on physical comedy, the mise-en-scène prioritizes shots in which her full or nearly full body is visible.

Through her characters, Moore often interacts with objects (such as telephones in *Orchids and Ermine*, film set props in *Ella Cinders*, clothing in *Irene*) and in situations that are more reminiscent of those situations faced by the characters played by Buster Keaton or Harold Lloyd. These are characters who are intelligent and inventive but generally baffled by social rituals, especially those concerning work or romance (in *Orchids and Ermine*, Moore's character is even romantically paired with a character played by an actor made up to look like Lloyd). This doesn't mean that gender or age are irrelevant to their comic outlook or that they are sexless, but typically all three comic performers create characters who don't live up to the gender ideals that are supposed to make them attractive and have power over others, especially over the opposite sex. For a female star, some of those ideals include the normative feminine beauty ideal of the time. Moore later claimed that she helped change how non-normative beauty of the time was valued, exemplifying through her style that "a girl who had straight hair, who was not buxom and not a great beauty" could have a chance for career and romance (*New York Times*, 26 October 1971, 36).

The *Photoplay* articles "Colleen Moore Wins Prize" and "The Cinderella Girl" provide their own version of the Cinderella narrative as a coming-of-age narrative in relation to Moore's career success. The former announces that Moore has been voted to be the former WAMPAS "baby" star who has advanced the most as a film performer in the past four years (September

1926, 125).[3] The latter emphasizes that her ability to handle roles as disparate in type as Pat in *Flaming Youth*, Selena in *So Big*, and Ella in *Ella Cinders* is the result of both hard work across the many studios in which she has worked and the intensity of her own dreams for success (August 1926, 30–31, 134). Both articles demonstrate a delight in Moore's successful "coming of age." In that way, the promotional press is compatible with visual and narrative aspects of the films that position the spectator to take delight in her characters' eventual "coming to knowledge" after many mishaps: for example, Pinks in *Orchids and Ermine* finally getting wise to the "come-on lines" of the various men who flirt with her at the hotel switchboard where she works (she yells after one, "I'm sick of this Sweet Mama, Baby-doll, Bright-eyes, Honeybunch, Sweet Patootie stuff!"); Irene in *Irene* figuring out how to get her girlfriends jobs as models and how to put on a successful fashion show; Ella in *Ella Cinders* inventively crashing the gates of a movie studio and eventually realizing that she would rather marry her small-town boyfriend (who, unbeknownst to her, is a millionaire) than continue acting. Moore's characters and their comic coming-of-age adventures, while exemplifying a sexuality "safe" to censors or to patriarchal society in general, still suggest that ideas of the "new woman" are relevant even to the ordinary small-town girl who actively projects herself into a dreamed-of future.

The on- and offscreen personas of Clara Bow, whose career was rising as Moore's was peaking between 1926 and 1928, position the star as a human dynamo who skips dreaming and goes right into action to get what she wants. Bow's flapper characters also engage in masquerade or posing, but they don't need to role-play as more sexually knowing than they really are—her flapper *is* the sexually knowing woman who is simultaneously "innocent," which is often a source of other characters' misunderstanding of her. Instead of being the innocent who (comically) comes into knowledge, as the Moore character typically was, the typical Bow character has to struggle to make others revise or reevaluate their knowledge of her. For this reason, even when her films are comedies, pathos often emerges from their narrative situations.

Clara Bow was born into a poor Brooklyn family in 1905. Her father was a waiter at Coney Island, but often unemployed; her mother was mentally ill and died in an institution not long after Bow went to Hollywood. In 1921, Bow won a "fame and fortune" contest co-sponsored by several fan magazines. This led to a series of sittings for photo portraits and a screen test that Bow tried to hide from her puritanical and increasingly insane mother—Bow would claim that when her mother found out that she was

Clara Bow in her most famous role, Betty, in *It* (1927). Publicity still.

pursuing an acting career, she tried to stab her to death. Bow's scenes in her first film, *Beyond the Rainbow* (1922), were cut out of the final print (to be replaced later when Bow became a big star), but she was given good press for her performance in her second, *Down to the Sea in Ships*, in which she played a young girl of perhaps twelve (Bow was sixteen) who stows away on a whaling ship.

Bow was brought to the attention of J. G. Bachmann, who was a partner in Preferred Pictures. Along with agent Maxine Alton, he lobbied the other partner of the company, B. P. Schulberg, to bring her to Hollywood. Schulberg had once been part of Paramount and at the moment he took Bow under contract he was biding his time, producing mostly low-budget pictures until he could return to a position at a more powerful studio. Schulberg recognized her talent but did little to treat her equitably or develop her as an actress. Compared to Swanson and Moore, it is clear that Bow—who by the end of the 1920s would equal and even surpass them in box office popularity—had little control over her career. She was not able to take advantage of her film appearances to negotiate with studios for higher salaries or strategically develop an acting versatility that would help her construct distinguishable character types. Schulberg cast her in his pictures, but he often loaned her out to other studios of varying quality and budget and let them bankroll her exposure in both large and small roles throughout the mid-twenties. This exploitation initially resulted in a haphazard construction of Bow's onscreen persona: she might play a wealthy flapper in one high-quality film, such as *Black Oxen* (in 1924, at First National), in which she was given key scenes and opportunities to construct an individuated character rather than a type; then play a low-class nightclub entertainer (with a heart of gold) in another, as she did in *The Primrose Path* (in 1925 at low-budget Arrow); or play a jailbird waif adopted by the judge of her case, as in *Free to Love* (in 1925 at Preferred), and in either of the latter films not have a close-up or even significant medium shots (not to mention direction) to register emotion and create individuated, distinct characters.

Schulberg did come through with one important, relatively high-quality film for Bow at Preferred in 1925, and partly because of its box office success, he was able to parlay contracts for them both at Paramount, his old company and perhaps the most prestigious studio at that time. The film was *The Plastic Age*. Bow played Cynthia Day, a collegiate flapper whose immense popularity (read: sexual reputation) among the male co-eds is perhaps only surpassed by the immensity of her good heart. This was the role in which Bow could finally develop the most significant aspects of her acting style to create characters who were an identifiable type (the flapper as sexually knowing woman) *and* unique individuals. Her acting style was characterized by a kind of "full-body" physicality—but unlike the deadpan, reactive physical style of Moore in her playing of the flapper or young dreamer, Bow expressed delight in her own character or in others through, among other movements, running, skipping, jumping, widening her eyes (which were already incredibly large and round naturally), doing double-takes, giggling, clapping, and running her hands through her hair. She constantly touches herself (on the breasts, hips) or others. If sensual enjoyment was understood as inextricably linked to the sexual or to the animalistic, Bow's characters could be associated with an exuberant sexuality before an intertitle even appeared to describe her or express her words.

The plot of *The Plastic Age* might render flapper Cynthia "safe" as she nobly gives up chasing young collegiate athlete and scholar Hugh Carver (Donald Keith) so that he can focus on his study and sports, but not before it establishes that she enjoys dancing, necking, drinking, and smooching with him (always followed by Bow looking directly into the camera with a smile on her face). The film and the way in which Bow constructs the flapper character seem to embody the contradictions associated with the flapper in social discourse—threatening approved sexual and gender values in her uninhibited, physical expressiveness, yet moral in her rejection of hypocrisy and in her commitment to the peer group; conforming to trends yet forging an individuality not tied to past tradition. Whatever social containment might be effected by the narrative (Cynthia is shown to have self-restraint when she gives up her love, at least temporarily, so that he might succeed at school), Bow creates a flapper who, by the sheer pleasure she inspires and experiences while holding true to a moral code, cannot be dismissed by any social discourses that would only condemn this kind of youthful "new woman."

Bow's version of the flapper would be developed over the course of the next four years in *Dancing Mothers* (1926), *Mantrap* (1926), *It* (1927), *Wings* (1927), *Get Your Man* (1927), *Red Hair* (1928), *The Wild Party* (1929), and *The Saturday Night Kid* (1929), all of which were successful at the box office. Only in *Dancing Mothers* would she play a character punished for the self-centeredness of her sensuality, yet even this character is shown to be "innocent" in that she is unaware of how her actions hurt others. In *The Wild Party*, which uses college as a setting for the flapper lifestyle, her character is chastened but ultimately rewarded. *It* has received the most attention from film critics and historians, and for good reasons: it brought the flapper type and Bow's particular version of it into an association with Elinor Glyn, and its story sets the terms for the success of the flapper character in relation to class, romance, and female masquerade.

Glyn reportedly received $50,000 to endorse Clara Bow as the "'It' Girl" (she appears in the film as herself to proclaim Betty, the character played by Bow, as possessing "It"). While neither Glyn nor Paramount reminded the public that Glyn had previously designated Swanson and other (mostly male) stars as having "It," the fan magazines did take notice: a *Motion Picture* magazine article from the time of the film's release in 1927 reveals that "'our Flaming Flapper Clara' has been chosen to have 'It.'" The author expresses surprise that Glyn would give the title to Bow. If the ideal Glyn heroine is exemplified by the "mature" actress with "regal manners," like Swanson, who can act the "'Lady in the Tiger Rug with a Rose in Her Teeth,'" Bow "would eat the rose, and the tiger rug, too, just to be doing something" (*Motion Picture*, February 1927, 42–43). But the article ultimately reassures readers about the appropriateness of the designation—for Bow has that unselfconscious magnetism, that unflappable focus on getting what she wants from life, that all possessors of "It" supposedly have. This press was consonant with the patterns of promotion that constructed Bow's offscreen persona between 1926 and 1931. She is frequently described as "untamed"—like a wild "young animal" (*Photoplay*, January 1931, 65) whose motivations and effects are known only through bodily force. She is described to have kissed one of her boyfriends so hard that his jaw was "sore for two days" (*Photoplay*, September 1926, 84). Her eyes are "two dance-floors of sparkling liveliness" (*Motion Picture*, November 1928, 44), while her hair is more than once compared to a riot and/or to the ocean—a "tempestuous riot" (*Motion Picture*, November 1928, 34) in one instance, a "riot of waves as free as the sea" (*Motion Picture*, November 1928, 45) in another. She is described, as early as 1926, before she was crowned the "It Girl," as an "overcharged" human "dynamo," who reads almost "feverishly" (*Motion Picture Classic*, June 1926, 90).

Film historians have pointed out that the flapper "dynamo" Betty in *It* gets what she wants through masquerade (Landay; Ross "Hollywood Flapper"; Orgeron). Betty works in the lingerie section of a department store and is attracted to her wealthy boss, Cyrus Waltham (Antonia Moreno). After catching his eye by inventively refashioning her work dress into a party frock and arranging to be at his restaurant, she secures a date with him for a joyous evening at Coney Island. Through a series of errors (set in motion by Cyrus's friend Monty, who has read Glyn's stories about "It" in *Cosmopolitan* magazine), Cyrus believes her to be the mother of an illegitimate child, and thus fallen. (The mother of the child in question is Betty's roommate, who serves the additional narrative functions of showing Betty's loyalty to other women and alluding to the sadness of fallen women familiar from earlier iterations of the seduction plot.) When Betty discovers this misunderstanding, she masquerades as an upper-class woman in order to get on his yacht to reeducate him about her virtue but also to win him back.

While Ross sees the masquerade in the flapper film as demonstrating that the flapper is really something else—that is, the good girl—Landay emphasizes the function of female trickery as a "tactic for negotiating the public sphere" to which, prior to the age of the flapper, women had been denied access except within strict constraints (Landay 92). Covert exercises of power are still necessary for women to get what they want, even in the liberated twenties, and Betty exemplifies this through her use of cosmetics, fashion, and masquerade. If the film can be seen as a comic representation of the economic basis of sexual exchange and of one way women can negotiate power in the age of the "new woman," it also confirms romance and companionate marriage through the characters' mutual recognition of one another's "Itness."

Get Your Man, which Bow made the same year as *It*, also involves comic masquerade. Bow plays Nancy Worthington, an American girl in Paris, who meets Robert (Buddy Rogers), an aristocrat, at a wax museum. Trapped there overnight, they fall in love. She later pretends to crash her car outside his family's villa. When rescued, she pretends to his family to be an aristocrat. Her plan is to break up Robert's engagement to another woman, an aristocrat to whom he was betrothed as a child. Nancy succeeds but only by first seducing the father of Robert's fiancée, helping the fiancée get together with her own love, and then finally, in a scene in which Bow displays the kind of physicality that made her flapper unique, tearing up her bedroom to convince Robert's father that Robert tried to assault her, thus forcing his hand to assent to a marriage to save her reputation. Like *It*, *Get Your Man* is a comic romance that exposes the contractual basis of marriage (the belief of Robert's family that he must marry another aristocrat to strengthen the family's status) and patriarchal expectations about female purity and reputation (Nancy manipulates the family's belief that women must be "saved" from a fallen state through marriage to the man who failed to uphold male chivalry). Both films comically rework the "seduction plot" popular in the teens (Jacobs 180–215).

In *Hula* (1927), Bow is a wild child of a Hawaiian planter and rancher. Hula (Bow) pursues Anthony (Clive Brook), a married engineer who comes to the island to build a dam. When his gold-digging wife shows up, Hula pretends to have blown up Anthony's dam to convince the woman he has no money. The film gives Bow a role to match the promotion that had consistently associated her with nature and animals—she is first seen swimming nude in a pond; she plays with monkeys, talks to her dog, and rides horses. Divorced from the urban atmosphere of the flapper, Bow's character is nonetheless the woman who goes after her man and appeals to him in part on the basis of her departure from genteel, traditional notions of femininity, specifically white Anglo femininity. She is a "savage" whose best friends are her father's native ranch hand and her little terrier.

This association between the "new woman" and the exoticism of the racial other/"savage" circulated widely in cultural discourses of the time, and the public's fascination with a variety of entertainers, such as the African American chanteuse-dancer Josephine Baker, is relevant in this context (Petro, *Aftershocks* 138–43). In Bow's first sound film, *The Wild Party* (1929), which, like *Get Your Man*, was directed by Dorothy Arzner, she plays Stella, a hard-partying and hard-drinking flapper at a women's college who falls in love with an anthropology professor, Gil (Frederic March), who calls her his "little savage." The two leave the college together to study foreign "savages," but only after Gil has both loved and tamed Stella's wildness by instructing her of the seriousness of women's education. Bow's last film, *Call Her Savage* (1932), would also associate her with "savagery"—she plays a "half-breed" Native American whose sexuality cannot be tamed. The film is clearly exploiting both racist fascination with the "other" and what was by now the public's conception of Bow as a woman of scandalous sexuality and perhaps mental instability. In 1928, Adela Rogers St. Johns had published a multi-part article in *Photoplay* that detailed the poverty and mental illness in Bow's background (*Photoplay*, February 1928, 30–31, 78, 104–06; March 1928, 38–39, 116–20; April 1928, 56–57, 108, 124–27). Fan magazines and the press reported Bow's broken engagements, suggesting she was involved in simultaneous love affairs and perhaps had a gambling problem (*Motion Picture*, November 1928, 44–45; *Motion Picture*, January 1931, 28–30; *Photoplay*, October 1930, 60–61, 138). In 1931, the star accused her secretary Daisy DeVoe of stealing, and details of Bow's love life were revealed by DeVoe at the trial.

Although both Swanson and Moore had less than successful sound films in the late 1920s and early 1930s, they had to make little adjustment in their acting style in the transition—in the way they used their bodies, for example. Bow's style was characterized by free and relatively unpredictable movement; with the restricted blocking of actors caused by early sound recording technology, the actress and her directors were forced to reconceive her style. Bow doesn't seem to know what to do with her hands in her early sound films: she swings her arms too much and clenches her fists as if she were channeling into those parts of her body her intense desire to move freely regardless of microphone range. Her obvious Brooklyn accent makes her characters of other class and backgrounds less credible. A few times, as in *The Saturday Night Kid* (1929), her accent aids her performances of characters of her own background; she soon developed a less accented and more modulated speaking voice.

The studios generally exploited the coming of sound in relation to their talent by creating a sense of panic among actors over the potential suitabil-

ity of their voices to the new technology. Actors were forced into voice lessons and sound screen tests, and new talent was brought in (often at a
lower price than established silent stars). Swanson made the transition as a
"talkies" actress with relative ease; ironically, it was her waffling as a producer over whether to make *Queen Kelly* a sound film that set career problems into motion. Moore was sent to voice lessons; when she was deemed
"sound worthy," she and husband-producer McCormick quickly picked two
unfortunate projects for her: the outdated, schmaltzy *Smiling Irish Eyes*
(1929); and *Footlights and Fools* (1929), in which she displayed the usual
verve and charm, but not the critically approved "Gallic accent" for her role
(Crafton 278). Before she retired from films in 1934, she did make a few
successful sound pictures, such as Fox's *The Power and the Glory* (1933).

The careers of Bow, Swanson, and Moore exemplify how Hollywood
faced industrial challenges, opportunities, and transitions in the 1920s
through capitalizing on actresses whose personas resonated with topical
social discourses about gender and sexuality. If these stars were less visible or
successful in the transition to the thirties, this was due, in part, to individual

Paramount gave Clara Bow or, as Schulberg now called her, "crisis-a-
day Clara," only a few weeks to prepare for her first sound film (Stenn
202). Bow was one of the few stars of that period who had successfully
rejected a morals clause in her contract, so while she couldn't be fired for
"scandalous" behavior, she could lose a studio-provided trust fund (which
she did) and she could be forced into material she didn't like (which she
was). Paramount did little to control the scandalous stories published by the
press and was almost certainly a source for some of the reports about Bow's
troubled transition to sound: fan magazines reported that Bow had "mic
fright" in addition to "nerves" over love affairs, and rumors circulated about
on-set breakdowns (*Motion Picture*, September 1930, 48–49, 108; *Movie Classic*, September 1931, 20–21; *New Movie*, August 1930, 56–58, 97; *Photoplay*,
July 1931, 31, 120–22). Instead of firing her—or helping her—the studio
stood by while she self-destructed, eventually giving into the troubled star's
request to be released early from her contract. Although Bow became comfortable with the "mic" and found a way to speak out about her "slave-like"
treatment at Paramount, she ultimately chose an exit from the industry
(*Photoplay*, October 1929, 29, 128–29; *Motion Picture*, September 1930,
48–49, 108; *New Movie*, January 1931, 36–37, 118; *Motion Picture*, January
1931, 28–30; *New Movie*, June 1932, 40–41; *Modern Screen*, August 1934,
58–59). She spent time in sanitariums, married, and after two superb performances in films for Fox Studio, including *Call Her Savage*, she retired for
good to have children.

The careers of Bow, Swanson, and Moore exemplify how Hollywood
faced industrial challenges, opportunities, and transitions in the 1920s
through capitalizing on actresses whose personas resonated with topical
social discourses about gender and sexuality. If these stars were less visible or
successful in the transition to the thirties, this was due, in part, to individual

circumstances (i.e., the end of Moore's production unit at First National when her contract was not renewed because she was a part of a package with her alcoholic producer-husband; Bow's personal problems; Swanson's loss of her production company resulting from the *Queen Kelly* debacle; the desire of all three to move on to other things). However, the patriarchal social matrix of their individual circumstances—reliance on male business partners for economic and artistic "autonomy" (Swanson and Moore) or on the studios' acceptance of their sexual expressiveness (Bow)—exemplify the limits of economic and industrial power for even the most popular female stars of the era. Swanson, Moore, and Bow had developed highly individuated versions of contemporary female types, mostly in films that avoided sentimentality. It is possible that had they continued their acting careers farther into the thirties, they would have profited from the preparation that their flappers, shop girls, wives, and Cinderellas would have given them for the screwball heroines and fallen women who were crucial to the following decade's filmic representations of femininity.

NOTES

1. Swanson also does an impersonation of Chaplin in *Sunset Blvd.* (1950). Her character, Norma Desmond, impersonates Chaplin to entertain her gigolo/screenwriter, Joe Gillis (William Holden).

2. This line is often quoted but not sourced, as for example, in Basinger, Zeitz, and many internet site entries on Moore or Fitzgerald. The Wikiquote entry for F. Scott Fitzgerald lists it as "unsourced"; http://en.wikiquote.org/wiki/F._Scott_Fitzgerald. As far as I have been able to ascertain, Diane Negra (31, 184) is the only writer who has given the quote a source; she claims that the line is what Fitzgerald wrote in an inscription in the miniature volume of *This Side of Paradise* that is part of the library in Colleen Moore's famous "fairy-castle" dollhouse.

3. WAMPAS is the acronym for Western Association of Motion Picture Advertisers. In the 1920s and 1930s, the organization elected annually several young actresses as "baby stars," i.e., upcoming stars. Both Colleen Moore and Clara Bow were elected "baby stars" early in their careers. Although "baby stars" yielded a few majors over the years—besides Moore and Bow, Janet Gaynor, Mary Astor, Ginger Rogers, and Joan Blondell were all WAMPAS picks for stardom—most who were chosen never made it past a "starlet" status. See Manners 56–57, 74–75, 78.

6 ☆★★★★★★★★★★

Greta Garbo
Fashioning a Star Image

LUCY FISCHER

> Woman is the mold into which the spirit of the age pours itself, and to those with any sense of history no detail of the resulting symbolic statue is without importance.
>
> —James Laver, *Costume and Fashion: A Concise History*

    In the quotation above, historian James Laver notes that an era's zeitgeist is often reflected in the vision of woman it proposes. In the modern age, this image was typically registered on the silver screen through the appearance of the female star. In the 1920s, Greta Garbo was one such cinematic icon, an actress whose "star text" was, in part, tied to her link to

---

Two sides of Garbo: the light and the dark—the direct and the mysterious. Publicity still.

broad social changes. She embodied a new type of film persona—one that invested aspects of the classic Temptress (an evil but alluring female) with elements of the new woman (a sophisticate who operated with sexual and social autonomy). Garbo was also a beacon of contemporary style, tied to a novel and cutting-edge design aesthetic that enjoyed much popular currency: Art Deco. Both aspects of Garbo's persona are evident in her movies of the 1920s.

★★★★★ From Mannequin to Movie Star

Garbo's connection to fashion began long before her debut in American movies. As a working-class teenager, living in Stockholm, Greta Louisa Gustafson was employed by Bergstrom's department store (Paris 23). When the establishment wanted a salesgirl to appear in *How Not to Dress* (1921)—a promotional film for their women's apparel line—they selected the beautiful Gustafson. She also was featured in the store's catalogue, modeling hats like those she sold in the millinery boutique. Years later, she recalled that amongst all her customers, she most "envied the actresses!" (Paris 24, 26).

Gustafson, of course, eventually achieved the status of the women she so fancied, leaving Sweden in 1925 to become the film star Greta Garbo at MGM Studios in Hollywood. What is especially intriguing about the early years of her screen career is her continuing relationship to fashion. Her identification with *moderne* style (and her constitution as one of its pivotal emblems) is especially clear in those Garbo films of the era that are set in the modern period, where her character is seen in contemporary context and garb.

In *Torrent* (1926), Garbo's first American release, she plays Leonora Moreno, a Spanish peasant girl with an extraordinary singing voice. As a young woman, she is spurned by Don Rafael Brull (Ricardo Cortez) because his betrothal would displease his overbearing mother. Leonora leaves her village and travels to Paris, where she becomes "La Brunna"—a famous opera singer. In early scenes, when Garbo is playing a simple rural maid, her demeanor is subdued and Victorian. But when Leonora appears in Paris, Garbo's bearing is totally transformed. Not only does Leonora become "La Brunna," but Greta Louisa Gustafson becomes "Greta Garbo." Significantly, the film's narrative moves dramatically between these two characterizations. When Leonora bids farewell to her town, she sits on the back of a horse cart, a shawl draped over her head, Madonna-style. We are then told that "a curtain of gray years" intervened, and that "behind it, Leonora Moreno vanished" and "from it emerged a new star—La Brunna, the idol of Paris." We next see Leonora performing on an opera stage. Shortly thereafter, she goes

In her first American film, *Torrent* (1926), Garbo emerges as an Art Deco icon. Publicity still.

to "The Café American in Paris," a tony night club decorated in a contemporary mode, with concentric arches and a tiered stairway. La Brunna is shown in a stunning medium close-up, her hair slicked back androgynously, wearing a dazzling metallic full-length evening coat, trimmed with white-and-black striped fur. Here, in Greta Garbo's first cinematic "glamour shot," she is adorned in chic fashion and inhabits a modernist space. An Art Deco Diva is born. Throughout *Torrent*, at heightened moments of the text, she returns to wearing Art Deco couture. After Leonora is reunited with Rafael in Madrid, the two plan to elope. But, again, Rafael is too cowardly to fulfill his promise. As Leonora futilely awaits him in her apartment, she wears a black-and-white geometrically patterned cape dress, with a stiff, round, ruffled collar. Thus, as she plays the "fool" to Rafael a second time, she looks like a Deco Pierrot or Harlequin (figures popular in the era).

★★★★★ Modern Design and the Cinema

But what specifically was Art Deco and what was its relation to the film medium? Deco was a popular international trend that surfaced between 1910 and 1935. In its ubiquity, it affected all aspects of the design world: fashion, crafts, housewares, jewelry, statuary, architecture, and interior decoration. The term itself was not coined until the 1960s (as an abbreviation of the hallmark International Exposition of Decorative and Industrial Modern Arts staged in Paris between April and October 1925). During the twenties, the movement was known as *modernism* or the *style moderne*.

Art Deco had many branches and influences. First, it was a highly current style, with its streamlined, geometric, and symmetrical patterns—traits associated with the industrial age. In keeping with Deco's stark, high-tech façades, color was often reduced to the basics: black, white, and silver. Deco was tied to the modern city; hence many movies marked by the mode took place in chic night spots and luxury dwellings. Deco also echoed various avant-garde movements. From constructivism and cubism, for example, it derived its passion for pure, abstract, form.

Despite its resolute contemporaneity, however, Art Deco also entertained an alternate theme that contradicted its futurist tendencies and bespoke the influence of traditional and primal forms. Specifically, Deco evinced a fascination with the "Ancient" and the "Primitive" as rendered through a litany of tropes. From the broader Middle East, for example, it recycled the Babylonian ziggurat structure; from Native American culture, it utilized myriad geometric symbols. Deco also courted the "Exotic." Oriental motifs were registered not only in the movement's iconography (for example, lotus flowers), but in its materials and palette (for instance, ebony wood and Jade Green). In Deco's American incarnation, its discourse also evinced a particular fascination with things European (especially French), a logical development, given that the 1925 Paris exposition ushered in the style. Stores like Bonwit Teller and Bergdorf Goodman named departments with French terminology: the *vingtième* shops, or the *salle moderne*.

Given Deco's theatrical orientation, it is hardly surprising that the mode would become linked to the movies and, starting in the late 1920s, every aspect of the cinema was affected by the style. First, it influenced set design, through the work of art directors like Cedric Gibbons at MGM. Second, Deco left its stamp on film costuming, especially for women, with designers like Adrian also contracted by MGM. Third, even the physiognomy of actors was used to create Deco-inspired constructions. As Mark Winokur notes, through blocking, "stars became generic Deco works [and] sculpturesque pieces" (204). In fact, many chryselephantine sculptures in the Deco era (popular mantel ornaments taking a female form) were modeled on real or imagined performers. Fourth, a Deco aesthetic influenced the graphic idiom of many movie posters as well as the font and layout of studio logos (RKO and Twentieth Century–Fox, for example). Finally, Deco had a tremendous effect on the architectural design of American movie theaters, especially those upscale establishments known as "picture palaces" (like New York's Radio City Music Hall or Oakland [California's] Paramount). As Donald Albrecht has noted, the cinema's Art Deco mode "successfully promoted the modern style to the general public, making it both more accessible and more palatable" (xii). The image of Greta Garbo (and the films in which it circulated) was part of that aesthetic "promotion," and it is necessary to analyze the "semiological" role played by the Deco style in her films and the manner in which it "fashions" her twenties' broader star persona.

★★★★★ Modernity and Garbo's Press Reception

The publicity that circulated around Garbo in the 1920s highlighted her urbane persona and its association with the contemporary woman—precisely the kind of female associated with the Art Deco style. Muriel Babcock called her "the new-type siren . . . a sophisticate" (*Los Angeles Times*, 8 January 1928, C19). A photograph announcing Garbo's appearance in *The Single Standard* noted that she plays an "ultra-modern character" (*Los Angeles Times*, 8 August 1929, A11), and another article notes how the film's heroine "casts aside convention and lives her life as her heart dictates" (*Los Angeles Times*, 18 August 1929, 20). A piece entitled "Old Styles in Heroines Passé" quotes film director Fred Niblo (referencing Garbo), who declares "the banishment of the demure little heroine the screen has done so well by for a generation." As he continues, the new female "has outgrown her ginghams and is all dressed up in evening gowns now. Her innocence is put away with her curls and dimples" (*Los Angeles Times*, 15 July 1928, C29). Finally, a *New York Times* article states that "in the greater number of her pictures [Garbo] has gone her own way . . . and has bothered not for tradition" (4 August 1929, X4).

Garbo's independent image also seems associated with her "foreignness," as though Americans could only tolerate such a risqué figure if she were not an "All-American Girl." When Garbo arrived in Hollywood, a piece mentioning her noted how one-third of the players at MGM were "foreign born" and that "the Scandinavian races are in the majority" ("Americans Hold Own in Pictures," *Los Angeles Times*, 28 December 1925, C4). Leonard Hall calls her a "Stockholm siren" and a "Stockholm storm" (60), and a photo of her in the *Los Angeles Times* is captioned "From Far-Off Northland" (15 October 1926, A11). In line with this, a *Time* reviewer notes that the "Swedish Greta Garbo . . . infuses [movie screens] with a cold white glow" (12 December 1927).

Significantly, most of the roles that Garbo plays in the 1920s are those of European women. In *The Torrent*, she is Spanish; in *The Temptress* (1926) and *The Kiss* (1929), she is French; in *Love* (1927) and *The Mysterious Lady* (1928), she is Russian; and in *Flesh and the Devil* (1926), she is German. In fact, when she first incarnates an American woman in *Wild Orchids* (1929), an article touts that fact as though to mark a new phenomenon (*Los Angeles Times*, 11 November 1928, C30). Significantly, however, the film's heroine travels to Java, so she is invested with foreign exoticism nonetheless. The same is true of Garbo's next American role, Arden Stuart in *The Single Standard* (1929), who sails to the South Seas.

In addition to stressing Garbo's sophistication and alterity, print media of the twenties emphasized her modern erotic appeal. A *Time* column calls her "the greatest living exponent of female sex appeal" (30 September 1929). The *Los Angeles Times* talked of her "seductive grace" (3 February 1927, A7) and also deemed her the "lotus flower of languor" (5 February 1927, 7), "alluring," and a woman of "fatal fascination" (her eyes "reach out and pull one in") (17 October 1926, C19).

As with other female stars of the period, her professional dedication (an aspect of her status as New Woman) was subject to question. Some wondered why she shunned the nightlife to prepare for early morning studio calls. One article quotes Garbo as stating: "Ne-ver [*sic*] until two months ago do I go out in evening. . . . I cannot work when I go to this party and that. I have not energy enough. People take energy from me and I need it for pictures" (*Los Angeles Times*, 17 October 1926, C19). Garbo's demands on the studio were also treated with skepticism. In a 1926 piece subtitled "Two New Temperamental Outbursts Bring Stir for M.-G.-M. Officials," it is rumored that "Garbo has rejected a script and wants adjustments in her salary" (*Los Angeles Times*, 11 November 1926, 14). An article in February 1927 reports "Miss Garbo in New Row With Studio" (*Los Angeles Times*, 10 February 1927, A22). Similarly, a piece in April 1927 asks, "What's the Matter with Greta Garbo," noting how MGM is threatening to deport the actress if she does not sign a new contract (*Photoplay*, April 1927, 28). Finally, one reporter notes that "there have been times when [Garbo] has been accused of 'temperament,'" but permits the star to deny this: "When you say temperamental you mean that I am very angry [and] I show it by doing awful things. Like in a picture in which I was in and a woman threw a telephone. That is terrible. I am not temperamental. I could not do that" (*Los Angeles Times*, 8 January 1928, C19).

✩✩✩✩✩ Garbo's Deco Films

The specter of the independent, sexually liberated, modern woman is apparent in numerous Garbo films of the period in which she plays a nontraditional female on both the sensual and moral plane. Not surprisingly, many of these works are cast in the Art Deco style. *Wild Orchids*, for example, invokes the Oriental strain of the movement—one that has

Garbo as Lillie Sterling in *Wild Orchids* (1929), "going native" in Java. Publicity still.

licentious overtones for the portrayal of Garbo's heroine. It is significant that when Lillie Sterling (Garbo) meets up with the roguish Prince de Gace (Nils Asther), she is accompanying her elderly husband, John (Lewis Stone), on an ocean voyage to Java. When the prince romances Lillie on shipboard, he compares her to Javanese women: "You are like the orchids of your country—you have the same cold enchantment. . . . In Java the orchids grow wild." Later, when the ship docks, and she and her husband vacation at the prince's palace, she playfully dons a native costume, which he abruptly rejects. Clearly, in the film, Deco's championing of an Oriental aesthetic is meant to infuse the staid Western world with the alleged carnality of the East. As the prince tells Lillie, "The East is a country of the senses—warm, mysterious—like the kiss of a lover." Though desirable, such sensuality can be suspect when attached to a Western female. Fittingly, a photo advertising the release of the film is captioned: "Oh, Yes! Very Exotic." Augmenting the movie's ambience is the fact that it played at Los Angeles's Egyptian Theater (a monument to architectural Orientalism).

Wild Orchids sees Lillie Sterling as somewhat justified in her adulterous fantasies, given that her elderly, asexual husband completely ignores her and refuses to heed her warnings about the lascivious prince. In a shipboard scene, for example, as she and John retire to bed, she confesses that the prince has tried to kiss her. John fails to react because he has fallen asleep. In allowing a certain sympathy for Lillie's conflicted desires, the film reflects cultural changes in contemporary attitudes toward marriage and female eroticism that placed greater expectations on the conjugal bond. A newspaper article of 1919 states: "The rock on which most marriages split is the failure of the husband to continue to be the lover" ("What Makes an Ideal Husband?," *Cumberland Evening Times*, 29 October 1919). This is, evidently, the situation confronting Lillie in *Wild Orchids*, as her atrophied passion is awakened by the seductive Eastern prince. While, on one level, exoticism in the film has a positive valence, it also has a negative one; and the narrative validates the latter view by having Lillie remain with her Western husband at the film's end.

The Single Standard projects Garbo's modernity and independence without recourse to exoticism. It casts Garbo as Arden Stuart, a free spirit. As the movie opens, an insert reads: "For a number of generations, men have done as they pleased—and women have done as men pleased." Clearly, this statement makes ironic reference to the film's title and the fact that there is a *double* standard in morals and behavior. Arden is introduced to us at a fancy party set in a grand but traditional mansion. She is described by other guests as "a good sport," the kind of female to whom "a man would never need to lie." After announcing herself "sick of cards and hypocrites," she leaves the gathering, declaring that she wants "life to be honest [and] exciting." She commands a chauffeur to drive her away at "70 miles per hour," and he obliges by taking her to a scenic spot. The two become amorous. He cautiously asks, "What will people think?" and reminds her that, as a girl, she "can't get away with the things a man can." She responds disdainfully: "What difference whether girl or man? Both have the right to—life."

When Arden and the chauffeur return to the party, a scuffle ensues, as the mansion's owner fires the driver for overstepping his bounds. In a shocking development, the chauffeur rides off and crashes his car. An intertitle informs us abruptly that "the first chapter in Arden's life" has closed and that "months later she [is] still trying to understand it." Certainly, this is a radical way for a film of 1929 to begin. Not only is the heroine immediately portrayed as promiscuous, but her first lover is dropped entirely from the narrative and his fate is left hanging. The fact that he is below her stature in class only makes matters worse.

It is significant that, in the sequence that opens the "second chapter" of Arden's life, she resides in a Deco home—one adorned with elegant pedestals and statues, geometrically patterned doors, modernist vanities, boudoir lamps, and platform beds. Furthermore, in another scene she wanders into a gallery that advertises (in Deco font) "Modern Art." It is there that she meets the artist/sailor Packy Cannon (Nils Asther)—a playboy/adventurer with whom she becomes smitten. In Packy's portrayal, there are clear references to Paul Gauguin. One of Cannon's paintings portrays exotic Polynesian women, and he is about to set sail for the South Seas. On a whim, Arden accompanies him and we see her onboard his yacht wearing masculine attire. But, after weeks of "strange lands . . . lonely seas . . . the fiery tropic sun," Packy asserts his maverick status as a man who refuses to be tied down.

Arden leaves him and when she returns home, people snub her. When one of the town matriarchs decides to invite her to a party, another inquires: "You're not going to invite Arden Stuart after that disgraceful scandal?" Displaying a liberal spirit, the matron replies: "You'd be proud to entertain Packy Cannon, right? Well what's sauce for the gander is no longer apple-sauce for the goose." The soirée occurs in a rather traditional home—making clear how the Deco aura is associated *selectively* with Arden. That evening, she reencounters a former friend and suitor, Tommy Hewlett (Mack Brown). He confesses his love and his wish to "take care of" her.

Years pass and we find her married to Tommy and the mother of a young boy. Having failed as a wild Deco woman, she "settles for motherhood" (Paris 163). While Arden's home is now decorated in a conventional style, in one particular scene she wears a Deco-inspired lamé coat/dress—a signal that trouble lurks. (Significantly, a *Time* review of the film calls her role that of a "fashionable woman" [8 August 1929].) When Arden learns that Packy has docked in town, she agrees to meet him, and her ardor is rekindled. At first, she pledges to run away with him. But, upon second thought, she declares, "One man must always be first in my life—and he is—my son. My life belongs to others now—not myself." Though she eventually decides to stay with her family, it is shocking that this wife and mother is almost ready to abandon them. Even when she decides to stay home, her vow is to honor her son, not her husband.

In the film's final segment, we surmise that Tommy has learned of Arden's renewed affection for Packy but is unaware that she has decided to remain with her family. Being a noble man, he intends to set her free by staging a hunting "accident" (really a suicide) to release her from her marital bonds. In the scene in which Arden realizes that Tommy's hunting trip is a morbid ruse, she wears the most blatantly Deco outfit of the film: a black-and-silver knit top, with zigzag design. Here, as things are most chaotic and unstable, she appears in *moderne* couture. As in so many American melodramas, the film's denouement brings a conservative resolution. Tommy is saved and the family unit is preserved. This conservatism was noted by the *New York Times*, which said that the film (in which Garbo plays "a 100% American role") is "one of the first in which she is led to respect the current legends about morality" (4 August 1929, X4).

Garbo's final silent film is *The Kiss*, which broke box office records (*Los Angeles Times*, 28 November 1929, A10). It was directed by Jacques Feyder, a Belgian-born cineaste who had been brought to the United States by MGM specifically to work with Garbo. Here, she plays Irene Guarry, an independent French wife who has become romantically entangled with another man, André Dubail (Conrad Nagel). Like *The Single Standard*, the story opens with Irene meeting her lover, once again in an art museum, which seems self-reflexively to highlight the film's modernist decor. Though Irene and André temporarily terminate their affair out of a sense of propriety, another man immediately becomes enamored with Irene—Pierre Lassalle (Lew Ayres), the young son of her husband's friend. Though Irene is not truly interested in Pierre, she enjoys a flirtation with him and promises him a photograph of herself to take back to college.

One night, he appears at her home unannounced while her husband is out. When Pierre requests a farewell kiss, she obliges. In the heat of the moment, he becomes carried away and embraces her against her will. Her husband returns unexpectedly and witnesses the ambiguous scene. A fight ensues between Pierre and Monsieur Guarry and the latter is shot and killed. Since the homicide takes place offscreen, the viewer does not know who has fired the gun. When the police investigate the crime, Irene lies to them—pretending that she was alone that night and asleep when her husband was murdered. A trial follows and André, a lawyer, defends her. When it is revealed that Monsieur Guarry was despondent over financial problems, his death is mistakenly ruled a suicide. After Irene is cleared of culpability, she tells André the truth: that Pierre visited on the fateful night and that, when her husband attacked Pierre, she grabbed a gun and shot him. Despite her confession, she goes free with André as her companion.

Many aspects of *The Kiss* are quite extraordinary, both on a narrative and a stylistic level. Again, the characterization of Irene is audacious: the opening scene shows her having an affair, and she feels no guilt about it. It is her lover, not she, who decides they should no longer "defy convention." We comprehend from the start that Irene's husband is an insensitive bore and we root for her liberation. But one illicit relationship does not suffice for Irene. When her liaison with André is forestalled, another immediately ignites with Pierre. Again, she skirts the borders of indiscretion, but this time her seductive games lead to death. At the end of the story (after telling the jury that she is "indifferent to public opinion"), she literally gets away with murder and is allowed to depart with her suitor. As she does so, a courtroom cleaning lady declares: "I don't blame her! Half us women would shoot our husbands—if we only had the nerve."

The narrative structure of the film is especially noteworthy for the manner in which it presents Irene's "testimony" about the facts of the crime. When the shooting takes place, the camera remains behind the closed door of Monsieur Guarry's study, as the three central characters (he, Irene, and Pierre) battle it out. Hence, the spectator does not see what happens. When the police later question Irene about the murder and she recounts her story, we see "flashbacks" from her perspective to the crime scene. Obviously, they are meant to illustrate her deposition.

When the police command her to tell them "exactly what happened," we see a shot of Irene on the evening of the crime, reclining on a sofa, with a clock visible on a table nearby. From her positioning, we deduce that she can see it. The clock reads 9:25. When the police ask her, "What time was it exactly?" we see a close-up of Irene (at the present moment) looking worried, responding: "Let me see." In her flashback, the clock's hands spin wildly from 8:55 to 9:15 to 9:05—a trope that signifies she is deceiving the police by changing her story. We then return to an image of the murder night, as she crosses the living room and hesitates at the front door. An intertitle states: "I left the door open—no, I . . ."—again revealing the slipperiness of her recollection. As the flashback continues, she walks into her bedroom and an intertitle states: "The windows were open, no I think they were. . . ." At this point, the panes of glass magically move from open to closed (through a process of pixilation).

Clearly, through these inventive formal strategies, Feyder suggests that Irene is practicing deception, though at this point we do not know the facts of Guarry's demise. If we suspect she is lying, we assume it is to protect Pierre and not her. Whatever the case, these images violate the inherent "veracity" of screen imagery and instead communicate fraudulence. When, after the trial, Irene recounts her tale to André, we finally see what really happened that night in the study: in the heat of the fight, Monsieur Guarry reached for a blunt object. Afraid he would kill Pierre, Irene took a gun from Guarry's desk drawer and fired upon him. It is crucial that the instability of the text attaches selectively to the figure of Irene—a questionable New Woman. As in other Garbo vehicles of this period, the prime means for signaling her threatening modernity is through her association with an Art Deco aesthetic.

Certain events in *The Kiss* take place in the home of someone other than the heroine. In an early sequence, Irene and her husband dine at the Lassalles' staid and traditional country estate. The Lassalle residence contrasts starkly with that of Irene, which is decorated in what one review deemed an "ultra-modernist" mode (*Los Angeles Times*, 24 November 1920, B15). Hers is such a complex domestic space that the viewer is never clear whether the terrain is geographically coherent. In the Guarry living room and entry way are flights of stairs done in zigzag style. A Deco female dancing figure rests on a console in one corner of the salon. The floors are made of black polished material, a tone echoed in the archway to another room. Bold geometric patterns are found on a wall hanging, a sofa, and some curvilinear chairs. Black triangular sconces adorn a wall. An exotic ceramic camel sits on a rectangular cabinet. When Pierre visits, he enters through French doors that are decorated with stained glass that might have been conceived by Frank Lloyd Wright. Monsieur Guarry's study has a geometric desk that holds a triangular lamp. His bedroom walls are decorated with a linear ceiling border.

But it is Irene's boudoir that is most radically Deco—as though the more a room is associated with the female body, the more avant-garde its environment becomes. Her bed—whose base is done in black striped lacquer—is set on a raised platform. At headboard level is a brash geometric design that is reminiscent of Native American iconography. A wall sconce echoes the

Her adulterous affair ended, Irene Guarry (Garbo) in *The Kiss* (1929) admires herself in
her chic, modernist boudoir. Publicity still.

same theme. An abstract black sculpture stands on a pedestal by the bed, and
the window panes bear traces of an Arts and Crafts aesthetic. Some of the
curved chairs are done in a fabric with a linear pattern; lamp shades reflect
a geometric design, while others draw upon an African motif.

In one bedroom scene, the connection of woman and decor is made
quite forcefully. It opens with an extreme close-up of Irene's face as she
adjusts her lipstick with her finger. As the camera pulls back over her
shoulders, we realize that we are peering into the mirror of a luxurious
Deco vanity with a mirrored base. On its surface are several modernist
objects and above it are V-shaped wall sconces. Irene herself wears a black
and metallic one-sleeved dressing gown that lends a modernist touch to
her body.

The sets for *The Kiss* (as well as for *The Torrent*) were designed under the
auspices of Cedric Gibbons—the head of MGM's art department for some
thirty-two years.[1] Under his contract with the studio, Gibbons was credited
for all MGM films produced in the United States, although he played a
prominent role in the creation of only some (Heisner 341). The man who
was actually assigned to *The Kiss* was Richard Day.

While Gibbons did not work on all 1,500 projects for which he is credited, his broad aesthetic dictated the "look" of studio production and it was one that was decidedly up to date. As Gary Carey notes: "All [Gibbons's] designs were drawn in accordance with . . . his philosophy of the uncluttered—they were clean, functional and often highly stylized, a look that was to cause a major revolution in movie decor" (Heisner 75). Of his philosophy of set design, Gibbons once said: "In the past the designer of settings has built a notable background for the action of a story. Now he must go one step further; *he must design a dramatic background of corresponding value to the theme of the picture* . . . [one] that augments the drama transpiring before it. *The keynote of this is making the set act with the players*" (Gibbons, *New York Telegram*, 9 March 1929; my emphasis). Several things are interesting about this statement. First, Gibbons imagines a set as "dramatic" as well as reflective of the narrative "theme." Second, he envisions the set "acting" in a manner commensurate with the players—establishing an equivalence between them.

It is precisely this kind of "equity" that we sense in *The Kiss* and other Garbo films of the 1920s. The Art Deco sets do not merely provide an artistic backdrop for the actress, nor do they simply fulfill the need for screen realism. Rather, they bear great symbolic force: establishing parity between decor and heroine, marking both as avant-garde and perilous. In truth, modernism seems not only to affix to Garbo in these films but to *emanate from her*—to *constitute itself at the moment she commands narrative space*.

But an Art Deco aura attends not only to the architecture around Garbo but to her costumes. In *The Kiss* (as in *A Woman of Affairs*, *Love*, *The Single Standard*, and *Wild Orchids*), her wardrobe was designed by Adrian,[2] who worked in Hollywood between 1925 and 1952 and was the chief costume designer for MGM. His outfits were strongly associated with the Deco style that derived from the fact that he studied in Paris and was a great admirer of the work of Erté. It is interesting that, as Hollywood's invocation of the *style moderne* grew stronger, America's influence on the fashion world began to supplant that of France. As James Laver notes, the French woman "did not fit into the new fashions as easily as her contemporaries in . . . the United States" (234).

The most modern outfit in *The Kiss* is the dressing gown Irene sports as she sits at her vanity after breaking up with André. But in other scenes she wears more tailored contemporary couture. When she and André have their tryst in the museum, she sports a simple, form-fitting, V-necked dress, accompanied by a fur stole. On her head is the requisite "cloche" hat that all but hides her hair. Such millinery (which looks best with a short coiffure) makes of the female face a simplified, abstract sculpture, and Garbo's stark bone structure is ideal for this look. On the fateful night of her husband's murder, however, Irene wears a lounging dress whose modernity is registered in its multi-toned geometric patches and the asymmetry of its lapels. Significantly, when Irene stands trial for her crime and a court reporter draws the scene for the newspaper, his sketches look more like fashion prints than forensic documents.

For Adrian, Garbo's modernist costumes were not meant to be sensational for their own sake; rather, they were tied to the theme of the film and to the actress's role within it. As he notes: "If modern clothes are to be worn [in a movie], I must know at what point in the story each dress will be worn, and the type of personality the star will portray" (Watts 55). Likewise, he remarks elsewhere that all costumes must "mirror some definite mood," must "be as much a part of the play as the lines of the scenery" (57).

At heightened moments of her films (when she is most audacious and tempting), Garbo appears in full Deco regalia. At times when the drama requires that she "pay" for her self-determination and eroticism, her demeanor and her attire entirely alters. When Irene is arrested for murder and awaits trial, she wears a simple black dress. When she takes the stand, she appears in another dark outfit, one with a flowing cape and a hat with a trailing veil. Significantly, when André visits her in prison, two nuns (in long black robes) accompany her into the room. Indeed, as the narrative progresses and Irene confronts her crime, she herself seems to wear religious habits.

Beyond functioning within the drama, it is likely that both the Deco look of Garbo's costumes and the radical nature of the women she played attracted female audiences (*Los Angeles Times*, 13 January 1928, A9), even though she was known for appealing almost equally to men and women. Leonard Hall makes this point when he says, "Women flock to her pictures, to wonder, admire, gasp and copy. In every county of the country, slink and posture a score of incipient Garbos" (270). Another article mentions a popular coiffure known as a "Greta Garbo cut" (*New York Times*, 29 December 1929, SM4); and a young woman of the period is quoted as saying: "I bet every girl wishes she was the Greta Garbo type" (quoted in Ware 179).

Clearly, her costumes sometimes occasioned fashion uproars. One writer speaks of Adrian's role in creating the popularity of Garbo-style hats: "Garbo's Adrian-designed hats gave the millinery industry a needed boost. The most spectacular one was what is referred to today in American millinery as 'A Garbo.' Adrian's cloche hat that has become a classic came from the film *A Woman of Affairs*. [It was] widely copied here and abroad"

(*Costume* 1974, 15). Adrian himself comments on the star's effect on fashion: Garbo, he says, "wears the unexpected. It is out of the unexpected that style is born, and the influence comes" (*Ladies' Home Journal*, June 1932, 8). For his creation of her startling costumes, Adrian leaped beyond the confines of present-day apparel in order to create something more radical: "I get entirely away from current trends, for screen fashions must, of necessity, be designed so that they will be, dramatically, months ahead when they will be seen on the screen by the world at large" (Watts 55).

What is ironic is that, despite Garbo's screen influence on fashion, in her private life she did not resemble the cutting-edge, dashing females she played. Adrian comments on his initial view of her: "When I first saw Garbo . . . she was wearing narrow shoulders, [and] high Elizabethan collars. She was hiding her youth and her real self" (qtd. in Peak 8). Similarly, the *Los Angeles Times* noted that clothes "bore the blonde Miss Garbo" and quoted the actress as saying: "For the screen I must be fitted so mooch [*sic*]—so when I am at home, I don't dress like [that]" (17 October 1926, C19). Finally, as another journalist wrote:

> Oddly enough Greta Garbo, called one of the most exotic women on the screen doesn't give a rap about her clothes. She is known to the gatemen at Metro-Goldwyn-Mayer studio by her somewhat battered and worn mannish overcoat with a huge turned down collar, which she wears with an old felt hat. Off the screen she wears very little make-up . . . and never dresses up.
> (9 September 1928, C14)

Also at issue in Garbo's personal raiment (and obvious from the above use of the term "mannish") was the question of its androgyny. Adrian touches obliquely on this topic when he writes: "Her wardrobe consists of tailored suits, various top coats of the sport variety, sweaters, slacks, berets, sport hats, stocking caps . . . and sport shoes. I don't think she has an evening gown and if she has I'm sure she has never worn it" (qtd. in Griffith 272). Invoking the subject more directly, Garbo's niece, Gray Reisfeld, states: "She had a great interest in fashion, but it was her *own* fashion. . . . The pants, the walking suits, the lack of jewelry—all that contributed to what was thought of as 'masculine' but what was really just uniquely *her*" (Paris 268). Clearly, the focus on Garbo's androgynous dress would fuel eventual rumors of her lesbianism.

★★★★★ Garbo as Mythic Temptress

At the same time that Garbo pioneered a modern screen image, some films harkened back to the more traditional Temptress, the mysterious seducer of men. In line with this, Edwin Schallert once described the actress as both a "modern screen *siren*" and a "modern *Circe*" (*Los Angeles Times*, 18 October 1926, A9; my emphasis). Though ostensibly set in the present day, the films that depict her in this fashion do not foreground their contemporaneity. Rather, many seem to take place in the old world. Moreover, several of their narratives create an archetypal dichotomy between the conventional domains of Man and Woman—conceived as two incompatible realms whose clash leads to personal and social tragedy.

The Temptress is notable for casting Garbo in a role that approaches the classic Vamp. Significantly, one of the film's lobby cards brags that its heroine has "added another to her list of victims." The movie is replete with intertitles that proclaim the generic danger of Woman, in this case Elena, Garbo's character. One, for instance, intones: "God makes men and women make fools." Directed by Fred Niblo, *The Temptress* was originally assigned to Mauritz Stiller, Garbo's Swedish mentor and the man who accompanied her to the United States. He was, however, eventually relieved of his duties on the picture, which left Garbo "broken to pieces." The drama takes place in Paris and involves the chance meeting (at a masked ball) of Manuel Robledo (Antonio Moreno) and an unidentified woman. Robledo is immediately smitten with her, and she leads him to believe that she is free to return his affections. Shortly thereafter, he visits an old acquaintance, the Marquis de Torre Bianca (Armand Kaliz), and is shocked and distraught to find that the woman he has previously met is his friend's wife, Elena.

Robledo soon reencounters the couple at a party in honor of Elena hosted by a wealthy banker, M. Fontenoy (Marc McDermott). Robledo is again stunned when Fontenoy announces that he is financially ruined and that Elena, his lover, is the cause—a statement that is followed by his suicide. We later learn that the Marquis has known about his wife's tryst, but has allowed it so that she might have the luxuries she desired. A few days later, Robledo departs for Argentina where, as an engineer, he is building a dam. An intertitle represents the locale as masculine domain: "The Argentine! Far from the artificial life of the old world—land of Men—and the work of Men!" With Robledo immersed in labor, "the memory of the temptress becomes fainter each day"—that is, until the Marquis and his wife arrive for an unannounced visit. Robledo warns Elena that Argentina "is not a country for European women" and she is visually contrasted with his shoeless, peasant maid, who has a grimy toddler in tow. When Elena retreats to her room and uses an atomizer to spray perfume, the maid runs away in fear—as though Elena were using a witch's potion. Then, it is Elena's turn to be disturbed when the distorted looking glass of the rustic room returns to her a warped image, one she immediately "revises" by using her own elegant vanity mirror. While in the Argentine, Elena captures the heart of another man, Manos Duras (Roy D'Arcy), a local bandit. When Manos romances Elena, Robledo tries to thwart him, but Elena boldly asserts that she does not fear the outlaw. When Manos grabs her in an embrace, Robledo defends her, and a vicious whip fight breaks out between them. As the brawl continues, we see Elena excitedly clutching her throat and bosom as she watches, chest heaving, seemingly titillated by the sight of bloodied men fighting over her. (Significantly, an article about the film sensationally proclaims: "Bull-Whip Duel Lends Realism to 'Thrill' Film" [*Los Angeles Times*, 31 October 1926, C12]). Robledo eventually prevails, but Manos dynamites the dam in retaliation and causes a flood—one that seems metaphorically associated with the discharge of sexual energy unleashed by Elena's presence. Eventually, Robledo saves the day and vows that "this woman shall destroy no one else." Though Elena ultimately wins him over, she departs, leaving a note that reads: "To love me would destroy you. It has always been so. It is my legacy from God—or the devil."

A similar Manichean structure of male vs. female rules the narrative of *Flesh and the Devil*, whose title makes clear its religious overtones. Though set in the modern era, it bears a decidedly old-fashioned stamp—including ancestral estates and transportation by horse and carriage. The film, directed by Clarence Brown, concerns two German friends, Leo von Harden (John Gilbert) and Ulrich von Eltz (Lars Hanson), pals from childhood who are now officers in the army. Arriving home on leave, Leo meets Felicitas (Garbo) and is immediately taken with her—a fact that is subtly expressed when, after she drops her bouquet, he retrieves it, sensuously smells it, and keeps one of its flowers. He reencounters her at a ball (where a moving camera dizzily follows their waltz together). When the couple goes outside for fresh air, they are bathed in romantic lighting that simulates the rays of the moon. In an understated, erotic sequence, she puts a cigarette in her mouth, transfers it to his, then asks for a light, whereupon he strikes a match and the two are dramatically lit from below before kissing. In a later scene, Felicitas entertains Leo at her home while indolently lying on a chaise longue; his head rests in her lap and the two are framed in close-up as they kiss. Then, suddenly, a man enters the room and we learn that he is Felicitas's husband, Count von Rhaden (Marc McDermott). He challenges Leo to a duel but requests that it be attributed to a disagreement at cards rather than to a tryst with his wife. The contest takes place, though we do not view its conclusion. We only learn about its outcome when the narrative cuts to Felicitas trying on black hats and veils—a clear sign that she is now a widow. Of course, her vanity in this enterprise only helps to portray her as heartless. Despite the pain she has caused him Leo secretly arranges to see her again, but the couple is observed by the town minister. As a result of Leo's misbehavior, the army sends him to Africa for five years. As he leaves, he asks Ulrich to watch over Felicitas.

After three years, Leo is allowed to return to Germany. When he learns of this, he stands in the African landscape as images of Felicitas's face are superimposed over the scene, along with letters that spell out her name—as though to represent his thoughts. When he arrives home and is met by Ulrich at the train station, Felicitas is there as well but as Ulrich's wife. Leo returns to his ancestral manor but avoids seeing the couple until Felicitas seeks him out to announce that Ulrich is heartsick at his absence. Leo decides to visit Ulrich despite his pastor's warning that "when the devil cannot reach us through the spirit . . . he creates a woman beautiful enough to reach us through the flesh." In a later scene, we see Leo, Felicitas, and Ulrich entering church together. When the pastor spots them, he selects as his sermon topic David's seduction of Uriah's wife. Alternate shots depict Leo and Felicitas listening—he horrified, she adjusting her makeup. Eventually, Felicitas comprehends the pastor's message and faints. Later in the service, Leo and Felicitas take communion, though she drinks rather sensuously from the sacred wine cup. Chastened again, Leo avoids Ulrich and Felicitas until the latter visits him again and lures him to a small shed where, by a blazing fire, she confesses her wish to abscond with him, despite the scandal it will cause. Leo succumbs to her ardor and they plan to flee that very evening since Ulrich is away.

Felicitas packs her bags to go, but instead of Leo, Ulrich appears at her door—having come home unexpectedly. He gives her a diamond bracelet and she pretends that there is nothing amiss; soon, he retires for the night. When Leo arrives for their journey, Felicitas reveals that Ulrich has returned and pleads with Leo to stay in town and carry on their affair surreptitiously. He is so horrified that he begins to choke her. Hearing the fracas, Ulrich breaks in and Felicitas cravenly claims that Leo has attacked her. To save her reputation and spare Ulrich's pride, Leo takes the blame. A duel between the men is set for the next morning at the "Isle of Friendship," a locale where the two had played as children and declared their eternal brotherhood. Artfully silhouetted images of Leo and Ulrich preparing for the duel are intercut with those of Felicitas languishing in bed. Ulrich's sister Hertha (Barbara Kent) appears and begs for Felicitas to tell Ulrich the truth and stop the fight. While at first Felicitas refuses, the sight of the girl innocently praying leaves her distraught (an emotion brilliantly realized through

Garbo's tortured facial expressions and frenzied bodily gestures). Eventually, guilt transforms her and she embraces Hertha. We return to the scene of the duel and see that the men have failed to fight. Ulrich has realized that Felicitas has been at fault, both in her recent encounter with Leo and in Leo's earlier argument with her first husband. Felicitas frantically dresses and trudges through the snow toward the Island of Friendship, ostensibly to stop the duel. However, a patch of ice breaks and she sinks into the water below; air bubbles on the surface reveal that she has drowned.

Though Garbo incarnated the Temptress here and in other films, she was not fond of that role. She disliked the term "vampire" and wanted instead to play "charming interesting women who are natural who are themselves [sic]." Neither, however, did she wish to be "flapperish" or just "sweet and pretty" (*Los Angeles Times*, 8 January 1928, C19).

Flesh and the Devil was an extraordinarily popular film. The *Los Angeles Times* reported that its exhibition represents the first time in seven years that a picture had been held over for a third week at the Capitol Theater in New York (25 January 1927, A11). Another article (written after the film's Los Angeles opening) noted that it broke box office records there as well (5 February 1927, 7). Of course, *Flesh and the Devil* was famous not only for being a profitable and masterful silent love story but as the first film in which Garbo starred with John Gilbert—an actor with whom she had a notorious offscreen romance. Its sex scenes were deemed "smoulderingly fervent" and "volcanic." One critic called the two a "screen combination that [would] doubtless cause many heart palpitations" (*Los Angeles Times*, 18 January 1927, A11). The press coverage that Garbo received for this liaison countered her desire to preserve an iron wall between her personal and professional existence. As she told the *Los Angeles Times* in 1928, she did not "see why anyone should be interested in whether she eats oatmeal for breakfast or whether she is going to marry this person or that." Garbo continues: "Why do they ask me so many questions? . . . That is for me . . . and I do not want to say things about it" (8 January 1928, C19). Rumors of her affair on the set of *Flesh and the Devil* were already at play in October 1926. By February 1927, the *Los Angeles Times* reported the couple's denial of an engagement. Even so, a review of their next film together, *Love*, remarked on how the screen duo remained "synonymous . . . with amorous abandon in love making" (*Los Angeles Times*, 4 December 1927, C15). The gossip finally ended in May 1929 when the press reported that Gilbert had wed another actress, Ina Claire.

Of course, the entire tumult about the Garbo-Gilbert affair was contrasted to other aspects of her press coverage that portrayed her as a hermit. A *Los Angeles Times* writer noted that Garbo lived by herself in a hotel and did not find "any particular companionship" there. Garbo is quoted as saying: "I just go to my room . . . I do not know many people . . . in Hollywood." Babcock ultimately deems Garbo "a very lonely individual." Similarly, Garbo was called "Greta the Recluse" and one reporter noted the actress "doesn't care much for people." Finally, Garbo was famous for stating she never wanted to get married. And, she never did.

★★★★★ Epilogue: Garbo Talks

As the 1920s came to a close, critics noted how Garbo was at the peak of her career, the reigning queen of the movies. *Photoplay* deemed her one of the "big five" in Hollywood (January 1929, 64). Of course, the coming of sound (a process that had begun in 1926) was looming larger and larger on the cinematic horizon. On the one hand, the press reported as late as 1929 how "Silence [Was] Still Golden" and how many stars (among them Chaplin, Lon Chaney, Dolores Del Rio, and Garbo) remained reluctant to appear in talkies. Supporting this were reports that "Silents [Could] Withstand [The] Onslaught" of the sound film, as witnessed by the popularity of works like *The Single Standard* (*Los Angeles Times*, 8 September 1929, B11). Nonetheless, it was felt that "the stressing of personality as it was known in silent film [was] becoming a rather lost art." Critics proved especially curious about the fate of émigré performers who spoke in accented English. As one journalist asked, "Will the foreign motion picture star be able to withstand the shock of the talkies?" (*Los Angeles Times*, 13 January 1929, C13).

Soon, of course, it was reported that Garbo would make the fated transition. In an article from January 1929, Garbo was reportedly working on her first sound film, *Anna Christie*. When her vocality was finally evaluated, it was said that her tonal pitch was low but "perfectly modulated." Other articles in the press testified that more and more actors were beginning to "scale the Tower of Babel" with Continental performers capitalizing on their linguistic facility to make foreign-language films. Garbo spoke Swedish, French, and German, and was already popular in Europe.

Critics, of course, wondered who the true "Voice Stars" would be, and one commented on the specific case of the Swedish actress:

> Perhaps even the fitness of a Greta Garbo might be demonstrated through the characterization of her voice in the film medium. It will be a different Garbo that will come before the audience, though, and it is a question whether this new Garbo will be the idol that she was known only through the silent form. That's where the risk is involved in her transition to the dialogue feature.
>
> (*Los Angeles Times*, 13 October 1929, 15)

We know now, of course, that for Garbo the "risk" paid off and that she (unlike John Gilbert) was successful in her talkie debut as well as in other movies of the 1930s. Though *Anna Christie* was not officially released until 1930, it was previewed in December 1929 in San Bernardino, California, and received sensationally. It was indeed a "different Garbo" that came before the sound film viewer but an "idol" nonetheless—one who remained a timeless icon of female modernity, autonomy, and style.

NOTES
1. Merrill Pye also worked on *Torrent*.
2. He was also known as Gilbert A. Adrian, but was born Adrian Adolph Greenberg.

7 ☆☆☆☆☆☆☆☆☆☆☆

Anna May Wong
Toward Janus-Faced, Border-Crossing, "Minor" Stardom

YIMAN WANG

Anna May Wong, one of the pioneering Chinese American actresses in Hollywood, remains a conundrum nearly half a century after her death. She is alternatively tokenized as an embodiment of Oriental appeal, disavowed as a painful reminder of Asian American subjugation in the American film industry, and recuperated as a resistant, minority cosmopolitan figure of the early twentieth century. One difficulty in assessing

---

Anna May Wong in a portrait for *Dangerous to Know* (1938)—Wong's quasi–Peking Opera gear evokes Myrna Loy's costume as the daughter of Fu Manchu. Publicity still.

Wong's impact is that, despite receiving adulation from the press, she remained a minor "Chinese actress," often mentioned as auxiliary to the white leading stars. The prolonged and passionate gaze that Wong aroused, *without* being a conventional "star" in Euro-America, raises important issues regarding the visual pleasure of cross-racial spectatorship. Wong's globe-trotting across the United States, Europe, and China demands that we examine spectatorship as an audience activity both in constant interaction with the actress's shifting self-positioning and varying with specific cultural-political conditions of production, reception, and interpretation. These conditions could be summarized as colonialism and Orientalism in Euro-America, and nationalism and Occidentalism in China.

In order to decipher the overlapping influences of race, gender, nation, and spectatorship, I compare American and Chinese media coverage of Wong's performance of Chinese roles with that of Hollywood's yellowface acting. The 1920s are important for assessing Wong's career for three reasons. First, the silent era coincided with Wong's career both in Hollywood and in Europe; second, during the twenties, her performances displayed Art Deco aesthetics that exerted a strong influence on Hollywood film style and ideology; third, these years witnessed the emergence of Chinese film culture in the chaotic Warlord Era (1916–1928) when China's internal factions blended with anticolonialist resistance. These factors made the 1920s a period of extensive interpenetration between colonial-national politics and modernist aesthetics. By juxtaposing Wong's screen and public performance with Hollywood's yellowface acting and placing them both in the 1920s geopolitical context, I offer a new conceptual framework for describing "minor" yet border-crossing ethnic stardom.

In reference to Anna May Wong's "Chinese" acting and Hollywood's yellowface practices, I have argued elsewhere that the central problem in understanding her performances is the mimetic fallacy. Wong, a Chinese American actress, was simplistically equated with her "Chinese" characters, leading to reductive interpretations—her acting either represented (for Western Orientalists) or misrepresented (for Chinese nationalists) "authentic" Chineseness. To correct this mimetic fallacy, I propose to read Wong's "Chinese" acting as a form of "screen passing" or "yellow yellowface," that is, as a calculated strategy that "denaturalized the category of the Asian by mimicking and highlighting the process of producing stereotypical Asian images" (Wang, "Art" 171). Yellow yellowface acting induced what Josephine Lee calls "an illicit pleasure that sets up a key tension between stereotype and performer" (Lee 101). More specifically, I argue that Wong's yellow yellowface acting hinges upon her mobilization of dramatic "Chinese" costuming, mannerist body language (in emoting, dancing, *and* dying), and sporadic use of the Taishan dialect (inserted in talkies as an Oriental marker). This, combined with her extensive efforts (and financial investment) in attaining a British accent as well as the most recent Western fashion, allowed her to flirt with multiple identities while maintaining a level of distance and irony. Thus, Wong's "yellow yellowface" acting constituted a process of "becoming minor," which, according to Gilles Deleuze and Felix Guattari, means to become "a sort of stranger within his own language" and to act from a marginalized or minority position within the dominant frame, which effectively deterritorializes the latter (Wang, "Anna May Wong" 99–100). By comparing the disparate reactions to Wong's acting in both America and China, I examine the ways in which the media fascination with yellowface may help to explain her "minor" stardom within global colonialism and Chinese nationalism.

★★★★★ Myrna Loy and Loretta Young Are Not Chinese; They Out-Chinese the Chinese

The contrast between casting an ethnic actor like Wong and yellowface white actors was recognized in 1922 by the *Los Angeles Times*. A commentary entitled "Oriental Make-up Defies Detection" began by pointing out the difficulty of making up a white actor to appear convincingly as Chinese. The difficulty increased when the white actor had to be photographed beside "real Chinamen with slanted eyes, pig tails and the inscrutability of the Oriental." Despite these barriers to authenticity, the commentator judged the four yellowface actors in Sidney Franklin's *East Is West* (1922)—including Constance Talmadge and Warner Oland—to be successful, "as oriental on the screen as the real Celestials appearing with them" ("Oriental Make-up," *Los Angeles Times*, 13 December 1922). This commentary followed the Orientalist logic of racial authenticity, and highlighted two aspects of yellowface—its fundamental lack of indexicality or reference to the real, and its deployment of the real through the art of make-believe (via the skillful makeup that obviated indexicality).

But if yellowface acting lacked representational accuracy and risked incredibility, and since ethnic actors were available (they were cast in supporting roles), why then did yellowface become a routine Hollywood practice? Furthermore, what distinguished yellowface from an ethnic actor's performance? Was the former more desirable than the latter? This conundrum has been addressed by several film scholars. Both Lucy Fischer and Mark Winokur have attributed this to Wong's "unacceptable realism" (as an "authentic" Chinese) as opposed to the artificiality of yellowface, which liberated the Orientalist audience from history and realism. Yet contrary to Winokur's contention that "Wong's career must fade in a climate in which [Myrna] Loy's can flourish" (*American Laughter* 233), the fact that Wong obtained good publicity in American media, even with her minor roles, suggests that her career as the "little Chinese actress" or "Chinese flapper" did not actually fade next to the luminous yellowface performers. How, then, were Wong and her contemporaneous yellowface actors mediated for their American audiences? What kind of dialectical tension existed between them despite the apparent opposition between authenticity and artificiality?

During the 1920s, the *Los Angeles Times* consistently covered yellowface acting. Conversely, Wong's minor Chinese roles in American productions were often mentioned only in passing. Nevertheless, she did receive coverage as a token Oriental ("Bits of Old and New China," *Los Angeles Times*, 15 August 1926), a model for artists ("Photograph as a Fine Art," *Los Angeles Times*, 14 December 1924), and a public figure ("Film Stars Open Work on Theater," *Los Angeles Times*, 5 January 1926). To get a sense of the public perception of Wong in 1920s Hollywood, let us examine two newspaper stories. A 1921 article, "Dip Her Ivory Hands in Suds," portrays Wong as quintessentially Chinese, not only in her physical appearance (her ivory hands and petal-like cheeks), but also through her working-class background and the family business. For the American directors, Wong was "a pip of a type" who readily fit into roles ranging from "a Chinese slave girl" to a "Chinese princess" (Timothy Turner, *Los Angeles Times*, 24 July 1921, 2:8). The author further singles out a "Chinese" trait that enabled her to felicitously cross between home and Hollywood, laundry and film. Her family's laundry "industry" had trained her to do what she was told, never to "give back any chin," and to understand the studio routine, which "may not be much different after all from the routine of a Chinese laundry." The article affirms Wong's "hopelessly, commendably old-fashioned . . . Chinese ways," which made her an asset in Hollywood. It presents the relationship between Hollywood and the Chinese laundry business as mutually beneficial. Hollywood periodically needed an Oriental/Chinese type that Wong readily fit, thereby enhancing her own status.

The illustrations in the article effectively juxtaposed Wong's two worlds. The top left image shows her in elaborately embroidered Chinese costume, tiptoeing (mimicking the gait of bound feet) in front of the movie camera. The bottom left shows her in plain clothing and high heels, wearing an apron, sleeves rolled up, skillfully ironing a shirt below hanging laundry, her father working in the background. On the right side, a large image shows her in a Chinese jacket, "ivory" hands folded in front of her chest, eyes cast downward, as if watching herself "acting" in both worlds. Interestingly, Wong is pictured with cropped hair, not the "China Doll" bangs that were to characterize her public and screen image later in the decade.

Nine years later, upon her return from Europe as a major success (having starred in a range of multilingual talkies as well as silent films and stage plays), the U.S. media started to blame Hollywood for failing to do justice to Wong. One 1930 article specifically attributed Wong's marginalization to her family and frank admission that she was a laundry man's daughter, rather than pretending to be an oriental princess (Grace Kingsley, "Anna May Wong Returns to Hollywood," *Los Angeles Times*, 18 November 1930, 12). Relishing Wong's vindication after her European success, the article presents an ironically critical perspective on the Hollywood economy. It suggests that the American dream of rags to riches might find its home not in America, but in Europe. Furthermore, while the Chinese laundry man's daughter may don the Orientalist appearance to pass as a Chinese princess or slave girl onscreen (where the "Chinese look" was all that counted), race, class, and gender issues became a real concern in relation to the actress's professional status and social mobility. Wong's marginalization, according to the article, had to do with her challenge to Hollywood's Orientalist illusion.

These two articles demonstrate that Wong's working-class Chinese background was harnessed for various purposes. It could represent her Chinese discipline and industriousness, making her the useful and desirable Other in Hollywood. It could also signify the social inequity that Hollywood (and mainstream ideology) would rather disavow. Importantly, both articles omitted Wong's American upbringing. The prevalent appellations of "little Chinese actress" and "Chinese flapper" ostensibly set her apart as a cultural and racial Other. Unsurprisingly, most reviewers of Wong's 1920s American movies positioned her as a mere icon or prop incorporated into the spectacular set—"an intriguing Chinese girl" with "authentic power" (see "Film Banquet Is Dazzling," *Los Angeles Times*, 11 July 1924, A9; "The Silent Drama," *Life*, 10 April 1924, 24).

Contrary to the brief coverage of Wong in minor roles, movie reviews frequently included detailed descriptions of yellowface leading actors with whom Wong appeared. The most notable examples include William Nigh's *Mr. Wu* (1927), Alan Crosland's *Old San Francisco* (1927), and Archie Mayo's *Crimson City* (1928). The leading yellowface actors in these films were, respectively, Lon Chaney, Renee Adoree, Warner Oland, and Myrna Loy. Against Wong's perceived racial authenticity, yellowface was seen as flirting with the line between being and seeming. Yellowface actors did not become Oriental;

rather, looking Oriental made them Occidental. This paradoxical logic was made abundantly clear in a "warning" against misidentifying Myrna Loy in *Crimson City*—"Despite her name [Loy], however, Myrna isn't Chinese . . . in fact, an oriental wig and costume makes her look decidedly more occidental than she has heretofore in a modern evening dress" ("'Good News!'—It's Still Running," *Los Angeles Times*, 6 August 1928, A7). This observation suggests two things regarding audience reception of yellowface. First, it affirmed Loy's convincing yellowface acting—so convincing (especially with her deceptive last name) that the commentator deemed it necessary to expose the illusion. Second, it reassured the audience of Loy's whiteness by arguing that whiteness was paradoxically reinforced by yellowface.

By focusing on racial masquerade as the means of reinscribing an untainted white "essence," the commentator both reinforced white hegemony and allowed space for cross-racial fantasy. Thus, racial masquerade not only drew upon Art Deco aesthetics that granted Caucasian actors unparalleled freedom in crossing racial lines (Fischer 254), but also endorsed its underlying racial politics. The white audience was invited to believe the masquerade (to temporarily suspend its disbelief) while simultaneously seeing through the illusion. This peek-a-boo titillation adjusted the spectator's position so as to reconfigure the relationship between the viewer, the yellowface actress, and the Oriental role. In her study of "ethnic drag" in West Germany, Katrin Sieg links race to the "spectatorial activity of decoding (and thereby producing) difference" rather than the physical properties of particular bodies (Sieg 257). Furthermore, Sieg sees race relations as being signified by mimetic masquerade, which "dramatizes social conflicts in the manner of a dream, through condensations, displacements, and distortions. Its relation to reality is indirect, its outcome in many ways counterintuitive" (255).

By emphasizing the convoluted production and reception of racial masquerade or "ethnic drag," Sieg's study usefully complicates the performative processes of race politics. Yellowface acting allowed white audiences to simultaneously blur and reinscribe racial boundaries because yellowface was positioned in contradistinction to the audience's assumptions about Wong's racial authenticity. If her fetishized Chinese personae made her a defused Other, strangely foreign yet palatable, then yellowface portrayed a defamiliarized Self, simultaneously expanding the plasticity of the Self while fortifying its parameters. Consequently, the attraction of yellowface was due to an impossible act of "drag" and the resultant spectatorial amazement at its near success. The attraction of Wong's "Chinese" acting was associated with an authentic exotica that was considered inalienable if not inimitable.

To achieve close "ethnic drag," yellowface heavily relied upon makeup, costuming, and mannerist body language. The 1922 commentary "Oriental Make-up Defies Detection" teasingly mentioned the competition between yellowface and "authentic" Asian actors, between the "fake" and the "true," only to posit the use of oriental makeup as the solution. With makeup, Loy could become the ideal "China girl! No one better knows how to impersonate the oriental than Myrna Loy" ("This Question of Nationality!," *Los Angeles Times*, 13 February 1927, H4). The secret, according to an "exotic" revelation, was not to "look like anybody else" but to "achieve an oriental atmosphere with a slow lift of her eyelids" ("Exotic," *Los Angeles Times*, 10 April 1927, I3). Not only Loy but a number of other actresses (including Sally Rand, Frances Lee, Vera Steadman, and Dorothy Dwan) were also lauded for flirting with "this question of nationality." Such imagery systematically exploited and reinforced the schism between being and seeming, so that readers and viewers were able to fantasize about exotic femininity while remaining fully assured of the fundamental American universal—the sporty Caucasian girl in a bathing suit, so to speak.

Another article, "Cosmetics Will Endow Girl of Future with Many Personalities," assigned makeup (without the need for costume change) with the magical power of satisfying the "natural craving of women for self-expression" (*Los Angeles Times*, 17 October 1926, B6). Echoing the "startling prediction of Max Factor," the article declared that screen actresses' shifting characters had stimulated "the constant desire of womankind to be versatile and different," or to experience "a mysterious fascination about hiding one's own identity in another personality." Such desires for self-fashioning could be satisfied by "the possibilities and the elasticity of the art of make-up." The projected utopian vision for girls of the future was "[a] different face for every occasion" and "her repertoire of faces will be like a stock of beauty masks." To achieve the repertoire of faces, one would need no more than a makeup kit composed of beauty plaster, powder, mascara, and wigs. According to Max Factor's vision, yellowface, now understood as an achievable and fashionable "personality," could be accomplished by an "every-day American girl." "With a little bit of beauty plaster, skillfully covered with cosmetics, she can lift the corners of her eyes to give them an oriental cast." The potency of makeup was illustrated by portraits of Yvonne Chappell, a minor silent era actress whose fame had largely faded by the 1920s. The images showed her posing as her "natural self," as an "oriental charmer," as a French noblewoman during the Louis XIV era, and finally, as a Hawaiian girl.

Published in 1926, this article expressed euphoria over the possibility of everyday "ethnic drag." Significantly, "ethnic drag" was associated with modern womanhood, despite the fact that some prominent male actors routinely applied elaborate makeup as well. Lon Chaney, for instance, was most noted for his self-designed facial makeup that produced disfiguration. In Tom Forman's *Shadows* (1922), his makeup and oriental mannerisms made him an "artist" ("Alhambra Reshows Chaney's *Shadows*," *Los Angeles Times*, 19 December 1922, 3:3). In *The Road to Mandalay* (1926), set in Singapore, where Tod Browning deployed "racial polyglot" made up of different "types," Chaney stood out as a "Creature of Terror" in grotesque yet sympathy-inspiring makeup (*Los Angeles Times*, 22 August 1926, C25). In *Mr. Wu*, Chaney's dual roles made him "the greatest make-up and character actor in motion pictures" (*Los Angeles Times*, 9 July 1927, A7). The makeup for Mr. Wu's grandfather, a one-hundred-year-old mandarin, took four to six hours to apply. The procedures included cheekbones and lips built up with cotton and collodion, the ends of cigar holders inserted into his nostrils, long fingernails made of strips of painted film stock, Oriental eyes fashioned with fish skin, and a Fu Manchu mustache and goatee made of gray crepe hair.

Max Factor's disregard for male actors' shape-shifting makeup, and his privileging of a feminine desire for versatility, suggested two things. First, it implied that the true purpose of makeup was to play an exotic charmer rather than to embody disfigured masculinity (as was the case with Chaney). Second, it emphasized easy application, practical on an everyday level, as opposed to Chaney's laborious and time-consuming routine. If the makeup resulted in "a stock of beauty masks" that left the original American face largely unaffected, Chaney's makeup produced total transformation. Max Factor's euphoria thus suggested that female yellowface could enter into everyday fantasy, allowing the female audience to don racial stereotypes, which reinforced racism and "universal" Americana at the same time.

The oriental fad reached a climax in 1932 with the release of four female yellowface films: Myrna Loy as the sadistic and seductive daughter of Fu Manchu in Charles Brabin's *The Mask of Fu Manchu*; Helen Hayes as Lotus Blossom in Clarence Brown's *The Son-Daughter*; Sylvia Sidney as Cho-Cho-San in Marion Gering's *Madam Butterfly*; and Loretta Young as Toya San in William Wellman's *The Hatchet Man*. In addition, Frank Capra's *The Bitter Tea of General Yen*, featuring the Danish Nils Asther, was to be released in January 1933. Meanwhile, Wong's return to the United States in 1930 following her European success led some commentators to question yellowface. Nevertheless, instead of striving at genuine re-recognition of Wong as a minority as well as "minor" actress and "internal-foreigner," detractors of yellowface still subscribed to the orientalist assumption of racial authenticity.

Harry Carr, a *Los Angeles Times* columnist, described Wong's value (which he said was fully recognized in Britain) in terms of "subtle, alluring orientalism" (*Los Angeles Times*, 15 November 1930, A1). Grace Kingsley's excitement with Wong's casting as Fu Manchu's daughter in her first Hollywood film, *Daughter of the Dragon* (1931), similarly reinforced the persistent myth of racial authenticity. It was only by referencing authenticity that she could describe female yellowface as no more oriental than French high heels, and that the "daughter of a Chinese laundryman" made a perfect fit for the daughter of Fu Manchu (*Los Angeles Times*, 3 April 1931, 11). Four months later, Kingsley reviewed another film with Wong, in which Wong's heroine was "Chinese to her fingertips, and a perfect and beautiful example of the subtleties and mental and emotional reflexes of a Chinese woman" (*Los Angeles Times*, 21 July 1931, A9). Kingsley surmised that Wong's increased work opportunities indicated that Hollywood was starting

Myrna Loy playing the daughter of Fu Manchu in yellowface in *The Mask of Fu Manchu* (1932). Publicity still.

to realize that "gluing an actor's eyes back and putting him in oriental clothes do not suddenly transform him into an Oriental. There are subtle qualities of mind and feeling that no Occidental can convey." In 1932, Harry Carr, responding to the "epidemic" of oriental films, suggested that Wong should replace Greta Garbo as Mata Hari, for Wong could flirt in ways that the gloomy, solemn Swede could not (*Los Angeles Times*, 21 November 1932, A1). Importantly, Wong's comeback was paralleled by Sessue Hayakawa, who co-starred with Wong in *Daughter of the Dragon*. Riding on the crest of oriental vindication, Kingsley declared that Chaney's yellowface should give way to Hayakawa and "orientals should play oriental roles" (*Los Angeles Times*, 14 May 1931, A9).

The racial authenticity that supposedly granted Asian heritage actors special privilege and enabled the critique of yellowface was problematic on two accounts. First, it was undermined by the logic of mimeticism or realism. If yellowface actors were disqualified on account of their racial mismatch, then the same logic would bar Hayakawa from playing Ah Kee in *Daughter of the Dragon*; racial authenticity would stipulate that a Japanese actor should not play a Chinese character. Second, criticism of yellowface failed to stop the practice, or make it less desirable. The proliferating yellowface films in 1932 and 1933 proved yellowface's continued attraction for audiences. Media coverage continued to laud yellowface actors as well as imaginary, oriental spectacles. After rejoicing over Wong's casting as Fu Manchu's daughter, and her edging out of yellowface actresses, Kingsley then pronounced Ramon Novarro a "screen oriental" who qualified himself by studying "things oriental" (*Los Angeles Times*, 3 April 1931, 11). In *The Son-Daughter*, featuring Helen Hayes, Novarro, and Warner Oland (who was Swedish) in yellowface, the old question of how to make the (apparently) white actors (Novarro was Mexican) "appear not too unreal" next to the "real" Chinese extras resurfaced. This time, it was solved by using predominantly white extras, which made the film "single tone" and the yellowface actors "more real" (*New York Times*, 27 November 1932, X5).

If this example betrayed the "secret" that yellowface was unrealistic and could work only at the expense of Asian heritage actors, then the *New York Times* defended the advantage of yellowface in its review of *Daughter of the Dragon*, criticizing Hayakawa for speaking indistinctly and Wong for performing only reasonably well. Yet there was praise for Oland for "get[ting] under the skin" of his character (Fu Manchu), and Oland's "purring tones" and "mysterious" movements suited his characterization "splendidly" (30 August 1931, X5). Thus the "real" paled next to the fake. The positive review of Oland's yellowface acting echoed the audience's reaction to his earlier

Anna May Wong playing the daughter of Fu Manchu in yellow yellowface as opposed to Warner Oland's yellowface Fu Manchu in *Daughter of the Dragon* (1931). Courtesy of Elaine Mae Woo.

portrayal of the same character in *The Mysterious Dr. Fu Manchu* (1929). S. R. Kent described the film's preview in New York in these terms: "The audience shivered, gasped, thrilled, laughed, applauded, ate it up and loved it. . . . Warner Oland is tremendous and as Fu the evil genius has given the screen one of its outstanding characterizations" (*The Whole Show*, 21 May 1929, 6). For both Hall and Kent, Oland's yellowface acting was exciting not because of its verisimilitude, but rather because of the hyperbolic, sensational performance that elicited intense affect and psychosomatic responses from the audience. In other words, whereas the discourse of racial authenticity, buttressed by Wong's European endorsement, started to throw yellowface into question, the latter continued to thrive as a fantasy system of iconography that appealed to the white American audience. The sound era further instigated a form of "acoustic yellowface" via adoption of pidgin English. Not only were European émigré actors (such as Greta Garbo and Maurice Chevalier) advised to retain and groom their foreign accents, Wong, who had "bought" her sophisticated British accent, was reportedly asked to practice some pidgin English (*Los Angeles Times*, 21 July 1931, A9).

In some cases, Wong's "racial authenticity" was seen as reproducible and improvable by yellowface. In a 1932 publicity piece on Loretta Young's yellowface acting in *The Hatchet Man,* the author highlighted the difficulty of transforming Young into "a Chinese woman." At the price of "working time, two hours! Discomforture, pretty heavy! Patience—a lot of that," Perc Westmore succeeded in "making people what they aren't" ("Loretta Young Goes Oriental," *Photoplay* 1932, 71). To underscore the superior artificiality, the publicity piece reassured readers that "the finished job might make you think Loretta was Anna May Wong" and "Loretta Young could fool us into thinking she was the mandarin's daughter." In anticipation of the question of "why didn't a real Chinese girl get the part," the publication explained that Young was under contract to First National, and that "her tests are as excellent as her make-up, so they thought you wouldn't know the difference." Of course, in addition to makeup and body language, Young would need the proper "accent" (namely, pidgin English). This piece explicitly played with the duplicity of Young's "ethnic drag." On the one hand, it reminded the audience that Young was not Anna May Wong, not a mandarin's daughter, not a "real Chinese girl," and did not speak Chinglish. On the other hand, she was supposed to be just as good (as the "original") thanks to the art of makeup and her acting skill (presumably manifested in her screen tests). Or, she could be perceived as better than a "real Chinese girl" like Anna May Wong, since she (rather than Wong) got the role. Following Art Deco aesthetics, and taking advantage of the rapidly developing makeup techniques, Young's publicity material exploited the audience's fascination with the permeability *and* intransigence of the racial divide.

★★★★★ Chinese Media: Loy "Belongs to the Orient"; Hepburn Is a "Miracle"; Is Wong Chinese?

When Wong's "Chinese" image was viewed as replaceable, reproducible, and even improvable by Caucasian yellowface, her special status as an embodiment of racial authenticity was not only fetishized but also usurped. Consequently, yellowface remained the dominant iconography in Hollywood's oriental fantasies. If Orientalism and Art Deco aesthetics determined the American audience's reception of Wong and yellowface, how then did 1920s Chinese cultural politics shape the reception of Wong—a Chinese heritage actress who did not speak Mandarin Chinese, the "national language"? As mentioned, the 1920s were dominated by warlord politics intermingled with anticolonial resistance. Meanwhile, the decade also witnessed the emergence of native Chinese cinema and Chinese film magazines. The rapid development of the film industry and celebrity culture in China facilitated a representational link between China and the West (especially in Hollywood after World War I). Given the combination of nation-building, anticolonialism, and modern commercial culture, 1920s China can be characterized as a form of "colonial modernity."[1] The core of this "colonial modernity," or, we could say, "colonial nationalism," ultimately involved the demarcation and reconfiguration of the Self and the Other, as necessitated by the global colonial encounter and its resulting inflection of the Self-Other relationship. One direct consequence was the intense concern with China's national image in the global arena, which led to frequent protests against Western films deemed humiliating to China.

Understood in this context, Wong's status unsurprisingly shifted according to the commentator's perspective and the context of reception. She was introduced to the Chinese audience as a fashionable, cosmopolitan, celebrity figure. On the other hand, she was often described as a Chinese person "traveling in America" (*lumei huaren*), an appellation that implicitly denied her American/transnational identity and disavowed her estrangement from China. The clash between the prescription of "Chineseness" and her non-Chineseness made her inadequately "Chinese," failing therefore to properly represent China to the West. Her stereotypically Oriental roles were seen as problematic in the 1920s and 1930s.

With the exception of some positive reviews,[2] most magazine commentaries in the 1920s focused on white leads (such as Lon Chaney in *Mr. Wu*, Douglas Fairbanks in *The Thief of Bagdad*) while mentioning Wong and her minor roles in passing. Some reviewers explicitly described her roles as disgraceful and humiliating to the Chinese. An early denouncement of Wong appeared in a 1927 diatribe, "Denouncing Anna May Wong" (*Bu chengren Huang Meiyan*). The author, Lang Shan, criticized *Xue Pinggui quanzhuan* (*The Complete Biography of Xue Pinggui*), a Hollywood production based on a Tang Dynasty story, for its nonsensical rendition of China.[3] What he found most problematic were precisely the Chinese actors, including Wong. Recognizing that the completely Westernized Wong was no different from a foreigner, the author contended that Wong's exploitation of Chineseness as a selling point in America was deplorable. The author ended with a serious protest against the American film industry: "Anna May Wong does not qualify as a Chinese star in America" (Lang 322).

Constrained by nation-centered geopolitics and the burden of representation, Wong's subversive "yellow yellowface" acting could only be taken at face value as a despicable mimetic Orientalism. Thus, despite the disparate orientations of the American and Chinese media (Orientalism for one, anticolonialism for the other), they paradoxically arrived at the same essentialist understanding of Wong's "Chinese" performance, albeit with divergent evaluations. On the other hand, just as American white hegemony combined with Art Deco aesthetics fueled and facilitated the craze for yellowface acting and other forms of racial masquerade (such as blackface and brownface), Chinese popular *and* intellectual discourses from the 1920s to the 1940s also demonstrated a remarkable fascination with yellowface acting, as Maria Cambon notes in her study of American cinema in Shanghai (Cambon 36–37). Such bifurcated reception of Wong's "Chinese" acting and yellowface indicated China's ambivalent self-positioning vis-à-vis Western filmic (as well as economic and political) hegemony.

To further examine this phenomenon, it is crucial to explore the following question: if American discourses on yellowface stressed the *apolitical* miracle of make-believe, how should we understand the Chinese interest in yellowface that coexisted with nationalist protests against Wong's Orientalist roles and films humiliating to China? Did the Chinese failure to see through racist yellowface representations contradict anticolonial politics? Could this phenomenon be explained through the intersection of political circumstances and specific filmic concerns? What exactly was the relationship between acting/technique/aesthetics, on the one hand, and the politics of colonial modernity on the other? These questions direct us to the context of reception, which can help explain the multivalent interpretations of Wong's acting.[4]

From their very inception, Chinese film magazines "educated" the audience in how to derive "visual pleasure" from the projected and mediated visual spectacle, especially those with Western film stars. The first issue of the earliest Chinese film magazine, *Yingxi zazhi* (*The Motion Picture Review*), introduced Bebe Daniels as a star with black hair and black eyes, who more closely resembled "one of our Oriental beauties" than the blond, blue-eyed Euro-American stars (*Yingxi zazhi,* qtd. in Jiang and Jing 6). In January 1934, shortly before Paul Muni was cast in *The Good Earth,*[5] *Dianying huabao* (*The Screen Pictorial Semi-Monthly*) described his makeup technique, marveling at this "man with a thousand faces," just like Lon Chaney (21).

Myrna Loy also attracted a devout Chinese following. As if infected by the American audience's enthusiasm for her yellowface acting, the Chinese media described her as quintessentially oriental, with a study of "beauty on the screen" using her Chinese name, *"Man na lai,"* to suggest hyperfemininity and Western flair and calling her *"yiguo hua de"* (exotic). "She belongs to the Orient; her delicate, bejeweled hand is most suitable for offering incense in a temple; her legs dance to the rhythm of the Oriental drum and gong. Her beauty is bright and sensitive. Her witchlike eyes suggest Circe reincarnate. Her job is to charm men with her magic" (Huang 65). By linking Loy with the "Orient," this conceit reproduced Western Orientalism in which the "Orient" signified myth and fantasy. The difference was that the "Orient" was now the exotic Self embodied by the racial Other—a Hollywood actress. Here, Loy is legitimized in her yellowface acting as a compelling form of re-recognizing and re-Orientalizing the Self via the Other.

The Chinese public's infatuation with yellowface resurfaced in the 1940s, following Katharine Hepburn's performance in MGM's *Dragon Seed* (1944). Hepburn's rendition of a Chinese folk song, "Mengjiang Girl Looking for Her Husband" (*Mengjiang nu xunfu*), was praised as a "miracle" (*qiji*), even though the reviewer admitted that a Chinese actress doing this would have been commonplace. In other words, Hepburn's yellowface acting was noteworthy precisely because of its strange, wondrous performative quality rather than its verisimilitude. This was also indicated in the reviewer's critique of Pearl S. Buck's original fiction as inauthentic and simplistic ("The Leading Actress," in Jiang and Jing 480). The fact that Buck's writing was subjected to the principle of mimeticism, whereas Hepburn's screen acting was largely exempted from it, suggests that acting was privileged as a domain of performance. In this domain, performance was in dialectical tension with representation, and yellowface served as the iconographic site for playing out and balancing the representational need and the performative interests.

Beyond popular discourses, intellectuals were also attracted to yellowface. Lu Xun, the founding father of modern Chinese literature and one of the most scathing critics of Chinese national characteristics, observed, "[Warner Oland's] performance of the Chinese character was quite vivid and realistic, and his films contained some likeable comic relief" (see Xu "Mr. Lu").

Among the multiple voices of fascination, we may detect two instances where yellowface was called into question. The first was a negative review of *The Complete Biography of Xue Pinggui*, which featured a Caucasian actor (as the Tang Dynasty emperor) as well as Anna May Wong and Jimmy Leung. The basis of the critique was a violation of "realism," which should be derived from an intimate understanding of Chinese history and not simply a racialized Chinese look. By this logic, the target of critique included Wong and Leung as well, who were deemed too Westernized and modernized for a film set in ancient China (Ba, qtd. in Jiang and Jing 226). The second objection to yellowface came from the Chinese government's attempt to shape the MGM project *The Good Earth* (1937). Following a series of protests against Hollywood films that portrayed Chinese as opium-smugglers/eaters, evil-doers, scheming servants, pig-tailed men, and bound-footed women, the Kuomingdang (KMT) government decided to monitor the MGM mega-production, to which MGM acquiesced in the interest of obtaining the Chinese market as well as acknowledging the American government's concern with the project. As a result, an agreement was reached between China and MGM, in which MGM would "intend" and "hope" to use an all-Chinese cast. This, however, was ultimately abandoned for being "impracticable" (Chung 97). The government's compromise on casting (but not on other terms) suggested its lack of a decisive position against yellowface, despite its vague discontent.

In his study of Chinese protest against *The Bitter Tea of General Yen* (1933), Eric Smoodin suggests that the film's dialogue and China-related situations became the focus of discontent, while the film's narrative structure was ignored (Smoodin). In view of the overall fascination with and occasional suspicion of yellowface, Smoodin's argument might be usefully extended. I contend that the Chinese audience's differential assessments of the representational and performative dimensions of Hollywood productions allowed them to follow the nationalist discourse, protesting against certain Hollywood productions, while also enjoying those "quality" films and their orientalist fantasies (which included yellowface makeup and acting). This meant that Chinese audiences had to constantly negotiate with the films' modes of address in order to achieve flexible self-(re)positioning. Such negotiation was necessitated and facilitated by two factors: (1) the development of international race politics and Chinese self-racializing discourses, and (2) the passion for filmmaking techniques, including makeup, costuming, and body language that were perceived as means of refashioning the body and cultural-political identity.

Since the mid-nineteenth century, China's encounter with the colonial West had involved all these factors: economic, political, cultural, psychic, *and* somatic. The most direct result of the physiognomic-somatic encounter was the emergence of racial discourse and self-racialization, often framed as unscientific impressions of different racial physiognomies and physiques gleaned from various geographical locations.[6] The medium of cinema further enabled racial comparison due to its border-crossing mobility and heavy reliance on the visual (especially close-up shots). The widespread discourses on "face" and "body" indicated the Chinese audience's efforts to articulate and negotiate the hyper-visualized gap between its self-perception and the Western faces projected on the screen. Such an encounter led to self-re-recognition via self-racialization in the context of colonial modernity.

One instance of self-racialization came from Wen Yiduo (1899–1946), now a canonized patriotic poet. While studying fine arts in America in the 1920s, Wen reportedly stated, "The Caucasian (white) face [is] the original print, with clearly defined features, contrary to a Mongolian (yellow) face—blurred due to multiple generations of photocopying" (see Liang 30). Views like this led to the common belief that flat-faced Chinese actors were inferior to their Western counterparts. In an article entitled "Qualifications of an Actress" (*Nuzi tousheng dianying jie de zige*), Lady Jingxia deemed a prominent nose a plus, whereas a flat nose should be redeemed by makeup (Jing, qtd. in Jiang and Jing 560–67).[7] Another author wrote in 1927 that the contemporary "Chinese cinema" was only nominally Chinese. With all the technological, filmic, and makeup materials being imported, the only remaining "Chinese" marker was the flat-faced, flat-nosed, and bulging-eyed Chinese actors (Ying 10–13). The implication here was twofold: (1) a cinema relying upon local cast alone could hardly qualify as an indigenous cinema; and (2) Mongolian facial features could hardly contribute to the aesthetics or respectability of cinema.

One negative consequence of such self-racialization, according to critic Lu Xun, was that Chinese audiences resorted to Western movies to compensate for their perceived deficiencies. With his trademark acerbic cynicism, Lu Xun wrote, "Our noses are flat and small, whereas the European nose is uplifted. We cannot help this. However, once we have a few coins to spare, we can go watch movies. Should we become fed up with detective stories, romance, war films and comedies, we can choose *Tarzan, An African Adventure*, etc. . . . Of course, we could always enjoy the barbarian curvy body of some barbarian woman on a barbarian land" (Lu 423). Here Lu Xun listed the Caucasian and the barbarian as the diametrical opposite of the Chinese. Western cinema (especially Hollywood) was seductive because it proffered what the Chinese lacked and had come to recognize as desirable.

According to Lu Xun's diagnosis, the Chinese attraction to Western cinema reinforced self-racialization, which in turn led to a slave mentality. This, however, did not mean that he had no use for racial differences. By acknowledging Warner Oland's convincing yellowface (quoted earlier), Lu endorsed precisely the essentialized racial differences that Oland effectively mimicked and sensationalized. The flip side, however, was that to the extent that Oland's yellowface came across as amusing and convincing, racial boundaries were revealed as both permeable and malleable.

The performative dimension of racial difference was reinforced by media attention to makeup and facial and bodily performance, and both were seen as instrumental in racial transformation and in fashioning early Chinese cinema. Evoking the American public interest in makeup techniques, semi-technical articles on makeup methods were featured regularly in various film magazines by the late 1920s. Many specifically focused on makeup methods for actors of different races. According to a 1924 article by Xu Hu, who studied makeup in France, the Chinese face was flat while the Western face had more pronounced features. Different complexions should also be matched with different grease paint. Xu observed that Africans were too dark for any color of grease paint to be useful; Caucasians were fair and rosy, most amenable to makeup; and the Chinese complexion was yellow and pale, hence the use of "*Baton Teint Maladif*" (sick-looking grease paint) (Xu H., qtd. in Jiang and Jing 351–52). Other writings described methods of makeup for characters whose age or physical appearance differed drastically from that of the actor. Lon Chaney and Paul Muni were admired as "men of a thousand faces" within this context (Shen, qtd. in Jiang and Jing 772; *Dianying huabao* 21).

In addition to articles on makeup methods, film magazines also devoted generous space to basic acting instruction. Dramatist Xu Gongmei wrote "Methodology of Acting in Motion Picture" (*Yingju de dongzuo shu*), consisting of six installments, detailing how to act with the hands, arms, and legs, how to balance the entire body, how to position legs and feet, how to use the eyes and the gaze, and finally how to practice walking (Xu, "Methodology" Epi. 1, qtd. in Jiang and Jing 211–25). Xu described the "Methodology of acting" (*dongzuo shu*) as a handbook for building the body language that would convey the meaning of the script and character. Xu reasoned that film (in the silent era), unlike drama, did not have dialogue, and thus relied heavily upon complicated sets of facial and bodily language that corresponded with specific emotional states and would elicit the appropriate audience response (Xu, "Methodology" Epi. 2, qtd. in Jiang and Jing 323–28). Xu's theory directly influenced teaching at the Star Studio Film School (Mingxing yingxi xuexiao). In a 1924 sample test of excellence, a student regurgitated at length how to achieve facial expressions such as glances, laughter, and tears (Cao, qtd. in Jiang and Jing 43–46).

While such acting manuals had no direct connection to yellowface or any form of racial masquerade, it did help to foster public interest in performance (including yellowface). Moreover, many acting instructions carefully distinguished "naturalistic" film acting from "conventionalized" stage acting. By stressing the connection between film acting and contemporary reality (as opposed to the outdated stage acting), these instructions strove to monitor and modernize everyday urban physical culture. They helped to fashion a new body language, one that was produced and circulated between the Western screen culture and Chinese urban spheres, mediated by movie-viewing activity. The paradox, however, was that the pursuit of a naturalistic body language was often a highly hyperbolic performance, epitomized by yellowface.

The Chinese audience's encounter with and enjoyment of yellowface raised an epistemological question: namely, how to recognize and reposition the Self through encountering the colonial Other that was now made up to suggest a defamiliarized self. The juxtaposition of resemblance and disjuncture fractured the Chinese viewing position, foregrounding the possibility as well as the discomfort of identifying with an image of self-difference (or Otherized Self). This discomforting identification provoked the viewer to re-recognize the Self via (if not in) the Other, to become aware of the plasticity of the body, and ultimately to contemplate reconfiguration of the self-image. The media hype of Myrna Loy's "Oriental" appeal and Oland's "realistic" Chinese acting demonstrated precisely how yellowface simultaneously reified and defamiliarized the "Oriental," thereby producing the ambiguity and tension that was already characteristic of China's shifting self-image at the time. To encounter a performing body (especially as epitomized by yellowface) on the screen thus coincided with and facilitated identity performance and transformation off the screen. In this light, when Chinese discourses described yellowface as intriguing or even convincing, it did not simply mean that racist stereotypes were internalized, or that the Chinese face was seen as a fixed model that the Caucasian face could only mimic. Rather, by going behind the screen, revealing and popularizing the techniques of makeup and acting, the screen image came to be understood as an assemblage of visual constructs. Specifically, racial differences (as highlighted in yellowface) became manageable as performative effects. Such physiognomic plasticity suggested that the Chinese face, as racialized as it was, was also capable of transformation.

★★★★★ Wong's Actor-Text in Search of a Viewer-Text

Historically, the bifurcated Chinese reception of both yellowface performance and Wong's acting emerge from dual standards. Whereas yellowface was appreciated as an embodiment of versatile acting and sophisticated makeup techniques, Wong's acting was inevitably judged according to its political value for the nation-building project. As a commentator wrote in 1934, Chinese reception of Western films in the early twentieth century vacillated between two fallacies—ideological supremacism and technological fetishism (Jun). What caused the apparent contradiction between such depoliticizing and compulsive politicizing moves?

Arguably, yellowface was explicitly associated with excessive makeup and acting, which stressed an iconography of caricature rather than that of indexicality or verisimilitude. As a result, figuration (or fantasy substitution) was decoupled from realistic representation and politics were displaced by technical interest. Consequently, a space emerged for viewers to go beyond representation to interpret non-indexical figuration. Wong's "Chinese" acting, on the other hand, was largely judged in indexical terms due to the unproblematic collapsing of her on- and offscreen persona with Chineseness. The iconographic or figurative dimension of Wong's yellow yellowface acting was absent in both Chinese and American media coverage. Under such circumstances, the juxtaposition of Wong and her contemporaneous yellowface actors in Hollywood conveniently allowed the Chinese audience to simultaneously assert nationalist essentialism and enjoy racial performance. Likewise, the same juxtaposition played off the tension between racial authenticity and racial masquerade for the American audience.

These multiple determinants suggest that Wong's "Chinese" acting should be understood on at least four levels: acting in Chinese roles, acting *as* Chinese, acting *like* Chinese, and playacting supposedly Chinese roles. These levels drew upon, paralleled, mimicked, and implicitly critiqued yellowface racism. To fully understand these multiple levels, we need a more nuanced conception of the politics and agency that unfolded under nationalism and colonial modernity. Eli Rozik's concept of "actor-text" is instructive here. Challenging the conventional dyadic structure of the actor and the character, Rozik proposes a triadic structure by inserting a third term, the actor-text. Rozik sees the actor as a producer of signs, the actor-text as the sign system produced by the actor, and the character as a result of the enactment and reference of the sign system (Rozik 122). To act means that "a producer of signs (W0) [the real world] inscribes on matter a description or 'text' [the actor-text] that enacts or refers to and describes a character (W1) [fictional world]" (122). The intermediate space inscribed in the actor-text or the sign system provides the site of performativity that allows for the incongruity between the actor and the character. If the character is overdetermined (as in the case of Wong's Orientalist roles), then the actor's agency should be understood not in terms of how he/she may deliver a character against all odds, but rather in terms of his/her ability to create an actor-text and thereby re-inflect the character. Such an actor-text becomes meaningful only when the viewer exercises agency and produces a corresponding viewer-text that enables alternative readings.

Look-alikes? Renée Adorée and
Anna May Wong in *Mr. Wu* (1927).

The Chinese reception of yellowface demonstrated a felicitous meeting between the actor-text and viewer-text. I describe yellowface as an actor-text because it was created by the Caucasian actor on his/her physical body but it did not spontaneously emanate from him/her. It was constructed to evoke an Oriental character type but it did not naturally fit with the character. It was a hyperbolic mask standing between the actor and the character, simultaneously suggesting and blocking their connection. When the Chinese audience experienced the distance between the yellowface actor and the Oriental character, it perceived a miracle suggestive of impossible possibility. Instead of summarily dismissed as racist humiliation, a viewer-text was born, enabling self-reflection and transformation both on and off the screen.

Wong's "Chinese" acting also constituted an actor-text. In contrast to yellowface actors who produced their multivalent actor-text inadvertently as part of the mainstream institution, Wong's yellow yellowface actor-text resulted from her self-conscious negotiation with mainstream positions in Hollywood, Europe, *and* China. Instead of merely impersonating her roles, Wong used her roles as the palimpsest on which she inscribed her "actor-text," constantly gauging and adjusting the distance between them. To the extent that her "actor-text" was largely drawn from the matrix of Art Deco Orientalism (that also formed the basis of yellowface), it both recycled Orientalist iconography and strove to maintain ironic distance (however infinitesimal) from the "minor" perspective.

To recognize Wong's "actor-text," we need to complicate the narrow political imperatives that confined her to the embodiment of either exotic Chinese femininity or the mysterious (often backward) China. This is not to depoliticize her acting or to adopt a pure auteurist conception of her work. On the contrary, the new viewer-text challenges us to more fully address the implications of nationalism, colonialism, and Orientalism that operated in Wong's bi-cultural background and border-crossing experiences, and thereby circumscribed her "actor-text."

After all, the Chinese viewer-text for yellowface was by no means an instance of mere techno-fetishism. Rather, it registered profound political concerns related to China's colonial modernity. It was in the context of colonial modernity that cinema—as a new Western technology and popular medium—was simultaneously admired for embodying modernity and condemned for trafficking in Western hegemony. Thus, if yellowface was treated as a fascinating showcase of cinema's latest developments in makeup, costuming, and hyperbolic body language, this fascination was subtended by a political anxiety with Wong and films humiliating to China. Ultimately, objection to Wong's acting and attraction to yellowface constituted two sides of the one coin of colonial modernity by registering different yet interrelated political desires. Thus, a new viewer-text, attentive to Wong's actor-text, would crystallize the relationship between politics, agency, and screen figuration.

Once we recognize the fundamental linkage between ideological supremacism and technological fetishism (as Jun put it in 1934), we can start to break away from the politics/technique binary and mobilize the Chinese fascination with "yellowface" to develop a new viewer-text. This viewer-text would fully address the overdetermined and multivalent border-crossing stardom achieved by a non-star who was minor, marginal, *and* who self-consciously mobilized geopolitical constraints for her calculated performance. By juxtaposing the reception of Wong's "Chinese" acting and her yellowface contemporaries, we can foreground, disentangle, and historicize multiple yet interrelated geopolitical concerns. These concerns remind us that alternative interpretations of Wong's acting have long been overdue. The development of such alternative interpretations would not only recast Wong's legacy in a productive light, but also provide a new framework for understanding the significance of border-crossing "minor" stardom under today's global geopolitical inequity.

NOTES

1. For discussions of "colonial modernity" in East Asia and popular music culture in China, see Barlow; Jones.

2. A 1924 article carried in a Hong Kong newspaper, *Chinese Mail* (*Huazi ribao*) (31 May 1924), introduced Wong as a Chinese actress who attained an important position in the Western film industry and thereby became the pride of China. See "Haiwai zhi Zhongguo nu mingxing Huang Meiyan jianlue" (A Sketch of Huang Meiyan, an Overseas Chinese Female Film Star) (qtd. in Yu).

3. Very little production information was given in the review. However, based on the very vague description, Elaine Mae Woo, director of *Anna May Wong: Frosted Yellow Willows* (2008), speculated that this referred to Harry Revier's *The Silk Bouquet* (1926), financed by Chinese Americans and renamed *Dragon Horse* in 1927.

4. Catherine Cole addresses a similar conundrum. Namely, Ghanaian concert party performers have historically enjoyed deploying blackface (à la Al Jolson) as a framing device for "creating a comic distance between the actors and their characters" (Cole 206). Cole argues that this conundrum should be studied in relation to global distribution and appropriation.

5. Per the Hays Code, Muni's casting as the male lead virtually ruled out the possibility of casting Wong as his wife, the female lead. This fact did not seem to disconcert Chinese media.

6. For a study of the development of racial discourse in the early twentieth century in China, see Dikotter.

7. Lady Jing Xia was introduced by the editor as a Western woman in the film industry; hence her views were considered useful to Chinese filmmakers despite China's difference from the West.

8 ★★★★★★★★★★★★
Emil Jannings
Translating the Star

GERD GEMÜNDEN

I'm going to America for six months. . . . That needs to happen. Everyone needs to have done that, to have had that experience. I need to have seen all of that with my own eyes, the way of working, the production methods, that pace of existence, of functioning.
—Emil Jannings in *Das Tagebuch*, October 1926

In the spring of 1929, Emil Jannings became the first actor to win an Academy Award.[1] A now famous photo shows him proudly holding the statuette.[2] This shot, however, was not taken at the 29 May inau-

---

Emil Jannings holding his Oscar in a Paramount publicity shot. Courtesy of Filmmuseum Berlin—Stiftung Deutsche Kinemathek.

gural awards ceremony, but several months earlier in the Paramount publicity department. That first year the winners were announced about three
months ahead of time.³ By the time the awards were officially celebrated,
Jannings was already back home in Germany. His highly successful two-
and-a-half-year run at Paramount had come to an abrupt end when the
studio converted to sound. By the time Hollywood professionals wanted to
crown the best male actor among them, he was no longer in their midst.

Jannings had come to Hollywood in October 1926, the last and most
celebrated star in a long line of German and other European film professionals to sign a contract with an American studio. A character actor who
had gained an international reputation with Ernst Lubitsch's two features
Madame DuBarry (*Passion*, 1919) and *Anna Boleyn* (*Deception*, 1920), he was
invited on the strength of two films in particular, F. W. Murnau's *Der letzte
Mann* (*The Last Laugh*, 1924) and E. A. Dupont's *Varieté* (*Variety*, 1925). During his time in Hollywood, Jannings acted in six feature films, including Victor Fleming's *The Way of All Flesh* (1927) and Josef von Sternberg's *The Last
Command* (1928)—the two films that won him the Oscar—as well as Ludwig Berger's *Sins of the Fathers* (1928), Lubitsch's *The Patriot* (1928), Mauritz
Stiller's *Street of Sin* (1928), and Lewis Milestone's *Betrayal* (1929). A number of other projects were cut short by Jannings's sudden departure, including a bio-picture of Paul Kruger, the leader of the South African resistance
against the British. When he left, Edwin Schallert wrote in the *Los Angeles
Times*, "[Jannings's] leaving culminates [an] exodus of foreign stars. The
king of them all has gone. The king of the European film stars. . . . [Jan-
nings's] pre-eminence as a pantomist actor is unquestioned, and in a sense
his going marks the close of a picturesque phase of Hollywood's history" (28
April 1929).

In a career that spans almost fifty years on stage and screen and appearances in almost eighty movies, Emil Jannings's six American films appear to
be a mere interlude. But his time in Hollywood was indeed a central and
pivotal experience for him, greatly augmenting his status in the film industry of Weimar Germany and on into the Nazi regime, while also providing
considerable personal enrichment and professional perspective.⁴ At the
same time, his American films, particularly *The Last Command*, *The Way of All
Flesh*, and *The Patriot*, have claimed their place in U.S. silent film history,
primarily, as contemporary reviews demonstrate, because of the dominating performance of Emil Jannings. Schallert's farewell, quoted above, was
indeed representative of the high regard in which many Hollywood film
professionals held Jannings as well as of the tremendous popularity he
enjoyed with the American public; Schallert was also quite prophetic about

the fact that Jannings's departure signaled not only the end of silent film as an era in which stars had enjoyed the status of kings and queens, but also the end of a period of intense internationalization of the American and German film industries.

The case of Emil Jannings is unique among all the stars discussed in this volume, because he is the only one to have been imported to America on the strength of his success abroad; he is the only actor whose American star persona and screen roles were grafted onto an already established image, and much of Paramount's energy was invested in the process of "translation," while the public's and critics' attention was focused on the similarities and differences between "the German" and "the American" Jannings. Even more unusual is that in this process of translating Jannings, the studio gave the star extraordinary control over scripts, roles, and choice of directors, allowing him power in the artistic creation of his films that few domestic stars and no other foreign stars enjoyed at the time. His American career thus raises a particular set of questions about how this imported star was incorporated: What image of Jannings existed in the United States prior to his arrival here, and how did Paramount employ that image to promote their latest property? How did casting decisions, promotional strategies, and directorial assignments help to shape Jannings's transition from one national cinema to another? What role did Jannings play in the larger international rivalry between the American and German film industry? And how does his American career differ from that of other famous imports, particularly Pola Negri, who, like Jannings, gained star status through *Deception* and *Passion*?

☆☆★★★ Between Competition and Compatibility

When Emil Jannings first stormed onto American cinema screens as Louis XV in *Passion*, he did so incognito because neither his name nor that of director Ernst Lubitsch was included in the credits. Because anti-German sentiment was still strong so shortly after World War I, the film's origins were intentionally obscured, and in some places it was advertised as a Polish production.[5] But by the time Jannings arrived in person in the fall of 1926, matters could not have been more different. The success of *Passion* and *Deception*, together with the critical acclaim for *The Cabinet of Dr. Caligari* and *The Golem* (both 1920), had overcome hostility toward German cinema, while Jannings, now a major international star, was welcomed as royalty. New York journalists reported the simultaneous docking of ships carrying Jannings and the Queen of Romania with the headline, "Welcome the

Queen Maria of Romania! Welcome the King of Dramatic Actors!"
(Munkepunke 101), while Hollywood film professionals greeted Jannings
and his wife, Gussy Holl, with a banner that read, "American Screen Guild
Welcomes Emil Jannings/Screen's Foremost Dramatic Actor." Jannings's
meteoric rise to international fame must certainly be attributed to his individual talent, but first and foremost it must be understood as part of the
German film industry's stunning postwar recovery, making it Hollywood's
fiercest rival but also its frequent collaborator. Indeed, the competitiveness
between German and American film studios was also the guarantee for the
German film professionals' compatibility within the U.S. studio system and
a reason for their success there.

It is important to recall that Weimar cinema, like Weimar culture in
general, was truly international, and its film industry presented both a commercial and artistic alternative to Hollywood, the only European cinema to
do so at the time:

> After the war Germany was the one nation which could pretend to present a
> European answer to Hollywood. For a fleeting moment in the first half of the
> postwar decade it even appeared to mount a frontal assault on American
> hegemony. For a comparably brief period in the second half of the decade it
> became the rallying point of a pan-European movement aimed at checking
> American inroads. However beleaguered, it thus presented a commercial as
> well as artistic alternative to American domination.   (Saunders 6)

Hollywood, in turn, was well aware of this competition, both because of the
German film industry's artistic and technological advances, and because of
its own failure to make the same inroads in Germany that it had made in
other European markets after the war. Hollywood's continued efforts to
reach German audiences were closely observed by German cultural critics as
well as the public at large, and *Amerikanismus* became a buzzword for the
contested reception of American culture, be it cinema, music, fashion,
sports, or lifestyle in general. While some Germans claimed that American
mass culture foreshadowed a homogenization of the world, others considered it to be a force that could subvert the pretentiousness of traditional elite
culture. Particularly in the discourse surrounding the film industry, the pros
and cons of American popular culture were of central importance, and German filmmakers had a very close eye on Hollywood, making it a measuring
stick for their domestic achievements. Yet rather than a one-way street of
one national culture influencing another, there was considerable two-way
traffic between the two nations' film industries. While German studios imitated American standardization of production, the emphasis on publicity, and
the star system, American producers were not only interested in conquering

a German market (often by setting up subsidiaries in Germany) but also in importing know-how and personnel. While the latter led to a genuine enrichment of the American film industry, it also often seemed aimed at weakening its competitors by depriving them of their strongest talent.

The long list of professionals who left Berlin for Los Angeles for stays of various lengths reveals only a few whose forays met with real success. The only true long-term success story is that of Ernst Lubitsch and his entourage, which included scriptwriter Hanns Kräly (who would win an Academy Award for his script for *The Patriot*), his personal assistant Henry Blanke, later to become an important producer at Warner Bros., and his main female star, Pola Negri, who would become one of the best-paid stars of her time. Lubitsch himself became one of the most consistently acclaimed directors of that decade, successfully straddling the conversion to sound, and even heading up production at Paramount for a short while. Most others who followed in their wake were far less successful, including the star producer Erich Pommer, who was brought in to repeat the feats that had made the German studio Ufa famous but who would return to Germany at the end of the decade; director Dimitri Buchowetzki, who had cast Jannings in *Danton* (1921), *Othello* (1922), and *Peter der Grosse* (*Peter the Great*, 1922), but who failed to gain recognition with his American films; F. W. Murnau, whose films with Jannings (*Tartuffe*, *Faust*, and *The Last Laugh*) made him Weimar's premier director of art film, but who struggled to preserve his artistic integrity in Hollywood, ultimately finding himself disenchanted with the studio system; not to mention E. A. Dupont and Ludwig Berger, who for various reasons did not meet the high expectations that their German works had created. Paul Leni's promising beginnings were cut short by his untimely death. Among the actors and actresses besides Negri, who arrived soon after Lubitsch, only Jannings and his friend Conrad Veidt acquired major star status, while Lya de Putti (Jannings's co-star in *Variety*), Lil Dagover (of *Caligari* fame), and Camilla Horn (the Gretchen in *Faust*) had short-lived careers. (One may add that Germany had, from the 1910s onward, likewise tried to make stars out of imported American actors like Fern Andra, Betty Amann, and Louise Brooks, also with rather different individual results.)

Both the American and the German trade press followed the import and export of talent closely. From the beginning of the decade, American voices, deeply mistrustful of Germans after the war, warned of "the German invasion," "the deluge," and "tidal waves"—all terms that very much echoed the anti-immigration sentiment described in Amy Lawrence's contribution on Rudolph Valentino in this volume—while by mid-decade, when the numbers of Europeans increased significantly, the rhetoric shifted toward protectionism, and *Variety* headlined in June 1927, "400 Aliens in U.S. Films. Majority Leads of Foreign Birth." German observers, on the other hand, were wary of the perceived drain on the film industry and frequently commented on the "talent raids" by Carl Laemmle, William Fox, Adolph Zukor, and other moguls. In March 1927, the renowned theater critic Herbert Ihering took stock of the German film industry and came up with a dire pronouncement: "Jannings, Conrad Veidt, Murnau, in the near future Ludwig Berger—the last year has cost Germany its most significant film artists. At the same time, the German cinemas have been swamped by an uncontrollable flood of mediocre American films, while German products have not been able to make inroads over there. The German film is destroyed" (Ihering, *Von Reinhardt* 388).

Despite the rhetoric of tidal waves, the actual number of German film professionals in Hollywood was small in proportion; what was big was the interest they created:

> In 1927 the influence of German cinema was felt everywhere in Hollywood, but neither the actual numbers of German filmmakers and actors on the West Coast nor the box office success (or lack thereof) of German films distributed in the United States justified its reputation. The rising stock of German film, particularly among Hollywood technicians and artists, was based on the reception of a handful of films. But word of Ufa's giant studio facilities in Babelsberg and its technical superiority, to say nothing of ingenuity, had trickled back to the West Coast. It was the technical and aesthetic innovations of the Germans that kept Hollywood abuzz.   (Horak 243)

It was this buzz that greeted Jannings when he arrived in October 1926, and that explains the extraordinarily warm welcome that he received in both New York and Los Angeles. Yet despite the numerous imports from Berlin, there were few German film professionals who could serve as a role model for successful integration into the American studio system; the majority illustrated the difficulties that actors in particular had to reckon with, making Jannings's success in Hollywood an intriguing case study for the translation of the star image.

★★★★★ The Americanization of "*König* Emil"

To describe Emil Jannings upon his arrival in New York as a king was an obvious reference to his supreme status among dramatic film actors at the time, as well as an allusion to the roles of historical leaders that had made him famous (Ludwig XV, Henry VIII, Nero, Danton, Peter the

Great, among others). Yet while "royalty" was the dominant metaphor, not to say cliché, at the time for film star publicity, it was also important to stress how human these kings and queens were after all. Thus, while the studio carefully orchestrated a glamorous welcome for Jannings, they also put an emphasis on showing him as a normal *mensch* without airs. Much was made of the fact that Jannings traveled not only with his wife, a maid, a chauffeur, a Viennese cook, and two Mercedes automobiles in tow, but equally important was the publicity that emphasized his eagerness to blend in—a famous shot shows him waving American flags on his front lawn—and to begin working. A willingness to be Americanized was important to undercut the stigma of being "difficult" that attached to foreign stars, because they were allegedly unable or unwilling to comply with American working methods, felt culturally alienated, or held so-called elitist views about film as art. Jannings was no exception. A 1927 editorial, "Mr. Jannings in Hollywood," singles out the recently arrived actor in warning of films that, by relying on "symbolism, highfalutin' notions, and profound abstractions," proclaim to be art but address only the privileged few (*Motion Picture Magazine*, January 1927, 5).

Similarly, in an article with the telling title "Spanking the Stars: High and Mighty Temperamental Geniuses Told Where to Get Off," a number of European stars are taken to task for their pretentiousness and lack of work ethic: "Jannings, a great artist, works in the deliberate German manner. He likes to sleep for an hour or two after lunch. He likes to pause for coffee and a chat in the middle of the afternoon. He was stunned at the suggestion that he work at night" (*Motion Picture Magazine*, November 1927, 21). Yet in comparison to Garbo's reclusiveness (a major challenge for publicity efforts, but also of course playing into the construction of her "mystery") and Negri's antics—the two stars most often mentioned in the same sentence as Jannings—he came across as a likeable, uncomplicated human being whose penchant for good food and pilsener beer, and much-advertised craze for dogs and birds, elicited sympathy and like-mindedness.[6] At the same time, publicity stressed that Jannings was a distinguished and invited visitor who, one hopes, would not return to Germany too soon, and he was therefore never linked to the discourse of immigration, which, as Lawrence shows, was central for understanding Valentino.[7]

How ordinary and "average" Jannings's offscreen persona really was becomes apparent when contrasted with that of Negri. Their respective careers share similar origins but then move in strikingly different directions. Like Jannings, Negri became a major star through Ernst Lubitsch, and her strongest films were those made under his direction. Negri, not Jannings, was the true star of *Passion*, which established her image as openly sexual and sensuous, a characterization that would dominate her U.S. career. Columnist Harry Carr described her in 1923 as an absolute novelty:

> For the most part our native screen stars are sweet and winsome but rather namby pamby. They tinkle; they never crash. Pola is a hurricane in a mountain canyon. She has color and depth and a sweep of emotion that is simply terrific. . . . Negri may be more biteable than kissable as someone has suggested; but it looks as though she were due to be one of the great actresses of all time. (*Motion Picture Magazine*, June 1923, 86)

Defying Puritan morals, Negri's vamps resonated with American audiences searching for the new American woman, and critics described her in terms that stressed her vitality and wildness, her ready wit, and her resolute manner. In stark contrast to Jannings's Hollywood image of devoted family man and serious film professional, which supported rather than contradicted his roles, Negri's offscreen antics, which included her infamous rivalry with Gloria Swanson and affairs with Chaplin and Valentino, completely obscured her films (and her real talents). Fan magazines and the yellow press were full of reports about her troubled love life and her extravagant lifestyle, which film historian Jeanine Basinger describes as a series of attention-grabbing idiosyncrasies:

> She wrapped herself in ermine and chinchilla and mink and draped herself with diamonds and rubies and emeralds and sat up straight in the back [of her white Rolls-Royce], staring stonily ahead, drawing all eyes. (She also kept a pet tiger on a leash, and frequently paraded down Sunset Boulevard with him.) She had her dressing room strewn daily with fresh orchid petals. Her wardrobe was dramatic, either black silk, black velvet, or sable, or the opposite—white silk, white chiffon, and ermine. She started the fad for toenails painted fire-engine red. (243)

Whether despite or because of her flamboyant offscreen persona, she was among the top-grossing stars of the early 1920s. But unlike Jannings, Negri appeared in too many films with silly or weak stories, while she exercised much less control over her scripts and directors, despite projecting an image of a woman who gets what she wants. If Jannings was cast repeatedly as an American of German origin in films that were set in present-day America, Negri was presented as utterly foreign and exotic in historical dramas and period pieces set in Europe. Her American films are usually considered inferior to her work in Germany, and when she left Hollywood in 1928, she was thoroughly disenchanted with its working methods and lack of cultural sophistication.[8]

Another reason why the continuities between Jannings's German and American roles are far greater than in the case of Negri and other imported stars is that Jannings, having arrived at the height of his fame, had negotiated a very favorable contract that not only paid him the handsome salary of $10,000 per week, but more importantly assured him the right to choose his directors and have a say in the script. He thus worked predominantly with European directors (Lubitsch, Stiller, Berger, von Sternberg) and writers (von Sternberg, Lajos Biró, and Hanns Kräly); he even claims to have successfully pushed for an alternate ending to *The Way of All Flesh*, since the original one seemed too contrived, and to have come up himself with the idea for *The Last Command* (Jannings, *Theater-Film* 184–86)—a claim contested by von Sternberg, who writes that the idea came from Lubitsch (126).[9] The fact that art director Hans Dreier, another important German import, worked on three of Jannings's six American films assured them the unifying "European" look that the studio strove for.

The offscreen persona created for Jannings by Paramount was very much in synch with the roles that they had in mind for him. His two most successful German films in America had been *The Last Laugh* and *Variety*—in both of which he had shifted from kings and other dignitaries to playing everyday men and their everyday plights—and Paramount's roles for him were meant to be an American extension on the fallen man type he had portrayed there.[10] With the exception of *The Patriot, Street of Sin,* and *Betrayal,* his U.S. films are set in present-day America and, as mentioned above, often cast him as American with a German-language background. In *The Way of All Flesh,* he plays the German American cashier August Schiller, an ideal father and loyal husband, who loses everything through one fateful misstep; similarly, in *Sins of the Fathers,* he plays a German American restaurateur who inadvertently blinds his son through his bootleg gin, serves a prison sentence, and is redeemed through an unlikely happy ending; and in *Betrayal,* Jannings is a mayor of a small Swiss town involved in a jealousy drama. In these roles, as well as the crime boss Basher Bill in the London-set gangster drama *Street of Sin,* and as Sergius Alexander, a former Russian general now toiling as an extra in Hollywood in *The Last Command,* he plays individuals who strive high and plunge deep—often through the smallest fault—eliciting our compassion for their all-too-human shortcomings. These are stories of degradation and humiliation that allowed Jannings full range of his melodramatic repertoire, making them of a piece with not only the German films that preceded them but also *The Blue Angel,* his German comeback.

These continuities in roles and characters were underscored by the recurrent use of key motifs. Many of his German roles are about the power of

Jannings in *Street of Sin*. Courtesy of Filmmuseum Berlin—Stiftung Deutsche Kinemathek.

clothes and foreground the act of dressing, be it the trapeze artist in *Variety* or the professor-turned-clown in *The Blue Angel*. Both *The Last Laugh* and *The Last Command* revolve around the uniform as the anchor of the self. For the hotel porter in *Laugh*, the uniform is the garment that makes his neighbors treat him like a general, and its loss implies the loss of his existence. At the beginning of *The Last Command*, we dwell for some time on Sergius Alexander, ex-Russian general and now a Hollywood extra, picking up the very kind of uniform that he used to wear in the war as part of his costume. Featuring a protagonist whose fate it is to have become a simulacrum of his former self, *The Last Command*, like *The Last Laugh*, is an extended reflection on performance and identity. At its center resides Jannings's huge body. Rotund, robust, but also vulnerable, it takes up a lot of space physically and visually; physical strength and frailty are often inseparable in Jannings's roles, making him human. The dramas of degradation, both in their German and American inflection, always leave their very visible scars on his enormous physique.

At the heart of the question of how to judge Jannings's American films lies the challenge of defining his overall achievements as an actor. Before assessing his performance in America, it is necessary to review how critics assessed his work prior to his departure for Hollywood. Like most German

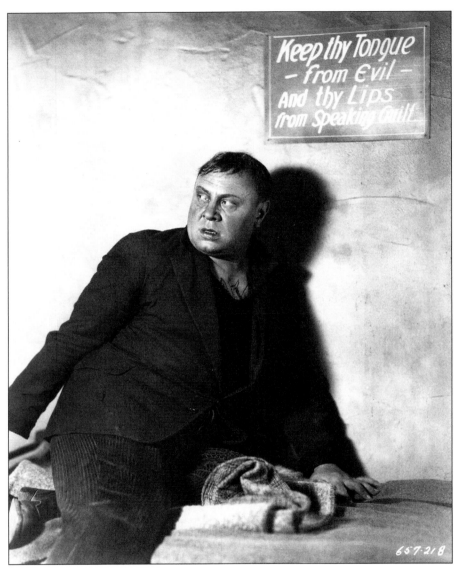

Jannings in *The Last Command*. Courtesy of Filmmuseum Berlin—Stiftung Deutsche Kinemathek.

actors of the 1920s (but unlike many of his co-workers in Hollywood), Jannings was stage trained, and he would return to the stage throughout his career. He therefore had a penchant for theatricality, for grand gestures and grimaces that were common in German films of the beginning of the decade but looked awkward and unnatural to American viewers. His kings and dignitaries of that period were very much his own creations, and he imposed his personality on the role, rather than attempting to disappear into them. In his early films, "he slipped into historical masks like into a second face. One no longer saw Henry VIII but Emil VIII" (Schulz 67). Yet in his work with Murnau, a transition toward naturalism became visible, reaching a climax in Dupont's *Variety*. Reviewing this film Rudolf Arnheim coined the term "Janningsesque" to describe the actor's new style:

> The most rapturous Schiller gesture is far more easily attainable to the novice than is one of those simple scenes where Emil Jannings changes his baby, looks at a woman lustfully, or slaps playing cards on the table with naïve enthusiasm. Something like this has an immediate certainty that cannot be taught in acting school. They are the convincing gestures of the boorish, good-natured artist. . . . They have the clumsy, heavy rhythm that is his characteristic. (116)

Most contemporaries agreed that Jannings's acting was that of a "Vollblutschauspieler"—the kind of thoroughbred actor who seems to be on stage at all times[11]—but some came to different conclusions as to what this implied about the actor's relationship to his roles. Lotte Eisner faulted him for his theatrical acting as late as *Faust*, taking him to task for "flaunting his usual fatuity once the demon [Mephisto] descends to earth, and exasperating the non-German spectators as much as ever" (285), and the reproach of overacting was a common one. In an analytic essay about Jannings's body, Ken Calhoon has offered an interpretation of his acting (and his roles) as an implied resistance to the evolution of screen acting:

> Certain of Jannings's roles make explicit his affinity to the gestural and pantomimic practices that grew out of mystery cycles, street theater, and the carnival: a trapeze artist in *Variety* and the devil-trickster Mephisto in *Faust*, not to mention the clown in *The Blue Angel*. Silent cinema necessarily entailed a high degree of gesture and pantomime, though with Jannings this is reinforced by the roles themselves and carries over into the age of sound. It is as if Jannings were there to embody, as an alien presence, the popular tradition that early cinema revived but that the naturalistic impulse of cinema was striving to eliminate. (89)

To be sure, and as Jannings was well aware, there was very little room on American screens for such an "alien presence," as the aversion to pantomimic acting was very pronounced, and paying homage to the bygone era of early cinema was out of the question. In his autobiography, Jannings describes how he had to adjust to this different acting tradition when Victor Fleming, his first director there, taught him to avoid unnaturalistic acting: "'Don't do anything!' he [Fleming] told me. 'Be as you are! If you do this,' and he lifted his little finger, 'it's like somebody else doing this!' and he suddenly raised his fist. . . . Slowly I became aware how a different Jannings emerged from within me—a simpler one, less encumbered, and more self-assured" (183).[12] Jannings's compatriot Ludwig Berger, the director of *Sins of the Fathers*, also recalls changes in Jannings's self-perception; only one year later, when preparing the film, a print of *The Last Laugh* was screened and Jannings was aghast about his own performance: "'That is awful, look at this acting job!' He [Jannings] was referring to his own play. He hit his fists against the screen and could not contain his indignation: 'Ludwig, what do you say to this terrible over-emphasizing?'" (53).

To American viewers, these adjustments of Jannings's style must have been too minuscule to be noticed. Contemporary reviews of his first American feature, *The Way of All Flesh*, underscored the continuities with his German performances—"He does here what anyone will expect of him if familiar with his work" (*Variety*, 27 June 1927, 22)—while attesting that high expectations have been met: "One cannot say of Jannings that this or that is his greatest performance, because he is so uniformly good; but it is certainly one of his best" (*Kinematograph Weekly*, 22 September 1927, 72). Reviews of Jannings's acting in *The Last Command* and *The Patriot* were also uniformly positive, but with subsequent films negative voices began to be heard, as the formula began to show signs of wear. Reviewing *Betrayal*, *Photoplay* wrote that there are moments when "Jannings tries at times to hold the screen" (May 1929, 55) while others put the blame elsewhere: "Jannings is not nearly as well directed as usual, but he manages to rise superior to both direction and story" (*Kinematograph Weekly*, 23 May 1929, 38). With *Sins of the Fathers* he seemed to have reached a low point; this film, wrote *Variety*, "represents mediocre stuff for the giant reputation of Emil Jannings" (30 January 1929, 34).

German critics, in contrast, frequently focused in their comments on whether or not Jannings's films (and his performance) upheld any artistic integrity in what was perceived to be an impersonal industry driven by the almighty dollar. While they continued to admire his performances and felt pride for his success "over there," they also voiced concerns that the scripts left much to be desired. Rudolf Arnheim, who had emphatically stated "*Variety* is one of the best films there is" (117), largely because of Jannings's performance, withdrew any sympathy for *The Way of All Flesh*, "an old-fashioned thing with out-of-date problems, and we closed the door on the down-at-heels beggar Emil Jannings: 'We can't give anything!'" (139). Herbert Ihering, an early advocate of Jannings who would go on to publish a monograph on him in 1941, zeroed in on his acting in this film: "Instead of the art of acting, we have a begging for pity. Instead of agitation through creativity, we have tear-jerking as around Christmas time, baggy pants, an ice-gray beard, a stooped back" (Ihering, *Von Reinhardt* 2:543). In similarly unambiguous terms, Harry Kahn condemned the experiment of infusing the American screen with Berlin's biggest star: "Neither fish nor fowl, neither Hollywood nor Babelsberg, but a sugary, schmaltzy mixture of both" (*Die Weltbühne* [1927], vol. 2, 867). Kurt Pinthus went so far as to say that the characters depicted in the film reminded him of the films made twenty years earlier (*Das Tagebuch* 8 [1927], 1036–37). If one compares these reviews to what *The Bioscope* wrote about the film—"[Jannings] has unique opportunities of displaying every phase of his art. The humors of his uneventful family life, the boyish delight in the company of his friends, the more hectic scenes of his night of wild dissipation, his tragic despair at the ruin which suddenly overtakes him, and his resigned pathos when his self-sacrifice is complete—all are depicted with the restraint and certainty of the great actor" (22 September 1927, 48)—one understands that what was really at stake here was something altogether different from just Jannings's acting. Instead, it was a debate about which motion picture industry—the German or the American—was more advanced and sophisticated, using Jannings as the big target he was to make one's point. While Americans insisted that they, too, could do art cinema, Germans argued the opposite—that at the hands of the studio machinery even a talent like Jannings's had no chance of survival.

What was true about the completely divergent reception of *The Way of All Flesh* was also true for Jannings's other American films, though to a lesser degree, as American critics became more critical of his subsequent performances and German critics seemed to pay less attention to them. Surprisingly, both shared praise for *The Patriot*, which in terms of setting, plot, and acting style stands in pronounced contrast to Jannings's five other American films. Directed by Lubitsch, *The Patriot* harks back to Jannings's costume dramas and seems almost an anachronism. Of this lost film only a three-minute trailer has survived, but together with the synopsis and contemporary reviews it clearly indicates that *The Patriot* was a return to the historical epics that Lubitsch and Jannings created, with Jannings impersonating the role of the paranoid Czar Paul I of Russia much in the ponderous, overtly dramatic manner of *Passion* and *Deception*, with arms flinging and eyes rolling. In his memoir, Lubitsch's costume designer Ali Hubert creates a vivid impression of how Lubitsch instructed his star: "Lubitsch jumps down from the camera platform in order to play vividly for Emil Jannings his scene with Florence Vidor. Suggestively, with penetrating gestures and exact timing he embodies precisely how the insane Czar courts the terrified

Countess Ostermann" (Hubert 35). While already filmed with some sound effects—"Hear Jannings's agonized roar!" promises the trailer—*The Patriot* was seen as the last film of its kind, as was Jannings's acting style: "When in days to come we foregather and discuss the dying days of the silent drama and the dawn of the sound device era, we will talk of the glorious performance that Emil Jannings gave us just before the old style went out" (*Film Spectator*, 28 April 1928, 7).

Jannings in *The Patriot*. Courtesy of Filmmuseum Berlin—Stiftung Deutsche Kinemathek.

⭐⭐⭐⭐⭐ **Between Berlin and Hollywood: *The Blue Angel***

When Jannings returned to Berlin in the spring of 1929, he was reportedly in culture shock. Plunging from sunny, prosperous, and politically isolated California into economically, socially, and psychologically depressed Berlin (with the economic crash of Black Friday yet to come), he found the "So what?" attitude ("Nu, wenn schon!") that Berliners had adopted to deal with chaos to be profoundly unsettling (Jannings, *Theater-Film* 194). In his memoir, written during the Third Reich but not published until after his death in 1950, he took his compatriots to task for their lethargy and lack of national pride—thereby reiterating the terms the Nazis used to describe the mindset of the Weimar Republic, but also demonstrating clear signs of an Americanization undergone while abroad.[13] It is because of the lasting impression that American professionalism made on him (and which he already expressed in 1930) that Jannings actively sought the opportunity to work under an *American* director in the film that would not only be his German comeback but was also to launch his career in sound.[14]

Beyond these autobiographical dimensions, there is, of course, ample evidence to consider *The Blue Angel* a film belonging to more than one national cinema.[15] Initiated by Erich Pommer, Ufa's erstwhile star producer who also had just returned from Hollywood, it was meant to be a synthesis of Hollywood and Babelsberg—a multiple-language film made for an international audience by a producer intimately familiar with the tastes of both the American and the German public; an American star director able to draw on his Austrian roots; a major international star capable of playing both the German- and English-language versions; and introducing a new star in the making, Marlene Dietrich. In a recent article on the differences between the English and the German versions of the film, Patrice Petro has read *The Blue Angel* as a film that wants to be *neither* American nor German, reinstating in sound film a transnational dimension that was believed to have been lost with the demise of the silents. As Petro shows, this is a film that "reflects upon the tensions—cultural, aesthetic, economic, social—that so define the hybridity of this period: the tensions between theater and cinema, Europe and America, the Old World and the New, youth and age, high and low culture" (156).

By bringing an American director to Berlin, *The Blue Angel* also reverses the decade-long pattern of German film professionals emigrating to Hollywood, which as Harry Kahn had written in his review of *The Way of All Flesh* (cited above) had *failed* to create a synergy between German and American talent. The plot, significantly reworked from the Heinrich Mann novel on which it is based, is familiar Jannings territory: a respected man falls for the "wrong" kind of woman and his life goes to pot, recalling the dramas of degradation that were central to his star persona and that had most recently been rehashed in Hollywood. There is some irony in the fact that in his role as English teacher Jannings tortures his students by drilling their proper pronunciation of the *th*-sound, while his own inadequate mastery of English had cut short his lucrative U.S. career. What is also remarkable about the English-language version is that it shows us a Jannings with a fine command of English, inducing some doubt about whether the language barrier would indeed have been as insurmountable as he always claimed.

As is well known, *The Blue Angel* would become Jannings's biggest success ever, yet his performance was overshadowed by that of Marlene Dietrich, for whom the film inaugurated a Hollywood career unprecedented by that of any German actor; meanwhile, Jannings would not celebrate a major success again until Joseph Goebbels had been installed as minister of propaganda.[16] The divergent futures of these two stars are prefigured in their two very different acting styles, and were understood as such by prophetic contemporary reviewers. While Dietrich was praised for her cool and restrained acting, which underlined her calculating sexuality and would be at the forefront of her subsequent films with von Sternberg, Jannings's theatricality, while in keeping with the psychology of his character, came across as anachronistic, a naturalism that reviewers described as "fussiness" (*Vossische Zeitung*, 2 April 1930) and clearly belonging to a tradition whose time, just like that of Professor Rath, had come. Ihering, always a hard critic to please, simply stated: "Jannings acts too obtrusively" (Ihering, *Blue Angel* 25). The internationally acclaimed Emil Jannings suddenly seemed of a piece with the provincialism and pettiness of his character while the mondaine upstart Dietrich would go on to conquer Hollywood in ways that no German actor, not even Jannings, had dreamed of.

It is perhaps no coincidence that one of the first successes Jannings would have under the new political regime in Germany would be a film meant to recast *The Blue Angel* in a decidedly German fashion—Carl Froelich's *Traumulus* (1936). Here Jannings plays another teacher, a boarding school headmaster named Niemeyer, in a drama that also involves students on the prowl and the protagonist's personal and financial downfall at the hand of a woman, Niemeyer's cunning second wife. In an intriguing reading of the film that focuses on Froelich's use of the camera, lighting, and stars, Erica Carter has argued that *Traumulus* is a decidedly antimodernist film that harks back to pre-Weimar film aesthetics. Particularly Froelich's use of Jannings as an actor-personality that serves as a vehicle for the experience of what Carter calls the *"völkisch* sublime" (110) stands in stark contrast to how Hollywood cinema had staged the star. It is as if Jannings were stripped of the internationalism that had marked his Weimar career and were reclaimed for a German national cinema; using an acting style that emphasizes symbolic gestures and static poses, Jannings returns to the stage traditions out of which he emerged. The script underscores the antimodernism of its visual style, instilling in the teacher figure the dignity and sympathy of which *The Blue Angel* had stripped it. Niemeyer is nicknamed Traumulus (faux Latin for dreamer) by his students because of his unworldly being—a far cry from the sadistic nickname "Unrath" (garbage) given to the Jannings character in *The Blue Angel*—but he proves to be an idealist who upholds humanistic values. As in *The Blue Angel*, the plot is set in motion by a student spending an evening in the company of an actress of questionable reputation at a dubious bar ("The Golden Peacock"!) and the professor's efforts to get at the truth, but it then deviates from von Sternberg's film by having the professor emerge as the father figure who wants to protect his student from harm. Like Rath, Niemeyer experiences disappointment and degradation, but his naïveté is ultimately vindicated, despite his failures.[17]

Yet not all films Jannings made during this period can be seen as critiques of international productions; indeed, the majority strove to emulate the production values of contemporaneous American films, and in the biopicture *Robert Koch, der Bekämpfer des Todes* (1939) Jannings plays the lead in a film made explicitly in response to the success of William Dieterle's *The Story of Louis Pasteur* (1935). For his lead in Veit Harlan's *Der Herrscher* (*The Ruler*, 1937), Jannings would win the State Award (*Staatspreis*) and was subsequently appointed cultural senator of the Reich and member of the governing board of the Reich's Film Committee. In 1939, on the twenty-fifth anniversary of his first film role, he received the highest cultural award, the Goethe Medal. As a member of the board of directors at Tobis, Jannings would have an instrumental role in creating *Ohm Krüger* (1941), an anti-British propaganda film in which he also played the lead, a project that Jannings had had to abort in Hollywood a decade and a half earlier. The patriarch figure of Uncle Kruger is here stylized as a political leader who, in Jannings's own words, "was chosen to begin a battle which will only be concluded in our days" (Jannings, *Gedanken* 9). Jannings was a king again.[18] After the war, Jannings narrowly escaped a prison sentence but was no longer allowed to act on stage or screen. In 1947, he assumed Austrian citizenship, retreating to his home on the Wolfgangssee. Withdrawn and embittered, he died of liver cancer in 1950. A subject of numerous books during his lifetime—three already by 1930, by Jean Mitry, Martini and Lange-Kosak, and Munkepunke—there exists to date no critical biography of this actor who embodies as few others do the history of twentieth-century German American film relations.

ACKNOWLEDGMENTS

I would like to thank Jörg Jannings, the son of Emil Jannings's younger brother, Walter, for fielding my questions and for sharing his rich archive on his uncle.

NOTES

1. The original German reads as follows: "Ich gehe für ein halbes Jahr nach Amerika. . . . Es muß sein, es muß einmal erlebt sein, man muß es einmal hinter sich haben, ich muß das alles, diese Art des Arbeitens, diese Methode der Herstellung, dieses Tempo des Daseins und Wirkens, das muß ich einmal mit eigenen Augen gesehen haben." What is remarkable here is the fact that Jannings describes his upcoming trip from the perspective of an anticipated experience, as if the expected Americanization of his professional skills is what matters and not the stay abroad.

2. Jannings won the Academy Award over Charlie Chaplin (for *The Circus*) and Richard Barthelmess (for *The Noose* and *The Patent Leather Kid*).

3. The results of the voting of the members of the Academy were published on the back page of the Academy Bulletin on 18 February 1929.

4. Jannings was fond of stressing his internationalism. Born in Rorschach, Switzerland, in 1884 to an American father of German origin and a German mother born in Moscow, Jannings for many years nourished the myth that he was actually born in Brooklyn, New York, and held an American passport.

5. The *New York Times* wrote that the German origin of the film was to be excused considering that its star was Polish and its subject matter French (quoted in Prinzler and Patalas 31).

6. His pat answer for why it took him so long to visit America was "Prohibition kept me away!"

7. Reviewing *The Way of All Flesh* for the *Film Spectator*, Welford Beaton wrote, "I hope he [Jannings] remains in this country a long time. . . . If Paramount can maintain such a pace we have in store for us some rare cinematic treats" (4 August 1927, 11).

8. Relations between the two stars seem to have been less than affectionate. Jannings gets short shrift in Negri's autobiography, significantly titled *Memoirs of a Star*, where she only comments on his lack of humor (179), while he provides a short paragraph of her bursting onto German movie screens (Jannings, *Theater-Film* 126).

9. Both von Sternberg's and Jannings's autobiographies are highly selective affairs and are quoted here only to illustrate the authority *claimed* by them. Jannings chose to mention only three of his six American films (*The Way of All Flesh*, *The Last Command*, and *The Patriot*), thus suggesting that the other three were of no significance or best forgotten. Interestingly, while Jannings speaks highly of von Sternberg, the latter provides an extended rant on the difficulties he had with the German star while working on *The Last Command* (but provides no explanation of why he agreed to work with him again in Germany a few years later).

10. Interestingly, in Nazi Germany Jannings would return to playing kings (*Der alte und der junge König* [*The Old and the Young King*], 1935) and other forms of leaders in politics (*Ohm Krüger*, 1941; *Die Entlassung* [*The Dismissal*], 1942), industry (*Der Herrscher* [*The Ruler*], 1937), and science (*Robert Koch, der Bekämpfer des Todes* [*Robert Koch, Victor over Death*], 1939).

11. This was also von Sternberg's contention, who wrote about Jannings: "He was a master of make-up, not only of the outside of his head, but also of its inside. The mirror was his alter ego" (123).

12. In a letter to his brother Walter, Emil Jannings has a much less generous view of his first director, calling Fleming "a good-hearted, naïve boy who knows as much about acting as an elephant knows about peeling potatoes" (*Schriftgutsammlung* of the Filmmuseum Berlin—Stiftung Deutsche Kinemathek.)

13. When Jannings described the changes introduced by the Nazis after their takeover, he explicitly compared them to the working environment he so admired in Hollywood. And yet, it is in this period that Jannings began to retreat from Berlin and permanently settle in Austria. It should be pointed out that Jannings wrote his autobiography during the 1940s but withheld it from publication when he was forced to omit names of famous Jewish colleagues such as Lubitsch and Reinhardt. His wife oversaw the posthumous publication in 1950.

14. Shortly after his return to Germany Jannings wrote, "this name [Hollywood] is one of the most important markers for the new [film] art that spans the globe . . . where I spent important and formative years of my life" (Jannings, "Vorwort" iii).

15. One of the first critics to raise the question "How German is *The Blue Angel*?" was Gertrud Koch, who suggested reading the film as an auteurist work by von Sternberg (much in line with the director's self-understanding) that displays stylistic qualities also found in his later films with Marlene Dietrich, while the subject matter harked back to the director's difficult childhood in Vienna at the turn of the century (see Koch 64ff).

16. Jannings was not the only major star who struggled to find adequate roles in the early 1930s. Commenting on the disappearance of actors like Fritz Kortner, Asta Nielsen, and Paul Wegner from the screen, Rudolf Arnheim pronounced in 1932 "a crisis of the so-called character actor," which he tied to "the fact that the standard of film production and of the film public has sunk frighteningly low once again" (54).

17. In a scene that can only be read as an in-joke, Jannings tells off another character by suggesting to him, "Why don't you become a waiter in America?"—the very role he had played in *Sins of the Fathers*.

18. There still exists some uncertainty regarding how Jannings, who was half-Jewish, managed to be so successful during the Third Reich. Emil Jannings's friend Erich Ebermayer, who also wrote a *roman à clef* about the Jannings family, *Unter anderem Himmel* (1942), writes that during the 1920s Jannings called himself "a half-goy with a Jewish brain," but later "organized some papers" to prove his racial purity according to the Nuremberg laws. After the war, however, Jannings allegedly told American journalists that he could not have been a Nazi by virtue of the fact that he was half-Jewish (Ebermayer, *Eh' ich's vergesse* 214–15). Jörg Jannings explained to me that his uncle flaunted his Jewish heritage during the 1920s, because Jewish artists were at the forefront of the sophisticated urban culture of Berlin.

9 ✩✩✩✩✩✩✩✩✩✩✩

Al Jolson
The Man Who Changed the Movies Forever

KRIN GABBARD

Al Jolson did not want to be a movie star, at least not at first. But late in his career, when he did turn to the movies, he brought a promiscuous talent and an outlandish collection of gestures, moods, and expressions. If today we do not find his films deeply offensive because of their racial politics, we are just as likely to find them confusing, even incoherent. For this, blame Jolson's persona, not the films. As Rip Lhamon has written, "He is not an integrated personality but a mob of conflicts" (106).

Al Jolson, "an ego who walks and talks like a man." Publicity still. Courtesy of Jerry Ohlinger's Movie Materials Store.

But somehow Jolson made his conflicting identities work in the cinema. With *The Jazz Singer* (1927), he almost single-handedly transformed the sound cinema from an experiment into an inevitability. *The Singing Fool* (1928), his second full-length film, was his greatest success, even becoming the nation's box office champion for the next eleven years. (It was finally knocked out of first place by no less than *Gone with the Wind* [1939]). After his triumph with these two semi-talking films, however, it was all downhill until he loaned his singing voice to Larry Parks in *The Jolson Story* (1946). Jolson's biopic kicked up some nostalgic gold dust and inspired *Jolson Sings Again* (1949), perhaps the only sequel to a biopic ever made. Jolson may have been as popular as ever in those last years before his death in 1950.

★★★★★ **Jolson's Career in Moving Pictures Prior to 1927**

The Vitagraph Company of America was launched in 1898 to distribute films about soldiers leaving for the Spanish American War. By 1907 the company had built studios in the Midwood section of Brooklyn and within a few years was releasing hundreds of short films each year. In 1916 Vitagraph asked Jolson to star in a film. Because Jolson knew that his body and not his voice would be the attraction, he was reluctant to appear before audiences without one of his greatest assets. The studio talked him into the deal, assuring him that the film would be shown only to the Policemen's Benefit fund to raise money. When Jolson found out that Vitagraph had plans for larger distribution, he ordered up all copies of the film and destroyed them himself (Freedland 74). So far as we know, no prints of this early Jolson footage exist.

Jolson could afford to put an abrupt end to his movie career in 1916 because he was one of the most popular, if not the most popular, entertainers in the country. In 1914, after several years of rising steadily through the ranks in vaudeville, he took a small role in a Broadway show called *Honeymoon Express* and quickly made it his own, regularly stopping the show with his exuberant delivery of songs. Even at this early stage, he would abandon the script and sing directly to the audience for as long as thirty minutes at a stretch. The other performers surely did not enjoy waiting in the wings, wondering when and if they would return to the stage. Jolson was already becoming known as self-obsessed and narcissistic, "an ego who walks and talks like a man" (Goldman 3). But audiences loved Jolson and his gleeful transgressions against theatrical tradition. In *Honeymoon Express* Jolson also blacked up to play Gus, the African American trickster he would repeatedly portray onstage and in the film *Big Boy* (1930).

Gus was the direct descendant of the *servus dolosus*, "the witty slave" of Roman comedy, as well as the Signifyin' Monkey of African American oral tradition. There may be no connection, but a year after Jolson introduced audiences to Gus, D. W. Griffith cast Walter Long as the lustful former slave who pursues the young and innocent Flora (Mae Marsh) to her death in *The Birth of a Nation* (1915). Like Jolson, Long played the part in blackface. And his character was named Gus.

When *Dancing Around* (1915) opened at the Winter Garden Theatre, Jolson again played Gus, but this time he received top billing. With *Robinson Crusoe, Jr.* (1916), in which Gus becomes Friday in a long dream sequence, the publicity machine labeled Jolson "America's Greatest Entertainer." All three of these shows toured extensively, and no other entertainer was as sure to fill the house, regardless of where it was. Back in New York, the Winter Garden had become Jolson's shrine, and a runway was specially installed so that he could walk directly into the audience and absorb its adulation. For at least the next ten years he had no need of the movies.

In 1923, D. W. Griffith had need of Jolson himself. The same director who had dominated and perhaps even defined the American cinema had not made a successful film since *Way Down East* (1920). In 1924, he had two of his biggest flops, *America* and *Isn't Life Wonderful*, soon to be followed by *Sorrows of Satan* (1926), an even bigger disaster. A film with the magic of Jolson might turn his career around, or so he hoped. Of course Jolson would appear in blackface, and of course there would be a reference to the song "My Mammy," which he had introduced to Broadway audiences in the 1921 production of *Sinbad* and which had already sold thousands of copies for Columbia Records.

The script that Griffith presented to Jolson was called *Mammy's Boy*, which was later changed to *Black and White*. Jolson was on the set long enough to shoot six reels of film, but he was offended by the absence of Griffith, who claimed that he was not the man to direct a comedy. When Jolson saw the first set of rushes, he knew that this was not the right project for a man now billed not just as America's but as "The World's Greatest Entertainer." Watching the rushes brought new superlatives—Jolson's wife, Ethel, declared them "the worst thing I ever saw." Jolson sailed for Europe on the *Majestic* the next day. After a few days at sea, he sent Griffith a telegram claiming ill health, even insisting that he was "on the verge of a serious collapse" (Goldman 129–30).

Fortunately for Jolson, he had gone to work on Griffith's film without signing a contract. This did not prevent Griffith from suing, however. The

case circulated through the courts for several years, with Griffith demand-
ing more than a half million dollars in damages at one point. Jolson had
smart representation, especially Nate Burkin, who was also Charlie Chaplin's attorney. When the case was finally settled in 1926, Jolson was ordered
to pay the director a mere $2,627.28, the amount of salary he had collected
before leaving for Europe. By then, Griffith had already worked with his
brother, Alfred Gray Griffith, to turn the Jolson vehicle into *His Darker Self*
(1924). The film starred Lloyd Hamilton as a white lawyer who puts on
blackface to clear a black man of murder (Goldman 130). So great was Jolson's star power—even in a medium in which he had yet to appear—that
several newspapers advertised the film as one in which Jolson was *supposed*
to star.

Although Griffith may have still been hoping that he would eventually
make a film with Jolson, it's also possible that the director himself succumbed to Jolson's appeal on at least one occasion. Griffith scholar Russell
Merritt has found what amounts to a fan letter written to Jolson by Griffith's attorney. Jolson probably provided complimentary tickets to Griffith
and his lawyer for a 1925 revival of *Big Boy*. The attorney wrote that Jolson's performance of "Keep Smiling at Trouble" moved both men to tears
(author's interview with Merritt, 12 August 2008).

The earliest surviving film footage of Jolson is a 1926 Vitaphone short
called *A Plantation Act*. Lee de Forest had developed a practical method for
simultaneously recording sound and image by connecting a camera to a
disc-cutting machine. For playback, a record-player worked in close synchronization with a movie projector. The system was far from perfect, as
those memorable parodic scenes in *Singin' in the Rain* (1952) attest; if the
record skipped, the synchronization was lost. But the process did allow for
the satisfying re-creation of a performance, much more so than the subsequent practice of pre-recording voices that may or not belong to performers who then lip-sync while the cameras roll. Jolson surely knew that his
highly spontaneous talent for connecting with audiences could now be
reproduced on film. He happily accepted an offer to appear in one of the
hundreds of short films that Warner Bros. was making with the new Vitaphone process.

In *A Plantation Act*, a blacked-up Jolson emerges from behind a cabin on
a primitive set meant to represent the rural, antebellum South. Cotton and
watermelons are growing in the foreground, and chickens are pecking
nearby. The background is a painting of a pastoral landscape. Jolson is wearing striped overalls, a tattered checked shirt, and an equally distressed straw
hat. But he emerges with a jaunty walk and a carefree grin. He immediately

begins singing "When the Red, Red Robin Comes Bob, Bob, Bobbin'
Along." (Michael Rogin observes that the song may have been the inspira-
tion for "Jack Robin," the stage name that Jolson's character adopts in *The
Jazz Singer* [53].) Like all three of the songs in the short film, "When the
Red, Red Robin" had received the Jolson treatment years earlier, and it is to
his credit that all three songs are still well known today. They might have

Jolson in blackface as he appeared in his first film, the Vitaphone short *A Plantation Act*
(1926). Publicity still. Courtesy of Jerry Ohlinger's Movie Materials Store.

been forgotten had Jolson not first brought them to life. As he sings about the bobbin' robin, his arms and legs are in constant motion, his hips swivel rhythmically, and his eyes bulge. When the music stops, he utters his signature phrases, "Wait a minute, folks" and "You ain't heard nothin' yet." He had long since made these words his own at the Winter Garden, and audiences would have been surprised if he did *not* speak them here and the next year in *The Jazz Singer*.

The next song in *A Plantation Act* is "April Showers," delivered at a slower tempo and with the highly emotional, pseudo-operatic, quavering-voice delivery that Jolson had perfected. Before he begins his third song, he again tells us to "wait a minute" and that we haven't heard anything yet. In an unusually long introduction, he adopts an epicene tone to justify singing a "mammy song" to those who consider the songs old-fashioned. He attempts to redeem the genre by insisting that even the famous Irish tenor John McCormack—Jolson calls him a "radio singer"—performs mammy songs. He then breaks into "Rock-a-Bye Your Baby with a Dixie Melody," beginning with a lighthearted, upbeat approach, but soon switching to his more melodramatic style, putting his fist on his heart and imploring the audience as if he were desperate for them to "sing that lullaby." He then speaks over the music, talking about his Mammy and how much she is loved by "Old Black Joe." After he has finished his third song he reappears for two curtain calls, each time after the shot fades to black. The first fade ends one long, unbroken shot of him in action singing the three songs. At his first curtain call, he bows and blows kisses. In the second he exaggerates the blowing of kisses, and when he grins sardonically at the camera there is an unmistakable air of contempt, completely incompatible with the character who had obsequiously apologized moments earlier for singing a mammy song. It's all over in ten minutes, but the Jolson film persona, with all its extreme and conflicting impulses, has been established.

A Plantation Act was one of several short subjects that preceded screenings of the first full-length film to be distributed with Vitaphone Sound. *Don Juan* (1926), with John Barrymore as the title character, was released with sound effects and a musical score, all recorded on discs packaged with the film. No one spoke in *Don Juan*, however. It was still done with intertitles. At this stage, Warner Bros. was not yet prepared to make a full commitment to sound film. But when the Jolson short was among the best received by audiences in that small group of theaters equipped with the Vitaphone system, a revolution was under way. Writing in the *New York World*, a critic embraced talking cinema while dismissing the film: "You may have the 'Don Juan.' Leave me the Vitaphone" (Hochheiser 23).

⭐⭐⭐⭐⭐ *The Jazz Singer*

Even before his success with the Vitaphone short, Jolson was so famous that an undergraduate at the University of Illinois knew his biography. Samson Raphaelson would later write some of the best films directed by Ernst Lubitsch—*Trouble in Paradise* (1931), *One Hour with You* (1932), *The Shop around the Corner* (1940), *Heaven Can Wait* (1943), and more—as well as Alfred Hitchcock's *Suspicion* (1941). As a college student he saw the road company production of *Robinson Crusoe, Jr.* in Urbana, Illinois, in 1917 (Carringer 11). He was, like so many others, completely taken with Jolson. He said that seeing Jolson perform was like watching "a duck hitting water" (Goldman 81).

Raphaelson knew that Al Jolson was born Asa Yoelson in Lithuania before his family moved to the United States (more precisely, Jolson was born in 1886 in a small, mostly Jewish village called Srednik, now part of Slovenia). The writer also knew that Jolson's father was a cantor, and that young Asa had left home to perform in vaudeville in spite of his father's profound disapproval. The boy also had an adoring mother, but she died when Asa was eight. With Jolson's biography in mind, Raphaelson wrote a short story called "The Day of Atonement," about a young man who runs away from home, passes into gentile society, and, just as he is on the verge of Broadway success, is called home on his big opening night to sing the Kol Nidre prayer on Yom Kippur, the Day of Atonement and the most sacred day in the Jewish calendar. The story was published in 1922 in *Everybody's* magazine.

Jolson himself read the story and had met Raphaelson. Before his aborted collaboration with D. W. Griffith in 1923, Jolson had even approached the director about working with him on a film version. But he also encouraged the young writer to turn the story into a play, even offering to help him see the show through to production. Although Jolson surely entertained fantasies of playing the lead role, when Raphaelson's play *The Jazz Singer* opened in Stamford, Connecticut, in July 1925, the part was played by George Jessel, a vaudevillian who was just beginning a career on the stage. The play eventually ran for a full season on Broadway and then toured the country for several months in 1926 and early 1927. Significantly, the play followed the plot of the short story by ending with the protagonist leaving show business and beginning a new life as a cantor. And although there were a few songs, it was a play, not a musical.

With the success of the Vitaphone shorts—Jolson's *Plantation Act* as well as many others—Warner Bros. was determined to make a full-length talking film. They chose *The Jazz Singer*, though at first the lead role in the film was to be played by Jessel, not Jolson. There are conflicting accounts, but Jessel probably alienated Warners with too many demands, including an unusually high salary. Jolson was happy to jump in when the offer came to him, and Warners paid him a total of $75,000 in installments throughout his time on the set.

Once Jolson was on board, the film became a musical. He would perform many of the songs that he had already made famous, just as he had done in the Vitaphone short. The one new song, written specifically for the film by Irving Berlin, was "Blue Skies," the tune that Jakie Rabinowitz/Jack Robin sings to his mother in one of the film's bizarrely incestuous scenes between Jolson and Eugenie Besserer. Another significant change was added at the last minute, presumably by one of the Warners. Alfred A. Cohn's shooting script for *The Jazz Singer* (published in Carringer 49–133) ends in much the same way as the play and Raphaelson's short story. At home with his mother and his dying father, Jack Robin is told that he will ruin himself as well as the producer if he walks out on opening night. Nevertheless, at the very end of the shooting script, while Jack is singing "Kol Nidre," his co-star Mary Dale (May McAvoy) says to the producer, "Don't you understand? It's his last time in there. He *has* to come back to us." The script then directs the producer to look at her in a "puzzled manner" and nod. The final image in the shooting script remained in the film: the ghost of Jack's father appears behind him and raises his hand in a blessing. Fade out. The jazz singer has found his true self and come home.

The "My Mammy" finale was added to the film to give it a more upbeat ending. After the ghost of Jack's father fades out of the picture, a title card reads, "The season passes—and time heals—the show goes on." We then see Jack back in show business. Earlier, when the producer had warned Jack about leaving the show, his line is even more emphatic than in the shooting script: "You'll queer yourself on Broadway—you'll never get another job." Mary literally hangs on his neck begging him to come back, asking, "Were you lying when you said your career came before *everything*?" But the film makes no real attempt to explain how Jack bounces back so quickly from walking out on an opening night. Suddenly he is alone on the stage of the Winter Garden Theatre singing directly to his adoring mother while the love-struck Mary looks on from the wings.

On the one hand, even though the plot does not explain Jack's return to the stage, the "My Mammy" finale makes perfect sense in terms of the conflicts the film has expressed with music, beginning when the young Jakie is caught singing "raggy time songs" in a beer hall, and continuing with many other musical moments such as the old cantor's instructions to a young pupil. Linda Williams has thoroughly explored this dialectic, pointing out that the film's songs come in matched pairs. Young Jakie sings the nostalgic "My Gal Sal" and then the upbeat minstrel tune "Waiting for the Robert E. Lee." At Coffee Dan's, Jack Robin sings the maudlin "Dirty Hands, Dirty Face" and then the bouncy "Toot, Toot, Tootsie." At home with his mother, he sings a lively, jazzy version of "Blue Skies" in stark contrast to the melodrama of "Mother of Mine, I Still Have You," the first song he sings in blackface. Unlike "Toot, Toot, Tootsie" and "Blue Skies," the final performance of "My Mammy" is not at all jazzy. According to Williams, it "triumphantly resolves the tensions between the musically new and the musically old, between the sexual liberty of syncopation and the familial constancy of Jewish sacred music" (147).

On the other hand, as one wag put it, the original ending of the script had to be changed because it's impossible to imagine Jolson giving up show business. In fact, Jolson's star identity makes the ending of *The Jazz Singer* much less incoherent. He was a white entertainer who performed as a black man. He was an immigrant Jew who spoke in a dialect that was pure American street argot. And he was extremely successful at invoking a plantation idyll that he could never have experienced. Why shouldn't Jakie/Jack have the love of a *shiksa* goddess, the congregation at a Lower East Side temple, and a cheering audience on Broadway, not to mention a father whose way of life he had completely renounced? There was never any question that he would have the unconditional love of his mother.

This model of all-embracing reconciliation is entirely compatible with American myths of inclusiveness, part of the still-widely shared conviction that options are eternally available in the New World. As Robert B. Ray has written, "Often, the movies' reconciliatory pattern concentrated on a single character magically embodying diametrically opposite traits. A sensitive violinist was also a tough boxer (*Golden Boy*); a boxer was a gentle man who cared for pigeons (*On the Waterfront*). A gangster became a coward because he was brave (*Angels with Dirty Faces*); a soldier became brave because he was a coward (*Lives of a Bengal Lancer*)" (58). The wildly successful Jolson, with none of his contradictions holding him back, was the perfect model for a film that definitively established the power of Hollywood's myth of inclusiveness.

The Jazz Singer was nevertheless a departure for Jolson, and not just because he was speaking lines in a film instead of on the stage. For one thing, he was playing a Jew, and for most of the film he was *not* in blackface. Although Jolson's blacked-up characters had numerous chances to express sadness in his stage vehicles, they had never encountered anything as profoundly distressing as what Jack Robin faces at the film's end. Many audiences were moved by *The Jazz Singer* because they understood what it means to choose between your own aspirations and the demands of family. Indeed, the film was not just Jolson's story; it was also that of many first-generation immigrants. It was also the story of the brothers Warner and the many other Jews who left behind an insular immigrant culture, married gentile women, and, as Neal Gabler has suggested, "invented Hollywood."

The film's success was also facilitated by Jolson's irrepressible need to improvise in the middle of a performance. Originally there was to be no talking in the film, only singing. On the first day of shooting with sound, he was to sing "Toot, Toot, Tootsie" at Coffee Dan's, where he first meets Mary Dale. But Jolson could not restrain himself, bursting out with the usual "Wait a minute" and "You ain't heard nothin' yet." He announces that he is going to sing and whistle "Toot, Toot, Toosie"; he then addresses his pianist Lou Silvers by name and tells him and the band what to do: "Now give it to 'em hot and heavy." Sam Warner, who was on the set, liked Jolson's ad-libbing and agreed that Jolson should once again talk as well as sing in the later scene with his mother when he returns home for the first time as an adult.

Warner and Jolson could not have known that they were setting up something momentous at the heart of *The Jazz Singer*. While Jolson sits at the piano ad-libbing, and as Eugenie Besserer desperately tries to hide her discomfort, the talkies are being born, the Jazz Age has reached its culmination, and the possibilities for ethnic assimilation are radically affirmed. The actors are arranged in the master shot so that the front door of the apartment is in the background but directly between Jolson and Besserer. Suddenly it opens and Jack's father (Warner Oland) shouts out his one and only syllable in the entire film: "Stop!" Any number of readings can be applied to this moment. Allegorically, the old order has asserted itself in hopes of stopping progress, whether it be the rise of jazz, the introduction of sound cinema, or young people's rejection of their parents' culture. Psychoanalytically, the scene represents the oedipally charged moment when the father, posed directly between Jolson and Besserer, attempts to reclaim the mother from a son who has violated taboo and approached her as an erotic object. (Michael Rogin is especially attentive to the sexual slang that Jack speaks to his mother, as when he asks her if she likes "that slappin' business" he has added to his piano playing [83].) And dramatically, this is the *coup de théâtre* when someone other than Jolson breaks into a scene and speaks for the first and only time in a film and then, at least temporarily, terminates all speech. After Oland's "Stop," the film switches to its Tchaikovskian nondiegetic score.

Audiences, however, had never seen and heard anything like it. Delivered in Jolson's hyperactive style, his stream of patter is ethnic humor at its most exuberant. Constantly in motion, he teases his mother, rolls his eyes, and deploys his own bizarre array of facial expressions as he jazzes it up with "Blue Skies." Writing about this scene in 1927, Robert Sherwood observed, "I for one suddenly realized that the end of the silent drama is in sight" (Carringer 41).

Much else can be said about this watershed moment in American cinema. For one thing, the father's wrath is the most important obstacle to Jack's success, and not just with his attempts to seduce his mother. At no point in the film does Jack Robin face antisemitism. The film completely elides the long history of Jew-hating and locates all conflict among the Jews themselves. In *The Jazz Singer* as well as in the vast majority of Hollywood films since, real problems that give Americans significant anxiety—whether they be war, racism, juvenile delinquency, mental illness, or antisemitism—are displaced into the struggles of individual characters. Unlike the larger problems, these struggles can be resolved. The old cantor will eventually give in and tell his son that he loves him. He may even come around to believing what the film has been saying all along, "that Jack's jazz singing is fundamentally an ancient religious impulse seeking expression in a modern, popular form" (Carringer 23). Or as the film itself states in its first title card, "Perhaps this plaintive, wailing song of jazz is, after all, the misunderstood utterance of a prayer." Rogin has gone even further in seeing the film as displacing not just antisemitism but white-on-black racism as well. In an advertisement for *The Jazz Singer*, the head of Jolson smiling in blackface overlaps slightly with a dolorous Jolson without makeup. Rather than address real problems of racial exclusion in the United States, the film locates the conflict within the body of a single performer, allowing him to express his own unique sorrows that are in turn resolved by the film.

In *The Jazz Singer*, blacking up is the unspoken solution to the unspoken problem of how the Jew can assimilate. A Jewish jazz singer has a better chance of success if, like the many Jews, Irish, and other white ethnics who worked as minstrels in the nineteenth and early twentieth century, he becomes more "white" by wearing the mask of a black man. As Susan Gubar phrases it in her imitation of Jolson's patter, blackface is the white ethnic's way of saying, "You thought those guys with beards and prayer shawls in the synagogue looked *verkocktah*, but wait a minute: at least they're not *schvartzehs*" (73). More specifically, in *The Jazz Singer*, Jolson puts on more than just a black mask. Playing his most emotionally charged scenes under cork, he has essentially become a new man. No wonder the

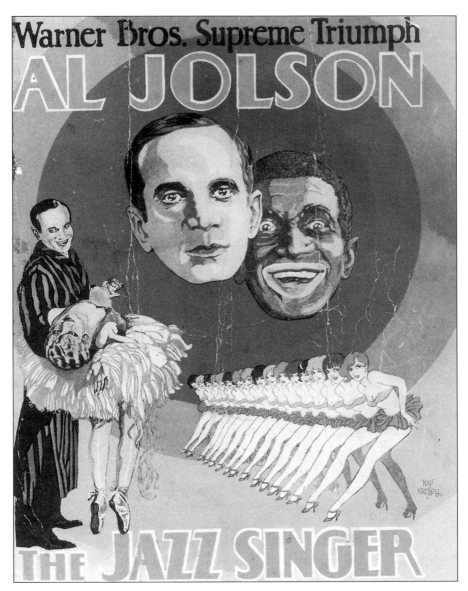

The notorious poster for *The Jazz Singer* (1927). Publicity still. Courtesy of Jerry Ohlinger's Movie Materials Store.

film is in no hurry the first time Jolson smears his face, ears, and neck with burnt cork. Critics regularly commented on the startling effect that this transformation produced. The sexual dimensions of blacking up are underscored by the presence of Mary Dale, herself in the elaborate masquerade of the showgirl.

The scene in which Mary watches Jack blacken his face raises other questions as well. Jack may be in special need of disguise at this moment because he has just been visited by Yudelson, the *kibitzer* from his old congregation, and it is now obvious that Jack is Jewish. Could it be that Mary Dale is only now making this discovery? And what about Mary herself? Is "Mary Dale" as much a made-up name as "Jack Robin"? At Coffee Dan's she was a brunette, but by the end of the film she has become a blonde. Has she been passing for something she is not, just like Jack? Is the showgirl outfit, with its huge feathered headdress and scanty blouse, as much a disguise as Jack's blackface? These questions may have been too much a part of the industry's own secrets to be answered in the film. Regardless, the film was a hit. It earned $3.5 million nationwide and was one of the top box-office attractions of 1927. Jolson was a bigger star than ever.

★★★★★ Jolson's Career from 1928 to 1930

Eager to capitalize on the formula that worked so well with *The Jazz Singer*, Warners went right to work on *The Singing Fool*. Like *The Jazz Singer*, the film was very much a hybrid. There were multiple scenes with intertitles instead of dialogue, even when Jolson was onscreen. Of course, Jolson could always be heard when he was singing. If *The Jazz Singer* was about 20 percent a talkie, *The Singing Fool* was about 40 percent. The plot of *The Singing Fool* strongly recalled that of the earlier film, casting Jolson as an aspiring singer who works his way to the top with the help of a more established female performer. There are plenty of backstage shots with chorus girls hustling about. And instead of mourning the death of a father, the film wrings pathos out of the Jolson's character's marriage to an unfaithful woman and then more fulsomely out of the death of his three-year-old son.

A blind person would have known it was a Jolson film from the moment *The Singing Fool* opens with the sounds of "Rock-a-Bye Your Baby with a Dixie Melody," one of several songs that he essentially owned. The action begins in a restaurant called Blackie Joe's, a clear echo of Coffee Dan's. When the owner calls for a new table, a waiter appears, but the table he carries in front of him covers his face. The table is lowered, and as the nondiegetic score quotes directly from "My Mammy," the face of Jolson appears, smiling broadly at the camera as if he were sharing a joke with the audience. "You knew it was me all along, didn't you?" his smile seems to say.

For some reason Jolson's character in *The Singing Fool*, Al Fuller, is never explicitly identified as Jewish. But regardless of Al's ethnicity, as in *The Jazz Singer* he moves from extreme vitality to the depths of depression,

Jolson in his most successful film, *The Singing Fool* (1928). Publicity still. Courtesy of Jerry Ohlinger's Movie Materials Store.

always in a style much more appropriate to the stage than to the screen. In his first singing scene, he is once again the ingratiating overachiever as he addresses the customers in the restaurant. He repeats his catch phrases "Wait a minute" and "You ain't heard nothin' yet" multiple times, adding several repetitions of "Hold your horses" as well. Later, when his character has become a star, he repeatedly tells the audience, "I'm gonna sing a thousand songs tonight."

The great success of the film was probably due to Jolson's scenes with young Davey Lee, whose performance as Sonny Boy must have had considerable appeal in 1928 but is nearly unwatchable today now that the craft of the child actor has been so thoroughly professionalized. A large degree of credit (or blame) must also go to the song "Sonny Boy," which Jolson sings to young Lee and then to an audience at the bathetic finale after the child has died. The song has much in common with "Mother, I Still Have You" in *The Jazz Singer*, and Jolson gives both the full emotional wallop. According to his biographers, "Sonny Boy" was written in haste and in jest by the team of DeSylva, Brown, and Henderson. The three would eventually write "You're the Cream in My Coffee," "Button Up Your Overcoat," and "The

Thrill Is Gone," among many others. For Jolson they would create "I'm Sitting on Top of the World" and "It All Depends on You," both of which he performs in *The Singing Fool*. But when he was not satisfied with the song the trio had written for his scenes with Davey Lee, he asked them for a show-stopping tearjerker that a father sings to his dying child. This request sent the songwriters into fits of hysterical laughter. It took them one hour to produce "Sonny Boy," a song into which they dumped every maudlin cliché they could blurt out in between bursts of laughter. They had to call a bellboy to mail the sheet music to Jolson because they were too embarrassed to carry it out of the hotel on their own. Jolson, however, loved it. So did audiences. It became the first disc to sell a million copies. Eventually it would sell three million (Freedland 133). What was it that H. L. Mencken once said about underestimating the American people?

Another fascinating similarity between *The Singing Fool* and *The Jazz Singer* is the presence and nonpresence of African American performers. In both films, a single black woman in a maid's costume appears briefly during one of the backstage scenes. In *The Jazz Singer* the only other black people are Jolson's impersonations. But toward the end of *The Singing Fool*, we find a black valet in Al's dressing room. As was usually the case in films of this era, even in films without Jolson, the black man is asleep on the job. Al is not angry, but he mischievously tickles the porter's face with bristles from a broom. When he awakens, Al congratulates him on his ability to sleep. With Joel Chandler Harris diction, the valet replies, "When a man's sleepin,' he ain't gettin' in no trouble." Al agrees but adds that he should also be careful where he sleeps. Later, intentionally or not, the porter is a silent presence when a blacked-up Al is about to take his place on the stage for the final performance of "Sonny Boy." As Arthur Knight has observed, placing a *real* black man next to Jolson in blackface might have raised embarrassing questions about the practice of whites imitating blacks. But for some audiences it might have actually authenticated Jolson's impersonation by casting the black porter as silently supportive (Knight 59).

Jolson is only in blackface during these final moments of *The Singing Fool*. Al arrives at the theater, inconsolable at the loss of his son. Even though it's still Jolson, there is real doubt whether or not he will have the strength to perform before the audience. A stage manager tells him that it might make him feel better if he goes on. As in the previous film, the camera lingers as Jolson applies burnt cork to his face, ears, and neck. Once in blackface, Al completely gives himself over to his emotions. Although tears are running down his face as he sings "Sonny Boy," he seems to take heart as he "sees" the image of his child superimposed over a shot of the audience. He even smiles as he sings the line, "I don't mind gray skies, if you make 'em blue, Sonny Boy." Does Al's impersonation of a black man turn him into someone who can grieve with all his heart but also take simple pleasure in memories? And does it give him license to sing with an intensity he never exhibited in scenes when he performed without burnt cork? Regardless, his performance of "Sonny Boy" appears to have taken a toll on Jolson's character, and he collapses when the curtain closes.

The Singing Fool was Jolson's most popular film, but he immediately faded as a film star. Actors were adopting more naturalistic acting styles for the new realism that the sound cinema suddenly made possible, and of course Hollywood was populated with actors who, unlike Jolson, had learned how to act in front of a camera, not in front of cheering crowds. On stage, Jolson could look right past the other actors, ignoring them while he appealed directly to the audience. In his film roles, he retained the practice, seldom looking directly at the other actor in a two-shot. He is always looking off to the side, even when he is speaking lines directed specifically to the character. It's bad enough that he's overacting; he seems to be emoting toward cue cards just outside the range of the camera.

Say It with Songs (1929) is in some ways even more depressing than *The Singing Fool*. If audiences loved to see Jolson suffer, and if they did not like watching him in blackface, this was the film for them. As boxer turned radio singer Joe Fuller, Jolson spends a large stretch of the film in prison after he strikes a friend who made overtures to his wife. Furious about this betrayal, the former pugilist throws just one punch. His would-be rival hits his head on a lamppost and dies. Convicted of manslaughter and imprisoned, Joe tries to cheer up his fellow inmates, at one point singing several choruses of "Why Can't You." The performances are supposed to be inspirational, but Jolson does not inspire.

An even bigger source of pathos in *Say It with Songs* is Davey Lee, now five years old and reappearing as "Little Pal," the Jolson character's ultracute son. Although the child doesn't die in *Say It with Songs*, he is run over by a car. At first the child is paralyzed and deaf, but after an operation he recovers all his faculties except his speech. As in *The Singing Fool*, Jolson pulls out all the stops when he puts the child on his knee and sings "Little Pal." And he does it without burnt cork. Although there is no blackface in *Say It with Songs*, there is an early scene in which Jolson's character acknowledges his Jewishness. In a clear reference to the real-life Jolson, Joe is asked by the bosses at his radio station to sing "another Mammy song." He agrees but he facetiously rejects the lyrics "I'll smother my mother with kisses when I get back to Tennessee" in favor of "I'll smother my father with *bedushkas* when I get to Odessa." The Jewish humor returns at the happy ending when, joking that he is having a private conversation with his wife while performing on his radio, Joe tells her he wants to come home to an elaborate dinner complete with ham and eggs. He then catches himself and adds, "Just the eggs, never mind the ham."

Jennifer Fleeger has ingeniously argued that the lack of blackface in *Say It with Songs* was part of Warner Bros.' defense of their continued reliance on the Vitaphone sound-on-disc system. While other studios were moving toward sound-on-film, the technology that would soon become the industry standard, Warners stayed with the system that had brought them great success, including the two hugely popular vehicles for Jolson. In a scene that must have been written specifically to endorse sound-on-disc, we see Little Pal lying awake in bed, still unable to speak. When he hears the sound of his father's voice on a phonograph record, the film superimposes an image of Jolson next to the child's bed. Seamlessly, the song on the record is picked up by Jolson's image. Believing that his father is in the room singing to him, Little Pal suddenly regains the power of speech. The film is suggesting that the sound of Jolson's voice on disc is so authentic that it passes for the real thing and even produces a medical miracle. The authenticity of Jolson on disc is further enhanced by the suggestion that other technologies for reproducing the voice are somehow suspect. Jolson does his most heartfelt singing when he sings without amplification to the other prisoners and of course when he sings "in person" to Little Pal on a disc. The fact that the man who propositioned Joe's wife was an executive in the radio industry further demeans a technological system that is supposedly inferior to Vitaphone. Significantly, RKO *Radio* Pictures at this time had already switched to sound-on-film.

Press books for *Say It with Songs* made much of Jolson's abandonment of blackface. He had matured from a comic to "an emotional actor," they said. The emotional authenticity that he gained when he blacked up to sing "Mother of Mine, I Still Have You" in *The Jazz Singer* and "Sonny Boy" in *The Singing Fool* now resided in the Vitaphone technology. But as Fleeger points out, Warners' gambit was a failure. Critics panned the film and audiences stayed away. The response of the unnamed critic at *Time* magazine was typical: "Jolson sings well, although without burnt cork, which he really needs" (19 August 1929, 39).

After the failure of *Say It with Songs*, Jolson starred in two films in 1930, both of them striking out in new directions. Actually, the new directions led backward toward his previous career on the stage. *Mammy* cast him as the star of a traveling minstrel troupe and gave him several opportunities to bring to the cinema some of the successful vaudeville bits that had followed him to Broadway. And of course, blackface returned. *Big Boy* was even more retro, for the first time bringing Jolson's can't-fail portrayal of Gus and one of his old stage vehicles to the big screen.

If nothing else, *Mammy* provides a good history lesson on minstrelsy, the most popular form of American entertainment for more than a hundred years, even if we're all too embarrassed to acknowledge it today. We actually see the minstrel troupe marching into a town where they are about to occupy the local theater, and we get an extended representation of a minstrel show, with its crowd of blacked-up whites arrayed across the stage. The stars or "endmen" are accurately identified as Tambo and Mr. Bones (Jolson's role), and the Interlocutor, the only character not in blackface, is at the center. But more so than any of Jolson's films to date, *Mammy* is a series of sketches barely held together by plot. Surely the most memorable scene in the film has Jolson and several other members of the troupe in outfits clearly associated with the operas of Richard Wagner and Giuseppe Verdi. In this bizarre garb they sing, "Yes, We Have No Bananas" in a broad parody of high opera. The plot, such as it is, has Al falsely accused of attempted murder. He hides out with his mother before she inspires him to do the right thing and give himself up. Returning to the scene of the crime, he discovers that the real perpetrator has confessed. A romance plot between Jolson and a winsome blonde (Lois Moran) never really takes off. As at the finale of *The Jazz Singer*, Moran gazes at Jolson singing his big number, but by this time she has become engaged to Westy, the Interlocutor. Also as in *The Jazz Singer*, the real love affair in *Mammy* is between Jolson and his mother (Louise Dresser).

In *Big Boy* Jolson returned to his roots, playing Gus, the character that had brought him so much success in so many shows at the Winter Garden. In the film, Gus is a would-be jockey who takes a job as a groom in the stables of a rich Kentucky family's plantation. He is most devoted to a horse named Big Boy. Audiences are asked to accept Jolson as an actual African American right up until the final moments when he suddenly appears as himself. Even more so than *Mammy*, *Big Boy* is a set of songs and vaudeville riffs with only the barest wisp of a plot to pull it all together. The songs seldom come in a logical order, as when Gus, for no particular reason, joins a group of singing blacks sitting on the grass and leads them in a version of "Go Down Moses (Let My People Go)" in which he seems to be channeling Paul Robeson.

Each incident in *Big Boy* provides an opportunity for Jolson to display his talent with words and music, even if they occur in no discernible order. For example, when the mustachioed villain, "Bully John" Bagby (Noah

Beery), arrives at the plantation, he abducts Annabel (Claudia Dell), the beautiful daughter of the plantation owner. Gus takes off after them on horseback, quickly returning with an unharmed Annabel and the perpetrator tied up with rope. And yet a few minutes later Gus is expelled from the plantation for a mild transgression of which he was not at all guilty. With no transitional scenes showing him moving to the city or hunting for jobs, he is working as a waiter in a large urban restaurant and trading comic insults with customers. By the end, he returns to the plantation to ride Big Boy to victory. The horse race is presented so ineptly that we don't even see the horses crossing the finish line.

The ending is even more incoherent. With the villains punished and the just rewarded, Gus turns around and with a quick lap dissolve is replaced by the smiling Jolson, his face no longer black. As the camera pulls back, we see that he is on a stage set in front of a live audience. As in *Say It with Songs*, he takes a jab at his own persona. When he offers to sing "Sonny Boy," the audience starts to walk out. After crying out, "Wait a minute, wait a minute," he then recapitulates "Tomorrow Is Another Day," which he had earlier sung to another blacked-up character as a lesson in how to deal with trouble. At the finale the song is an anthem for a jokey stage performer rather than for a happy-go-lucky stable boy.

☆☆★★★ Jolson under Cork

Early in his career, Al Jolson worked exclusively with his brother Harry. Mostly they did dialect humor, making fun of Jewish immigrants with an incomplete grasp of the English language. They labored for several years without much success until they managed to impress a songwriter named Ren Shields, undoubtedly the most important figure in Jolson's early career. Shields was instrumental in landing the boys a good booking at a vaudeville house on Fulton Street in Brooklyn. There they met James Francis Dooley, who regularly performed as a blackface comedian at the theater. Seeing that Al lacked confidence on stage, Dooley suggested that he try blackface. Wearing burnt cork was essentially an elaborate costume, the older comedian explained, and it would help him get into character (Goldman 36). By all accounts, Jolson was completely transformed by blackface. He suddenly felt spontaneous, transgressive, and carefree. He became Al Jolson. Blackface would always be an essential part of his work, more so onstage than in films.

The harshest critic of blackface in the cinema is probably Susan Gubar, who unites *The Birth of a Nation* and *The Jazz Singer* in a chapter entitled

"Spirit Murder in the Movies: Blackface Lynchings." She sees blackface in the Jolson vehicle as a means of emasculating the hero, turning him into a pathetic momma's boy, even more pathetic than the unblacked-up Jakie Rabinowitz who is devoted to his mother and expelled by his father. Of Jolson in blackface she writes, "His outstretched arms, his pleading on bended knee, his passionate declaration of loyalty and love, his whitened and widened mouth, his effort to gain the approval of his mother and girlfriend. All these unman as effectively as hypermasculinization and castration do in Griffith's film" (70–71).

For me, the most useful work for understanding blackface and what it could do for Jolson is Eric Lott's *Love and Theft: Blackface Minstrelsy and the American Working Class*. The book is a thorough inquiry into the ambivalent view of blacks that white Americans held in the first half of the nineteenth century and in many ways continue to hold today. Although minstrelsy allowed whites to indulge their contempt and even hatred for blacks, Lott argues that white people in the early nineteenth century, especially working-class males, regarded black men as sexual role models: the minstrel shows regularly played to white obsessions with the supposed phallic power of black men. For the white minstrel man, "to put on the cultural forms of 'blackness' was to engage in a complex affair of manly mimicry. . . . To wear or even enjoy blackface was literally, for a time, to become black, to inherit the cool, virility, humility, abandon, or *gaîté de cœur* that were the prime components of white ideologies of black manhood" (Lott 52). Lott could be speaking of Jolson, who discovered the power of blackface at an early age and never gave it up. When he dances as Gus in *Big Boy*, he is more uninhibited than in any of his other films. And although Gubar sees blackface as emasculation in *The Jazz Singer*, there is no mistaking the flirtatious sexuality that Jolson directs at Mary Dale as he blacks up.

Lott also connects white fascination with black men to nineteenth-century ethnic and class anxiety. Significantly, many minstrel performers were Irish immigrants, perhaps the one ethnic group in America whose members could identify with the powerlessness and poverty of blacks during the early decades of the nineteenth century. Minstrel songs in the North, especially those that expressed nostalgia for the plantation or "Old Folks at Home," were easily conflated with the Irishman's sentimental longing for his own homeland (191). In addition, "blackface acts had the effect of promoting socially insecure Irishmen (actors as well as audiences), an 'Americanizing' ritual by which they distanced themselves from the people they parodied" (96). During harsh economic times, white working-class males of all ethnicities found consoling pleasures in watching counterfeit black men. The working man, who frequently saw himself as a "wage-slave," his masculinity in question, may have taken some comfort in the minstrel man's mimicking of the *real* slave who seems oblivious to hard times and indefatigable in his sexuality.

The case was very similar for recently arrived Jews, who, like the Irish, also worked in minstrelsy. Jolson was definitely not the first. Michael Rogin has applied the research on minstrelsy to the American cinema in general and to Jolson in particular. Like Gubar, he connects *The Birth of a Nation* with *The Jazz Singer*, but he adds an earlier film, *Uncle Tom's Cabin* (1902), and a later one, *Gone with the Wind* (1939), to create a sequence of crucial documents in cinema history, all of them relying on the "surplus symbolic value" of black Americans to connect with large audiences (73). Like Lott's minstrel man in the nineteenth century, Jolson's Jack Robin acquires a more overt sexuality at the same time that he has eased his path to assimilation by concealing his Jewishness under cork. Rogin is highly critical of what Lott calls minstrelsy's "dialectic of romance and repulsion" (Lott 86). For Rogin there is a great deal more theft than love: "The film does no favors to blacks" (Rogin 80). The blacked-up Jewish minstrel in *The Jazz Singer* is neither a jazz singer nor black. Rogin argues that the project of the film is to bring together an assimilating Jew with a gentile woman, a goal achieved more easily by momentarily stealing African American sexuality. Just as important, the film covers over the material on which much of anti-semitism was built. By somehow suggesting that Jolson had a southern mammy, films like *The Jazz Singer* counteracted myths of "the ambitious, rootless, cosmopolitan Jew, the anti-Semitic turn taken by agrarian nostalgia in the Jazz Age" (Rogin 109).

Writing at least partially in response to Rogin, Linda Williams rethinks Jolson's blackface, largely in terms of her ongoing research on the centrality of melodrama to American entertainment. For Williams, white Americans tend to conceive of race relations primarily in terms of exaggerated virtue and villainy and the staging of innocence; in other words, as melodrama. Blacks are either heroically suffering models of moral excellence, like Harriet Beecher Stowe's Uncle Tom, or vicious defilers of white women, like the renegade Gus in Griffith's *Birth of a Nation*. Williams designates these categories as Tom and anti-Tom, both of which comfortably accommodate a large body of melodramatic books, plays, and films. Rather than demonize one and exalt the other, Williams sees Tom and anti-Tom as two sides of the same melodramatic coin that feed off each other and are still with us today. She convincingly presents the media treatment of the Rodney King beating in 1991 as the creation of a Tom figure and the handling of O.J. Simpson's 1997 murder trial as an anti-Tom spectacle.

Williams also explains the crucial importance of black music to white Americans, especially in films such as *The Jazz Singer*: "white characters acquire virtue by musically expressing a suffering that is recognizable as 'black'" (137). Rogin sees Jolson blacking up in order to hide his Jewishness, assimilate, and then become more white. At no point does he pay back a debt to real blacks. For Williams, there is a more complex connection between Jews and blacks. "*The Jazz Singer*'s achievement was to take another group unfamiliar to dominant mass culture as objects of sympathy—recently emigrated, rapidly assimilating Jews—and to ennoble their travails of assimilation through association with the by now thoroughly conventionalized afflictions of slaves" (148).

Williams's formulation may help explain why Jolson was spared any real criticism for blacking up in the first half of the twentieth century. White liberals mostly assumed that blackface was another instance of cross-racial sympathy, at least before contemporary notions of race-consciousness were formed during World War II and its immediate aftermath. Indeed, blackface performance disappears almost completely from the American cinema in the early 1950s, most notably in the 1952 remake of *The Jazz Singer*, released by Warner Bros. to celebrate the twenty-fifth anniversary of the original film. As the title character in the 1952 film, Danny Thomas never wears blackface. (In the 1980 remake of *The Jazz Singer*, Neil Diamond does in fact black up, but only after an African American singing group insists that he substitute for an imprisoned member of their group.)

We can never really know what actual African Americans thought about Jolson and blackface. Arthur Knight, however, has come to some conclusions after an exhaustive reading of black newspapers. Of Jolson's appearance with Cab Calloway in *The Singing Kid* (1938), he writes, "Jolson's meaning for African Americans might not have been clear in 1938, but few blacks seem to have doubted that he and the range of complex practices he embodied had a meaning, one that had to do with African American culture and one that they should actively attempt to extract and (re)shape" (Knight 81). Even earlier, in 1927, this is exactly what happened when *The Jazz Singer* played at Harlem's Lafayette Theatre. Black Americans in the audience cried during the screening, and the black press was enthusiastic. On the one hand, the *Amsterdam News* called it "one of the greatest pictures ever produced" and wrote of Jolson, "Every colored performer is proud of him" (Rogin 196). On the other hand, the owners of the Lafayette Theatre did more than just show the film. Because the theater was not equipped with Vitaphone technology, they invited a local cantor to sing "Kol Nidre" and the other holy chants, but they brought in a black singer named Willie Jackson to perform Jolson's numbers (Rogin 197).

Jolson may not have enjoyed hearing another performer replacing his voice, but the spectacle at the Lafayette is entirely consistent with the Jolson persona, itself a crazy quilt of substitutions and appropriations. Asking us to see Jolson as much more than a blackface minstrel, Linda Williams insists that we actually listen to him. His style of speaking is an authentic, working-class patois, not just a white imitation of Negro dialect. It is Jewish, Irish, and Lower East Side with echoes of minstrelsy, Tin Pan Alley, and opera (Williams 145). Lhamon goes a step further, arguing for a richer identity in Jolson's blackface. Lhamon takes issue with Rogin's argument that Jolson is simply "replacing" black people. "Assimilation is negotiated in a moving ratio that always retains traces of the previous identity. *The Jazz Singer* shows this process in exceptional detail. The film figures it by the act of blacking up. Indeed, blackface is the means by which a good bit of Atlantic acculturation has negotiated a compounded identity, fuller than replacement" (108).

One scene in particular reveals Jolson's "compounded identity" in all its contradictions and desperate thrusts at assimilation. *Big Boy* was the only film in which he played Gus, the black trickster who had been essential to his stage success. In this film, Gus is cowardly, confident, despairing, sarcastic, maudlin, insulting, enterprising, and consoling. In the scene with Bully John Bagby, Jolson runs through all these positions in just a few minutes. When Bagby first arrives, Gus is with Tucker, a character played by another blacked-up white actor, Tom Wilson. As far as I can tell, Wilson is the only other white actor in the film who wears blackface, and although Jolson has conversations with a few African American actors in *Big Boy*, his character seems closer to Tucker than to anyone else.

Bagby, who has already identified himself as "The Tornado of New Orleans" and "The Fire Eater," belligerently addresses Gus as "Ink Spot" and demands that he dust off his boots. Incensed, Gus tells Bagby that he is a free man and that he won't do it. Bagby points a six-shooter at Gus's stomach and once again demands that he clean his boots. Gus immediately becomes servile and smiles broadly, saying, "Why didn't you say you wanted your boots dusted off? I never heard ya, no suh!" While cleaning Bagby's boots, Gus engages in a kind of call and response with the braggart. As Bagby orates each of his achievements, Gus throws in a short comment. With Bagby only a few feet away, Tucker upbraids Gus for kowtowing to a white man, telling him that he's a free man and that he has the Constitution on his side. Gus responds, "When you got a gun in your abDOmen, ha ha, you ain't got no constitution." When Bagby says, "Hey, you black soul," Gus turns to Tucker and says, "He must mean you. I'm a Creole." Bagby tells Gus that he is talking too much and that he put a bullet through the throat of the last man who talked too much. Gus replies, "From now on, I'm a clam." After Bagby tells Gus that he is a member of the "Night Riders of the South," Gus fiddles nervously with his hat and asks innocently, "Are you paid-up, Mr. Bagby?" This infuriates Bagby who says, "Where I come from, we string up alligator bait like you." He then turns to his manservant and says, "Remind me to horse whip him tonight at six o'clock." Bagby departs, leaving Gus to engage in a kind of minstrel show dialogue with Tucker, trading insults and then consoling each other with biblical aphorisms. Alternately terrified and indignant at Bagby's threats, Gus finally breaks into a chorus of "Tomorrow Is Another Day." Later, of course, Gus will have his revenge, doing to Bagby what he threatened to do to Gus.

In the Bully John Bagby scene, *Big Boy* directly confronts the issue of white racism and even acknowledges the reality of lynching. At least at first, Jolson behaves like a powerless victim of racial violence. But Noah Beery plays Bagby with such bluster and overstatement that it's difficult to take anything he says seriously, and the background music suggests that the scene is purely comic. The fact that threats are made to a blacked-up minstrel figure further denies the real violence that white men were still perpetrating with impunity. Indeed, if Gus is the *servus dolosus* of Roman comedy, Bagby is the *miles gloriosus*, the boasting soldier, constantly making threats but always outsmarted and thwarted. The film makes the actions of the Ku Klux Klan part of a series of idle threats.

Just as the film asserts and disavows the worst excesses of American racism, so Jolson claims and disavows his various identities, most notably when he briefly claims to be a Creole, still another role in a long list. As Gus, he both is and is not a black man, just as he both is and is not an actor. Thus he can switch back and forth between defiance and servility, pathos and comedy. Bagby, his foil, hits the same note again and again, thus freeing up Jolson to adopt all these positions at will. *Big Boy* is about a scrappy black man who consistently overcomes adversity in a world where violence and injustice are always looming. But at the conclusion, Jolson appears as himself and assures the audience that the villains aren't really villains and that the actor who played an English jockey was neither an Englishman nor a jockey. He may also be reassuring them that his black character was not really overpowering and ridiculing whites. It's even possible that he's telling black people not to be insulted because it was all make-believe.

Also in the finale, Jolson recapitulates his introduction to "Tomorrow Is Another Day" along with the song itself. Originally, Gus had said that his Mammy used to sing the song to him. As himself, Jolson says that he heard the song from his grandfather, who he says was named Moishe Pippick. Before he says the last name, he loudly pops the first "P" in Pippick. Talking his way through the last chorus of the song, he switches character again, becoming a white-face version of the minstrel longing for his "old Kentucky home." He rhapsodizes about going back to his "little house on the hill in Kentucky" to see his Mammy. He says he sees her at the door of his house, but then he switches once more, turning the speech into a Jewish joke when he spots a big ham in the window of his house. "That ain't my house," he says. And the film ends.

Whether as Gus, as a minstrel, as a Jewish entertainer, or as himself, Jolson both embraces and disavows these identities, always with so much glee that we are caught up in it, even if we're not entirely sure what it all means. In a confessional moment, Lhamon says that he finds Jolson's work "nakedly earnest and poignant" (103). The Jolson of *The Jazz Singer* and *The Singing Fool*, his two huge successes, was much more coherent. Movie audiences could respond to an ambitious young man facing family crises. The Jolson of the Winter Garden—the Jolson who was Gus until the man behind the mask broke character and talked to the audience as intimates—could not negotiate the transition to the screen. As a film, *Big Boy* was not a hit. Neither were the films he made in the 1930s. As Andrew Sarris pointed out (39–41), Jolson made talking pictures a reality only to become one of their first victims.

10 ☆☆☆☆☆☆☆☆☆☆☆

African American Stardom Inside and Outside of Hollywood

Ernest Morrison, Noble Johnson, Evelyn Preer, and Lincoln Perry

PAULA J. MASSOOD

If it is true, as Richard Dyer suggests, that stars "articulate what it is to be human in society," what do we make of the almost whole-sale exclusion of African American performers from Hollywood star dis-course of the 1920s? What does it mean, in effect, to discuss stars at a time when most black performers were not even credited for the small roles they

Noble Johnson, independent filmmaker and Hollywood actor. Collection of the author.

played in studio productions? Indeed, if they were credited, it was often for roles such as Uncle Toms and Mammies that denied the full range of black humanity. There were only two choices open to African American performers in the film industry at this time: Hollywood or the independent "race film" industry that produced films for black audiences and exhibited them in mostly segregated venues. The transition to sound also affected the involvement of black performers in Hollywood and the race film industry. Since star personas are as much a product of the studio's marketing department as they are of the individuals themselves, it is essential to consider the ways in which both mainstream and African American newspapers presented narratives of "Black Hollywood."

★★★★★ Silent-Era Hollywood: Pickaninnies and Noble Savages

With the proper handling . . . we could soon develop in our race a rival to Mary Pickford, Douglas Fairbanks, Charles Chaplin, and Rudolph Valentino.
—*Baltimore Afro-American*, 11 June 1927

In many ways, African American participation in film during the twenties was influenced by tropes that had been solidified a decade earlier in D. W. Griffith's *The Birth of a Nation* (1915). To be sure, Griffith himself relied upon a racial mythology that preexisted the cinema and that had been transferred from page and stage to screen at cinema's beginnings. Griffith's infamous epic of antebellum bliss and Reconstruction-era devastation was built upon caricatures that ranged from the black brute and the dangerous mulatto to docile Uncle Toms and Mammy figures. Borrowing from vaudeville and minstrel performance, his black characters were played by white performers in blackface, with only inconsequential bit parts filled by African American extras.

This situation did not change significantly over the next decade, even in the wake of black soldiers' distinguished service during World War I and what is now called the Great Migration. The African American populations of cities like Chicago, Detroit, and New York increased rapidly, as rural black migrants, looking for better living conditions and an escape from southern racism and peonage, flocked to northern industrial centers. During this time, neighborhoods like New York's Harlem became a symbol of African American artistry, industry, and modernity as young writers, artists, musicians, and dancers were drawn to its streets, theaters, and salons, flush with hope that they would finally be accepted by white America. This was the era of Alain Locke's "New Negro," and yet Hollywood did not incorporate these larger social and political dynamics into its stories.[1] "As late as the mid-twenties," argues Thomas Cripps, "major Negro roles went to white men in blackface. Not until after 1925 would a small cadre of Los Angles Negroes replace the old white actors" (118).

Donald Bogle concurs with Cripps and argues that during the early part of the decade the most visible black performers in Hollywood were children associated with the "Our Gang" series. In fact, by mid-decade, no adult had yet achieved the level of stardom of some of the series' black child actors (Bogle 41). In some ways, such prejudicial casting made sense, for the "Sunshine Sammys" (Ernest Morrison), "Pineapples" (Eugene Jackson), "Buckwheats" (Billie Thomas), "Farinas" (Allen Clayton Hoskins), and "Stymies" (Matthew Beard) drew from one of the nation's most enduring stereotypes, the pickaninny. Based in part on Topsy, from Harriet Beecher Stowe's *Uncle Tom's Cabin* (1852), the pickaninny figure was a well-established character on stage and screen by the 1920s. In fact, Stowe's novel was well known throughout the late nineteenth and early twentieth centuries through serialization and numerous stage and screen adaptations in which Topsy, following minstrel traditions, was played by a white performer in blackface.

As Sunshine Sammy, Ernest Morrison continued this tradition, first as a sidekick to comedians Harold Lloyd and Harry "Snub" Pollard, and later as one of the original members in the "Our Gang" series produced by Hal Roach. And yet Morrison was an anomaly at the time, partly because he appeared in films at a very early age. His first credit dates to 1916, when he would have been three or four years old (although some say he started in film as an infant). By 1919 he became the first black actor to sign with a studio when he was offered a contract with Hal Roach Studios.

Morrison's early work was mostly as an adjunct to Lloyd and Pollard, but in 1921 Roach cast the nine-year-old as the lead in *The Pickaninny*, the first in a planned series of shorts featuring the Sunshine Sammy character, who had gained popularity as Lloyd's sidekick in films such as *Haunted Spooks* (1920). The series was short-lived, however, because Roach was informed by exhibitors "that mainstream theatres would not show shorts featuring a colored star" (Bogle 33). Regardless of his age and his roles as a harmless, comedic pickaninny, white audiences, or at least the exhibitors who catered to them, refused to support an African American lead—a lesson that Bert Williams had learned a decade earlier when the popular Ziegfeld Follies performer tried unsuccessfully to transfer his talent from stage to screen. Morrison's role in the "Our Gang" series followed the very next year. In the series he was part of an ensemble cast of children—which included Peggy Cartwright, Jackie Condon, and Mickey Daniels—the only black in an early version of cinematic diversity (although the ensemble soon added Allen "Farina" Hoskins). As such, he proved to be less of a threat to white audiences.

The black press celebrated Morrison's success, and details of his business relationship with Roach were touted as an example of Hollywood's inclusion of black performers. In one example, the *California Eagle* reported on Morrison's five-year contract and "yearly salary of $10,000," suggesting that it was "indeed pleasing to the thousands of admirers of the seven-year-old Race [*sic*] lad who is now the highest salaried member of the Race movies today" (qtd. in Bogle 33). Morrison was treated like a celebrity, with the black press following his activities and roles in detail. He himself remembered being treated as the first black movie personality to be featured in fan magazines and the first black to become a millionaire because of the movies.[2] While the latter claim is difficult to substantiate, Morrison stayed with the "Our Gang" series until 1924 before moving on to a successful and lucrative career on the vaudeville stage. He made brief returns to the screen, most notably in the 1940s as part of the "East Side Kids" series produced by Monogram Pictures. In this, as in his previous film work, he was the sole African American performer in an all-white though ethnically marked cast.

While Sunshine Sammy may have been "the most well-known Negro actor in the early twenties" (Leab, *Sambo* 55), Noble Johnson was the performer who worked most consistently, if often inconspicuously. Johnson's acting career spanned the years 1915 through 1950, and he was known in two somewhat differing and contradictory capacities. First, he was the president and the principal star of the Lincoln Motion Picture Company, a short-lived black independent filmmaking concern. Second, he was a versatile character actor who played a variety of roles, many of which were not African American. Throughout his career, Johnson's light skin was often unreadable as "black" in the visual ideology of the day, and so he was cast in a variety of brown-skinned, or "swarthy," roles, including Native Americans, Asians, Pacific Islanders, and other exotic characters.[3]

Not long after beginning his career in film, Johnson founded the Lincoln Motion Picture Company with his brother George, with the intention of providing black audiences with dramatic stories of African American accomplishment. Firmly ensconced in the uplift ideology embraced by W.E.B. Du Bois's "Talented Tenth," the company was celebrated by the black press for its "dedication to technical merits and thematic integrity in depicting black life and culture" (Everett 117). In his capacity as top talent for the company, and before he left in 1918, Johnson appeared in Lincoln's three releases, *The Realization of a Negro's Ambition* (1916), *A Trooper of Troop K* (1917), and *The Law of Nature* (1917). He often used the money he earned from his work in studio films along with other sources to bankroll Lincoln's operations. His abrupt resignation from the company was rumored to be the result of an ultimatum set by Universal Studios, which had him under contract. The studio saw revenue from films with Johnson fall in theaters where Lincoln films were also shown (Bogle 23).[4] Whether it was its own productions or independent films, Hollywood seemed reluctant to bestow stardom on a black dramatic actor, and yet it used the contract system to limit his outside options.

The Lincoln Motion Picture Company continued under the leadership of George Johnson for a few more years, finally going out of business in 1923 after making its last film, *By Right of Birth* (1921), featuring Clarence Brooks, another of Lincoln's featured male leads. Noble Johnson continued working as a character actor throughout the 1920s, appearing in nearly sixty films by the end of the decade and enjoying abundant opportunities in the industry even after the transition to sound. Despite often functioning as "atmospheric furniture"—Thomas Cripps's apt description for the roles offered to black actors during the twenties (*Slow* 127)—Johnson appeared in minor roles in a number of prestige pictures, including Rex Ingram's *The Four Horsemen of the Apocalypse* (1921), Cecil B. DeMille's *The Ten Commandments* (1923) and *The King of Kings* (1927), and Raoul Walsh's *The Thief of Bagdad* (1924). Throughout the early 1920s, the black press functioned as boosters, reading Johnson's work experiences as a sign of black achievement and an example of the ways in which Hollywood's institutional racism could be countered from within.

☆☆☆☆★ The Silent Race-Film Industry: Stars from the Stage on the Screen

> Moving Pictures have become one of the greatest vitalizing forces in race adjustment, and we are just beginning.   —Oscar Micheaux

The Lincoln Motion Picture Company was one of the earliest race film companies—along with the Foster Photoplay Company (est. 1910) and the Ebony Film Company (est. 1918)—to make films for black audiences (see Stewart). Unlike the Foster and Ebony companies, which produced comedy shorts with subject matter and situations mined from vaudeville and variety shows, Lincoln was committed to making dramatic films.[5] This was no small feat, as accepted roles for African American performers tended to be confined to comic buffoons with performance styles to match. Lincoln's heroes, played in the early days by Noble Johnson, were educated, accomplished, and, above all, dignified. Unlike the comic stooges, Johnson's performances were restrained and subtle.

A number of race film companies were established in the late 1910s and early 1920s. According to D. Ireland Thomas, writing in 1923, arguably the most influential outfits were the Lincoln, the Micheaux Book and Film Company (est. 1918), and the Norman Film Manufacturing Company (a white-owned, highly respected company established in 1920) (Regester, "African-American" 41). After the demise of the Lincoln Company, Micheaux and Norman were joined by the Colored Players Film Corporation in 1926. The latter, another white-owned enterprise, also boasted the involvement of showman Sherman H. Dudley, a well-known vaudeville performer and theater owner based at that time in Philadelphia. At different times in the decade, each of these companies was in competition with the other, attempting to capture some share of the black box office from Hollywood productions, which had more money, more reach, and higher production values.

While companies like Lincoln, Micheaux, Norman, and the Colored Players were invested in presenting quality dramas, not only as an alternative to Hollywood, but as more or less successful business ventures, they were significant for other reasons as well. First, with their focus on dramatic content, they began to explore new genres in African American filmmaking. While black film is often thought of as a single genre (see Cripps, *Black*), the fact is that from very early in its history, it developed along a number of paths, spanning the generic range to include physical comedies, uplift melodramas, westerns, boxing films, and action films. For example, the Norman Company's race titles featured the African American cowboy star Bill Pickett as himself in *The Bull-Dogger* (1921) and *The Crimson Skull* (1922), the latter of which was described as "a typical picture of the old swash-buckling west, with the added attraction of a cast composed of our actors and actresses who could ride and shoot in true Western style" (qtd. in Klotman 168–69). Norman also produced an aviation film, perhaps capitalizing on the popularity of aviatrix Bessie Coleman, in *The Flying Ace* (1926), which also featured Lawrence Criner and Katherine Boyd.

The second important function of race films relates to the companies' practice of casting, for it is here, especially with Micheaux, that we begin to see an attempt to capitalize on the name recognition and popularity of actors from the dramatic stage rather than from vaudeville. Founder and prime force behind the Micheaux Book and Film Company, Oscar Micheaux is today a famous figure in early cinema history, largely as a result of the meticulous research of scholars like Pearl Bowser, Louise Spence, Charles Musser, and others. A former Pullman porter, homesteader, and novelist, he moved into filmmaking after George and Noble Johnson refused his request to direct their adaptation of his novel *The Homesteader* (1917). Instead, he produced his own adaptation, enlisting a young, relatively unknown actress, Evelyn Preer, as the film's heroine. The film inaugurated Micheaux's decades-long filmmaking career, along with Preer's tragically short career (she died in 1932) as a featured actress in film and onstage with the Lafayette Players.

The Lafayette Players, originally called the Anita Bush Stock Company, was established in Harlem in 1915 with the goal of "producing . . . legitimate dramatic productions" for black theatrical performers (Thompson, "Shadows" 20). The company changed its name when it moved to the Lafayette Theatre (another Harlem venue) and soon became a training ground for many actors who enjoyed long stage and screen careers. The original troupe included performers such as Anita Bush and Charles Gilpin, both preeminent stage players, and its alumni boasted such distinguished figures as Arthur "Dooley" Wilson, Andrew Bishop, Clarence Muse, Lawrence Chenault, and Edward Thompson. The company disbanded in 1932, but not before providing race filmmakers, especially Micheaux and the Colored Players, with the majority of their talent.[6]

Before the transition to sound, many of the Lafayette Players worked with race film companies in what can only be described as a mutually beneficial relationship: audiences outside the reach of live theatrical venues were exposed to dramatic players from the stage, and film producers could capitalize on the draw and talent of recognizable performers like Bush, Gilpin, and Chenault. Phyllis Klotman suggests that when Richard Norman first saw that Bill Pickett was older and "less prepossessing" than expected, the filmmaker assigned the cowboy a supporting role and cast Anita Bush and Lawrence Chenault as stars (168). The posters for the films, especially *The Crimson Skull*, prominently feature the performers' names and even identify Bush as the "Little Mother of Colored Drama." In a genre film with action sequences, Norman must have felt that the presence of Bush and Chenault would be a draw for audiences eager to see accomplished performers. It must not be forgotten that throughout their existence race films were compared to Hollywood films, since to have recognizable stars was a coup for the underfunded and often technically inferior race productions.

But the precedent of featuring black performers had already been set by Micheaux, the black independents' most famous and successful showman.

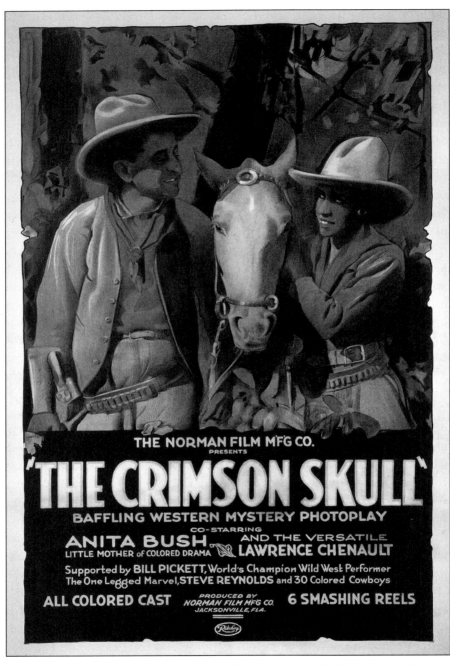

The Norman Film Manufacturing Company's *The Crimson Skull* (1922). Courtesy of Photofest, New York.

In his promotional copy for *The Homesteader* (1919), for example, the director advertises "an all-star Negro cast," which included the relative unknowns Evelyn Preer and Charles D. Lucas.[7] Micheaux continued this approach in the advertising for his second film, *Within Our Gates* (1920), which again focused on Preer's involvement, along with the film's more sensational elements, including lynching and attempted rape. Not long after its release, Preer joined the Lafayette Players, increasing her visibility in dramatic roles.

Throughout the decade, Micheaux helped to build the careers of a number of stage performers, often drawing his cast from the ranks of the Lafayette Players, whose home base was located near his Harlem office. Preer was probably his best and most consistent performer, and the pair worked together on a number of films during the 1920s, including *The Brute* (1920), *Birthright* (1924), and *The Conjure Woman* (1926), among others, while she was also starring in Lafayette productions. Between her stage and screen appearances, and despite the often critical reviews Micheaux's films received, Preer achieved stardom in the black community, a role bestowed on her by the black press and Broadway producers like David Belasco, who cast her as one of the players in his stage production of *Lulu Belle* in 1926. A writer for the *New York Age* described her as "an actress of rare ability and intelligence" (qtd. in Thompson, "Shadows" 28) and the *Pittsburgh Courier* announced, in 1927, that she "was the Colored Queen of the Cinema" (qtd. in Leab, "All-Colored" 334).[8]

Despite the praise, Preer's transition to Hollywood was less remarkable. Accounts differ, but she may have been an uncredited extra in a number of films for different studios, including Paramount, when she appeared in Josef von Sternberg's *Blonde Venus* (1932) alongside Marlene Dietrich. Her credited roles were equally small, especially considering her high status among African American audiences. For example, she appeared in a series of short sound films for Paramount.[9] While the press and the black community saw her as a "pioneer in the cinema world for colored actresses" (*Pittsburgh Courier*, 16 April 1927, 13), her Hollywood experiences were not all that different from Noble Johnson's. In both cases, their talent did not guarantee anything other than limited roles in Hollywood. Whereas Preer's characters in Micheaux's films were complicated and sympathetic and her performances were often subtle, her mainstream career pushed her into stereotypical roles that she had previously avoided.

The bind faced by Preer and many other actors (and race film producers) was worsened by their awareness of what their position meant to the entire community. They were not simply performers; they were also symbols of African American advancement and accomplishment. For example, while eulogizing Preer at her funeral after she died of complications from childbirth, fellow Lafayette Player Clarence Muse credited the actress with "uplifting the world" (qtd. in Thompson, "Shadows" 32). Such words were not spoken lightly at this time, because it was, at least according to Du Bois and the black bourgeoisie, the role of the best and brightest to uplift the race. Many other members of the Lafayette Players felt the same way, most famously Muse, who carefully chose his film roles and didn't appear on screen until the 1930s, and Charles Gilpin, who only appeared in one film, *Ten Nights in a Barroom* (1926)—the Colored Players' adaptation of Timothy Shay Arthur's nineteenth-century temperance tale.[10] Gilpin was also famous for changing the more egregious wording of the stage plays in which he appeared; for example, he famously irked Eugene O'Neill by altering the dialogue of *The Emperor Jones*.

Besides launching Preer's career, Micheaux provided work for other unknown and accomplished actors. In the former category was Shingzie Howard, Micheaux's sometime office assistant, who first appeared in *Uncle Jasper's Will* (1922) and was subsequently cast in a number of Micheaux and Colored Players productions over the decade, including *The Prince of His Race* (Colored Players, 1926) and *The House Behind the Cedars* (1927), Micheaux's adaptation of the Charles Chestnutt novel of the same name (published in 1900).[11] In the latter category were veteran actors like Lawrence Chenault, a member of the Lafayette Players, who became a ubiquitous presence in race films in the 1920s and 1930s. Chenault, a dignified, light-skinned leading man, appeared in some of the most significant silent-era race films made by Micheaux and the Colored Players, often starring opposite the leading black actresses of the time, including Anita Bush, Evelyn Preer, and Shingzie Howard.[12]

While Micheaux worked with an assortment of accomplished actors, he is perhaps best known for launching the screen career of Paul Robeson in *Body and Soul* (1925). There are many reasons for this critical focus on Micheaux's connections to Robeson, not the least of which is both the filmmaker's and the actor's future fame. Additionally, many silent race film stars did not successfully transition—for a variety of reasons—into sound film, where, at least initially, the demand in both Hollywood and race films was for entertainers who could sing and dance rather than for performers with dramatic talents. Robeson's film career, though it started in 1925, did not begin in earnest until the 1930s with the Dudley Murphy adaptation of *The Emperor Jones* (1933).[13] Still, his role in *Body and Soul* offers some insight into the relationship between the black stage and screen at this time in suggesting the ways in which a filmmaker like Micheaux used references to the stage to publicize his films and to add meaning to his cinematic narratives.

By the time Micheaux cast Robeson in *Body and Soul*, the young actor was already well known and well respected in both the black and white communities for his abilities as an athlete, a scholar, a vocalist, and a stage performer. In the months before he started working with Micheaux, Robeson appeared in stage productions of Nan Bagby Stephens's *Roseanne* (1923) and Eugene O'Neill's *The Emperor Jones* (1921) and *All God's Chillun' Got Wings* (1924). The plays themselves were both reviled and celebrated by the black press, who criticized them for their continuing use of demeaning stereotypes and yet also acknowledged them for the new opportunities that they gave to black performers. For example, Stephen's *Roseanne* was originally staged with white performers in blackface. It was later revived with black performers, including Charles Gilpin. O'Neill's plays were intended to feature black performers and, in fact, both Gilpin's and Robeson's reputations were made by their performances in *The Emperor Jones*. And yet, Robeson's involvement in the productions would have the black press referring to him as "one of the greatest actors of the Race" as early as 1925 (*New York Amsterdam News*, 11 November 1925, 5). Micheaux capitalized on Robeson's name and renown, for the actor brought a legitimate and recognizable star quality to the production and yet he was not so established as to be too expensive for an independent filmmaker. Furthermore, as Charles Musser has shown, *Body and Soul* loosely draws upon Stephens's and O'Neill's plays, and thus the director may have been using young Robeson's presence to "forge a crucial intertextual connection between the film and the much publicized and discussed plays" (324).[14] In other words, Robeson meant more to Micheaux than just box office potential.

It is unclear why Robeson agreed to play the part of the Reverend Isaiah T. Jenkins in *Body and Soul*. Perhaps it was, as Donald Leab suggests, simply because he wanted the money and the work ("All-Colored" 336). But surely there were other elements of the production that appealed to him. First, it provided him with the opportunity to work in film, and to do so with a well-known African American director, especially after having been involved with white stage productions. In addition, the film's focus on a corrupt preacher—actually an escaped convict masquerading as a man of the cloth—may have appealed because of the plot's similarities to *Roseanne*, which also told the story of a transgressive clergyman. It may also have been that Robeson's doubled role as the criminal and his upright brother, Sylvester Jenkins, provided him with the opportunity to play a range of roles that showed off his acting abilities. Finally, it might have been, simply, that Micheaux knew how to stroke the young actor's ego by giving Robeson top billing and describing him as the "World's Greatest Negro Actor" in advertising, a fact that would have pleased Robeson, who was still in Gilpin's shadow.

Regardless of Robeson's reasons for appearing in the film, there is no doubt that his performance as Isaiah Jenkins, a liar, a cheat, a thief, a drunk, and a rapist, was not only powerful but something new for African American screen roles. Unlike the heroes of the uplift tales produced by the Lincoln and Norman companies or even Micheaux's previous heroic, upstanding, and basically asexual male characters, Robeson's Jenkins is a man whose physical presence dominates the film. *Body and Soul*, according to Bowser and Spence, "is bursting with sexuality," and yet Jenkins is "not turned into a sexual object, exotic innocent, or savage primitive" (194). Robeson's performance is both subtly menacing and physically remarkable. He often fills the screen quietly or, when he shares the frame with other performers, he towers over them gracefully (especially in relation to Julia Theresa Russell, who plays Isabella, his young victim), ultimately controlling both narrative and mise-en-scène.[15]

Body and Soul was a critical failure, despite Robeson's and Micheaux's efforts. Although Robeson's performance was lauded in some reviews, the film's critical rendering of African American clergy went too far for many reviewers—and this even though accounts of crooked preachers had been the focus of many black newspapers and magazines throughout the decade. Even before the film was released, it was rejected by the New York Board of Censors for its "scenes of drunkenness and gambling" (Musser 342–43), which forced Micheaux to cut it from nine reels down to five. It is unclear, despite varying reports, which version was ultimately released to theaters and how this might have affected final reviews. Robeson was equally as dismissive of the film, returning to the stage in *All God's Chillun' Got Wings* and never mentioning the picture after its release (Musser 337).

Micheaux continued making films throughout the decade, often casting as leads his regulars, including Preer, Howard, and Chenault. During this time, the director began working with another relative unknown, Lorenzo Tucker, a handsome leading man. Tucker had a mostly undistinguished career as a dancer in traveling variety shows and then as a straight man before he was invited to join the Lafayette Players in 1927. He was approached by Micheaux and asked if he wanted to work in the movies. Tucker, who hadn't heard of Micheaux, agreed to act in the director's next film, thinking, "I'll do this; I'll do that. It doesn't matter to me, as long as I'm getting paid" (qtd. in Grupenhoff 50). Tucker worked with Micheaux on a number of silent and sound films, including *When Men Betray* (1928), *Wages of Sin* (1929), and *Ten Minutes to Live* (1932).[16]

It was during Micheaux's publicity campaign for the latter film that Tucker was given the moniker of "The Colored Valentino."[17] The actor would be associated with Valentino, at least in the black press, throughout his career; according to Tucker, "I never got any white press at all and very few people outside of the black community ever heard of me" (qtd. in Grupenhoff 66). Unfortunately for Tucker, his career as the "Colored Valentino" was short-lived. He worked with Micheaux through the early sound years and had a number of bit parts in race films before World War II.[18] After the war he appeared in one more race film, William Forrest Crouch's *Reet, Petite, and Gone* (1947), and then returned to the stage. During the early sound years, the Lafayette Players disbanded (1932), Evelyn Preer died (1932), and most of Micheaux's stock players, except for Chenault, left the business. It appeared to be the end of the collaboration between serious black theater and film.

★★★★★ *Uncle Tom's Cabin* (1927): A Breakthrough?

> It is scarcely possible to think of a black American actor
> who has not been misused.
> —James Baldwin

In film history, the year 1927 is often associated with the release of *The Jazz Singer*, the movie that has been long thought to mark the industry's transition to sound. The film had far-reaching impact upon the industry, not the least of which was the increased financial demands put on film companies wishing to conform to the new technology and what would quickly become the industry standard. It also had wide aesthetic impact, from changes in camera movement and editing styles, to the introduction of new genres, such as the musical, and in the reinvention of others; for example, the gangster film, a periodic production during the silent era, began to flourish in the early 1930s. *The Jazz Singer* also shaped the form that African American roles would take in Hollywood talkies at least in the short term. The irony, of course, is that the movie did not feature African American performers. Instead, it gestured backward toward nineteenth-century performance codes with Al Jolson's blackface musical routines, continuing tensions between modern cultural forms and nostalgic aesthetics.

The same year that *The Jazz Singer* premiered, *Uncle Tom's Cabin* and *In Old Kentucky*, both silents, were also released. In many ways, the films conformed to cinematic narrative conventions, incorporating black characters from previous decades. Both are set in the South, the former during the antebellum era and the Civil War and the latter during the Reconstruction period. Additionally, both films feature white performers, with minor roles of slaves and servants played by African American actors. Neither was a major success, although the former was Universal's attempt at a prestige picture, and yet both function as interesting examples of the advancement and regression of African American performance in the late silent era.

James B. Lowe, star of *Uncle Tom's Cabin* (1929). Courtesy of Photofest, New York.

From as early as 1903, Harriet Beecher Stowe's *Uncle Tom's Cabin* had been adapted repeatedly for the screen, a phenomenon that was based on the novel's massive readership and the popularity of traveling stage adaptations (called "Tom shows"). Universal's 1927 version was, in fact, the tenth time the novel had been adapted to film, and it was the second time that both Universal and director Harry Pollard had been involved with the story; Universal made a version in 1913, and that same year Pollard appeared in blackface as Uncle Tom in a version produced for another company.[19] In all but one of the preceding versions, Uncle Tom and the other principal black characters were played by white actors in blackface (including Edwin Porter, Sam Lubin, and Frank Losee). The 1914 version by William Daly was the only adaptation to feature a black stage actor, Sam Lucas, as Uncle Tom. And no version, including the 1927 *Uncle Tom's Cabin*, ever featured an African American performer in the part of Topsy.

Universal's 1927 adaptation differed from earlier versions. First, as a contract director with the studio, Pollard was given the go-ahead by studio-head Carl Laemmle to make a big-budget historical epic, replete with multiple locations, a large crew and cast of extras, and, significantly, an African American performer in the role of Uncle Tom. Despite this support, the production was plagued by problems, not the least of which were missing footage, inclement weather, and the director's illness, which almost resulted in the film being reassigned to Lois Weber. The initial casting of Tom was no less problematic. Initially, Charles Gilpin was contracted to play the part, but he was soon cut from the production. The actual cause for his dismissal is unclear, although Universal's official version credited his leaving to stage commitments in New York. Other reports suggested that Universal found Gilpin, who had a reputation for changing any dialogue he found offensive, too "aggressive" for the role. According to David Pierce, Universal press releases reported that "Gilpin has Indian blood in him and is proud of it. He refused to wear his hair in kinky tufts over his head, but slicked it back with grease" (25). Other rumors circulated that Gilpin's well-known drinking problem exacerbated the situation (Cripps, *Slow* 159).

After Gilpin's departure, Pollard briefly considered Robeson for the role before settling on James B. Lowe, a stage performer who appeared in the Los Angeles staging of *The Emperor Jones* and who had been a bit actor in Universal westerns. Lowe was actually one of the few Los Angeles–based black actors to have an agent, Jimmie Smith, and it may have been due to Smith's efforts that the actor got the part (Cripps, *Slow* 159). Unlike Gilpin, Lowe was not "problematic." If he had complaints about the production, he kept them to himself. In fact, Universal's press department described the actor as "respectful, courteous and conscientious," suggesting his willingness to conform to the production (*Universal Weekly*, 5 March 1927). Beyond Lowe's casting, the film followed the conventions of the times; the parts of George and Eliza Harris, both light-skinned black slaves, were played by white actors so as not to upset audiences that may have found a love story between African Americans, according to Universal, too "repulsive" (qtd. in Pierce 15). The role of Topsy went to Mona Ray, a petite white stage comedienne known for her physical performances. African American actors, such as Madame Sul-Te-Wan, Matthew "Stymie" Beard, and Louise Beavers, appeared as uncredited extras.

The film's narrative is just as conventional as the majority of the casting, with Pollard, a southerner, creating a tale that blamed the horrors of slavery on white interlopers like Simon Legree. Despite the film's southern sympathies and its continuation of plantation drama conventions, Uncle Tom, as played by Lowe, was a change from earlier characterizations of the role. Lowe gave Tom the vigor that was lacking in previous productions, a fact picked up by the press at the time: "Lowe, who is a young man, sturdy and not the popular conception of the 'Uncle Tom' of 'Uncle Tom's Cabin,' will go against all tradition and play the world's best known slave as a younger man" (unsourced press clipping, 1926, Special Collections, Wichita State University). Tom may be a slave, but he is also a husband and father, and the film's scenes in his home suggest a robust man with a rich and rewarding personal life. Furthermore, Lowe's distinguished features and upright bearing brought a dignity to the character lacking in blackface renditions, a fact evident in publicity stills. While Pollard's sympathies may have been with the white South, Lowe's performance suggested African American humanity and virility. In fact, it may have succeeded in accomplishing what Universal's press releases claimed; that is, to establish "a new standard for the Negro in the motion picture industry" (*Universal Weekly*, 5 March 1927, n.p.). Lowe was, if nothing else, the first black actor to play a leading role in a Hollywood film without resorting to comedy.

While the studio pushed the film and, at least in initial press announcements, Lowe's role in the production (later publicity packets focused on the sets, the story, and the white actors), the African American critical establishment was more lukewarm in its response. Alain Locke and Sterling A. Brown, for example, felt that the picture, despite Lowe's performance, "yielded little beyond the conventional values of blackface comedy and traditional sentiment" (25). Brown and Locke's criticisms, written in 1930, were expressions of a general unease voiced by many newspaper writers, who felt, like Floyd J. Calvin in the *New York Amsterdam News*, that Lowe was "caught in midair" between "a superb performance" and a "humility" in keeping with the Uncle Tom character (qtd. in Cripps, *Slow* 161). Thus was the general consensus of the black press: praise for Lowe's performance and disappointment at the industry's continuing reliance on outmoded racial conventions. Even the white press saw the movie as old-fashioned, an assessment due more to the narrative's inability to mesh with Jazz Age conventions than with any misgivings toward minstrelsy.

Another release from the same year, *In Old Kentucky*, offers an interesting counterpoint to *Uncle Tom's Cabin*. Directed by John M. Stahl for MGM, it was the fourth adaptation of a play by the same name written by Charles T. Dazey.[20] A horseracing film set following the Civil War, *In Old Kentucky* follows the efforts of a former Confederate soldier to recover emotionally from his war experiences and to prepare his horse for the Kentucky Derby. As this suggests, the narrative is not focused on African American characters, yet its southern setting guaranteed the inclusion of a few parts for black performers, including Carolynne Snowden and Lincoln Perry (aka Stepin Fetchit) as servants and extras. The film initially raised excitement in Los Angeles for the casting of Snowden, a Los Angeles–born performer who was signed to a five-year contract with Stahl's production company, Tiffany-Stahl Productions. Snowden was an experienced actress who had worked in the city's clubs, on stage with the Lafayette Players, and as an extra in studio films for directors such as Erich von Stroheim and Lois Weber (she also had a bit part as a maid in *The Jazz Singer*). Her contract with Stahl was celebrated in the black press, which described the actress as "the only Negro girl who is today taking important parts in leading film productions" (qtd. in Bogle 81) as a "Hollywood Movie Star" (Bogle 371n72).

Appearing as Snowden's love interest was Lincoln Perry, a vaudeville comedian who was attempting to break into films.[21] While *In Old Kentucky* received lukewarm reviews in both the black and white press, Snowden's and Perry's performances were praised by the latter; the *Chicago Defender*, for example, suggested that the pair had "opened wide the gates of a new field for Race talent on the screen . . . and producers and directors . . . are clamoring for their contracts" (qtd. in Regester, "Stepin" 506). But where Snowden's status effectively remained the same following the film's release, *In Old Kentucky* provided a breakthrough role for Perry, who transferred his signature shuffling and lazy Stepin Fetchit persona from stage to screen. After this film, he signed a five-year contract with Fox Film Corporation, and his success throughout the late 1920s, according to Bogle, "proved that there had to be a place for a black personality in Hollywood cinema. Moviegoers,

Lincoln Theodore Monroe Andrew Perry,
aka Stepin Fetchit. Publicity still.

black and white, knew him—and they went to his movies as much to see
him as to see the white stars" (Bogle 99). Perry's success guaranteed that he
would be covered extensively in the black press, and his screen persona and
offscreen antics became a lightning rod for critiques of black film stereotypes
for decades to come. More immediately, he provides the perfect conclusion
for a consideration of black stars during the 1920s because he typified the
conundrum faced by many talented black performers trying to succeed in
Hollywood at this time: play a role and risk the wrath of the black press or
don't act at all.

By the time Perry started appearing in movies, he was already a well-
known vaudeville performer, both as a partner with Ed Lee and then on his
own. What is less known is that at the same time he began making films he
was also an entertainment commentator for the *Chicago Defender*, for which
he penned "Lincoln Perry Writes" and "Lincoln Perry's Letter." That Perry
was not only the focus of the black press but was himself a columnist provides some insight into his career-long obsession with defining, for better or
worse, his image.[22] Early in his writing career, for example, he was a
booster of black cinema, urging theater managers to screen films with black
performers and providing advice to aspiring actors. Charlene Regester
argues that Perry was aware that he was playing demeaning roles on the
screen, and yet "off the screen he could and would continue his denuncia-
tion of segregated practices that existed for African Americans." However,
Regester points out that after the success of *In Old Kentucky*, Perry's image
started to change and his offscreen financial and personal excesses led the
black press to begin to criticize the actor ("Stepin" 506).

Perry appeared in small roles in a few silent films for Tiffany-Stahl Productions before signing with Fox, where he debuted in his first sound film,

The Ghost Talks (1929). It was Perry's next role, as Gummy in *Hearts in Dixie* (1929), however, that cemented the success of the Stepin Fetchit character, the role Perry would continue to play regardless of film or genre throughout his career.[23] Until the late 1930s when his appeal began to falter, Stepin Fetchit was a star and "the movies' most famous black actor" (Bogle 99). Critics at the time lauded his talent; for example, of his performance in *Hearts in Dixie*, Robert Benchley opined in *Opportunity*, "I see no reason for even hesitating in saying that he is the best actor that the talking movies have produced. His voice, his manner, his timing . . . is as near to perfection as one could hope to get in an essentially phony medium such as this" (*Opportunity*, April 1929, 122). A writer for the *Chicago Defender*, his old employer, described Perry as a "natural born comedian. He is funny without effort" (qtd. in Regester, "Stepin" 508).

However, while Perry's talent was the subject of praise and his Hollywood successes were extolled, he began facing increased scrutiny in the black press. By 1929, he was earning more than any other black actor in Hollywood and, according to Bogle, he "began to act and live in a manner befitting a star" (98). Soon the press was filled with reports of his ostentatious displays of wealth, including purchases of expensive cars, homes, and clothing.[24] Worse still were Perry's legal troubles, which landed him in courtrooms for assault, breach of contract, and, by 1930, bankruptcy. For the black press, which often voiced the ideology of the black bourgeoisie, Perry was a representative of the race, and his behavior made all African Americans appear to be undisciplined and foolish. Perry himself only fueled the flames, bolstering his offscreen persona in interviews. Ironically, however, the black press, which was vigilant in its coverage of Hollywood's production of stereotypes, took issue with Perry's offscreen behavior and *not* his onscreen performances. At this time, Perry was a movie star with some bad habits. He would not begin to be criticized for the types of roles he played until the following decade.

While the casting of James B. Lowe in *Uncle Tom's Cabin* suggested that Hollywood had begun to take legitimate black actors seriously, the success of Stepin Fetchit proved that the studios preferred a more familiar (and profitable) route for their African American talent. This was no more apparent than in the trajectories that both performers' careers took following their big breaks in film. Lowe, along with his agent, went to London to help with the European promotions for the film. At this time, Robeson also was enjoying success on stage in London. Afterward, Lowe made no more films despite his positive reviews. Stepin Fetchit, however, enjoyed a productive career in Hollywood, working almost solidly throughout the 1930s (most

famously with director John Ford) before his character succumbed to criticism and personal excess in the 1940s and his popularity diminished. In this
career trajectory, Stepin Fetchit became one of the few black actors working in Hollywood to survive the transition to sound.

★★★★★ Lift Every Voice and Sing: The Transition to Sound and the End of an Era

> The Negro voice achieves an artistic triumph and becomes a more purely
> Negro thing, for one—a true peasant gem in a genuine setting.
> —Alain Locke and Sterling A. Brown

The same year that *In Old Kentucky* introduced Stepin Fetchit
to movie audiences, Alan Crosland's *The Jazz Singer* appropriated performance modes from vaudeville and the musical revue, especially blackface
minstrelsy, for sound film. Between Hollywood's borrowings from the
vaudeville stage and a belief in the general "harmony" of African American
voices, sound film inspired—with the help of a cabaret vogue already associated with Harlem's cafes, clubs, and theaters—an almost instantaneous
demand for African American singers and dancers on screen (see Knight;
Massood; Weisenfeld). The immediate result was the production of short
sound films featuring African American stage performers like Bessie Smith,
Noble Sissle and Eubie Blake, and Ethel Waters. By 1929, Hollywood studios drew performers from the Chitlin' Circuit, siphoning off the race film
industry's talent, and capitalizing on the theatrical success of a number of
successful Broadway musicals (such as *Shuffle Along* and *The Green Pastures*).
In 1929, it released two popular feature-length musicals with all-black
casts, *Hearts in Dixie* and *Hallelujah!*

While African American intellectuals mostly avoided discussions of film
during the earlier part of the decade, the release of Paul Sloane's *Hearts in
Dixie* and King Vidor's *Hallelujah!* was heralded along with sound technologies more generally as a moment of great potential for African American
performers. Locke and Brown, for example, praised the former film for its
true "pictorialization of Negro [folk] life." In particular, the writers com-
mended Clarence Muse, Eugene Jackson, and Stepin Fetchit for their
"spontaneity, naturalness, unself-conscious charm" (26). In their opinion,
sound film and the all-black musical held great promise for African American performers in particular and race relations more generally, especially if
the technology was used to promote sensitive renderings of the "Negro folk
genius" (Locke and Brown 29). While contradictory in their logic, such
statements underscored the belief that modern technologies like sound

could help rectify the history of film stereotypes by providing more accurate portrayals of folk culture (see Everett).

At least initially, the hope expressed by intellectuals and the popular press about sound film saw its fruition in an increased number of roles for African American performers. Using numbers supplied by Floyd Covington in 1929, Bogle suggests that between 1927 and 1928 there was a "200% increase in placement numbers and almost a 300% increase in wages" in casting calls for black extras (100). Part of this increase can be credited to the production of musical shorts and song and dance segments in longer films, which showcased the technology's abilities as well as those of black entertainers, many of them fresh from the cabaret stages of Harlem or Los Angeles's Central Avenue. But the increase was also due to the overall appeal of the black voice for the studios, as suggested by Locke and Brown's claims for the achievement of the "Negro voice." White critics felt this way as well: "One of the chief obstacles in the advance of the 'talkies' has been the voices of the actors. . . . With the opening of *Hearts in Dixie*, however, the future of the talking movie has taken on a rosier hue. Voices *can* be found which will register perfectly. Personalities *can* be found which are ideal for this medium. It may be that the talking-movies must be participated in exclusively by Negroes, but, if so, then so be it" (*Opportunity*, April 1929, 122). Black performers, it seems, were "naturals" for sound film. According to Covington, while it was questionable that Hollywood ever produced a "Negro star" during the silent period, sound film brought "the Negro's real opportunity to produce stars in his own right" (125–26).

The opportunity existed, as least briefly, as black singers, musicians, and comedians began appearing in Hollywood productions at a greater rate than in the 1920s. But to end on such a note would ring false: first, because the vogue for black entertainers proved to be temporary and by the mid-1930s the studios had moved on to other fads; second, because such a conclusion overlooks the fact that the 1920s saw its share of African American stars, many of whom—like Ernest Morrison, Noble Johnson, Evelyn Preer, and Lincoln Perry—provided complex and often contested depictions of blackness within and outside of Hollywood. If it is true that "stars articulate what it is to be human in society," then the black stars of the 1920s, whether in independent race films or Hollywood productions, remind us of the ongoing struggle faced by African Americans to be recognized as human beings in an industry and a nation that has often been torn apart by racial strife. That many of the stars' images were riddled with contradictions—invisible to white audiences or forced to play stereotypes, for example—only underlines the conundrum of African American stardom during this time.

NOTES

1. The phrase "New Negro" refers to the title of Locke's anthology, *The New Negro*, along with his introductory essay to the collection. The anthology, a revision of the "Harlem" special edition of the sociological journal *Survey Graphic*, introduced the area and its residents to a broader audience. Published in 1925, *The New Negro* is considered to be one of the foundational texts of the Harlem Renaissance.

2. See "A Tribute to Sunshine Sammy Morrison," www.sunshinesammy.com.

3. Johnson occasionally played African American characters, including those from *Uncle Tom's Cabin*; for example, in 1927 he played Uncle Tom in *Topsy and Eva*, an adaptation of Catherine Chisholm Cushing's play of the same name and based on Stowe's novel.

4. For more on Johnson's resignation, see also Sampson 132–38.

5. Foster's two-reel comedy, *The Railroad Porter* (1913), starring Lottie Grady and Howard Kelly, "former members of the Pekin Stock Company," is considered to be the first black-directed motion picture (Sampson 174).

6. In the twenties, the Players expanded to other locations. In 1922, for example, Bush helped open a company in Chicago and by 1924 there were four companies, one of which was a traveling troupe (Thompson, "Shadows" 19).

7. Lucas was an unknown. He was not a member of the Lafayette Players and his only other screen credit was in Micheaux's second film, *Within Our Gates*.

8. The actress also wrote a series of columns for the *Pittsburgh Courier* detailing her "thrills in the movies." See, for example, "My Thrills in the Movies," *Pittsburgh Courier* (18 and 25 June 1927).

9. Some of the films were scripted by Spencer Williams and based on the stories of Octavus Roy Cohen. Williams appeared in the adaptations and went on to become a popular film actor in the 1930s and 1940s; he went on to play Andy in the "Amos 'n' Andy" television series in the 1950s. Williams was also an independent filmmaker who made a number of race films in the 1940s.

10. The choice to cast Gilpin and Lawrence Chenault in *Ten Nights in a Barroom* was ironic considering that both performers had well-known drinking habits. In Gilpin's case, excessive drinking led to dismissal from jobs, including the London run of *The Emperor Jones*, the Eugene O'Neill play that had made his reputation. Gilpin was replaced by Paul Robeson.

11. Micheaux also adapted Chestnutt's *The Conjure Woman* (1899) in 1926, starring Evelyn Preer. The director, who often included stories of characters either being mistaken for or passing for white, was drawn to Chestnutt's stories of mistaken identity and racial masquerade.

12. Chenault had an interesting background, which included years touring on the vaudeville circuit with Ernest Hogan, Bert Williams and George Walker, and the Pekin Stock Company (Sampson 508). Yet Chenault's screen performances were much more indebted to the dramatic style of the Lafayette Players than they were to minstrelsy. See, for example, his performance as Jefferson Driscoll, a self-hating and destructive black man passing as white in Micheaux's *Symbol of the Unconquered* (1920), where he provides a moving performance of a man being "torn asunder" by race.

13. Robeson appeared in two more films prior to *The Emperor Jones*: *Camille* (1926), an experimental short based on the Alexander Dumas original that also featured Sinclair Lewis, Anita Loos, Theodore Dreiser, and Sherwood Anderson, and *Borderline* (1930), a British production, directed by Kenneth MacPherson. The former film was a short, unofficial movie made by Dumas *fils*. The latter film, also experimental, was not released in the United States because its story of miscegenation was considered too volatile for American audiences.

14. The connections between the texts have been made by a number of scholars, including Hazel Carby in *Race Men* and Pearl Bowser and Louise Spence in *Writing Himself into History: Oscar Micheaux, His Silent Films, and His Audiences*.

15. Robeson's physique was well known by this point, which he used to great success as a football player for Rutgers University. In 1924, for example, Robeson posed for sculptor Antonio Salemme, whose "Negro Spirituals" featured a life-size nude of the performer. The same year that *Body and Soul* was released, Robeson sat for a series of nude photographs for Nikolas Muray.

16. Tucker's first film with Micheaux was called *A Fool's Errand*. It wasn't released in the United States because the director ran out of funds while the print was at the lab. Grupenhoff suggests that the film may have been based on a 1927 stage production of a Eulalie Spense play of the same name (62–63). Whether this is true or not is difficult to determine because no prints exist of this film or any other of Tucker's silent films with Micheaux.

17. Tucker is normally referred to as "The Black Valentino," although in Grupenhoff he argues "these historians today always say that I was called 'The Black Valentino.' Well, I was never called that because we never used the word 'black' like that in those days. Micheaux only called me 'The Colored Valentino,' nothing else" (66). Grupenhoff's book, *The Black Valentino*, does nothing to dispel this linguistic adaptation.

18. Tucker continued to work on the stage throughout the early 1930s, perhaps most famously with Mae West in a production of the actress's three-act play *The Constant Sinner*, in which he played West's pimp. The play, which featured a kiss between Tucker and West, received so much criticism in Washington, D.C., that it was forced to close. Tucker was removed from the role before *The Constant Sinner* could open on Broadway. He played a bit part as a waiter in the Broadway production (see Grupenhoff 98–101; Watts, *Mae West* 136–42).

19. The novel was adapted twice in 1903 by Edison and Lubin, twice in 1910 by Vitagraph and Thanhouser, three times in 1913 by IMP, Kalem, and Universal, by World Film Corp. in 1914, and by Famous Players–Lasky in 1918. These versions were fairly straightforward melodramatic adaptations of the novel. There were other films made that focused on certain parts of the narrative, especially the character of Topsy (See Williams "Versions"; Wallace).

20. The first screen version was directed by a young D. W. Griffith for Biograph in 1909.

21. Lincoln Theodore Monroe Andrew Perry was universally known by his stage name, Stepin Fetchit, from the late twenties onward; however, as late as 1927 he was still writing for the *Chicago Defender*, using his actual name in the byline. In this essay, the actor is referred to as Perry, the character as Stepin Fetchit.

22. As late as the seventies, Perry continued to write and defend himself in the black press.

23. The same year, Perry appeared in nine films, some of which include *Fox Movietone Follies of 1929*, *Innocents of Paris*, *Thru Different Eyes*, and *Show Boat*.

24. This was the decade of Hollywood excess, but Perry's behavior was treated differently from that of white stars because it allowed the mainstream press to present (whether intentionally or not) the actor as a buffoon who couldn't control his urges. Compare his treatment, for example, to the coverage of Rudolf Valentino or Douglas Fairbanks Sr.

11 ★★★★★★★★★★★

Marie Dressler
Thief of the Talkies

JOANNA E. RAPF

Voted by the Academy of Motion Picture Arts and Sciences as the greatest
woman actress; voted, unofficially by Hollywood, as the most beloved
member of the colony; voted by the picture public, as the great panacea
for depression; voted by society, as the most charming and witty of dinner
companions; voted, by studio workers, as the best scout who ever stepped
on a set—that is the record of this elderly woman of humble birth.
—Josephine Jarvis, 1932

Marie Dressler is a significant transitional figure between the
optimism and exuberant exaltation of youth in the post–World War I "Flapper Age" of the 1920s and the sobering realities that hit the United States

Marie Dressler, "the great panacea for the depression." Collection of the author.

with a jolt as the stock market crashed in 1929. She did not become a full-fledged motion picture star until 1930, after she "stole" Greta Garbo's first "talkie," *Anna Christie*. After that film, she was heralded as being "in a class with Charles Chaplin" and as "the only woman who ever played in the same picture with Greta Garbo and crowded the Swedish nightingale for picture honors" (*New York Graphic*, 21 November 1930). Recognizing that in 1930, Americans were "troubled by unemployment, domestic strife," and "cynicism," Ted Le Berthon, in the *Los Angeles Record*, wrote that Dressler can bring people a feeling "that will enable them to live with themselves, to feel that life is still good in some strange, secret way, even if one is poor and obscure, and picked about, and spat upon." She was, he reiterated, "the great panacea for depression" (9 December 1930).

★★★★★ What It Takes to Be a Star

The drive to become "a star" and maintain "stardom" was ostensibly foreign to Dressler. In interview after interview, she explains that she was a star onstage for so long before the movies, "that she cannot view the position through the covetous and beglamored eyes of youth" (Baldwin 54). She claimed that she was happy to play smaller roles and build them up through her skills as a performer. "Why should I be a star?" she asks in a 1930 interview after the release of *Anna Christie*. "Stars last two years, maybe longer, and then what can they do? Their pride won't let them go back to minor roles—they're out of pictures and out of the money. No thank you. I'd rather be a bit player with a chance of getting the laughs" (*Los Angeles Examiner*, 6 July 1930). A year later, after her Oscar-winning performance in *Min and Bill* (1930), and when directors Charles Reisner and George Hill were calling her "one of the world's greatest women" and "the greatest dramatic figure on the screen today" (*Los Angeles Times*, 4 January 1931), Dressler herself was still insisting, "I don't want to be a star. I would much rather support stars. All that I ask is a real part to play—if it's only a bit" (*Screenplay*, March 1931, 100).

Scholarship on stardom has tended to focus on the criteria of youth, beauty, and sex appeal. According to Richard deCordova, "The popularity of stars has always been linked with their 'sex appeal,' and the narrative cinema, practically from its inception, specialized in stories that presented idealized versions of men and women engaged in heterosexual romance" (141). Jeanine Basinger similarly stresses youth and beauty in talking about stars of the 1920s such as Gloria Swanson, Mabel Normand, Pola Negri, and Mary Pickford, who entered middle age as the decade drew to a close and did not translate well into "the harsher Depression era" (469). After the publication of Elinor Glyn's novella *It* in 1927, and Clara Bow's performance in the movie of the same name, wholesome, girlish movie stars like Pickford began to seem outdated. In an attempt to reinvent her image in 1928, Pickford cut her famous curls into the fashionable flapper bob, but this did nothing to revive her stardom. James Quirk wrote in *Photoplay* that five years earlier, audiences would have been shocked, "but today Mary's bob is of no . . . interest. Poor Mary is facing a new public that no longer believes in 'America's Sweetheart,' a public that thinks the word 'sweetheart' is a little ga-ga" (November 1928). As she neared forty in 1931, Pickford discussed in *Photoplay* "how to face forty gracefully." But by then, Dressler's star outshone hers, so the *Photoplay* story continues, "Marie Dressler has completed the cycle Mary is entering; She has accepted old age; furthermore, she has made her greatest success in it" (September 1931, 45). Although she lived until 1979, Mary Pickford made her last film in 1933.

In their discussions of stardom, neither Basinger nor deCordova deals with comedians, for whom the criteria may be different. Dressler's "extraordinary prominence in a business that sometimes seems like a big romance comic book" seems to suggest "some latitude in the casting of comediennes" (Mordden 128). Mae West is a good example. Like Dressler, a star onstage before she translated her outrageous, off-color plays and performance as a "female female impersonator" to screen, she parodied sex, and was forty years old when she appeared as the seductive Lady Lou in *She Done Him Wrong* in 1933. For a comic, youth, beauty, and sex appeal are clearly not crucial to screen success; a distinct personality is. And both West and Dressler had that and more.

Using the ideas about stardom in an interesting Hollywood book edited by Laurence A. Hughes in 1924, *The Truth about the Movies by the Stars*, the following criteria emerge as essential: personality, unselfishness, hard work, being true to oneself, having expressive eyes, patience, being liked, stage training, and luck or fate. In the short pieces by the stars, youth is only rarely mentioned, even though the so-called "Jazz Age" was seen as a time that exalted youth, and there is more emphasis in this book on the star's inner beauty than external appearance. Clara Bow acknowledges that "of course, you must have a certain beauty of face and form, but the beauty that lies within you is much more important" (163). Similarly, for Marie Prevost, "Not beauty, but personality, I would say, is the essential to screen success" (217). And Virginia Valli simply defines beauty as "unselfishness" (112). Norma Talmadge says it is "the girl with the eyes who wins out in motion pictures" (63). Chaplin stresses luck or "fate" (53). Conway Tearle, citing Rudolph Valentino's "years of apprenticeship" before he became a film star, asserts, "You cannot become a motion picture star without years of experience any more than you can become a lawyer without years of study" (115).

Marie Dressler fit all these criteria. She told her friend Adela Rogers St. Johns in 1932, "I believe in luck," and luck, the right meetings at the right time, was no doubt a factor in her comeback (*Photoplay*, October 1932, 57). In her sixties, she was praised for her unique beauty. Barrett C. Kiesling describes her arrival at the premiere of *Min and Bill*: "She turned around, showed to the crowd a beautiful face, wrinkled, age-worn, filled with experiences which have never embittered" (*Photoplay*, February 1931, 43). Dressler's beauty certainly came from within, and she had years of apprenticeship as a stage performer before devoting herself to films. In close-ups her eyes are wonderfully expressive, and in spite of her tendency to steal scenes from other performers, offscreen she had a reputation as one of the most unselfish people in Hollywood and a remarkable friend. Grace Mack comments on Dressler's "rare capacity for friendship" (*Screenplay*, March 1931, 100). Comparing Dressler to Mary Pickford, Jane Kutten writes, "Marie may not be the World's Sweetheart. But she *is* the World's Best Friend" (*Motion Picture*, January 1931, 31).

In *New Movie Magazine* in 1930, St. Johns suggests two reasons for Dressler's "power to dominate scenes and pictures": personality and experience. First, "she has a tremendous personality, vibrant with fascination, with sheer humanity. . . . Second, she has had forty years on the stage" (33). Dressler herself credits some of her success to her ability to be patient, to wait for the parts to come along. "I was patient. I said to myself, 'All these stars and prima donnas around here think they're mighty important, but you've been a star and a prima donna, Marie, and now you've only got one ambition. And that is to go into every picture you can and upset the plot at least twice'" (*New York Times*, 22 June 1930).

In the years between 1927 and 1930 that is exactly what she did, taking every part offered and making each memorable, no matter how small. Even onstage, Dressler was noted for stealing any scene she was in. On film, her scene-stealing was a significant factor in her emerging stardom. Victoria Sturtevant argues that "the ideological richness of the films of her starring years can be partly attributed to the ways she demanded centrality by disrupting any film that tried to push her into the background. . . . By refusing the marginality of the supporting actor's position, Dressler actively resisted the process of her erasure, and quickly graduated to the category of star" (Sturtevant 58). When she made *Caught Short* in 1931, a reviewer wrote, "Her portrayal of the belligerent landlady in 'Caught Short' was a riot. If they weren't so fond of her, other players would justifiably accuse her of grand larceny; no talent can safely share a scene with her. Instead, Garbo, Marion Davies, and Lillian Gish requested that not a bit of her work be cut from their films" (*Picture Play*, January 1931, 29).

★★★★★ Marie Dressler's Early Years

She was born Leila Marie Koerber in Cobourg, Canada. Her exact birth date is uncertain, but her biographer, Matthew Kennedy, suggests the most reliable year is 1868 (9). In her autobiography, *The Life Story of an Ugly Duckling*, she writes that it was "tripping over a rug as a fat, clumsy, three-year-old that really settled my career. I discovered that people laughed when I acted awkwardly, so I began to fall deliberately, from a desire to make my friends enjoy themselves" (3). She learned show business by touring all over the United States with various companies, playing in the chorus, doing bit parts, and moving on to larger roles. Her first New York appearance was in a musical spoof of Robin Hood, *The Robber of the Rhine*, starring Maurice Barrymore (father of Ethel, Lionel, and John), in 1892. It was Barrymore who told her, "You were born to make people laugh, Marie," and who encouraged her as a comic rather than a singer (Kennedy 19). With Dan Daly she starred in *The Lady Slavery* in 1896, "the most successful New York and road show of the generation" (*Liberty Magazine*, 20 May 1933, 15). When it came to Washington, D.C., the opening night audience included such diverse personalities as President Grover Cleveland and Buffalo Bill Cody.

By the turn of the century, she was the toast of Broadway, appearing with Joe Weber in the 1904 hits *Higgledy-Piggledy* and *The College Widower*, the latter a musical comedy in which she first created "Tillie," a character she would later develop in film. These were followed by *Twiddle-Twaddle* with Weber in 1906 and a trip to London in 1907, where she headlined at the Palace Theatre. But it was as Tillie that Marie Dressler first became a featured player onscreen.[1] *Tillie's Punctured Romance* (1914) was Sennett's first six-reel comedy and featured two other players in his Keystone stock company, Charlie Chaplin and Mabel Normand. Today, since Dressler is not as well known as Chaplin, it is often referred to as a "Chaplin film," but Dressler is very much the star. The film is a chaotic but affirmative exhibition of female strength, with Dressler as Tillie refusing to be a victim. Characteristically, she is unafraid to be unattractive, to kick a cop in the butt, and to dance for her own pleasure (see Rapf). *Tillie's Punctured Romance* ends with an "un-wedding" rather than the traditional romantic union, as Tillie removes her wedding ring and embraces her husband's girlfriend (Mabel Normand), who now also recognizes what a cad he is.

Dressler made two other "Tillie" features, although not for Sennett, *Tillie's Tomato Surprise* (1915) and *Tillie Wakes Up* (1917), the latter with a screenplay by Frances Marion. This marks the first collaboration between Dressler and Marion, who would be responsible, in large part, for reviving Dressler's movie career in the late 1920s. Dressler had met Marion in San Francisco during the run of *Tillie's Nightmare* in 1911 when the young journalist interviewed her and the two became life-long friends. *Tillie Wakes Up* takes advantage of the amusement park setting of Coney Island for its stunts and pratfalls.[2] Steve Massa suggests that *Tillie Wakes Up* "is the first film to take advantage of the dramatic talents behind Marie's clowning and it seems likely that this came from Frances Marion as it's a hallmark of the scripts, such as *Min and Bill*, that she wrote for Marie in the 1930s." The film is also the last feature Dressler was to do for ten years until Marion arranged for her to appear in *The Callahans and the Murphys* in 1927.

World War I found Dressler, who was of German descent, dedicated to drumming up support for America and the troops. She sold war bonds and toured the country with other performers such as Chaplin, Pickford, and Fairbanks as part of the Liberty Bond Drive. After the war, she immediately became involved in a different kind of political activity as the outspoken president of the Chorus Girls Union. She marched with actors, stagehands, and musicians in a successful strike that eventually brought the Actors' Equity Association recognition from the American Federation of Labor. But Dressler's union activism essentially blacklisted her in the New York theater world.

As the 1920s began, she did some revivals of her earlier shows, but they now seemed old-fashioned. Later, as she put it in the *Saturday Evening Post*, she looked back on that period as "one of the worst, I think, in our history—of the worship of the flapper." She wondered, "Maybe my public had turned to flapper worship, but had human nature so changed that it would look at nothing else it had approved before, even while preferring the other image of a woman?" (10 September 1932, 28–29). For a while, the answer to the question seemed to be yes. Youth was all the rage, beginning with Olive Thomas as Ginger King in *The Flapper* (1919), written by Frances Marion and with stars like Colleen Moore, Louise Brooks, Joan Crawford, and Clara Bow dominating the fan magazines as audience favorites. Although the flapper fad may have peaked around 1924, the dominance and appeal of these youthful stars, defying convention, dancing, drinking, smoking, and suggesting exciting erotic possibilities, endured throughout the decade until the exuberance of the Jazz Age fell with a crash in 1929. In Part III of "The Private Life of Marie Dressler," St. Johns comments on how the people who had starred with Dressler before the Great War—Eddie Foy, Lillian Russell, Joe Weber and Lew Fields—all faded as the flapper age descended, and that Dressler's "genius was swamped beneath the passion for youth" (*Liberty*, 27 May 1933, 36). At the age of fifty-five in 1923, "she found no producer wanted to hire a dumpy old lady with a face like a mud fence" (Thomas 151).

She traveled, got by with various odd jobs—working as a hostess at New York's Ritz-Carlton Hotel, selling peanuts at Coney Island—and, on the advice of friends, wrote her autobiography in 1924, *The Life Story of an Ugly Duckling*. But she was shrewd about publicity, even during this low point in her career, resisting the invisibility that beset many other actresses her age. She used friendships with prominent society women to keep her name and photograph in the newspapers, and when she returned to the movies as sound was coming in, friends such as Mrs. Stuyvesant Fish ("Mamie") and Elisabeth Marbury were models for some of the regal dowagers she played in *The Vagabond Lover* (1929), *One Romantic Night* (1930), and *Let Us Be Gay* (1930). In the Dressler scrapbooks in the Billy Rose Theatre Division of the New York Public Library there is a photograph of her, dated 8 February 1923, with the caption, "Marie Dressler at The New Winter Garden celebrating her fiftieth year as a funmaker." Another, dated April 1924, shows Dressler and a friend at the Coliseum in Rome. The *New York Herald* has a photo with the caption, "Mrs. Robert Morris Phillips and Dressler, both looking elegant" (14 November 1926). Dressler was well aware of how she was using her society friends, but she was unapologetic about it. A *Photoplay* article in 1930 notes that during her years of sporadic employment, she "kept her name in every newspaper in the country as though she were working daily." It quotes the actress as saying, "I played politics, but I played them on the level. My friends knew they were being used and did it to help me" (September 1931, 117).

She finally worked in film again during the summer of 1926 when her friend and astrologer, Nella Webb, arranged for her to appear in a series of shorts called *Travelaffs* funded by press agent Harry Reichenbach, and to be shot at various European landmarks. Only two were made and Dressler hated them. With no script and little direction, they simply showed beautiful historic places such as Fontainebleau and Versailles with Dressler entering the scene and trying to be funny. Her foray back into the movies, however, did generate quite a bit of publicity. The *New York Telegraph* in

September 1926 captioned a photograph: "Marie Dressler, Who Returns Today with Several Short Subject Films Made Abroad" (Billy Rose Theatre Collection Scrapbooks). A story in the same paper on 19 September announced, "The country is safe from boredom again. Marie Dressler is back home. . . . The Summer has been spent in Europe where she began her series of 'Travelaffs,' scenic pictures through which runs a two-reel plot featuring the idiosyncrasies of the fun-making woman."

Her next break came from director Allan Dwan, who had seen her onstage and asked her to appear in a small role as a society matron in *The Joy Girl* (1927). Again convinced by Nella Webb to take the part, Dressler traveled to Florida where the film was being shot. After just a couple of days of work, she returned to New York. But as biographer Kennedy rightly observes, "The minor assignment in *The Joy Girl* was less important as a role than as a promise of more employment in the movies" (123).

More employment came through Frances Marion, who convinced Irving Thalberg at MGM to hire Dressler for the part of Ma Callahan opposite Polly Moran in Marion's screenplay of *The Callahans and the Murphys*. Although the initial reviews were excellent—the *New York Times* called it "a

Polly Moran and Marie Dressler in *The Callahans and the Murphys* (1927). Collection of the author.

rough and tumble comedy that plays for loud laughs and occasional sentiment" (12 July 1927)—it was pulled from release just as it went into
national circulation because of vehement protests from Irish American
groups about the stereotypical portrayal of the Irish for their drinking and
fighting, and it is no longer available.

She next got a small part in *Breakfast at Sunrise* (1927), featuring Constance Talmadge. As Her Royal Highness Queen Sophia of Hernia, Dressler
drew on her ability to play regal matrons, the kind of elegant, queenly
women she would go on to portray in *The Patsy* (1928), *The Vagabond Lover*,
One Romantic Night, and *Let Us Be Gay*, and which she would spoof in her
routines in *The Hollywood Revue of 1929*.

★★★★★ Marie Dressler Begins Her "Golden Screen Career": 1927–1930

In the Dressler file at Lincoln Center's Billy Rose Theatre
Collection there is a clipping, with no newspaper or page indicated, of a story
by Harold Heffernan entitled, "An Actor Recalls: Some Memories of a Great
Trouper," in which Edward Everett Horton suggests that it was he who
"paved the way for the golden screen career" of Marie Dressler by offering
her the part in *The Swan*, a French farce by Ferenc Molnár. Horton could not
pay her much and apologized for this, but Dressler was happy to play the
dowager princess Beatrice, a role she would later reprise in *One Romantic
Night*. According to Horton, when "the show opened, and when Marie
Dressler stepped out on stage in the fourth act, the audience went wild.
People applauded, cheered, even stood up and whistled. It was the greatest
ovation I have ever witnessed." The story continues, "*The Swan* ran for nine
weeks. . . . In the ninth week, Marie Dressler signed her motion-picture
contract with Metro-Goldwyn-Mayer—one destined to make her the most-
loved comedienne the screen has ever known. . . . It was a mighty small
part I played in Marie Dressler's movie career, but I feel good every time I
think about it."

The film for which Dressler left *The Swan* was *Bringing Up Father* (1928),
another Irish comedy with a screenplay by Frances Marion in which she
was again paired with Polly Moran. Based on the well-known comic strip
characters, Maggie and Jiggs, drawn by George McManus, Polly Moran
played Maggie and Dressler played Annie Moore. But this time their slapstick routines did not rouse the ire of the Irish. MGM was careful to appease
any antagonism ahead of time, pointing out that the cartoon had run in
Hearst newspapers for the last twenty years with no problem, and in her

screenplay Marion avoided anything that was obviously ethnic. Although its "rolling-pin humor" did not excite the public, Dressler was praised for the "best performance" in the film, with "a style of comedy all her own" (quoted in Beauchamp 207).

For Sturtevant, the least-known period of Dressler's career, 1927–1930, "is among the most important for the ways it shows Dressler's active body slowly refocusing the narrative trajectory of her MGM films, so that the romantic entanglements of young characters are reframed, displaced, and overshadowed by Dressler's powerful reminders that life does not end at the altar" (Sturtevant 32). During those years she played a number of parts in unexpected ways. In *The Patsy*, for example, as Ma Harrington, Dressler is the domineering mother to Patricia "Pat" Harrington (Marion Davies), her Cinderella-like daughter, and to her favored sister, Grace (Jane Winton), the glamorous, ambitious one. The film allows Davies to shine as a lively, winsome comedienne who at one point cleverly imitates a number of the silent stars of the decade, including Mae Murray, Lillian Gish, and Pola Negri, in an attempt to capture the attention of the man she desires. But as the social-climbing matriarch, the inimitable Dressler outshines the younger performers. In a risqué scene, as mother and daughters get ready to go to a yacht club dinner, we first see Ma Harrington as she primps in front of a mirror in her underclothes. Once dressed, she enters the girls' room and pushes in front of them to get a full view of herself in their dressing table mirror. While all three try to see themselves in the glass and we watch their reflections, Dressler shoves her daughters out of the way in order to preen. This is almost a metaphor for what happens when Dressler is in a scene. All eyes go to her, in part because she is never still. Sitting with her family at the yacht club, she pokes at her hair, touches her hen-pecked husband's hand, fixes Pat's hair, bats her on the back to get her to sit up straight, fans herself, is infuriated when she is called "a big cow," and most famously, suffers the indignity of having a piece of celery fall down the front of her dress. The scene is filled with bits of business in which Dressler is the central player.

King Vidor, who skillfully directed this comedy following his success in more serious dramas such as *The Crowd* (1928), focuses extensively on expressive reaction shots from Dressler, especially during the scenes when she thinks her daughter Pat is crazy. The happy ending, when Pat gets her man and is reconciled with her sister, and Pa Harrington (Dell Anderson) finally stands up for himself and tells his wife to "shut up," allows Dressler a final bit of dominance. After he threatens a divorce from their twenty-five-year marriage, Ma Harrington is distraught. In a two-shot, they sit together on the couch and she starts to take off her wedding ring. When he doesn't let her, they embrace, but not calmly. Even in this tender moment of reconciliation, Dressler is not still. She pats his face and twists his ear, leaving the focus of attention not on a couple but on her.

Dressler's last silent film was *The Divine Lady*, released in March 1929, almost a year and a half after *The Jazz Singer*. Kennedy says it "was inconsequential to Marie's reemerging career," for her part was very small and did not attract much notice (133). She also appeared in the MGM all-star *Hollywood Revue of 1929*, directed by Charles Reisner and released in June of that year. Although also not of major consequence to Dressler's career, the emphasis on her performances in the film indicates that at the time she was considered an important studio property. Producer Harry Rapf rounded up old vaudeville friends and current MGM players to exploit the new sound technology, along with some Technicolor sequences, in a singing, dancing, and comedy pastiche over two hours long. Conrad Nagel and Jack Benny host a roster of participants that includes John Gilbert, Norma Shearer, William Haines, Joan Crawford, Lionel Barrymore, Bessie Love, Marion Davies, Buster Keaton, Cliff Edwards ("Ukulele Ike"), Gus Edwards, Laurel and Hardy, and, of course, Dressler and Polly Moran. *Hollywood Revue* is a chance to see just how captivating Dressler must have been onstage. She appears with Moran in four numbers and the finale, in which the whole cast sings "Singin' in the Rain." As rain pours down "onto MGM Sound Stage 15," and the camera tracks along the singing faces (except for Buster Keaton; he remains stone-faced and looks around baffled), she is the only one "jiggling a small umbrella" (Kennedy 139–40).

In her first number with Moran, she sings, "For I'm the Queen." One reviewer wrote, "When Marie sings 'For I'm the Queen' we listened to a bit of recording and saw snatches of pictures that will be lifted out of this revue one of these days and laid aside as part of the 'history' of the talkies" (*Theatre Magazine*, October 1933, 39). As her fame grew, she became known as "Queen Marie of Hollywood," the title of the *Photoplay* piece quoted at the beginning of this essay. Conrad Nagel introduces her as "her most gracious majesty, beloved Queen Marie Dressler," borne aloft onstage in a small carriage, followed by "that charming little princess, Polly Moran." Elaborately dressed and bedecked in feathers and jewels, Dressler mugs a bit with host Benny, who enters in a suit of armor and then, after both Benny and Moran exit, sings of all the powers she has as "queen." During the song we get a close-up of her expressive face and eyes, seeing her as stage audiences never could. At one point her shoulder seems to move spontaneously as the music suggests sex and flirtation, but she slaps it back into order. As the

An "incorrigible picture-stealer," Dressler sings "For I'm the Queen" in *The Hollywood Revue of 1929*. Collection of the author.

song comes to an end, she makes fun of her large size, comparing herself to Lady Godiva, but suggesting that in her case it was her "weight that killed the horse."

Dressler's size is referenced again as Jack Benny introduces her next number, this one with Polly Moran and Bessie Love. He describes the three as "five lovely girls." Dressler is certainly the largest and if for no other reason would stand out because of her size. They make fun of various vaudeville routines, and the balcony scene from *Romeo and Juliet*, with the balcony breaking under Dressler's Juliet.[3] The three then reappear wearing big baby bows on their heads and draped in sheets which, when removed, reveal little girl costumes. Bessie Love jumps into Dressler's arms as Polly Moran belts out a parody of Al Jolson. Moran is the centerpiece here with her vigorous renditions of "Sonny Boy" and "Mammy." Finally, in a third scene with the "five lovely girls," each is on the arm of a man and they enter singing, "While strolling in the park one day." This is Gus Edwards's number and he is, in fact, one of the three strolling men. But again, Dressler steals the stage, not only because of her size, but also because of her costume, which includes a large white jacket and a tall feather sticking up out of her hat. As the six sing, our eyes are drawn to the jacket and the feather and the grace with which a large woman makes herself a part of a chorus line and then disrupts the fluid motion by bumping her escort and knocking him over. *Hollywood Revue of 1929* is filled with memorable moments by MGM personalities, some who were stars during the 1920s, such as Buster Keaton, others who would become stars during the 1930s, such as Joan Crawford, and others, such as Bessie Love, who are largely forgotten today. Dressler was a well-known entertainment figure in 1929, but she was not yet the star she was about to become just one year later.

Still without the security of a long-term contract, Dressler did two more films released in 1929, *Dangerous Females*, a comic short for Paramount, again pairing her with Moran, and *The Vagabond Lover*, a Rudy Vallee musical feature for RKO. Neither Vallee nor Sally Blane (the love interest) was particularly strong as an actor, so Dressler, in another of her snobbish society matron roles, easily steals the screen, fiddling with her pearls, fidgeting with her scarf, shrugging and shaking her shoulders, and fainting when she discovers the band she has hired to play at an orphanage benefit is not, in fact, the famous Ted Grant band she had thought it to be.

Also made in 1929, although not released until January 1930, *Chasing Rainbows* reunites the "five lovely girls" from *Hollywood Revue of 1929*, Bessie Love, Polly Moran, and Dressler, along with others from that cast, including Charles King, Jack Benny, and George K. Arthur. An MGM picture, it was produced by Paul Bern and directed by Charles Reisner.[4] Perhaps best known for introducing what was to become Roosevelt's Depression-era theme song, "Happy Days Are Here Again," *Chasing Rainbows* is a backstage musical that, like *Hollywood Revue of 1929*, had some Technicolor scenes. Although they are now lost, one apparently included a number with Dressler singing "My Dynamic Personality." Playing a character actress named Bonnie, she squabbles with the wardrobe mistress, Polly Moran, in the warring friendship that began in *The Callahans and the Murphys*, was utilized in *Dangerous Females*, and would flourish in a series of topical comedies: *Caught Short* (1931), *Reducing* (1931), *Politics* (1931), and *Prosperity* (1932).

Dressler recognized she had at least two screen personalities: the imperious, regal dowager and the one MGM developed for her as a sentimental, down-and-out, self-sacrificing caretaker. In a *Screenland* story in June 1931 she said, "When I'm asked for my photograph I wonder whether I shall sign myself as a queen or a derelict" (June 1931, 119). But she really had three, the third being the shrewd, overbearing comic partner to the meeker and more diminutive Polly Moran, who once said of her co-star, "I admire her more than any one on earth" (*Picture Play*, January 1931, 29). "The queen" or imperious dowager dominated in the late 1920s. The raucous comic partner to Polly Moran straddled both decades. But it was as a "derelict" that she truly became a star.

★★★★★ The Stock Market Crashes and Dressler's Star Rises

The new technology of sound movies was accompanied by the stock market crash in 1929, wiping away the easy optimism of the roaring twenties. The country was looking for images of gritty survival that Dressler's "derelict" persona came to embody so well. Mae West's character was also a survivor, but hardly through a life modeled on traditional values. West was cynical; Dressler was not. Both do seem to challenge the traditional social restraints put on women, and both are comfortable with their formidable bodies. But West puts hers on display for the male gaze that she then returns with a sharp one-liner, whereas Dressler is deliciously indifferent to her looks. West's technique is essentially that of farce—hostile, aggressive. Dressler's comedy, on the other hand, like Buster Keaton's, is not mean, bitter, or hostile. Where there is an ambivalent shade of grey to Keaton's "damned if I know" worldview, Dressler's, unlike West's or Keaton's, affirms love, commitment, and family, a welcome relief from the rejection of sentiment that Lea Jacobs explores in *The Decline of Sentiment* as dominating the discourse of the 1920s.

Richard Dyer begins his book on stardom with a quotation from Raymond Durgnat: "The stars are a reflection in which the public studies and adjusts its own image of itself. . . . The social history of a nation can be written in terms of its film stars" (6). Marie Dressler's spectacular rise to the number one box office star in the first few years of the Great Depression is a stunning illustration. Like deCordova and Basinger, Dyer does not mention Dressler, but his points about Will Rogers, another unlikely star without youth or sex appeal, are also applicable to her. In their popular performances during the early thirties, both emphasize the possibility of material progress through the ethic of hard work, the importance of traditional values and attitudes, and, significantly, the "dignity of the common individual" (Dyer 28). In a version of her autobiography published just after her death, Dressler wrote, "Despite the fact that I am a comedy actress, I have a certain dignity that is sacred to me and that I will not allow abused" (*My Own Story* 83). She brought this dignity to every role, whether she was being kicked in the rear, having celery fall down her dress, or dancing in drunken abandon. This is a quality reviewers at the time recognized. In "A Greater Gift Than Beauty" in 1931, Myrtle Gebhardt writes in *Picture Play*, "But dignity rests serenely on her large shoulders. . . . With all her clowning she is never crude; there is a suggested delicacy" (January 1931, 28).

Dignity and delicacy help to define Dressler's favorite role, the one that made her a movie star, Marthy in *Anna Christie*. There had been an earlier silent version of O'Neill's play in 1923, starring Blanche Sweet. The new sound version was heralded as Greta Garbo's first talkie, but reviewers at the time all seemed to agree that Dressler stole the picture. "She stole the picture from Garbo. . . . She is homespun and past middle age and homely. But she is real" (*Motion Picture*, January 1931, 31). This is the role that

In her favorite role, as Marthy in *Anna Christie* (1930), Dressler peers into the saloon where she will first meet Anna. Collection of the author.

earned her the moniker "The Thief of the Talkies." *Photoplay*'s editor, James Quirk, observed in April of 1930, "It is no criticism of Garbo to say that it is lucky for her Marie Dressler was only in the first two reels. If she had remained throughout, it would have been a case of grand larceny." *Film Screen* sums up her achievement: "Her portrayal was one of the great triumphs of motion pictures, and it made her a star. She is one of Hollywood's great luminaries and she is 58 years old" (June 1931, 35). With even greater lyrical effusion, the magazine quotes a tribute to Dressler: "The writer had seen moonlight over the Taj Mahal. He had seen the warm glow of sunset on the Matterhorn. He had seen Duse at her height, and he had listened to the golden voice of Melba. All of these thrills had paled into insignificance at Marie's performance in the Eugene O'Neill play" (74).

Frances Marion, who continued to write for her friend, built up the part of Marthy, the abused, alcoholic mistress of the old sea captain, Chris (Anna's father, played by George F. Marion), to give Dressler significant screen time. Indeed, after some establishing shots of the foggy waterfront, the first character we see in the film is Marthy, listening to the horn of an old phonograph and tapping her hand on the arm of a chair. It is a simple scene, but Dressler milks it memorably with her body language and facial expressions as she gets up in annoyance after the record stops playing properly, hiccups several times, and then says "Excuse me" to herself, adding, "Always the lady."

Marthy became her favorite screen role. She once said to Vera Mason, "I loved doing that part because deep down beneath the sordidness of the character I wanted her fine soul to show through. That's the way I visualized her when I read the script" (*Shadowplay*, January 1934, 76). A good example is when she indulges in a bit of business with the front door of the local bar as she is talking with Chris about which entrance to use. The door of the bar hits her in the rump and she bumps it back several times, and then is surprised at one moment when the door remains open instead of springing back. When the two finally walk over to the "Ladies Entrance," and Chris goes around to let her in, she comments to herself, "Well, why not, says she, with all the *dignity* in the world" (emphasis mine). It's a brief moment in the film, but impressive enough to inspire one reviewer to write years later: "Who can forget Marthy, who managed an elegant nonchalance as she regarded the ladies-entrance at the waterfront saloon in 'Anna Christie,' straightened her hat, tossed her head and stepped in *like a queen*, with a 'Well, why not?'"(*Maclean's Magazine*, 15 March 1951, 52).

Dressler herself cites another bit of business in the film, when she and Anna first meet in the ladies' section of the bar. Anna has invited Marthy to sit with her, and as they talk and Marthy describes Anna's father ("as fine an old guy as ever walked on two feet"), she slaps the table hard with her right hand and then shakes her fingers in reaction to the sting. In an interview in which she describes some subtle ways of stealing a scene, she admits, "I'm foxy though. I slipped it over a couple of times. Remember that bit of business where I let my hand fall and I hit my finger on the edge of the table and hurt it and give it a little shake? Well he (Clarence Brown, director) didn't see that at all. He was watching Garbo all the time. He wasn't paying any attention to me." But in the projection room, looking at the rushes, "they flashed on that bit of business on the screen. He roared and roared. 'Marie,' he said, 'that was great'" (*Screenplay*, August 1930, 109).

In that same interview, she discusses a memorable moment in the film that Frances Marion added to O'Neill's play to open it up a bit and give Dressler another scene. It is set at an amusement park. Anna, who wants to impress Matt (Charles Bickford), pretends not to know the shabby, alcoholic Marthy, but finally admits, "Yeh, I know her." Even in this demeaning situation of embarrassment and rejection, Dressler plays her character with a pathetic dignity, and makes sure that the lines she wanted remained in spite of the censors.

> Well, we had to cut everything out of *Anna Christie*. Lots of grand lines had to go. Then we came to the farewell scene where I say to Garbo, "Well, kid, it's a hell of a life at best." "You know we can't keep that line. You'll have to cut it, won't you Marie?" they said to me. "Yeh, I'll cut it," I said. Then I came to that line, and I couldn't bear to let it go. So I times a hiccup so it would break just where the "hell" was to be and saved the line.   (Raider 227)

Sturtevant describes another subtle moment when Marthy joins Anna at her table in the bar. We have already twice seen Marthy eagerly gulp two big glasses of beer, leaving a white mustache that she wipes with her sleeve. When the barman brings her another glass as she now sits with Anna, she instinctively reaches for it, but then pulls back, recognizing that Anna does not yet have her drink. She reaches again, but again withdraws her hand until Anna can raise her glass with a small toast. Sturtevant writes, "This little piece of business, besides artfully drawing the camera's gaze away from Garbo, again bespeaks the generosity and dignity of Marthy" (57).

In *Screenplay* in 1931, Grace Mack writes, "It is easy to understand why a character like 'Marthy' would appeal to Marie Dressler. They have in common three rare traits: Sympathy, tolerance, and an understanding of human nature" (March 1931, 100). According to Irving Thalberg's biographer, Bob Thomas, her brief scenes in *Anna Christie* "provided that rare happening in films, when a performer makes a magical transference of humanity from screen to audience" and she was recognized "for what she had always been: a star" (153).

★★★★★ A Panacea for the Depression: Dressler's Last Years

Dressler did several films after *Anna Christie*, including the film version of *The Swan* (*One Romantic Night*) for United Artists with Lillian Gish (Gish's first talkie); it was the last picture she made away from MGM, for she was finally signed to a three-year contract in the spring of 1930. At the time, one critic wrote, "There is the bare possibility that Irving Thalberg, having signed Marie Dressler to a three-year contract, does not realize the full import of Miss Dressler's potentialities, not only as a great star, but as a formidable institution of the near future" (*Los Angeles Record*, 9 December 1930). An astute producer, Thalberg may not have known quite the impact Dressler was to have, but she indeed became the studio's most important star and biggest moneymaker.

Caught Short, in which Dressler was again paired with Polly Moran, and *Let Us Be Gay*, another Frances Marion screenplay, this one starring Norma Shearer, followed *One Romantic Night*. Then in the fall of 1930 came *Min and Bill* in which Dressler co-starred with Wallace Beery. The two became America's most beloved couple. Their romance of old age trumped youthful comedies; Dressler was nominated for Best Actress that year and won. By the spring of 1931 the publicity department at MGM was going full tilt to generate nonstop ballyhoo about its remarkable star:

> " . . . it is utterly impossible to put Marie Dressler on paper,
> to describe her in words"   (*Los Angeles Times*, 7 June 1931)

> " . . . the greatest female comic the screen has produced"
>   (*New Movie Magazine*, July 1931)

> " . . . she has brought to the screen a humanity never matched
> by any other personality"   (*Hollywood Magazine*, October 1931)

The publicity pieces, especially those by Adela Rogers St. Johns, and new screen roles, especially those fashioned by Frances Marion, transformed Dressler from a clumsy but lovable ugly duckling to a mother figure to nurture the country though the early years of the Great Depression. Sturtevant recognizes that although Dressler had had a public role in supporting the nation during the crisis of World War I, the post-1929 collapse allowed her films and her persona to have a greater relevancy because the crisis, unlike World War I, was experienced first-hand by U.S. citizens in their daily lives and in their homes. The survival of household and family became a kind of paradigm for the survival of the nation. Sturtevant sees Dressler's starring films of the early 1930s as prefiguring "the way the New Deal would reshape American ideas about the cooperative logic of domestic political and economic systems, the nation as family, and the leader as benevolent parent . . . creating maternal comic utopias from a Depression landscape" (Sturtevant 66). Dressler herself was a big fan of the Roosevelts and was a welcome guest at the White House after his election.

That election opened up the possibility of a brighter horizon for the country. In fan magazines and in her films, Dressler began to give homespun advice that emphasized the power of love and loyalty, the importance of family, and the evil of greed and corruption. With sentimental and good-hearted films of female sacrifice like *Emma* (1932) and *Tugboat Annie* (1933), she came to be seen as a moral beacon for the importance of bedrock American values. St. Johns wrote in *Liberty Magazine* on 13 May 1933, "Marie Dressler is not just an actress, a movie star. She is a woman from whom, above all others, this old world has borrowed its mirth during the darkest days any of us remember. . . . Marie Dressler is the greatest box-office attraction in the entire motion-picture industry" (21).

On 7 August 1933, Dressler was the first movie actress ever to be featured on the cover of *Time* magazine. The inside story called her "the most valuable performer in Hollywood," with a name "worth more at the box office than that of Greta Garbo, Janet Gaynor, Jean Harlow or Mickey Mouse." Ironically, today it is Garbo, Gaynor, Harlow, and Mickey Mouse whom we remember; Marie Dressler is largely forgotten. But her star helped a nation in crisis, and her perseverance, integrity, generosity, and, of course, artistry, are the very core of what makes a great performer and screen personality. Her last film, *Christopher Bean* (1933), another morally uplifting and sentimental drama like *Emma*, allowed a heart-warming farewell to her fans. Her last words in that film are simply, "Good night." She died of cancer in July 1934. The funeral, although private and appropriately "dignified," was still attended by Hollywood's elite, while hundreds of fans waited outside the gates of Forest Lawn. Tributes poured in, including these words from Mae West, another imposing woman with impeccable comic timing who had years ahead of her as Dressler's career came to an end: "Those of us who have been privileged to walk even near the path of Miss Dressler have learned something we shall not soon forget. We have learned to be more tolerant, to share with others and to show humility. Miss Dressler is gone but she left a lot for us to remember" (qtd. in Kennedy 218).

ACKNOWLEDGMENTS

For help in the preparation of this essay, I am grateful for travel support from the University of Oklahoma. I would also like to thank the wonderful people at the Marie Dressler House in Cobourg, Canada, Ned Comstock at the Doheny Library at USC, Barbara Hall at the Margaret Herrick Library at the Academy of Motion Picture Arts and Sciences, Matthew Kennedy, Rob King at the University of Toronto, Steve Massa at the Billy Rose Theatre Division of the New York Public Library of the Performing Arts, and my colleague at the University of Oklahoma, Victoria Sturtevant.

NOTES

1. Dressler had appeared in 1910 with some other vaudeville and traveling show stars such as Eddie Foy, Bert Williams, Lew Fields, George M. Cohan, and Annie Oakley in an *Actors' Fund Field Day*, a short made by Vitagraph.

2. Coney Island was a popular early location. Roscoe Arbuckle, while at Keystone, shot there in *A Bath House Beauty* (1914), and he and Buster Keaton used it again several months after Dressler in *Fatty at Coney Island* (1917). See Rabinovitz for a full discussion of the amusement park location.

3. *The Hollywood Revue of 1929* also includes a serious "balcony" scene in Technicolor with John Gilbert and Norma Shearer.

4. At the time, producers did not take screen credit. Harry Rapf's obituary notes that "he produced all of the late Marie Dressler's films" (*Variety*, 9 February 1949), but the *Chasing Rainbows* file in the MGM Collection at USC's Doheny Library has "Okayed by Mr. Bern" on the 15 July 1929 draft of the script, which would suggest Paul Bern produced this one.

★☆★☆★☆★☆★☆★

In the Wings

PATRICE PETRO

As prelude to significant shifts that would take place during the 1930s, I turn, in this coda, to a remarkable and elusive photographic image. Taken in Berlin by a young Alfred Eisenstadt, who was at the time an amateur photographer, it features three icons of twentieth-century cinema: Marlene Dietrich, Anna May Wong, and Leni Riefenstahl. Eisenstadt's photograph depicts twenties Berlin nightlife at its pinnacle. Here is a young, pre-Hollywood, sexually assertive Dietrich, looking directly into the camera, cigarette holder clenched in her teeth, hands on her hips, displaying an attitude at once defiant and playful. Here, too, is Anna May Wong, signature bangs framing her face, wearing a long string of pearls, a simple sheath dress,

The 1928 photograph of Marlene Dietrich, Anna May Wong, and Leni Riefenstahl. Alfred Eisenstadt/Time Life Pictures/Getty Images.

and a flower in her hair. Finally, there is Leni Riefenstahl, her arm around Wong's waist, more matronly or at least fuller figured than the other women—soft hair, strained smile, in a shimmering, sequined gown. The photograph conjures up worlds of flappers and glamour and lost sophistication. It also documents the circulation of artists and actresses and film personnel, which connected Hollywood, New York, London, Paris, and Berlin.

But when and where in Berlin was the photograph taken exactly? Historians and commentators list various dates for the photograph, ranging from 1928 to 1930.[1] Establishing the exact date, however, is crucial to understanding its circulation and consumption, especially within the quotidian contexts (the movie theater and the home-delivered photo magazine) that constructed a cosmopolitan imaginary in popular culture in the United States and abroad.

For instance, knowing that the photograph was taken early in 1928 (and not in 1930, as some commentators have claimed) allows us to understand something about the impulse behind its creation. This photograph was taken before Dietrich's performance in *The Blue Angel* (1930) crystallized her persona forever as a worldly woman with a cool and sardonic exterior. It was taken before Leni Riefenstahl became known as "Hitler's filmmaker," the much celebrated and later vilified documentarist of *Triumph des Willens* [*Triumph of the Will*] (1935) and *Olympia* (1938). Riefenstahl was a rising German star in 1928, having gained a reputation on Berlin's dance circuit before she quickly moved into making a series of *Bergfilme* or "mountain films" for Arnold Fanck. Indeed, at the time this photograph was taken, Wong was the only international film star among the three women pictured—which is why she occupies the center position in the image. As Yiman Wang points out in her contribution to this volume, Wong had made several films in Hollywood in the 1920s that garnered an international audience, appearing in stunning if still supporting roles (her breakthrough film was Douglas Fairbanks's *The Thief of Bagdad* in 1924, in which she played a Mongol slave). Frustrated with typecasting and the dearth of opportunities in Hollywood, Wong left for Europe in 1928. Like many female performers before and after her (notably, Josephine Baker and Louise Brooks), she was drawn to Berlin, which explains how she ended up in a photograph taken at a Berlin ball in 1928 with two up-and-coming but still national film stars.[2]

But if the 1928 date helps to explain why the three women appeared together in this photograph, it does not fully exhaust speculation about what it is they were doing there. A Berlin Film Museum newsletter, published in 2004, remarks on the revived interest in the Eisenstadt photograph, especially on the occasion of what would have been Wong's one hundredth birthday. The newsletter reports on several new books about Wong, but focuses on one in particular, Graham Russell Gao Hodges's *Anna May Wong: From Laundryman's Daughter to Hollywood Legend* (2004). The newsletter explains: "This one we got hold of. It looks serious, it reads seriously but it has its unserious moments. The famous Eisenstaedt photograph showing Anna May, Marlene and Leni Riefenstahl at a ball in Berlin makes the author speculate: Did Anna May have a love affair with Marlene in Berlin; did Marlene have a love affair with Leni; couldn't it possible be that there was a 'ménage a trios' [*sic*]? All this leads to the question which we have to ask the author: What kind of sex life do you have to ask questions like this? Certainly not one that satisfies your needs" (5 February 2004).[3]

After reading this, I turned to the Hodges book to see exactly what he had written. There, he references the Eisenstadt photograph as well as others taken at the time that featured Wong and Dietrich and claims that they "reveal an intimacy and warmth beyond a publicity friendship." "Were they lovers?" he asks, only to answer: "Biographers of Dietrich have assumed so and stated that Dietrich seduced Wong because she was an exotic personality. . . . No doubts are ever expressed; rather, Anna May was simply another conquest for Dietrich, who used sex to express casual friendship rather than deeper affection. Wong's reputation suffered greatly from rumors of the liaison. It was one principal reason for the shame her family felt toward her career. There is no definite proof that Dietrich and Wong, or, for that matter, Wong and Riefenstahl, were ever lovers. At the same time, Dietrich probably would not accept less of a public companion. Gay women were everywhere in Berlin, and arriving at a party with someone of the same sex simply proved one was modern" (87).

Although defensive on Wong's account and reluctant to explore the issue further, Hodges is onto something crucial. Being a lesbian or bisexual or gay in twenties Berlin (and outwardly appearing and performing as such) was not only proof that "one was modern" but was also indicative of an emergent form of cosmopolitanism, especially for women, newly enfranchised and eager to think, dress, and perform beyond national borders and traditional identities. Speculations about Dietrich's or Wong's or Riefenstahl's sexuality are thus not merely or simply voyeuristic and prurient (or evidence of a deficient sex life). They also testify to the circulation of images that bind features of a cosmopolitan imaginary to popular culture and everyday life.

In this regard, it is important to note that while the Eisenstadt photograph seems to document a singular moment in history, frozen in time, it is actually one of several photographs taken of the three women at a 1928 Berlin ball, which circulated well into the 1930s and beyond. As I have

Two versions of the famous trio. Alfred Eisenstadt/Time Life Pictures/Getty Images.

already described it, one photograph depicts a cigarette-smoking, hands-on-hips Dietrich, with a defiant, almost swaggering look at the camera. She is joined by Wong and Riefenstahl, and it is Riefenstahl who has her arm around Wong, which perhaps explains the speculation that they, too, were lovers. But there is another photograph of the threesome which seems nearly identical, although it is notable for its softening of Dietrich's image. Here, Dietrich's cigarette and holder are gone; her arms are at her side and her shoulders are bare. She is smiling, and glances beyond the photographer taking the picture, as if addressing someone outside of the frame. Wong's arms are now fully in view, hands clasped in front, while Riefenstahl's eyes seem somewhat vacant, her smile hesitant, even forced.

What are we to make of this second, nearly identical photograph? As Dietrich biographers have pointed out, long before her big break with *The Blue Angel*, Dietrich often approached photographers with this request: "Take some pictures of me that will make me a star" (Spoto 37). Clearly, Eisenstadt took multiple shots of the three women, who have obviously posed for the carefully constructed photograph. In any case, Dietrich's outfit in all of the photographs taken at the 1928 ball remains of special interest. A curator at the Dietrich collection at the Berlin Film Museum writes: "These were the years of costume balls. Everyone tried to outdo one another. Marlene arrived in her own creation of sexy pirate—assembled from odd pieces of her soon-to-be famous *Blue Angel* costume" (Naudet 6). That her "sexy pirate" costume would serve to shape the image of the mature Lola Lola in the final sequence of *The Blue Angel* testifies to the distinctive self-fashioning Dietrich brought to the movies, derived from her everyday life in twenties Berlin.[4]

Needless to say, other actresses of the period also incorporated their own styles into their screen personas. In her essay for this volume, for instance, Lea Jacobs points out that fashion was critically important to the success of the Talmadge sisters' star images; "the fact that Schenck's studio was in New York," she explains, "meant that the Talmadges had access to the best fashion designers, such as Lucile and Mme. Francis, and this gave them an edge on the actresses restricted to shopping in the more provincial Los Angeles." Fashion clearly played a central role in shaping and defining cosmopolitan culture—both for female stars and for their fans and audiences. It offered a route to influence, emulation, and a form of democratization for women, perhaps especially for women of color, as they experimented with and performed conventionalized roles and identities.[5] Indeed, Wong also used her own personal Chinese wardrobe in her performances. As Yiman Wang has shown, while this was "meant to reinforce her affinity and natural fit with her racialized roles . . . one may argue that by clothing her characters in her own Oriental costumes, Wong did not simply naturalize her transitive bond with the roles but also highlighted the constructedness of the Orientalist fantasy. In these terms, she achieved two things at the same time: collaborating in the production of the Orientalist fantasy and, more important, highlighting her self-conscious fabrication and reification of the fantasy" (Wang, "Art of Screen Passing" 175).

But just as fashion changes with the times, so do the contexts in which it is experienced and viewed. In this respect, the second photograph from 1928 is of special interest because its depiction of a more demure Dietrich was reproduced in the 1930s, notably in the pages of *Look*, a general interest magazine known more for its photographs than its articles. *Look* was considered by some to be the also-ran to *Life* magazine. Prior to World War II, it also specifically addressed itself to "women in the news" and news for women, and regularly covered issues of politics, ethnicity, and race.

Shirley Jennifer Lim is the first scholar to analyze the Eisenstadt photograph as it appeared in a 1938 issue of *Look*. She points out that extended coverage of Wong in this issue of *Look* established the star's hyphenated Chinese-American identity, while the inclusion of the Eisenstadt image underscored her cosmopolitan woman-of-the-world status for American audiences—precisely because it showed her in the company of world-famous (and in the case of Riefenstahl, politically infamous) German stars. Here, the tension between nationalism and cosmopolitanism in thirties U.S. culture comes into view: Wong is both American and Chinese American—a nationally hybrid star and woman of the world.

Lim traces Wong's career in Hollywood throughout the 1930s and shows how she ultimately moved beyond earlier exotic typecast characters to attain professional Chinese American film roles. She argues that various historical shifts in the United States and in its relationship to China laid the groundwork for this transformation by changing the way that "Orientals" were portrayed on the screen. Lim points out, for example, that the Sino-Japanese War, triggered in 1931 by Japan's invasion of Manchuria, resulted in greater sympathy for China and Chinese Americans. "The United States sided with China, which also signaled a turn in race portrayals. Thus in the 1930s, as the United States developed the image of China as a good ally, Orientals became ethnicity-specific. In films, Chinese and Chinese-Americans gained an identity distinct from that of the Japanese" (61). Wong took advantage of the improved image of China in the United States to pay a visit there, but Chinese audiences, or rather Chinese critics, did not embrace her, since Wong's modern cosmopolitanism was at odds with Chinese nationalism.

Lim emphasizes that changes in international relations had an impact on the representation of ethnic identities, but so did the Production Code, which was established in 1930. Although the Code did not prohibit ethnic stereotyping, there was a general stipulation, under the heading of "national feelings" (itself an interesting formulation) that the history, institutions, prominent people, and citizenry of all nations be treated fairly, a provision that clearly reflected the MPPDA's concern about the potential loss of foreign revenue from various national markets. According to Ruth Vasey, the Chinese government was keenly interested in Hollywood's depiction of Chinese characters at least as early as 1930. After 1934, the Hays Office was sensitive to changing political relations between the United States and China, and Production Code Administration practices reflected this. The more interesting point, however, is that the new distinction that emerged between Japanese and Chinese "Oriental" characters was drawn on national lines. That is to say, "ethnic" specificity was defined in terms of "national" differences, which speaks to the broader issue of the emerging power of national distinctions in the 1930s.

Lim's analysis led me to the pages of *Look*, where I discovered that the infamous Eisenstadt photograph had also appeared a year earlier in the inaugural February 1937 issue of the magazine, this time featuring Nazi commander Hermann Goering on its cover. The caption accompanying the image of Goering, shown giving a bottle to a docile full-grown lion, perched in his lap, reads: "Goering—Germany's Strange Bridegroom." Strange and perverse, indeed. Although not another word is written about Goering in this issue of the magazine, it nonetheless comments on the perversity of gender politics in Hitler's Germany. Recall that the 1938 issue of *Look* reprints the Eisenstadt photograph to underscore Wong's international star status (because she appears with now world-famous Dietrich and Riefenstahl who, ironically, were relatively unknown and certainly not of Wong's stature when the photograph was taken). In 1937, by contrast, the Eisenstadt photograph is enlisted not to call attention to Wong or Dietrich, but to an imminent danger in international politics—the threat of Hitler's Germany to world order as evidenced by its impact on these women's apparent friendships.

The title above the image reads: "Parted by a Nation's Hatred . . . and Hitler . . . Hitler Won't Like This Picture—It Can Never Be Taken Again." In three columns that line up under each woman in the photograph, we learn the following (the text is brief and worth quoting in full):

Women in the News   Page 3

Parted by a Nation's Hatred . . . *and Hitler*

. . . Hitler Won't Like This Picture—It Can Never Be Taken Again

Marlene Dietrich

When Marlene Dietrich, Anna May Wong and Leni Riefenstahl posed together for this remarkable photo a decade ago, Adolf Hitler had not yet come to power to tear apart their friendship. Today he hates two of them, bestows his favors on the third. Miss Dietrich and Miss Wong, almost unknown when this picture was taken, are now Hollywood stars, while Leni has become Hitler's favorite.

        v

In 1933 the Nazi government ordered German film artists abroad to return home to assist "in the great cultural upbuilding of Germany," by working for German film producers. Marlene declined to return, although Hitler warned German artists they would be regarded not only as unpatriotic but as actual traitors if they ignored the edict.

        v

Since then Marlene has never returned to Germany, because she says, "They don't like me." She insists she is Aryan. Her picture, "Song of Songs," was banned by Germany in 1934. Although Marlene was born and reared in Germany, she has sent her daughter to school in England.

Anna May Wong

Anna May, recently received most hospitably in the Orient, would not be allowed on a Berlin stage because she is not "Nordic." Hitler regards "non-Aryan" blood as a menace to Germany, but this does not worry Anna May. She once turned down a plastic surgeon who offered to operate on her nose to make her look "more Nordic."

        v

She ran into the same prejudice which Hitler holds, however, when she was making pictures in England. In spite of her good acting, British censors ruled that the lips of an English actor touching the mouth of a Chinese woman would offend the British public. All scenes of Anna May kissing were cut out.

Leni Riefenstahl is Hitler's ideal of pure German womanhood: energetic, good at sports and mannishly attractive. She had his permission to make exclusive cinema recordings of the 1936 Olympic games and with this power made herself unpopular with foreign cameramen. They would be all set to take certain pictures, then receive orders that it was forbidden by Fraulein Riefenstahl.

Leni Riefenstahl
(Pronounced "Lane-i Ree-fen-shtall")

She is 28, the daughter of a Berlin plumber. She began her career as a ballet dancer in Munich in 1923, progressed to the movies where she refused to have a double for dangerous film sequences. Fond of mountain climbing, she is nicknamed, not too prettily, "the Oily Goat."

        v

Hitler liked her screen work, engaged her to advise him when he posed for photographs. On Leni, Hitler has showered countless special privileges enjoyed by no other woman.

        v

Berlin gossips talked about her when she lived six months on Mount Blanc unchaperoned with eight men in a movie cast. She taught the men how to ski.

        v

Of her relationship with Hitler, even the most skeptical quote an article on "Hitler's Love," which a Paris newspaper published, to the great annoyance of the German dictator. The article quoted Miss Riefenstahl as saying, "The Realmleader could not love except platonically." The paper was banned immediately from the newsstands.

"Women in the News" section of the inaugural issue of *Look* magazine in February 1937. Collection of the author.

MARLENE DIETRICH

When Marlene Dietrich, Anna May Wong, and Leni Riefenstahl posed together for this remarkable photo a decade ago, Adolf Hitler had not yet come to power to tear apart their friendship. Today he hates two of them, bestows his favors on the third.

In 1933, the Nazi government ordered German film artists abroad to return home to assist "in the great cultural upbuilding of Germany," by working for German film producers. Marlene declined to return, although Hitler warned German artists they would be regarded not only as unpatriotic but as actual traitors if they ignored the edict.

Since then Marlene has never returned to Germany, because she says, "They don't like me." She insists she is Aryan. Her picture, "Song of Songs," was banned by Germany in 1934. Although Marlene was born and reared in Germany, she has sent her daughter to school in England.

ANNA MAY WONG

Anna May, recently received most hospitably in the Orient, would not be allowed on a Berlin stage because she is not "Nordic." Hitler regards "non-Aryan" blood as a menace to Germany, but this does not worry Anna May. She once turned down a plastic surgeon who offered to operate on her nose to make her look "more Nordic."

She ran into the same prejudice which Hitler holds, however, when she was making pictures in England. In spite of her good acting, British censors ruled that the lips of an English actor touching the mouth of a Chinese woman would offend the British public. All scenes of Anna May kissing were cut out.

While Dietrich receives three paragraphs and Wong two, Riefenstahl garners the greatest attention with five paragraphs devoted to her story. (Under her name in bold, proper English pronunciation of her German name is provided, further reinforcing her foreign, German origins and suggesting, too, that hers was not a household name in the United States.) The text reads:

Leni Riefenstahl is Hitler's idea of pure German womanhood: energetic, good at sports and mannishly attractive. She had his permission to make exclusive cinema recordings of the 1936 Olympic games and with this power made herself unpopular with foreign cameramen. They would be all set to take certain pictures, then receive orders that it was forbidden by Fraulein Riefenstahl.

She is 28, the daughter of a Berlin plumber. She began her career as a ballet dancer in Munich in 1923, progressed to the movies where she refused to have a double for dangerous film sequences. Fond of mountain climbing, she is nicknamed, not too prettily, "the Oily Goat."

Hitler liked her screen work, engaged her to advise him when he posed for photographs. On Leni, Hitler has showered countless special privileges enjoyed by no other woman.

Berlin gossips talked about her when she lived six months on Mount Blanc unchaperoned with eight men in a movie cast. She taught the men how to ski.

Of her relationship with Hitler, even the most skeptical quote an article on "Hitler's Love," which a Paris newspaper published, to the great annoyance of the German dictator. The article quoted Miss Riefenstahl as saying, "The Realmleader could not love except platonically." The paper was banned immediately from the newsstands.   (3)

What is stunning about these captions is the way in which they document how popular culture in the United States became increasingly nationalized in the 1930s, accompanied by a shift from outward signs of bisexuality and gender play to heavily laden gender, racial, and national stereotypes. Marlene "insists she is Aryan" even though Nazi Germany considers her a traitor for refusing to return to the Reich. Anna May isn't allowed on Germany stages because "she is not Nordic," refuses plastic surgery to make her appear so, but allegedly faces similar discrimination in Britain where the censors prohibit ethnic mixing. Ironically, as scholars have pointed out, this sort of censorship of Wong's films did not occur in Britain but prevailed in the United States.

But in what is perhaps the most striking formulation in the text, Riefenstahl is described as "mannishly attractive." This is remarkable, because in twenties Berlin and in at least one of the Eisenstadt photographs, it is Dietrich, and not Riefenstahl, who would seem to be the most mannishly attractive of all. She is the brazen, bisexual, troubling figure, donning a "sexy pirate" costume, cigarette holder in her teeth, defiantly addressing the camera. To be sure, Dietrich's image would be recast during World War II as the uniformed booster of the Allied cause, complete with WAC-like wide shoulder military blouse, jacket, and tie. Clearly, cosmopolitan androgyny was recast and modified under the pressure of wartime politics. But this is 1937, before the outbreak of war, and here the Eisenstadt photograph is enlisted to soften Dietrich's persona and feminize her image. The text itself then does the work of masculinizing Riefenstahl, who stands as a larger symbol for a censoring, aggressive German nationalism. This nationalism is strikingly anti-feminine and asexual (not only in the person of Hitler, who loves platonically, but also in the example of Riefenstahl, who receives favors unlike any other woman, and who lives unchaperoned with eight men on a film shoot, but engages in nothing other than teaching them how to ski). It is evidence of a nondecadent modernity—and an allegiance to masculine values of authority, discipline, athleticism, and sport.

While by no means uncomplicated, the nationalizing trend in the world film industry throughout the 1930s is unmistakable. For instance, although Dietrich refused to return to Nazi Germany, her popularity there nonetheless continued unabated until the latter part of the 1930s, when she applied for U.S. citizenship and publicly renounced Nazi racial policies. Historian Erica Carter observes that "Third Reich stars were modeled in part as replicas of Hollywood's counterparts, 'Germanicised American' prototypes of a hybrid star aesthetic." National differences, in other words, while understated, were nonetheless deeply understood by actors and audiences alike.

Carter explains: "Hollywood stars [in Germany] were admired for their spectacular quality, but denigrated also for their status as inauthentic, serially produced doubles or replicas, the manufactured products of a film industry oriented around profit, not art." Thirties German stars fashioned in Hollywood's image—actresses such as Hungarian Marika Rökk or Swedish-born operetta and revue diva Zarah Leander—therefore "always risked embodying a profane commercialism that the Third Reich film commentary abhorred. But German stars were uncanny doubles in a second, psycho-symbolic sense, representing as they did an imagined return to German screens of figures 'repressed' through mass purges and censorship" (16).

Dietrich's films were ultimately banned in Hitler's Germany. Wong's films were also banned in China for what were perceived to be their anti-Chinese sentiments. Even Leni Riefenstahl's 1935 film *Triumph of the Will*, which was a rousing success in Europe (receiving an award for the best foreign documentary at the Venice Biennale in 1935 and the gold medal and the Grand Prix from France in 1937), was widely banned in the United States. A purging and censorship of images occurred worldwide in the 1930s, as did a revision of the meaning and significance of images produced in earlier times. Thus, I return for a final time to the 1928 Eisenstadt photographs and to yet another Berlin Film Museum newsletter, which weighs in on the purported significance of the relationships between the two German stars.

The newsletter reports:

Yes, there are two photographs by Alfred Eisenstaedt taken at a Berlin journalists ball. . . . Marlene is chatting with Anna May Wong and Leni Riefenstahl. So what? Remember, the year is 1930 [this is incorrect, of course; the photograph was taken in 1928, and yet the newsletter further reports, with accuracy, that] *The Blue Angel* hasn't yet been shown in public and it took another three years till Hitler came to power. Leni Riefenstahl in her memoirs remembers that she suggested Marlene to Sternberg for the part of Lola Lola. The story was first published in the German yellow press journal "Bunte" in May 1987. Marlene cabled "Bunte" on June 3rd 1987: "The Riefenstahl story is so ridiculous that Sternberg and Remarque would have laughed themselves to death if they wouldn't be dead already." "Bunte" in reply offered Marlene as many pages as she would like to tell her version of the story. Awaiting the scoop of his lifetime "Bunte" editor told the biggest German daily "Bild" about the "Last showdown of the old ladies." But this did not happen as Marlene wisely did not react. In June 1991 Marlene was asked in a letter to meet Leni Riefenstahl. "She would like to clear up a few things which to the great regret of Leni Riefenstahl might be standing between her and you." Marlene just noted on that letter "Nazi." They never met again. The main difference between Marlene and Leni? Leni Riefenstahl fell for the Nazis, Marlene fought against the Nazis. And that sums up the whole story of their relationship.   (16 August 2002)

While presuming to be the final word on the matter, the newsletter's view of Dietrich and Riefenstahl has been further complicated by Elisabeth Bronfen, who briefly references the 1928 Eisenstadt photograph in an essay on stardom and German nationalism. For Bronfen, Wong remains a largely forgotten Chinese American film star who merely anchors "the two women from Berlin" in the photograph; in a kind of uncanny foreshadowing, Bronfen points out that it is telling that Dietrich and Riefenstahl studiously avoid

Marlene Dietrich, Hollywood star. Collection of the author.

touching one another. Bronfen further argues that Dietrich and Riefenstahl "would go quite different ways within two years after this photograph was taken," but would nevertheless share much in common in the postwar German imaginary. Their movie star status, she argues, is now "invariably seen in light of the attitude they assumed towards National Socialism: Marlene Dietrich—an icon of seduction—was one of the few Hollywood stars to speak out against the Nazis. Leni Riefenstahl—an icon of the seduced—was, according to Goebbels, the only one who understood the National Socialist politico-cultural project so perfectly that she could be entrusted, without misgivings, with the job of documenting the Reich Party convention in Nuremberg in 1934 . . . as well as the Olympic Games in 1936" (170). Bronfen is less interested in the Eisenstadt photograph itself than in Dietrich's and Riefenstahl's—and mostly Riefenstahl's—career after 1945. Her essay nonetheless underscores the ways in which images, especially star images, can be enlisted in symbolic fictions about women and nationalism as well as cosmopolitanism and political engagement.

In thinking about transitions across "star decades," this much is clear: the late 1930s ushered in an era of intensely nationalist rhetoric, despite the cross-cultural fluency of actors, directors, and audiences alike, who had long mastered a more complicated understanding of cinematic symbolism and meanings. The interwar years were nonetheless an auspicious time for thinking both within and beyond nationalism and for sustaining multiple and flexible attachments to more than one community. Women like Dietrich, Wong, and Riefenstahl were part of a deeply cosmopolitan cultural imaginary, forged in the interwar years, and disseminated across various popular, everyday, and quotidian forms, such as the movies and illustrated magazines. They helped to shape our ideas about gender, nationalism, and popular culture, and the sights and sounds of cultural mimicry and hybridity that remain with us today.

NOTES

1. For instance, Hodges dates this image to fall 1928, whereas the 2002 Berlin Film Museum newsletter lists the date as early 1930. Other sources identify the photograph as having been taken in January 1928 at the annual Press Ball at the Hotel Adlon, while still others identify the date as February 1928 at the Berlin Reimann Ball. For a contemporary account of the Reimann ball, see Wagner. For additional photographs of the three women at this event, see http://www.marlenedietrich.org.uk/id18.html. These additional photographs feature the trio preparing for the formal portrait; one features Wong playfully adjusting Dietrich's cigarette holder, another shows Dietrich and Riefenstahl with their arms around an unidentified man, and still another depicts Dietrich posing alone in her "sexy pirate" costume.

2. Werner Sudendorf remarks on Dietrich's status at this time: "Professionally, 1928 and 1929 were successful years for Marlene. She had played central figures in five films,

besides performing in plays and revues. And although her films were only received moderately well and her performances on stages outside of Berlin went almost unnoticed, she was no longer unknown. Nevertheless, she could not compete with the fame of an Olga Tschechowa, the beauty of a Brigette Helm or the class of a Louise Brooks. She was first choice for second-rate films" (138).

3. Various English-usage and spelling errors occur in the text, which appears to be an English translation from an original German text.

4. This was not the first or last time her style would find its way into pictures. Cast as an amoral flapper in a 1926 film, Dietrich arrived at the first rehearsal and was told by director Leopold Jessner that she looked just right in her own outfit—"silk trousers, a dark jacket and a startling monocle—and that she should wear all these in the performances" (Spoto 37).

5. On this point, see Lim and Wang. On Wong's career in Europe, with particular attention to the differences in the ways her films were received in Germany and Britain, see Bergfelder.

WORKS CITED

☆☆☆★★★★★★★

Fan magazines and other primary or archival materials are cited in the text of individual essays.

Agee, James. "Comedy's Greatest Era." *Life* 5 September 1949. Reprinted in *Film: An Anthology*. Ed. Dan Talbot. New York: Simon & Schuster, 1959. 130–47.

Albrecht, Donald. *Designing Dreams: Modern Architecture in the Movies*. New York: Harper & Row, 1986.

Allen, Frederick Lewis. *Only Yesterday: An Informal History of the Nineteen-Twenties*. New York: Harper, 1931.

Altman, Rick. *Silent Film Sound*. New York: Columbia UP, 2007.

Anderson, Mark Lynn. "1921: Movies and Personality." *American Cinema of the 1920s: Themes and Variations*. Ed. Lucy Fischer. New Brunswick, N.J.: Rutgers UP, 2009. 46–69.

Aranda, Francisco. *Luis Buñuel: A Critical Biography*. Ed. and trans. David Robinson. New York: Da Capo, 1976.

Arnheim, Rudolf. "The Artistry of Silent Film." *The Philosophy of Film: Introductory Texts and Readings*. Ed. Thomas E. Wartenberg and Angela Curran. London: Wiley-Blackwell, 2005. 50–59.

———. *Film Essays and Criticism*. Trans. Brenda Bethien. Madison: U of Wisconsin P, 1997.

Aron, Robert. "Films de révolte." *La Revue du cinéma* 5 (15 November 1929): 41–45. Reprinted in *French Film Theory and Criticism, Vol. I: 1907–1929*. Ed. and trans. Richard Abel. Princeton, N.J.: Princeton UP, 1988. 432–36.

Ba, Ling. "Is This Really a Hollywood Production" (Helihuo de chuping shi zheyang de ma?). *Yinguang* 4 (1 March 1927). Reprinted in Jiang and Jing, vol. 12, 225–29.

Bab, Julius. *Schauspieler und Schauspielkunst*. Berlin: Oesterheld, 1926.

Baldwin, James. *The Devil Finds Work*. New York: Dell, 1976.

Banner, Lois. *Women in Modern America: A Brief History*. New York: Harcourt Brace Jovanovich, 1974.

Barbas, Samantha. *Movie Crazy: Fans, Stars and the Cult of Celebrity*. New York: Palgrave, 2001.

Barlow, Tani. "Introduction: On 'Colonial Modernity.'" *Formations of Colonial Modernity in East Asia*. Durham, N.C.: Duke UP, 1997. 1–20.

Basinger, Jeanine. *Silent Stars*. New York: Knopf, 1999.

Beauchamp, Cari. *Without Lying Down: Frances Marion and the Powerful Women of Early Hollywood*. New York: Scribners, 1997.

Berger, Ludwig. *Theatermenschen: So sah ich sie*. Velber: Friedrich Verlag, 1962.

Bergfelder, Tim. "Negotiating Exoticism: Hollywood, Film Europe and the Cultural Reception of Anna May Wong." *'Film Europe' and 'Film America': Cinema, Commerce and Cultural Exchange 1920–1939*. Ed. Andrew Higson and Richard Maltby. Exeter: U of Exeter P, 1999. 274–345.

Bie, Richard. *Emil Jannings: Eine Diagnose des deutschen Films*. Berlin: Frundsberg-Verlag, 1936.

Blesh, Rudi. *Keaton*. New York: Collier, 1971.

Blum, Heiko. *Meine zweite Heimat Hollywood: Deutschsprachige Filmkünstler in den USA*. Berlin: Henschel, 2001.

Bogle, Donald. *Bright Boulevards, Bold Dreams: The Story of Black Hollywood*. New York: One World/Ballantine Books, 2006.

Bowser, Pearl, and Louise Spence. *Writing Himself into History: Oscar Micheaux, His Silent Films, and His Audiences*. New Brunswick, N.J.: Rutgers UP, 2000.

Brewster, Ben, and Lea Jacobs. *Theatre to Cinema: Stage Pictorialism and the Early Feature Film*. New York: Oxford UP, 1997.

Bronfen, Elisabeth. "Leni Riefenstahl und Marlene Dietrich: Zwei deutsche Stars/ Leni Riefenstahl and Marlene Dietrich: Two German Stars." *Filmmuseum Berlin*. Ed. Wolfgang Jacobsen, Hans Helmut Prinzler, and Werner Sudendorf. Berlin: Filmmuseum Berlin, Deutsche Kinemathek and Nicolaische Verlagsbuchhandlung, 2000. 169–190.

Calhoon, Kenneth S. "Emil Jannings, Falstaff, and the Spectacle of the Body Natural." *Modern Language Quarterly* 58.1 (1997): 83–109.

Calverton, V. F. *The Bankruptcy of Marriage*. New York: Macaulay, 1928.

Cambon, Maria. "The Dream Palaces of Shanghai: American Films in China's Largest Metropolis Prior to 1949." *Asian Cinema* 7.2 (Winter 1995): 34–45.

Cao, Yuankai. "A Detailed Account of What I Have Learned in School and Its Uses" (Xiangyan zai xuexiao zhi suo xue ji qi gongyong). *Movies Magazine* (*Diangying zazhi*) 6 (1924). Reprinted in Jiang and Jing, vol. 2, 43–46.

Carby, Hazel. *Race Men*. Cambridge, Mass.: Harvard UP, 1998.

Carringer, Robert, ed. *The Jazz Singer*. Wisconsin/Warner Bros. Screenplay Series. Madison: U of Wisconsin P, 1979.

Carroll, Noël. *Comedy Incarnate: Buster Keaton, Physical Humor, and Bodily Coping*. Malden, Mass.: Blackwell, 2007.

Carter, Erica. *Dietrich's Ghosts: The Sublime and the Beautiful in Third Reich Film*. London: BFI, 2004.

Chung, Hye Seung. *Hollywood Asian: Philip Ahn and the Politics of Cross-ethnic Performance*. Philadelphia: Temple UP, 2006.

Clark, Danae. *Negotiating Hollywood: The Cultural Politics of Actors' Labor*. Minneapolis: U of Minnesota P, 1995.

Cole, Catherine. "Reading Blackface in Africa: Wonders Taken for Signs." *Critical Inquiry* 23 (1996): 183–215.

Cott, Nancy F. *The Grounding of Modern Feminism*. New Haven, Conn.: Yale UP, 1989.

Covington, Floyd C. "The Negro Invades Hollywood." *Black Films and Filmmakers*. Ed. Lindsay Patterson. New York: Dodd, Mead, & Company, 1975. 122–27.

Crafton, Donald. *The Talkies: American Cinema's Transition to Sound 1926–1931*. Berkeley: U of California P, 1997.

Cripps, Thomas. *Black Film as Genre*. Bloomington: Indiana UP, 1978.

———. *Slow Fade to Black: The Negro in American Film, 1900–1942*. New York: Oxford UP, 1993.

Curtis, Scott. "Douglas Fairbanks: Icon of Americanism." *Flickers of Desire: Movie Stars of the 1910s*. Ed. Jennifer Bean. New Brunswick, N.J.: Rutgers UP, forthcoming.

Daniel, Robert L. *American Women in the 20th Century: The Festival of Life*. New York: Harcourt Brace Jovanovich, 1987.

deCordova, Richard. *Picture Personalities: The Emergence of the Star System in America*. Urbana: U of Illinois P, 1990.

De Grazia, Victoria. *Irresistible Empire: America's Advance through Twentieth Century Europe*. Cambridge, Mass.: Belknap Press, Harvard UP, 2005.

De Groat, Greta. "Rediscovering Norma Talmadge." *Griffithiana* 71 (2001). Available at www.stanford.edu/~gdegroat/NT/home.htm. Accessed 29 August 2008.

Deleuze, Gilles, and Felix Guattari. *Kafka: Towards a Minor Literature.* Minneapolis: U of Minnesota P, 1986.

Desnos, Robert. *Cinéma.* Ed.André Tchernia. Paris: Gallimard, 1966.

Dikotter, Frank. *The Discourse of Race in Modern China.* London: C. Hurst & Company, 1991.

Dos Passos, John. *The Big Money.* New York: New American Library, 1969.

———. *Facing the Chair: Story of the Americanization of Two Foreignborn Workmen.* New York: Da Capo, 1970.

Dressler, Marie. *The Life Story of an Ugly Duckling.* New York: Robert M. McBridge & Company, 1924.

———. *My Own Story, as told to Mildred Harrington.* Boston: Little, Brown, 1934.

Dumont, Hervé. *Frank Borzage: Sarastro à Hollywood.* Milan: Edizioni Gabriele Mazzotta, 1993.

Dyer, Richard. *Heavenly Bodies: Film Stars and Society.* London: BFI, 1986.

———. *Stars.* London: BFI, 1982.

Ebermayer, Erich. *Eh' ich's vergesse: Erinnerungen an Gerhart Hauptmann, Thomas Mann, Klaus Mann, Gustaf Gründgens, Emil Jannings und Stefan Zweig.* Munich: Langen, 2005.

———. *Unter anderem Himmel.* Berlin: Zsolnay, 1942.

Eisner, Lotte. *The Haunted Screen: Expressionism in the German Cinema and the Influence of Max Reinhardt* [1952]. Trans. Roger Greaves. Berkeley: U of California P, 1969.

Ellis, Havelock. *Little Essays of Love and Virtue.* New York: George H. Doran, 1921, 1922.

Érèbe, Judith. "Sur le film comique et singulierement sur Buster Keaton." *Crapouillot* (August 1927). Reprint, *Crapouillot* 59 (January 1963): 10–13.

Evans, Sara M. *Born for Liberty: A History of Women in America.* New York: Free Press, 1989.

Everett, Anna. *Returning the Gaze: A Genealogy of Black Film Criticism, 1909–1949.* Durham, N.C.: Duke UP, 2001.

Eyman, Scott. *The Speed of Sound: Hollywood and the Talkie Revolution, 1926–1930.* Baltimore: Johns Hopkins UP, 1999.

Faderman, Lillian, and Stuart Timmons. *Gay L.A.: A History of Sexual Outlaws, Power Politicos, and Lipstick Lesbians.* New York: Basic Books, 2006.

Fass, Paula S. *The Damned and the Beautiful: American Youth in the Twenties.* New York: Oxford UP, 1977.

Felando, Cynthia. "Hollywood in the 1920s: Youth Must Be Served." *Hollywood Goes Shopping.* Ed. David Desser and Garth S. Jowett. Minneapolis: U of Minnesota P, 2000. 82–107.

FilmMuseum Berlin Newsletter no. 42 (16 August 2002). Available at www.marlenedietrich.org/pdf/News42.pdf. Accessed 12 January 2009.

FilmMuseum Berlin Newsletter no. 60 (5 February 2004). Available at www.marlenedietrich.org/pdf/News62.pdf. Accessed 12 January 2009.

Finnegan, Margaret. *Selling Suffrage: Consumer Culture and Votes for Women.* New York: Columbia UP, 1999.

Fischer, Lucy. *Designing Women: Cinema, Art Deco and the Female Form.* New York: Columbia UP, 2003.

Fleeger, Jennifer. "How to Say Things with Songs: Al Jolson, Vitaphone Technology, and the Rhetoric of Warner Bros. in 1929." *Quarterly Review of Film and Video* 27.1 (December 2009).

Ford, Charles. *Emil Jannings*. Paris: L'Avant-scène du cinéma, 1969.

Fraenkel, Heinrich. *Unsterblicher Film: Die grosse Chronik—Von der Laterna Magica bis zum Ton-film*. Munich: Kindler, 1956.

Franklin, Robert, and Joan Franklin. "Interview with Buster Keaton." *Buster Keaton Interviews*. Ed. Kevin W. Sweeney. Jackson: U of Mississippi P, 2007. 62–102. Also in Oral History Research Collection, Columbia University Library.

Freedland, Michael. *Jolson: The Story of Al Jolson*. Portland, Ore.: Valentine Mitchell, 2007.

Friedberg, Anne. "Writing about Cinema: *Close-Up*, 1927–1933." Ph.D. diss., New York University, 1983.

Gabler, Neal. *An Empire of Their Own: How the Jews Invented Hollywood*. New York: Crown, 1988.

Gemünden, Gerd. *A Foreign Affair: Billy Wilder's American Films*. New York: Berghahn Books, 2008.

Gerstner, David A. "Ramon Novarro: The Performance of Deception." Unpublished manuscript.

Goldman, Herbert G. *Jolson: The Legend Comes to Life*. New York: Oxford UP, 1988.

Gomery, Douglas. *The Coming of Sound*. New York: Routledge, 2004.

Gramsci, Antonio. "Americanism and Fordism." *Selections from the Prison Notebooks of Antonio Gramsci*. Ed. and trans. Quintin Hoare and Geoffrey Nowell-Smith. New York: International Publishers, 1971. 277–318.

Gregor, Josef. *Meister deutscher Schauspielkunst: Krauss, Klöpfer, Jannings, George*. Bremen: Schünemann, 1939.

Grieveson, Lee. *Policing Cinema: Movies and Censorship in Early Twentieth Century America*. Berkeley: U of California P, 2004.

Griffith, Richard. *The Talkies: Articles and Illustrations from Photoplay Magazine, 1928–1940*. New York: Dover, 1971.

Grupenhoff, Richard. *The Black Valentino: The Stage and Screen Career of Lorenzo Tucker*. Metuchen, N.J.: Scarecrow Press, 1988.

Gubar, Susan. *Racechanges: White Skin, Black Face in American Culture*. New York: Oxford UP, 1997.

Gunning, Tom. "Crazy Machines in the Garden of Forking Paths: Mischief Gags and the Origins of American Film Comedy." *Classical Hollywood Comedy*. Ed. Kristine Brunovska Karnick and Henry Jenkins. New York: Routledge, 1995. 87–105.

Hall, Leonard. "Garbo-Maniacs." *The Talkies*. Ed. Richard Griffith. New York: Dover, 1971. 4–5, 270.

Hamilton, Mary Beth. *'When I'm Bad, I'm Better': Mae West, Sex, and American Entertainment*. Berkeley: U of California P, 1997.

Hansen, Miriam. "Pleasure, Ambivalence, Identification: Valentino and Spectatorship." *Cinema Journal* 25.4 (Summer 1986): 6–32.

Hastie, Amelie. *Cupboards of Curiosity: Women, Recollection, and Film History*. Durham, N.C.: Duke UP, 2007.

Heffernan, Harold. "An Actor Recalls: Some Memories of a Great Trouper." Marie Dressler clipping file at the Billy Rose Library for the Performing Arts, Lincoln Center, New York.

Hegeman, Susan. *Patterns for America: Modernism and the Concept of Culture*. Princeton, N.J.: Princeton UP, 1999.

Heisner, Beverly. *Hollywood Art: Art Direction in the Days of the Great Studios*. Jefferson, N.C.: McFarland, 1990.

Helker, Renata. "Kunst-Ausschuss: Emil Jannings als Schauspieler und Produzent." *Tonfilm-frieden/Tonfilmkrieg: Die Geschichte der Tobis vom Technik-Syndikat zum Staatskonzern*. Ed. Jan Distelmeyer. Munich: Text & Kritik, 2003. 150–58.

Higashi, Sumiko. *Cecil B. DeMille and American Culture: The Silent Era*. Berkeley: U of California P, 1994.

———. "Ethnicity, Class and Gender in Film: DeMille's *The Cheat*." *Unspeakable Images: Ethnicity and the American Cinema*. Ed. Lester Friedman. Urbana: U of Illinois P, 1991. 112–39.

Higson, Andrew, and Richard Maltby, eds. *"Film Europe" and "Film America": Cinema, Commerce and Cultural Exchange 1920–1939*. Exeter: Exeter UP, 1999.

Hochheiser, Sheldon. "AT&T and the Development of Sound Motion-Picture Technology." *The Dawn of Sound*. Ed. Mary Lea Bandy. New York: Museum of Modern Art, 1989. 19–33.

Hodges, Graham Russell Gao. *Anna May Wong: From Laundryman's Daughter to Hollywood Legend*. New York: Palgrave Macmillan, 2004.

Holba, Herbert. *Emil Jannings*. Ulm: Knorr, 1973.

Horak, Jan-Christopher. "Sauerkraut & Sausages with a Little Goulash: Germans in Hollywood, 1927." *Film History* 17 (2005): 241–60.

Huang, Banxiang. "Study of Beauty on the Screen" (Yingmu shang de mei de yanjiu). *Yingxi zazhi* (*The Film Magazine*) 1.11/12 (April 1931): 64–67.

Hubert, Ali. *Hollywood: Legende und Wirklichkeit*. Leipzig: Seemann, 1930.

Hughes, Laurence A. *The Truth about the Movies by the Stars*. Hollywood: Hollywood Publishers, 1924.

Hughes, Thomas P. *American Genesis: A Century of Invention and Technological Enthusiasm, 1870–1970*. New York: Penguin, 1989.

Hull, Edith M. *The Sheik*. Boston: Small, Maynard & Company, 1921.

Ihering, Herbert. "*The Blue Angel* and *An American Tragedy*." *Sternberg*. Ed. Peter Baxter. Trans. Maaret Koskinen. London: BFI, 1980. 24–27.

———. *Emil Jannings: Baumeister seines Lebens und seiner Filme*. Heidelberg: Hüthig, 1941.

———. *Von Reinhardt bis Brecht: Eine Auswahl der Theaterkritiken von 1909–1932*. 3 vols. Ed. Rolf Badenhausen. Reinbek: Rowohlt, 1967.

Israel, Betsy. *Bachelor Girl: The Secret History of Single Women in the Twentieth Century*. New York: Morrow, 2002.

Jacobs, Lea. *The Decline of Sentiment: American Film in the 1920s*. Berkeley: U of California P, 2008.

Jannings, Emil. "Correspondence between Emil and Walter Jannings." Schriftgutsammlung of the Filmmuseum Berlin–Stiftung Deutsche Kinemathek.

———. "Gedanken zu meinem Film *Ohm Krüger*." *Englischer Krieg vor 40 Jahren und heute*. Berlin: Tobis Filmkunst, 1941. 7–9.

———. *Theater-Film: Das Leben und ich*. Ed. C. C. Bergius. Berchtesgaden: Zimmer & Herzog, 1951.

———. "Vorwort." Ali Hubert. *Hollywood: Legende und Wirklichkeit*. Leipzig: Seemann, 1930. ii–iii.

Jay, Martin. *The Dialectical Imagination: A History of the Frankfurt School and the Institute of Social Research, 1923–1950*. Boston: Little, Brown, 1973.

Jiang, Yasha, and Li Jing, eds. *Zhongguo zaoqi dianying huakan* (*Compendium of Early Chinese Film Magazines*). Beijing: Quanguo tushu guan wenxian suowei fuzhi zhongxin, 2004.

Jing, Xia. "Qualifications of an Actress" (Nuzi tousheng dianying jie de zige). *Movies Magazine* (*Dianying zazhi*) (1924). Reprinted in Jiang and Jing, vol. 2, 560–67.

Jones, Andrew F. *Yellow Music: Media Culture and Colonial Modernity in the Chinese Jazz Age.* Durham, N.C.: Duke UP, 2001.

Jun. "Casual Comments on Film Reviews" (Yingping ouji). *The Screen Pictorial Semi-monthly* (*Dianying huabao*) no. 14 (20 September 1934).

Keaton, Buster, with Charles Samuels. *My Wonderful World of Slapstick.* New York: Doubleday, 1960.

Kennedy, David. *Over Here: The First World War and American Society.* New York: Oxford UP, 1980.

Kennedy, Matthew. *Marie Dressler.* Jefferson, N.C.: McFarland, 1999.

Kerr, Walter. "Last Call for a Clown." *Harper's Bazaar* (May 1952): 156–57. Reprinted in *Pieces at Eight.* New York: Simon & Schuster, 1957. 195–202.

Klotman, Phyllis R. "Planes, Trains, and Automobiles: *The Flying Ace*, the Norman Company, and the Micheaux Connection." *Oscar Micheaux & His Circle: African-American Filmmaking and Race Cinema of the Silent Era.* Ed. Pearl Bowser, Jane Gaines, and Charles Musser. Bloomington: Indiana UP, 2001. 161–77.

Knight, Arthur. *Disintegrating the Musical: Black Performance and American Musical Film.* Durham, N.C.: Duke UP, 2002.

Koch, Gertrud. "Between Two Worlds: Von Sternberg's *The Blue Angel* (1930)." *German Film and Literature: Adaptations and Transformations.* Ed. Eric Rentschler. New York: Methuen, 1986. 60–72.

Koebner, Thomas. "Von der Schwäche der starken Männer: Über Emil Jannings, Werner Krauß, Heinrich George und ihre Rollen." *Idole des deutschen Films: Eine Galerie von Schlüsselfiguren.* Ed. Thomas Koebner. Munich: Text & Kritik, 1997. 83–103.

Koszarski, Richard. *An Evening's Entertainment: The Age of the Silent Feature Picture, 1915–1928.* Berkeley: U of California P, 1994.

———. *Fort Lee: The Film Town.* Rome: John Libbey, 2004.

Kouwehoven, John A. *Made in America.* New York: Doubleday, 1948.

Kracauer, Siegfried. *From Caligari to Hitler: A Psychological History of the German Cinema.* 1947. Princeton, N.J.: Princeton UP, 2004.

———. *Kleine Schriften zum Film 1928–1931.* Ed. Inka Mülder-Bach and Ingrid Belke. Frankfurt: Suhrkamp, 2004.

Krämer, Peter. "Battered Child: Buster Keaton's Stage Performances and Vaudeville Stardom in the Early 1900s." *New Review of Film and Television Studies* 5.3 (December 2007): 253–67.

———. "The Making of a Comic Star: Buster Keaton in *The Saphead*." *Classical Hollywood Comedy.* Ed. Kristine Brunovska Karnick and Henry Jenkins. New York: Routledge, 1995. 190–210.

Kurtz, Rudolf. *Emil Jannings.* Berlin: Ufa-Buchverlag, 1942.

Landay, Lori. *Madcaps, Screwballs, and Con Women: The Female Trickster in American Culture.* Philadelphia: U of Pennsylvania P, 1998.

Lane, Christina Merrel. "Hollywood Star Couples: Classical-Era Romance and Marriage." Ph.D. diss., University of Texas, 1999.

Lang, Shan. "Denouncing Anna May Wong" (Bu chengren Huang Meiyan). *Yinguang* 5 (1 April 1927). Reprinted in Jiang and Jing, vol. 12, 322.

Latham, Angela. *Posing a Threat: Flappers, Chorus Girls, and Other Brazen Performers of the American 1920s.* Hanover, N.H.: Wesleyan/UP of New England, 2000.

Laver, James. *Costume and Fashion: A Concise History*. London: Thames & Hudson, 1995.

Leab, Daniel J. "'All-Colored'—But Not Much Different: Films Made for Negro Ghetto Audiences." *Phylon* 36.3 (1975): 321–39.

———. *From Sambo to Superspade: The Black Experience in Motion Pictures*. Boston: Houghton Mifflin, 1976.

Lee, Josephine. *Performing Asian American: Race and Ethnicity on the Contemporary Stage*. Philadelphia: Temple UP, 1997.

Leider, Emily W. *Dark Lover: The Life and Death of Rudolph Valentino*. New York: Farrar, Straus and Giroux, 2003.

Lhamon, W. T. Jr. *Raising Cain: Blackface Performance from Jim Crow to Hip Hop*. Cambridge, Mass.: Harvard UP, 1998.

Liang, Shiqiu. *On Wen Yiduo* (Tan Wen Yiduo). Taipei: Zhuanji wenxue chubanshe, 1967.

Lim, Shirley Jennifer. *A Feeling of Belonging: Asian American Women's Public Culture, 1930–1960*. New York: New York UP, 2006.

Lippmann, Walter. *A Preface to Morals*. New York: Macmillan, 1929.

Locke, Alain, and Sterling A. Brown. "Folk Values in a New Medium [1930]." *Black Films and Filmmakers*. Ed. Lindsay Patterson. New York: Dodd, Mead, & Company, 1975. 25–29.

Loos, Anita. *The Talmadge Girls: A Memoir*. New York: Viking, 1978.

Lorca, Federico Garcia. "Buster Keaton's Promenade." Trans. Tim Reynolds. *Accent* 17.3 (Summer 1957): 131–33.

Lott, Eric. *Love and Theft: Blackface Minstrelsy and the American Working Class*. New York: Oxford UP, 1993.

Lu, Xun. "The Future Glory" (Weilai de guangrong) [1934]. *The Complete Works by Lu Xun (Lu Xun quanji)*. Vol. 5. Beijing: Renmin wenxue chubanshe, 1987.

Lyons, Eugene. *The Life and Death of Sacco and Vanzetti*. New York: International Publishers, 1927.

Mahar, Karen Ward. *Women Filmmakers in Early Hollywood*. Baltimore: Johns Hopkins UP, 2008.

Mann, William J. *Wisecracker: The Life and Times of William Haines, Hollywood's First Openly Gay Star*. New York: Viking, 1997.

Marcuse, Herbert. "Social Implication of Modern Technology." *Studies in Philosophy and Social Science* 9.3 (1941): 414–39.

Mardore, Michel. "Le plus bel animal du monde." *Cahiers du cinéma* 130 (April 1962): 34–37.

Markle, Fletcher. "Telescope: Deadpan." *Buster Keaton Interviews*. Ed. Kevin W. Sweeney. Jackson: UP of Mississippi , 2007. 155–63.

Martin, André. "Le mécano de la pantomime." *Cahiers du cinéma* 86 (August 1958): 18–30.

Martini, Wolfgang, and Margarete Lange-Kosak, eds. *Emil Jannings: Das Filmgesicht*. Munich: Curt J. Andersen, 1928.

Massa, Steve. "I'm Glad Now That I'm Homely: The Downs and Ups of Marie Dressler." *Slapstick! Magazine* 13. Available at www.looserthanloose.com. Accessed 17 March 2009.

Massood, Paula J. *Black City Cinema: African American Urban Experiences in Film*. Philadelphia: Temple UP, 2003.

McGregor, Don. "An Interview with Raymond Rohauer." *The Buster Keaton Film Festival Album*. Staten Island: Eclipse Enterprises, 1982. 27–33.

Mitry, Jean. *Emil Jannings: Ses débuts, ses films, ses aventures*. Paris: Pascal, 1928.

Moon, Michael. "Flaming Closets." *October* 51 (Winter 1989): 19–54.

292 WORKS CITED

Moore, Colleen. *Silent Star*. New York: Doubleday, 1968.

Mordden, Ethan. *Movie Star: A Look at the Women Who Made Hollywood*. New York: St. Martin's, 1983.

Morey, Anne. "Elinor Glyn as Hollywood Labourer." *Film History* 18 (2006): 110–18.

Morris, C. B. *This Loving Darkness: The Cinema and Spanish Writers, 1920–1936*. New York: Oxford UP, 1980.

Mulligan, W. E. "The Man Who Never Smiles." *Pantomime* 1.2 (5 October 1921): 5. Reprinted in *Buster Keaton Interviews*. Ed. Kevin W. Sweeney. Jackson: U of Mississippi P, 2007. 7–8.

Mumford, Lewis. *The Brown Decades: A Study of the Arts in America, 1865–1895*. New York: Harcourt, Brace & Company, 1931.

———. *Sticks and Stones: A Study of American Architecture and Civilization*. New York: Norton, 1924.

Munkepunke [Alfred Richard Meyer]. *1000% Jannings*. Hamburg: Prismen, 1930.

Musser, Charles. "To Redream the Dreams of White Playwrights: Reappropriation and Resistance in Oscar Micheaux's *Body and Soul*." *Yale Journal of Criticism* 12.2 (1999): 321–56.

Musto, Michael. "The Glass Closet." Available at out.com/detail.asp?id=22392. Accessed 20 February 2009.

Naudet, Jean-Jacques. *Marlene Dietrich: Photographs and Memories from the Marlene Dietrich Collection of the FilmMuseum Berlin*. New York: Knopf, 2001.

Neale, Steve. "Melo Talk: On the Meaning and Use of the Term 'Melodrama' in the American Trade Press." *Velvet Light Trap* 32 (1993): 66–89.

Negra, Diane. *Off-White Hollywood: American Culture and Ethnic Female Stardom*. New York: Routledge, 2001.

Negri, Pola. *Memoirs of a Star*. New York: Doubleday, 1970.

Nenno, Nancy. "Femininity, the Primitive, and Modern Urban Space: Josephine Baker in Berlin." *Women in the Metropolis: Gender and Modernity in Weimar Culture*. Ed. Katharina Van Ankum. Berkeley: U of California P, 1997. 145–61.

Neville, John F. *Twentieth-Century Cause Célèbre: Sacco, Vanzetti, and the Press, 1920–1927*. Westport, Conn.: Praeger, 2004.

Nougé, Paul. *L'Experience continue*. Brussels: Éditions de la revue les lèvres neus, 1966. 175–76.

Nye, David E. *Electrifying America: Social Meanings of a New Technology, 1880–1940*. Cambridge, Mass.: MIT Press, 1990.

O'Dell, Scott. "Our Hospitality." *Representative Photoplays Examined*. Hollywood: Palmer Institute of Authorship, 1924. 296–301.

Orgeron, Marsha. *Hollywood Ambitions: Celebrity in the Movie Age*. Middletown, Conn.: Wesleyan UP, 2008.

Paris, Barry. *Garbo: A Biography*. New York: Knopf, 1995.

Parrish, James Robert. *The Paramount Pretties*. New Rochelle, N.Y.: Arlington House, 1972.

Perez, Gilberto. "The Bewilder Equilibrist: An Essay on Buster Keaton's Comedy." *Hudson Review* 34.3 (Autumn 1981): 337–66. Reprinted in *The Material Ghost: Films and Their Medium*. Baltimore: Johns Hopkins UP, 1998. 92–122.

Perry, Louis B., and Richard S. Perry. *A History of the Los Angeles Labor Movement, 1911–1941*. Berkeley: U of California P, 1963.

Petrie, Graham. *Hollywood Destinies: European Directors in America, 1922–1931*. London: Routledge, 1985.

Petro, Patrice. *Aftershocks of the New: Feminism and Film History*. New Brunswick, N.J.: Rutgers UP, 2002.

———. "*The Blue Angel* in Multiple-Language Versions: The Inner Thighs of Miss Dietrich." *Dietrich Icon*. Ed. Gerd Gemünden and Mary Desjardins. Durham, N.C.: Duke UP, 2007. 141–61.

Pickford, Mary. *Sunshine and Shadow*. New York: Doubleday, 1955.

Pierce, David. "'Carl Laemmle's Outstanding Achievement': Harry Pollard and the Struggle to Film *Uncle Tom's Cabin*." *Film History* 10.4 (1998): 1–53.

Pratt, Georges. *Spellbound in Darkness: A History of Silent Film*. New York: New York Graphic Society, 1973.

Prinzler, Hans Helmut, and Enno Patalas, eds. *Lubitsch*. Munich: Bucher, 1984.

Pupin, Michael. *Romance of the Machine*. New York: Scribner's, 1930.

Rabinovitz, Lauren. "The Coney Island Comedies: Bodies and Slapstick at the Amusement Park and the Movies." *American Cinema's Transitional Era: Audiences, Institutions, Practices*. Ed. Charlie Keil and Shelley Stamp. Berkeley: U of California P, 2004. 171–90.

Raider, Roberta (Sloan). "A Descriptive Study of the Acting of Marie Dressler." Ph.D. diss., University of Michigan, 1970.

Rampersad, Arnold. *The Life of Langston Hughes. Volume 1: 1902–1941, I Too, Sing America*. 1986. 2nd ed. New York: Oxford UP, 2002.

Rapf, Joanna E. "Queen of the Movies: Marie Dressler and *Politics*." *Quarterly Review of Film and Video* 19.4 (October/December 2002): 309–22.

Rathkolb, Oliver. *Führertreu und Gottbegnadet: Künstlereliten im Dritten Reich*. Vienna: Österreichischer Bundesverlag, 1991.

Ray, Robert B. *A Certain Tendency of the Hollywood Cinema, 1930–1980*. Princeton, N.J.: Princeton UP, 1985.

Regester, Charlene. "The African-American Press and Race Movies, 1909–1929." *Oscar Micheaux & His Circle: African-American Filmmaking and Race Cinema of the Silent Era*. Ed. Pearl Bowser, Jane Gaines, and Charles Musser. Bloomington: Indiana UP, 2001. 34–49.

———. "Stepin Fetchit: The Man, the Image, and the African American Press." *Film History* 6.4 (Winter 1994): 502–21.

Robinson, David. *Buster Keaton*. Bloomington: Indiana UP, 1969.

Rogin, Michael. *Blackface, White Noise: Jewish Immigrants in the Hollywood Melting Pot*. Berkeley: U of California P, 1996.

Rose, Paul. *Berlins große Theaterzeit: Schauspieler-Porträts der 20er und 30er Jahre*. Berlin: Rembrandt, 1969.

Ross, Murray. *Stars and Strikes: Unionization of Hollywood*. New York: Columbia University Press, 1941.

Ross, Sara. *Banking the Flames of Youth: The Hollywood Flapper, 1920–1930*. Ph.D. diss., University of Wisconsin-Madison, 2000.

———. "'Good Little Bad Girls': Controversy and the Flapper Comedienne." *Film History* 13 (2001): 409–23.

———. "The Hollywood Flapper and the Culture of Media Consumption." *Hollywood Goes Shopping*. Ed. David Desser and Garth S. Jowett. Minneapolis: U of Minnesota P, 2000. 57–81.

Rourke, Constance. *The Roots of American Culture and Other Essays*. Ed. Van Wyck Brooks. New York: Harcourt, Brace, 1942.

Rozik, Eli. "Acting: The Quintessence of Theatricality." *SubStance* 31.2/3 (2002): 110–24.

Sampson, Henry T. *Blacks in Black and White: A Source Book on Black Films.* 2nd ed. Lanham, Md.: Scarecrow, 1995.

Sands, Pierre Norman. *A Historical Study of the Academy of Motion Picture Arts and Sciences (1927–1947).* New York: Arno Press, 1973.

Sarris, Andrew. "The Cultural Guilt of Musical Movies." *Film Comment* 13 (September-October 1977): 39–41.

Saunders, Thomas J. *Hollywood in Berlin: American Cinema and Weimar Germany.* Berkeley: U of California P, 1994.

Schickel, Richard. *His Picture in the Papers: A Speculation on the Celebrity in America Based on the Life of Douglas Fairbanks, Sr.* New York: Charterhouse, 1973.

———. "Valentino: The New Romantic." *Stars.* New York: Bonanza Books, 1962. 42–47.

Schulz, Berndt. "Emil Jannings: Deutscher Mephisto in Hemdsärmeln." *Die Unsterblichen des Kinos: Stummfilmzeit und die goldenen 30er Jahre.* Eds. Adolf Heinzlmeier, Berndt Schulz, and Karsten Witte. Frankfurt: Fischer, 1982. 66–75.

Seldes, Gilbert. *The Seven Lively Arts.* New York: Barnes, 1962.

Shen, Xiaose. "On Setting and Make-up" (Tantan bujing he huazhuang). *Dianying yuebao (Movie Monthly)* 6 (September 1928). Reprinted in Jiang and Jing, vol. 3, 772–73.

Sherer, Maurice [Eric Rohmer]. "Le cinéma, art d'espace." *La Revue du cinéma* (June 1948): 6–7.

Sherwood, Robert. *The Best Moving Pictures of 1922–1923.* Boston: Small, Maynard & Company, 1923.

Shipman, David. *The Greatest Movie Stars: The Golden Years.* New York: Crown, 1970. 537–41.

Showalter, Elaine. *Sexual Anarchy: Gender and Culture at the Fin de Siècle.* New York: Penguin, 1990.

Shulman, Irving. *Valentino.* New York: Trident Press, 1967.

Sieg, Katrin. *Ethnic Drag: Performing Race, Nation, Sexuality in West Germany.* Ann Arbor: U of Michigan P, 2002.

Sinclair, Upton. *Boston.* 2 vols. New York: Albert & Charles Boni, 1927.

Slide, Anthony. *The Kindergarten of the Movies: A History of the Fine Arts Company.* Metuchen, N.J.: Scarecrow, 1980.

Slotkin, Richard. *Regeneration through Violence: The Mythology of the American Frontier, 1600–1860.* Middletown, Conn.: Wesleyan UP, 1973.

Smith, Greg. "Silencing the New Woman: Ethnic and Social Mobility in the Melodramas of Norma Talmadge." *Journal of Film and Video* 48.3 (1996): 3–16.

Smith, Terry. *Making the Modern: Industry, Art, and Design in America.* Chicago: U of Chicago P, 1993.

Smoodin, Eric. "Going Hollywood Sooner or Later: Chinese Censorship and *The Bitter Tea of General Yen.*" *Looking Past the Screen: Case Studies in American Film History and Method.* Ed. Jon Lewis and Eric Smoodin. Durham, N.C.: Duke UP, 2007. 169–200.

Spehr, Paul C. *The Movies Begin.* Newark: Newark Museum, 1977.

Spehr, Paul C., with Gunnar Lundquist. *American Film Personnel and Company Credits, 1908–1920.* Jefferson, N.C.: McFarland, 1996.

Spoto, Donald. *Blue Angel.* New York: Cooper Square Press, 2000.

Staiger, Janet. *Bad Women: Regulating Sexuality in Early American Cinema.* Minneapolis: U of Minnesota P, 1995.

Stella, Antonio. *Some Aspects of Italian Immigration to the United States.* New York: Putnam's, 1924.

Stenn, David. *Clara Bow: Runnin' Wild*. New York: Penguin, 1988.

Stenzel, Albert. *Vom Kinntopp zur Filmkunst: Menschen, die Filmgeschichte machten*. Berlin: Wendt, 1935.

Stewart, Jacqueline Najuma. *Migrating to the Movies: Cinema and Black Urban Modernity*. Berkeley: U of California P, 2005.

Studlar, Gaylyn. "Douglas Fairbanks: Thief of the Ballets Russes." *Bodies of the Text: Dance as Theory, Literature as Dance*. Ed. Ellen W. Goellner and Jacqueline Shea Murphy. New Brunswick, N.J.: Rutgers UP, 1995. 107–24.

———. "Oh, 'Doll Divine': Mary Pickford, Masquerade, and the Pedophilic Gaze." *Camera Obscura* 48, 16.3 (2001): 197–227.

———. "Out-Salomeing Salome." *Visions of the East: Orientalism in Film*. Ed. Matthew Bernstein and Gaylyn Studlar. New Brunswick, N.J.: Rutgers UP, 1997. 90–129.

———. *This Mad Masquerade: Stardom and Masculinity in the Jazz Age*. New York: Columbia UP, 1996.

Sturtevant, Victoria. *A Great Big Girl Like Me: The Films of Marie Dressler*. Urbana: U of Illinois P, 2009.

Sudendorf, Werner. "Marlene Dietrich: Von Kopf bis Fuss/Marlene Dietrich: From Head to Toe." *Filmmuseum Berlin*. Ed. Wolfgang Jacobsen, Hans Helmut Prinzler, and Werner Sudendorf. Berlin: Deutsche Kinemathek and Nicolaische Verlagsbuchhandlung, 2000. 131–68.

Swanson, Gloria. *Swanson on Swanson*. New York: Random House, 1980.

Sweeney, Kevin W. *Buster Keaton Interviews*. Jackson: UP of Mississippi, 2007.

Talmadge, Margaret L. *The Talmadge Sisters: Norma, Constance, Natalie*. Philadelphia: Lippincott, 1924.

Talmey, Allene. *Doug and Mary and Others*. New York: Macy-Masius, 1927.

Thomas, Bob. *Thalberg: Life and Legend*. New York: Doubleday, 1969.

Thompson, Sister Francesca. "From Shadows 'n Shufflin' to Spotlights and Cinema: The Lafayette Players, 1915–1932." *Oscar Micheaux & His Circle: African-American Filmmaking and Race Cinema of the Silent Era*. Ed. Pearl Bowser, Jane Gaines, and Charles Musser. Bloomington: Indiana UP, 2001. 19–33.

Thompson, Kristin. *Herr Lubitsch Goes to Hollywood: German and American Film after World War I*. Amsterdam: Amsterdam UP, 2005.

Valentino, Rudolph. "Keeping in Condition." *The Truth about the Movies by the Stars*. Ed. Laurence A. Hughes. Hollywood: Hollywood Publishers, 1924. 274–75.

Vance, Jeffrey, with Tony Maietta. *Douglas Fairbanks*. Berkeley: U of California P, 2008.

Vasey, Ruth. *The World according to Hollywood, 1918–1939*. Madison: U of Wisconsin P, 1997.

von Sternberg, Josef. *Fun in a Chinese Laundry*. New York: Macmillan, 1965.

Wagner, Horst. "Harfenjule, Penner und Patentluden beim Zilleball." *Berliner Tageblatt* (4 February 1928): 72–74. Available at www.luise-berlin.de/bms/bmstxt99/9902novd.htm. Accessed 12 January 2009.

Wallace, Michele. "Uncle Tom's Cabin: Before and after the Jim Crow Era." *Drama Review* 44.1 (Spring 2000): 137–56.

Wang, Yiman. "Anna May Wong: A Border-Crossing 'Minor' Star Mediating Performance." *Journal of Chinese Cinemas* 2.2 (2008): 91–102.

———. "The Art of Screen Passing: Anna May Wong's Yellow Yellowface Performance in the Art Deco Era." *Camera Obscura* 20.3 (2005): 159–91.

Ware, Susan. *Holding Their Own: American Women in the 1930s*. Boston: Twayne, 1982.

Watts, Jill. *Mae West: An Icon in Black and White*. New York: Oxford UP, 2001.

Watts, Stephen, ed. *Behind the Screen: How Films Are Made*. London: Arthur Barker, 1938.

Weisenfeld, Judith. *Hollywood Be Thy Name: African American Religion in American Film, 1929–1949*. Berkeley: U of California P, 2007.

Werner, Margaret. "How Buster Keaton Got That Way." *Movie Weekly* 3.40 (10 November 1923): 12, 26. Reprinted in *Buster Keaton Interviews*. Ed. Kevin W. Sweeney. Jackson: U of Mississippi P, 2007. 9–11.

White, G. Edward. *The Eastern Establishment and the Western Experience: The West of Frederic Remington, Theodore Roosevelt, and Owen Wister*. New Haven, Conn.: Yale UP, 1968.

Wid's Year Book, 1920–21. Hollywood and New York: Wid's Films and Film Folks, 1920.

Williams, Linda. *Playing the Race Card: Melodramas of Black and White from Uncle Tom to O.J. Simpson*. Princeton, N.J.: Princeton UP, 2001.

———. "Versions of Uncle Tom: Race and Gender in American Melodrama." *New Scholarship from BFI Research*. Ed. Colin MacCabe and Duncan Petrie. London: BFI, 1996. 120–23.

Winokur, Mark. *American Laughter: Immigrants, Ethnicity, and the 1930s Hollywood Film Comedy*. New York: St. Martin's, 1996.

———. "Improbable Ethnic: William Powell and the Transformation of Ethnic Hollywood." *Cinema Journal* 27.1 (Fall 1987): 5–22.

Wolfe, Charles. *Buster Keaton and American Modernism*. Berkeley: U of California P, forthcoming.

———. "On the Track of the Vitaphone Short." *The Dawn of Sound*. Ed. Mary Lea Bandy. New York: Museum of Modern Art, 1989. 35–41.

Xiao, Zhiwei. "Anti-Imperialism and Film Censorship during the Nanjing Decade, 1927–1937." *Transnational Chinese Cinemas: Identity, Nationhood, Gender*. Ed. Sheldon Hsiao-Peng Lu. Honolulu: U of Hawaii P, 1997. 35–58.

Xu, Gongmei. "Methodology of Acting in Motion Picture" (Yingju de dongzuo shu). Episode 1. *Movies Magazine* (*Diangying zazhi*) 7 (1924). Reprinted in Jiang and Jing, vol. 2, 211–15.

———. "Methodology of Acting in Motion Picture" (Yingju de dongzuo shu). Episode 2. *Movies Magazine* (*Diangying zazhi*) 8 (1924). Reprinted in Jiang and Jing, vol. 2, 323–28.

Xu, Guangping. "Mr. Lu Xun's Entertainment" (Lu Xun xiansheng de yule). *Lu Xun huiyi lu: zhuanzhu* (*In Memory of Lu Xun: Monographs*). Vol. 1. Beijing: Beijing chubanshe, 1999. 388–94.

Xu, Hu. "Make-up for Film" (Dianying huazhuang xue). *Movies Magazine* (*Dianying zazhi*) 1 May 1924). Reprinted in Jiang and Jing, vol. 1, 351–52.

Ying, Dou. "The Urgent Issue Facing the Producing Companies" (Zhipian gongsi ying jiqi zhuyi zhege wenti). *Yinxing* 16 (1928): 10–13.

Yingxi zazhi (*The Motion Picture Review*) 1.1 (December 1921). Reprinted in Jiang and Jing, vol. 1, 6.

Yu, Muyun. *Xianggang dianying shihua* (*Stories of Hong Kong Film History*). Vol. 1. Hong Kong: Ci wenhua tang, 1996.

Zeitz, Joshua. *Flapper*. New York: Three Rivers Press, 2006.

Zierold, Norman. *Sex Goddesses of the Silent Screen*. Chicago: Henry Regnery, 1973.

CONTRIBUTORS
☆☆☆☆☆☆☆☆☆☆☆

SCOTT CURTIS is an associate professor in the Radio/Television/Film Department at Northwestern University, where he teaches film history and historiography. His publications include "A House Divided: The MPPC in Transition," in *American Cinema's Transitional Era*, edited by Charlie Keil and Shelley Stamp (2004), and *Managing Modernity: Art, Science, and Early Cinema in Germany* (forthcoming).

MARY DESJARDINS is an associate professor of Film and Television Studies at Dartmouth College. She has published on stardom, feminist filmmaking, melodrama, and material culture in a variety of journals and anthologies. She is co-editor of *Dietrich Icon* (with Gerd Gemünden, 2007) and author of *Recycled Stars: Female Film Stardom in the Age of Television and Video* (forthcoming).

LUCY FISCHER is a professor of film studies and English at the University of Pittsburgh, where she serves as director of the Film Studies Program. She is the author of seven books, including, most recently, *Designing Women: Art Deco, Cinema and the Female Form* (2003) and *Stars: The Film Reader* (co-edited with Marcia Landy, 2004). Her most recent edited book, *American Cinema of the 1920s: Themes and Variations*, appeared in 2009. She has published extensively on issues of film history, theory, and criticism in such journals as *Screen, Sight and Sound, Camera Obscura, Wide Angle, Cinema Journal, Journal of Film and Video, Film Criticism, Women and Performance, Frauen und Film, Film Quarterly*, and *Biography*.

KRIN GABBARD is a professor of comparative literature and English at the State University of New York at Stony Brook. He is the author of *Black Magic: White Hollywood and African American Culture* (2004), *Jammin' at the Margins: Jazz and the American Cinema* (1996), and, with Glen O. Gabbard, *Psychiatry and the Cinema.* (1999). His most recent book, *Hotter than That: The Trumpet, Jazz, and American Culture*, was published in 2008.

GERD GEMÜNDEN is Ted and Helen Geisel Third Century Professor in the Humanities and a professor of German studies, film studies, and comparative literature at Dartmouth College. His volumes as editor include *Wim Wenders: Einstellungen* (1993), *The Cinema of Wim Wenders* (1997), *Germans and Indians: Fantasies, Encounters, Projections* (2002), and *Dietrich Icon* (with

Mary Desjardins, 2007). His most recent book is *A Foreign Affair: Billy Wilder's American Film* (2008), which was also published in Austria as *Filmemacher mit Akzent: Billy Wilder in Hollywood* (2008). He is series editor for "Screen Cultures: German Film and the Visual" at Camden House Press.

LEA JACOBS is a professor in the Department of Communication Arts at the University of Wisconsin–Madison. She is the author of *The Wages of Sin: Censorship and the Fallen Woman Film* (1997), *Theatre to Cinema* (with Ben Brewster, 1998), and *The Decline of Sentiment: American Film in the 1920s* (2008).

AMY LAWRENCE is a professor of film and television studies at Dartmouth College. She is the author of *Echo and Narcissus: Women's Voices in Classical Hollywood Film* (1991), *The Films of Peter Greenaway* (1997), and of numerous articles on star issues (James Stewart, Marlene Dietrich), experimental animation and gender, and Eadweard Muybridge.

PAULA J. MASSOOD is a professor of film studies in the Department of Film at Brooklyn College, the City University of New York (CUNY), and the Doctoral Program in Theatre at The Graduate Center. She is the author of *Black City Cinema: African American Urban Experiences in Film* (2003) and the editor of *The Spike Lee Reader* (2008). She served as the Film and Theater subject editor for the African American National Biography project. Her current work focuses on the cultural and historical legacy of Harlem, New York, in twentieth-century visual culture.

PATRICE PETRO is a professor of English and film studies at the University of Wisconsin–Milwaukee, where she also serves as vice provost for International Education. She is the author, editor, and co-editor of ten books, most recently *Teaching Film* for the Modern Language Association's Options for Teaching series (with Lucy Fischer, forthcoming), *Rethinking Global Security: Media, Popular Culture, and the 'War on Terror'* (with Andrew Martin, 2006), and *Aftershocks of the New: Feminism and Film History* (2002). She is currently the president of the Society for Cinema and Media Studies.

JOANNA E. RAPF is a professor of English at the University of Oklahoma. She is the author of *Buster Keaton: A Bio-Bibliography* (1995), *On the Waterfront* (2002), and *Interviews with Sidney Lumet* (2005). Her articles on film have appeared in such journals as *Film Quarterly, Literature/Film Quarterly, Quarterly Review of Film & Video, Film Criticism, Journal of Popular Culture, Studies in American Humor, Western Humanities Review*, and a number of critical anthologies, including an essay on feminism and Jerry Lewis praised by the comedian himself in *Hollywood Comedians: The Film Reader* (2003).

YIMAN WANG is an assistant professor of film and digital media at the University of California at Santa Cruz. Her areas of research include transnational/trans-regional Chinese cinemas of all periods, intra-Asian and cross-Pacific film remakes, Pan-East Asian celebrity culture, East Asian cultural studies, and Asian American cinema. She is interested in issues of translation as played out in border-crossing and cross-temporal contexts, including the cultural politics of border-crossing film remakes.

CHARLES WOLFE is a professor of film and media studies at the University of California at Santa Barbara. He is the author of two books on the films of director Frank Capra and has published widely on various aspects of commercial, independent, and documentary filmmaking in the United States. With Edward Branigan, he is the series co-editor of the American Film Institute's Film Reader Series, which to date has published nineteen volumes of critical essays on topics of contemporary concern in film, television, and new media studies.

I N D E X

Note: Featured stars in boldface; page numbers for illustrations in italic.